STEVE WASSERSTROM

BETWEEN ATHENS
AND JERUSALEM

JOHN J. COLLINS

BETWEEN ATHENS AND JERUSALEM

JEWISH IDENTITY IN THE HELLENISTIC DIASPORA

CROSSROAD · NEW YORK

1983

The Crossroad Publishing Company
575 Lexington Avenue, New York, N.Y. 10022

Printed in the United States of America

Library of Congress Cataloging in Publication Data

Collins, John Joseph, 1946–
Between Athens and Jerusalem.

Includes index.
1. Judaism—History—Post-exilic period—586 B.C.–
210 A.D.   2. Apocryphal books (Old Testament)—
Criticism, interpretation, etc.   3. Greek literature
—Jewish authors—History and criticism.   4. Jews—
Identity.   I. Title.
BM176.C64   1982   296'.09'014   82-14069
ISBN 0-8245-0491-7

For John Strugnell
Teacher and friend

CONTENTS

PREFACE

This study was undertaken as part of a research project on Normative Self-Definition in Judaism and Christianity, funded by the Social Sciences and Humanities Research Council of Canada. The project was coordinated by Professor E. P. Sanders of McMaster University. Responsibility for the area of Hellenistic Judaism was shared by Professors David Winston of the Graduate Theological Union, Berkeley, Professor Alan Mendelson of McMaster, and myself. Professors Winston and Mendelson devoted their attention to the extensive corpus of Philo's writings, while I undertook to review the numerous minor authors of the Hellenistic Diaspora. This division of labor accounts for the most obvious lacuna in the present volume: the lack of a substantial discussion of Philo and his philosophical approach to Judaism. Such a discussion could scarcely have been incorporated in a single volume in any case. The lacuna will be filled by the forthcoming studies of Winston and Mendelson.

I should like to express my gratitude to Professor Sanders, McMaster University, and the Social Sciences and Humanities Research Council of Canada for the support which made this book possible; to Professors Winston and Mendelson for their advice and cooperation at all stages of the project, and to Professor Thomas H. Tobin, S.J., of Loyola University, Chicago, for his helpful comments on the manuscript.

Professor John Strugnell first introduced me to the fragmentary Hellenistic Jewish writings in a memorable seminar at Harvard Divinity School in Spring, 1970. This book is dedicated to him in gratitude and friendship.

ABBREVIATIONS

AB   Anchor Bible
Ag Ap   Josephus, *Against Apion*
AGJU   Arbeiten zur Geschichte des antiken Judentums und Urchristentums
AnBib   Analecta biblica
ANRW   *Aufstieg und Niedergang der Römischen Welt* (Berlin: de Gruyter)
Ant   Josephus, *Antiquities of the Jews*
APOT   *Apocrypha and Pseudepigrapha of the Old Testament* (ed. R. H. Charles; 2 vols., Oxford: Clarendon, 1913)
BA   *Biblical Archeologist*
BASOR   *Bulletin of the American Schools of Oriental Research*
BBB   Bonner biblische Beiträge
BETL   Bibliotheca ephemeridum theologicarum lovaniensium
Bib   *Biblica*
BJRL   *Bulletin of the John Rylands University Library of Manchester*
BZNW   Beihefte zur Zeitschrift für die neutestamentliche Wissenschaft
CBA   Catholic Biblical Association
CBQ   *Catholic Biblical Quarterly*
CBQMS   Catholic Biblical Quarterly Monograph Series
CIJ   *Corpus inscriptionum judaicarum*
Compendia   *The Jewish People in the First Century* (Compendia rerum iudaicarum ad Novum Testamentum; 2 vols.; ed. S. Safrai and M. Stern; Assen: van Gorcum, 1974, 1976)
CPJ   *Corpus papyrorum judaicarum*
CTM   *Concordia Theological Monthly*
CQ   *Classical Quarterly*
ET   *Expository Times*
ETL   *Ephemerides theologicae lovanienses*
FGH   *Fragmenta der griechischen Historiker* (ed. F. Jacoby)

FRLANT	Forschungen zur Religion und Literatur des Alten und Neuen Testaments
GCS	Griechische christliche Schriftsteller
HDR	Harvard Dissertations in Religion
HE	Eusebius, *Historica ecclesiae*
HR	*History of Religions*
HSM	Harvard Semitic Monographs
HTR	*Harvard Theological Review*
HTS	Harvard Theological Studies
HUCA	*Hebrew Union College Annual*
JAOS	*Journal of the Americal Oriental Society*
JBL	*Journal of Biblical Literature*
JJS	*Journal of Jewish Studies*
JR	*Journal of Religion*
JRS	*Journal of Roman Studies*
JSHRZ	Jüdische Schriften aus hellenistisch-römischer Zeit
JSJ	*Journal for the Study of Judaism*
JSNT	*Journal for the Study of the New Testament*
JTS	*Journal of Theological Studies*
JW	Josephus, *The Jewish War*
KBW	Katholisches Bibelwerk
NovTSup	Supplements to Novum Testamentum
NRTh	*La nouvelle revue théologique*
NTS	*New Testament Studies*
OCD	*Oxford Classical Dictionary*
PE	Eusebius, *Praeparatio evangelica*
PGM	*Papyri graecae magicae* (ed. K. Preisendanz)
PL	Patrologia latina (ed. J. Migne)
PVTG	Pseudepigrapha Veteris Testamenti graece
PWRE	Pauly-Wissowa, *Real-Encyclopädie der classischen Altertumswissenschaft*
RAC	*Reallexikon für Antike und Christentum*
RB	*Revue biblique*
REJ	*Revue des études juives*
RHR	*Revue de l'histoire des religions*
SANE	Studies in the Ancient Near East
SBLASP	*Society of Biblical Literature Abstracts and Seminar Papers*
SBLDS	Society of Biblical Literature Dissertation Series
SBLMS	Society of Biblical Literature Monograph Series
SBS	Stuttgarter Bibelstudien
SC	Sources chrétiennes
SCS	Septuagint and Cognate Studies
SJLA	Studies in Judaism in Late Antiquity
SNTS	Studiorum Novi Testamenti Societas
SPCK	Society for the Promotion of Christian Knowledge
SUNT	Studien zur Umwelt des Neuen Testaments

SVT	*Stoicorum veterum fragmenta*
SVTP	Studia in Veteris Testamenti pseudepigrapha
TAPA	*Transactions of the American Philological Association*
TDNT	*Theological Dictionary of the New Testament*
T&T	Texts and Translations
TU	Texte und Untersuchungen
TZ	*Theologische Zeitschrift*
VC	*Vigiliae christianae*
Vita	Josephus, *Life*
VT	*Vetus Testamentum*
WMANT	Wissenschaftliche Monographien zum Alten und Neuen Testament
WUNT	Wissenschaftliche Untersuchungen zum Neuen Testament
ZAW	*Zeitschrift für die Alttestamentliche Wissenschaft*
ZDPV	*Zeitschrift des deutschen Palästina-Vereins*
ZNW	*Zeitschrift für die neutestamentliche Wissenschaft*
ZTK	*Zeitschrift für Theologie und Kirche*
ZRGG	*Zeitschrift für Religions- und Geistesgeschichte*

INTRODUCTION

How shall we sing the song of the Lord
in a foreign land?

Ps 137:4

The plaintive question of the psalmist by the waters of Babylon is a moving testimony to the ageless homesickness of the exile and the depth of human longing to be rooted in a specific place which can be recognized as home. It is also a classic expression of one of the major problems of Jewish history. The "song of the Lord" was primarily the recitation of the mighty acts of Yahweh, the story of how Israel had come to exist as a people and to occupy the promised land. It was not only the song of the Lord, but the story of the people. Religion and national identity went hand in hand, and both were deeply rooted in the land of Israel itself. For much of the history of Israel the identity of the people had been shaped and supported by a number of complementary factors—common territory, political loyalty, ethnic continuity, common language, religious observance and tradition. After the exile, the people was scattered geographically, subject to various political authorities, and diverse in language. Religious tradition and observance assumed an ever greater role in maintaining distinctive identity. Even ethnic considerations were subordinated in importance, in the case of proselytes and renegades. The problem of singing the song of the Lord in a foreign land was the problem of maintaining the identity of the people and its survival as a distinct entity.

Identity, whether of a people or of an individual, is a matter of knowing who one is, where one is coming from, and where one is going. Such knowledge is a practical necessity if one is to proceed to any purposeful action in life.[1] But such knowledge is inevitably shaped by social context. It is "a social-scientific platitude to say that it is impossible to become or to be human, in any empirically recognizable form that goes beyond biological observations, except in society."[2] Peter Berger has gone so far as to say that "the individual becomes that which he is addressed as by others."[3] This is undoubtedly an oversimplification, if only because any individual is likely to be addressed in conflicting ways, but Berger's valid point is that the identity of any individual is built up in interaction with others and must be confirmed by others if it is not to be merely idiosyncratic or solipsistic. Any society must provide the framework within which individuals can share a common view of reality and confirm each other's convictions as to where they are coming from and where they are going. Society "provides a world for man to inhabit"[4] by propagating common assumptions about the nature and purpose of life, and institutions which regulate common modes of action. These assumptions and institutions are frequently religious in character both in the sense that they are concerned with ultimate reality and in the more obvious sense that they involve the worship of divine beings.[5] In the ancient world in general, and in Israel in particular, the dominant beliefs and institutions were explicitly religious and were embodied in traditions passed on from generation to generation. The power of such traditions to shape the identity of people derives from the fact that they are commonly taken as objective reality, within a given society.[6] If they are to function at all they must at least be plausible enough to the members of the society to retain their belief. Now plausibility depends to a great extent on social and cultural support. Few people question what everyone else takes for granted. By contrast, any group that holds unusual views is inevitably under pressure to establish their plausibility, not only to win the respect of outsiders, but primarily to maintain the allegiance of its own members.

THE DIASPORA SETTING

The basic problem in the Jewish Diaspora was how to maintain the Jewish tradition in an environment dominated by gentiles. Quite apart from actual persecution, which was extremely rare before the Hellenistic age,[7] the very juxtaposition of diverse beliefs challenged the plausibility of minority views. The people who made up the majority in Babylon and other centers of exile were, for better or worse, "significant others,"[8] and Jewish identity would inevitably be modified by interaction with them.

In the case of the Babylonian exile, the crisis of plausibility was especially severe, since the exile was an enforced one, and might be attributed to Yahweh's inability to protect his people: "We have become a taunt to our neighbors, mocked and derided by those round about us. . . . Why should the nations say 'Where is their God?'" (Ps 79:4, 10). Yet the very direct threat to the traditional Jewish faith entailed a certain simplicity. At least in the beginning, the lines of conflict were clearly drawn and invited firm unambiguous decisions.

The situation was different in the Diaspora of the Hellenistic age. The Jews were no longer exiles against their will; their exile was no longer a cause of derision. Already in the Babylonian exile there were many who heeded the advice of Jeremiah to "seek the welfare of the city where I have sent you into exile, and pray to the Lord on its behalf, for in its welfare you will find your welfare."[9] At the time of the restoration under the Persians, not all the Jews in Babylon chose to return.[10] Jewish communities persisted and flourished in Babylonia throughout the Hellenistic and Roman periods.[11] The Jewish Diaspora in the West did not originate in compulsory exile at all. At the time of the conquest of Judah by the Babylonians many of the "remnants of the nation" (Jer 41:16) sought refuge in Egypt, and even the prophet Jeremiah was taken along despite his protests.[12] The community at Elephantine, which survived for over a hundred years, had apparently originated in a voluntary migration to serve as mercenaries.[13] It is possible that some of those who went down to Egypt in the time of Ptolemy I were coerced,[14] but the subsequent growth of the Jewish community in Egypt and throughout the Hellenistic world was not due to any external compulsion. The Jewish population of Egypt grew steadily in the third century BCE, when Palestine was under Ptolemaic rule and there was constant commercial intercourse between the two countries.[15] Similarly, a large Jewish population arose in neighboring Syria.[16] There was a major migration of Jews to Egypt in the wake of the Maccabean revolt, including Onias IV and his supporters,[17] and there is some evidence that the political enemies of the Hasmoneans continued to seek refuge there.[18] By the first century CE, Philo could claim that "the Jews dwelling in Alexandria and Egypt from the Libyan slope to the borders of Aethiopia do not fall short of a million" and that "no single country can contain the Jews because of their multitude."[19] While Philo's figures are not reliable,[20] there is no doubt that the Jewish population had grown vast. While the general impression from the papyri "is that of a hard-working people earning its living by tenacious labour," there were many who prospered, and no branch of economic life was closed to them.[21]

It is evident from the literature of the Diaspora that Jews were educated, by whatever means, in Greek literature and philosophy.[22] The open attitude of the Diaspora Jews to their Hellenistic environment is amply shown in their use of Greek names and their recourse to Hellenistic law.[23] The struggle of the Jews in Alexandria for parity with the Greek citizens typifies the aspirations of the Hellenistic Diaspora. The Hellenistic Jews were not reluctant exiles. They were attracted by Hellenistic culture, eager to win the respect of the Greeks and adapt to their ways.

Yet the Jews were a distinct people with their own peculiar traditions, and a certain degree of tension was inevitable. The tension arose from both sides. Greek interest in Judaism was superficial. In the period immediately after Alexander's conquests a number of Greek historians and philosophers wrote on the Jews (Hecataeus of Abdera, Theophrastus, Megasthenes, Clearchus of Soli). Their attitude was respectful, determined by Greek stereotypes of eastern peoples rather than by observation. However, when the actual Jewish scriptures became available in Greek translation, they were ignored.[24] In general, the Greeks of the Hellenistic age looked upon Judaism as a strange superstition.[25] Agatharcides of Cnidus in Asia Minor, writing in the mid-second century BCE, claimed that Jerusalem had fallen to Ptolemy I Lagus because of the Jewish observance of the sabbath, and regarded this as a prime illustration of the folly of superstition.[26] Another second-century writer from Asia Minor, Mnaseas, alleged that the Jews worshipped an ass's head.[27] It is unlikely that Mnaseas invented the story. It is embedded in an account of a conflict between the Idumeans and the Jews and may have originated as Idumean propaganda.[28] In any case, the story was designed to ridicule the Jews, and could only augment their reputation for superstition. We learn from Josephus that the Egyptian polemicist Apion drew material for his ridicule of the Jews from Posidonius and Apollonius Molon.[29] These were two of the great men of their age. Posidonius of Apamea in Syria (135–51 BCE) was a philosopher, historian, and scientist, and was a prolific writer. Unfortunately, his work is almost completely lost, and attempts to reconstruct his thought from others who may have been influenced by him have been controversial. Consequently we can say little about his attitude to the Jews.[30] Apollonius Molon was a rhetorician who came from Caria but taught in Rhodes and numbered Cicero and Julius Caesar among his disciples. According to Josephus, Posidonius and Apollonius "charge us with not worshipping the same gods as other people" and "tell lies and invent absurd calumnies about our temple." He goes on to specify the calumnies about the temple: the story of the ass's head and the allegation that the Jews annually murdered a Greek. Josephus is responding to the polemic of Apion and it is not certain whether these charges were already found in Posidonius and Apollonius. According to Josephus, Apollonius "has not grouped his accusations together, but scattered them here and there all over his work, reviling us in one place as atheists and misanthropes, in another reproaching us as cowards, whereas elsewhere, on the contrary, he accuses us of temerity and reckless madness. He adds that we are the most witless of all barbarians and are consequently the only people who have contributed no useful invention to civilization."[31] Apollonius was the first Greek writer after Hecataeus who was said to have written a special book on the Jews. The fragment of the book preserved by Alexander Polyhistor does not show a bias against the Jews but associates their origin with Syria.[32] We may suspect that his tirades against the Jews were rhetorical in character and that he was not greatly concerned to verify his charges.

Apollonius's distinguished pupil, Cicero, also inveighed against the Jews in two orations: his defense of Flaccus and "On the Consular Provinces." He characterizes the Jewish religion as superstition and contrasts it with the traditional religion of Rome. In his speech "On the Consular Provinces" he says that the Syrians and Jews were born to slavery. It has been pointed out, however, that ridiculing the enemy was a standard rhetorical tactic of Cicero. In the defense of Flaccus he also denounces the cities of Asia Minor, and elsewhere he ridicules the Sardi and the Gauls. Cicero was not motivated by any direct animosity toward the Jews, although one might infer from his speeches a general lack of respect for remote and alien peoples.[33]

The Roman attitude to the Jews around the turn of the era is perhaps best reflected in the gibe of Horace *credat Iudaeus Apella.*[34] The Jew was assumed to be credulous, because of his strange beliefs.

Later Roman writers were in general more hostile to the Jews.[35] Seneca's attitude to the Jews followed from his general resentment of the spread of eastern cults in Rome. He directed his criticisms at Jewish ritual and ceremonial in order to show the superstitious, irrational nature of the cult (e.g., that the sabbath observance wasted a seventh of a person's life). Seneca paid no attention to the moral side of Jewish religion. This was also true of the satirists of the later first and early second centuries. Persius ridiculed the sabbath. Petronius regarded circumcision as the main mark of the Jew and alleged that the pig was the Jewish deity. Martial comments on circumcision and the sabbath. Juvenal stresses the sabbath, circumcision, and abstention from pork. The relatively extensive comments of Tacitus are introduced in the context of the destruction of Jerusalem by Rome, but he does not denounce or even blame the Jews for their rebellion.[36] His dislike for Judaism was due to the same cause as that of Seneca and Juvenal. He resented the spread of Judaism and other eastern cults in Rome.

Judaism then appeared as a strange phenomenon with unfamiliar rites and observances in the Hellenistic and Roman world. As such it was liable to caricature and mockery and also to suspicion and occasional hostility. In Egypt another dimension was added to this. Already in the third century BCE the Egyptian priest Manetho wrote a highly derogatory account of Jewish origins. Since elements of that account are found even earlier in Hecataeus of Abdera, there is some reason to believe it was drawn from old traditions.[37] According to Manetho, Jerusalem was founded by the Hyksos who had been expelled from Egypt. These were low-born people who had committed outrages in Egypt, including the destruction of temples. Moses, however, known as Osarsiph, was the leader of a group of lepers and unclean people who had been set to work in the stone quarries. These joined forces with the settlers in Jerusalem, pillaged Egypt, and committed various acts of sacrilege against the gods. This account of Jewish origins was adapted by a succession of authors, Chaeremon, Lysimachus, Apion.[38] Lysimachus claimed that Jerusalem was named Hierosyla (from the Greek phrase for plundering a temple) because of the sacrilegious acts of the founders. The Egyptian version of Jewish origins also circulated outside of Egypt and left a clear imprint in Tacitus. Anti-Jewish polemic reached its apex in Alexandria in the first century CE, where Apion drew together the various historical and moral allegations which were hostile to the Jews.

In part, the negative perception of the Jews was rooted in ignorance. In large part, however, it sprang from social tensions. This was especially true in Egypt. Even in the Ptolemaic period, when Jews enjoyed the favor of a king such as Philometor, they inevitably incurred the resentment both of opposing factions and of other groups in the king's service.[39] In the Roman period, the Jews resented the fact that they were classified with the native Egyptians and denied the privileged status of the Greeks. Consequently, they often tried to emphasize their affinities with the Greeks and differences from the Egyptians, and were resented by both. Riots erupted in Alexandria in the reign of Caligula, and the problems between Greeks and Jews were laid before both Caligula and Claudius. The letter of Claudius, which confirmed the Jews' right to observe their own customs but reminded them that they lived in a city which was not their own, did not put an end to the racial tensions, as can be seen from the outbreak of fighting in 66 and the tragic revolt under Trajan.[40]

The social tensions between Jews and gentiles in Egypt were exacerbated by the nature of the Jewish religion itself. Much of the hostile propaganda focused on the "strangeness" of the Jews, their refusal to worship the gods of the land and their alleged hostility to other peoples.[41] In fact, the Jewish tradition insisted that Yahweh was a jealous god, who demanded that "you shall be holy to me for I the Lord am holy, and have separated you from the peoples that you should be mine" (Lev 20:26). The ideal of holiness by separation from the gentiles was especially prominent in postexilic Judaism.[42] The priestly laws in Leviticus were probably put in final form during the exile. The program for restoration in Ezekiel 40–48 provided clear boundary lines for preserving the purity of the temple and avoiding the errors of the past: "No foreigner, uncircumcised in heart and flesh, of all the foreigners who are among the people of Israel, shall enter my sanctuary" (Ezek 44:9). A century later, Ezra was outraged to find that "the holy race has mixed itself with the peoples of the land" (Ezra 9:2) and instituted a reform which included the divorce of foreign wives. The distinctive commandments, such as sabbath observance, circumcision, and dietary laws, were the hallmarks of Judaism which were most immediately obvious to gentile observers in the following centuries.[43] The fact that Jewish identity was so closely bound up with these observances obviously created obstacles for those who were attracted by Hellenistic culture—as is amply illustrated by the events which led up to the Maccabean revolt.

We should not of course conclude that the gentile reaction to Judaism was entirely negative.[44] The earliest Greek writers on Judaism, such as Hecataeus, wrote with respect for the Jews. They were especially impressed by the laws of Moses and by the rejection of idols. Megasthenes and Clearchus regarded the Jews as philosophers. Strabo's *Geography*, book 16, gives a very sympathetic account of Moses and says that he set up an excellent government, even though Moses' successors took a serious turn for the worse. Some scholars attribute the passage to Posidonius. Varro, a contemporary of Caesar and Cicero, was impressed by the aniconic religion and identified the God of the Jews with Jupiter. Pompeius Trogus credited the Jews with "uniting justice with religion," and the treatise "On the Sublime," attributed to Longinus, had high praise for Moses. It appears then that there was a dimension of Judaism which was quite attractive to the Hellenistic world. This was its philosophical dimension, its ethical code, and aniconic God.

The corpus of Jewish literature which has survived from the Diaspora may be viewed in part as a response to the assessments and polemics of the gentiles. Since much of this literature is explicitly devoted to defending a view of Judaism in Hellenistic categories, it is usually described as "apologetic." It is also commonly regarded as missionary literature—the propaganda which accompanied Jewish proselytizing.[45] Victor Tcherikover, on the other hand, argued in a celebrated essay that this literature is not properly apologetic but is directed to a Jewish rather than a gentile audience.[46] Much of the secondary literature since Tcherikover's essay has been concerned with choosing between these alternatives.

Some light can be thrown on this problem if we bear in mind the situation of the Diaspora Jews. The Hellenized Jew who aspired to participate in the cultural life of a city such as Alexandria experienced dissonance on two counts.[47] First, the Jewish tradition affirmed a certain account of Jewish origins and assessment of Jewish mores which was highly positive. In the Hellenistic world, the account of origins was often contradicted and Jewish mores were denounced as antisocial superstition. The Hellenistic view of Judaism was, thus, often dissonant with the Jewish tradition. Second, the Jewish tradition itself was far from ecumenical and strongly discouraged any form of syncretism. Mingling with the nations was thought to be bad. Yet for many Diaspora Jews, mingling with their Hellenistic neighbors was highly desirable. Again, dissonance arose, or, in other terms, the plausibility of Judaism in the Hellenistic world came under strain.

Where dissonance is present there is inevitably pressure to reduce or eliminate the dissonance.[48] Perhaps the simplest way to do this was by abandoning Judaism altogether. Philo's nephew, Tiberius Julius Alexander, is the most notorious example.[49] There were Jews who exercised this option, but they were always a minority. The majority sought ways to reduce the dissonance while remaining Jewish but without rejecting Hellenistic culture.

We will observe the various ways in which Jews accomplished this in the following chapters. Essentially, dissonance is reduced by modifying one or both of the conflicting bodies of opinion. In some cases, Jews take issue with the Hellenistic view of Judaism and refute it (as in Josephus's *Against Apion*) or simply contradict it. In other cases they highlight the aspects of Judaism which were most acceptable to cultured gentiles, e.g., by representing Judaism as a philosophy, while playing down the more peculiar customs and rituals. Conversely, they distinguished between the loftier elements of philosophical religion, with which rapprochement was possible, and the vulgar superstitions of the masses (especially the Egyptians). In this way the dissonance is admitted with some aspects of Hellenistic life, but is removed in a significant area. The allegorical interpretation of scripture by Philo and others is an evident method of reducing the dissonance between the Jewish scriptures and philosophical religion. The expression of traditional Jewish material in Hellenistic forms, such as tragedy and epic, again blurs the differences between the two traditions and serves to show that Judaism is not an alien body in the Hellenistic world.

When we realize that what was at stake was the plausibility of Jewish tradition in a new environment and the dissonance experienced by the Hellenized Jew, it is almost inevitable that the "apologetic" would be directed simultaneously to those within and to those outside. If gentiles could be persuaded to embrace Judaism, clearly the Jews need not feel social pressure to abandon it.[50] The outward movement of the propaganda simultaneously has the effect of bolstering the faith of the community. On the other hand, the concentration on those aspects of Judaism which were most acceptable in the Hellenistic world could also facilitate propaganda and proselytism, since it presented Judaism in terms which a Greek could understand and appreciate. Even if the apologetic had little impact on outsiders it still reduced the dissonance for the Jews since it showed how their tradition could be made compatible with the surrounding culture.

HELLENISTIC JUDAISM AND JUDEA

In this volume we are concerned with the Diaspora, and especially with Egypt, since that is the area for which we have the most ample documentation. However, the problems posed by Hellenization were not confined to the Diaspora. As has often been pointed out in recent years, Judea was also profoundly influenced by Hellenism.[51] The so-called Hellenistic reform which preceded the Maccabean revolt was only the climax of a long and gradual process. For a century and a half Judea had been governed by the Ptolemies and Seleucids. The lively contacts between Judea and Egypt in the Ptolemaic period, and the ease with which prominent Jews engaged in Hellenistic commerce and politics, are illustrated by the Zeno papyri and the tales of the Tobiads in Josephus.[52] We know of some thirty Greek cities within Palestine in the Hellenistic period.[53] The Hasmoneans, while they treated these cities harshly, rapidly "went the way of Hellenization began to resemble the normal type of Hellenistic monarch."[54] The names of the Hasmonean rulers are suggestive in this respect—Hyrcanus, Aristobulus, Alexander, Antigonus. From the time of Alexander Jannaeus the Hasmonean coins bear a Greek inscription in addition to the Hebrew. Aristobulus called himself *philhellēn*, lover of the Greeks.[55] Needless to say, the trend was continued by the Herods.

It is not surprising then to find that we cannot draw a clear line between the literature of the Diaspora and that of Judea. At least one of the Hellenistic Jewish writers preserved in Eusebius was a Judean, Eupolemus, and he was an associate of Judas Maccabee. In the case of some others, such as Philo the epic poet, Alexandrian provenance has generally been assumed without substantial evidence, but a Judean origin is also possible. In several other cases where the balance of probability favors a Diaspora setting, the evidence is extremely slight and arguments for Judean origins have also been put forward. (The Testament of Abraham is a case in point.) The Testaments of the Twelve Patriarchs are the ultimate monument to the failure of scholarship to pin down the literature of this period to definite historical settings.[56] On the one hand, there is an ongoing debate as to whether the Testaments are a Jewish composition with Christian redactional elements, or rather a Christian composition which incorporates Jewish traditions. Even those who regard them as Jewish disagree as to their provenance. Several recent studies have emphasized their contacts with Egyptian Judaism. Yet, fragments related to the Testament of Levi and the Testament of Naphtali have been found at Qumran and there are many parallel motifs in the Testaments and the Scrolls. The complex history of the Testaments cannot be confined to either Judea or the Diaspora. Similar problems are raised by the fact that much Judean literature was translated into Greek and circulated in the Diaspora. Sometimes, as in the case of Esther and Daniel, the Greek version expanded the original, but even these expansions did not necessarily originate in the Diaspora—the colophon of Greek Esther says that the Greek version was ascribed to "a member of the Jerusalem community."[57] 2 Maccabees claims to be the abridgment of a five-volume history of Jason of Cyrene. Yet it is prefaced by two letters from the Jews of Jerusalem to those in Egypt. The substance of the book is derived from Judea, although it is presented for a Diaspora audience. Such a book defies classification as either Palestinian or Hellenistic (= Diaspora). Similarly, the works of Josephus stand in the apologetic tradition of Hellenistic Judaism.[58] Yet he himself was Palestinian.

We should not, of course, conclude that there were no differences at all between Palestine and the Diaspora. Palestinian Judaism produced no philosopher analogous to Philo. The Diaspora has nothing to compare with the rabbinic corpus which was compiled from Palestinian tradition some centuries later. Hebrew and Aramaic were still widely used in the homeland.[59] Judaism was never a minority religion in Hellenistic Palestine, and the social and cultural support was obviously greater there than elsewhere. If Judaism was politically and militarily threatened in Palestine at various times, the cultural threat to the plausibility of the tradition was greater in the Diaspora. While even such reclusive areas as Qumran show Hellenistic influence,[60] attempts to express the Jewish tradition in explicitly Hellenistic forms are relatively few in Palestinian Judaism while they predominate in the Diaspora. In short, while the familiar opposition of Hellenistic and Palestinian Judaism cannot be maintained and while there is a considerable gray area where we cannot be sure of the derivation of particular works, the fact remains that the main evidence for the attempt to present Judaism in Hellenistic dress derives from the Diaspora.

THE CONSTRAINTS OF THE TRADITION

The Hellenistic Jewish apologists operated within certain constraints derived from an authoritative religious tradition. Before we proceed to the ways in which they formulated their faith, it is necessary to consider the nature and force of these constraints, and so to ask what were the parameters within which a writer had to operate if he was to remain Jewish at all.

We may begin by observing that at least from the time of Ezra, Judaism had a canon of scripture, of which the book of the Torah, the Pentateuch, was the authoritative foundation.[61] It is significant that the earliest literary activity of the Greek-speaking Diaspora was the translation of the book of the Torah, and its influence is pervasive throughout the Hellenistic Jewish corpus.[62] The translation inevitably involved some transformation of the material. We need only mention the celebrated rendering of the divine self-introduction in Exod 3:14, *eimi ho ōn* ("I am the one who is"). However, while Hellenistic sensibilities in theology and style inevitably left some imprints, the LXX of the Pentateuch is remarkably faithful to its prototypes, and is far removed from the free rendering of the tradition we find in some Hellenistic Jewish authors, or from the paraphrastic nature of the Targums.[63] There is no doubt that it aspired to render accurately the basic documents of the tradition and to a great extent it succeeded.[64] In short, Diaspora Judaism had the same canonical foundation as its Palestinian counterpart.

The canonical Torah provided a common basis for postexilic Judaism, in the sense that all forms of Judaism relate to it in one way or another. It does not provide a definitive norm in the sense of prescribing a single orthodox way of being Jewish. To begin with, the scriptural canon continued to grow well into the Hellenistic period. The latest addition to the Hebrew canon, Daniel, was composed only at the time of the Maccabean revolt. The Greek translation of some of the writings was later still. Further, the religious life of the people was always informed by the ongoing tradition and by influential though noncanonical writings. The tradition drew heavily on the canonical scripture, but nevertheless rewrote it freely and continued to provide new formulations and emphases. The ongoing process of reformulation points to a more basic problem with any canon—the possibility of diverse interpretations. The most celebrated conflict of interpretations in postexilic Judaism was located in the Egyptian Diaspora.

Philo defended his allegorical interpretation against the "unreflective" literalists on the one hand, but also against the extreme allegorists "who, regarding laws in their literal sense in the light of symbols belonging to the intellect, are overpunctilious about the latter, while treating the former with easy-going neglect."[65] It should be observed that the extreme allegorists are not denounced as apostates, even though Philo "blames" them. They are still said to be "overpunctilious" in their own approach. The diversity of interpretation was not always due to Hellenistic philosophy, as can be seen from the exegetical peculiarities of the Qumran scrolls.[66] In fact, the Torah itself was never a consistent systematic treatise, but a compilation of materials which embraced diverse attitudes and even contradictions,[67] and so by its very nature invited diversity of interpretation.

It is of course possible that a particular interpretation of the Torah, or an understanding of Judaism distilled from the Torah, could attain normative status. E. P. Sanders has proposed the expression "pattern of religion" for "the description of how a religion is perceived by its adherents to *function*," that is "*how getting in and staying in are understood:* the way in which a religion is understood to admit and retain members is considered to be the way it 'functions.'"[68] Sanders has further argued that the pattern of "covenantal nomism" was pervasive in Palestinian Judaism and was the "basic *type* of religion" there in the period 200 BCE to 200 CE,[69] but was also widespread in the Diaspora and was to a great degree "*the* religion of Judaism."[70] Covenantal nomism is defined as "the view according to which salvation comes by *membership* in the covenant, while obedience to the commandments *preserves* one's place in the covenant."[71] There is no doubt that the conception of a covenant with its attendant obligations was of major importance in Judaism and occupied a central place in the canonical Torah. Yet here again the question of understanding and interpretation is crucial. If we grant Sanders's claim that 4 Ezra diverged from the pattern of covenantal nomism and is instead legalistic,[72] the fact remains that 4 Ezra clearly presupposes the Mosaic covenant as the basis of Judaism. The divergence lies in the understanding of the covenant, and 4 Ezra is none the less Jewish because of it. Again, Sanders's brief treatment of Diaspora Judaism shows that the pattern of covenantal nomism could coexist with other patterns in a subordinate role: while Philo "did not renounce covenantal nomism"[73] he regarded "true Judaism" as a quest for the vision of the incorporeal.[74] It is not enough then to ask whether the elements of covenantal nomism are present. We must ask what is the dominant pattern, which determines the understanding of Judaism on the most significant level.

When due emphasis is placed on the element of understanding in "the way a religion is understood to function," it becomes apparent that Judaism in the Hellenistic age was not nearly as uniform as Sanders suggests. The traditional "covenant form" which has been outlined by Mendenhall and Baltzer,[75] entailed one particular understanding of Judaism. The obligations of the law arose from the history of the people, especially from the mighty acts by which God had given them the land. That history imposed a debt of gratitude and loyalty. Further motivation was supplied by the blessings and curses which promised well-being to the faithful and punishment for the rebellious. This understanding of the covenant persisted throughout the Hellenistic and Roman periods. It is clearly shown in a series of prayers of repentance, which review the history of the people, confess their breach of obligation, acknowledge their present distress as an appropriate punishment and then appeal to the mercy of God. These prayers are found in canonical texts (Nehemiah 9, Dan 9:4b–13), at Qumran (1QS 1:24b–2:1; CD 20: 28–30; 4Q Words of the Luminaries 1:8–7:2), and in the Diaspora, east and west (Tobit 3:1–6; 3 Mac 2:2–20; LXX prayer of Esther).[76] Yet, side by side with these traditional formulations we find other interpretations of Judaism. It is of the essence of the apocalyptic literature that the history of Israel is no longer a sufficient grounding for the covenant obligations. There is need of a higher, supernatural revelation. It is the vision of the apocalyptic seer, over and above the recollection of history, which provides the insight to support the faithful.[77] By contrast, in the wisdom literature there is no such appeal to higher revelation. Yet here too the traditional logic of the covenant is thrust into the background. Wisdom is derived from the observation of human nature which is potentially universal. Israel and its law may be the supreme embodiment of wisdom, but their status is appreciated in the universal categories of wisdom rather than asserted on the basis of Israel's history.[78] Wisdom and apocalypticism, then, to mention only two major examples, reflect different understandings of Judaism, each distinct from the traditional covenantal pattern. This is not to suggest that we can isolate rigidly separate and mutually incompatible patterns in postexilic Judaism.

Quite the contrary. As Sanders has shown in the case of Philo, distinct ways of understanding the religion can persist side by side with little attempt to clarify their implications for each other. Religion is notoriously resistant to attempts to reduce it to consistency.

A religion such as Judaism in the Hellenistic age is nourished by a long tradition, which inevitably contains an accumulation of diverse and often contradictory elements. The diversity which exists within the book of the Torah itself is well known. People remain within the religion as long as they continue to define their identity in terms of the tradition and find within it adequate resources for life.[79] Despite the undeniably central role of the covenant law in the Jewish tradition, not all strands of Judaism had their primary focus on the law, and even those that did understood it in various ways. None of the variants of Judaism actually rejects the law, although some pay little explicit attention to it. Since the purpose of a religion is to assemble resources for living rather than articulate consistent systems, we cannot be surprised to find that different ways of understanding the religion are commonly found in combination, although it is usually possible to speak of a dominant pattern.

In the light of the preceding discussion, the importance of the canonical Torah can be seen in perspective. The Torah was the basic component in the tradition and those who would remain within Judaism had to relate themselves to it in some way. This did not mean that all had to conform to a single pattern. Not all the laws were necessarily binding, and the element of law was not necessarily the focal point of the tradition which was most significant for establishing Jewish identity. Rather, a number of different approaches could be taken within the parameters of the tradition.

Further, we must beware of defining Jewish identity too narrowly in theological terms. As we noted at the outset, national identity was always built up by a number of factors. Ethnic continuity is evidently a matter of some importance, despite the acceptance of proselytes, and is a serious factor in the prohibition of intermarriage. Political allegiance and relations with the land of Israel are also significant factors in Jewish identity.

Finally, we must recognize that the Jewish identity of a cultivated man like Philo was not quite the same as that of the Roman Jew "taught by his mother to beg."[80] Social stratification undoubtedly modified Jewish understanding of the tradition and relations with the gentiles.[81] Unfortunately, the views of the lower classes are not well recorded in the literature. The distinct groupings which we can identify in Ptolemaic Egypt are political rather than social—e.g., as shown in the attitudes towards the various Egyptian rulers in the sibylline oracles—or are even simply theological. Only after the first revolt against Rome (66–70 CE) do we find significant social division within the Jewish community—in the rejection of the Sicarii by the Alexandrian Jews and the destruction of the Jewish upper classes in Cyrene.

PROSPECT

With these various factors in mind our study of the Hellenistic Diaspora is divided into two main parts:

Part One: National and Political Identity.

Part Two: Identity through Ethics and Piety.

I. Part One considers Jewish identity primarily in historical and political terms and is divided into three chapters:

1. The Uses of the Past: The retelling of history as a way of redefining identity, both by refuting hostile accounts and by modifying the tradition in the light of the Hellenistic environment. Several of the earliest documents of Hellenistic Judaism fall into this category.

2. Religion and Politics: The Ptolemaic Age: A number of documents from the second and first centuries BCE contain a significant element of political propaganda (Sib Or 3 is perhaps the prime example). These documents throw light on the conception of Jewish identity in political terms and the consequent attitudes towards gentile authorities and towards the land of Israel.

3. Religion and Politics: The Roman Age: Political aspects of Jewish identity are again reflected in the struggles in Alexandria in the first century CE and in the events leading up to the Diaspora revolt.

II. Part Two also has three chapters:

4. The Common Ethic: One of the best known characteristics of Hellenistic Judaism lies in the attempt to build bridges to Hellenistic culture by affirming Jewish values which were also appreciated by enlightened gentiles (e.g., rejection of idolatry and homosexuality) while playing down the more problematic rituals and observances. While we do not find strict consistency

in the various Jewish documents, there is a nearly universal trend in this direction, and we will find few exceptions.

5. Philosophical Judaism: The main representative of philosophical Judaism was Philo of Alexandria. We will not attempt an analysis of Philo's copious works here, but will be concerned with the preliminary stages of the attempt to translate Jewish tradition into philosophical terms, in, e.g., Aristobulus and the Letter of Aristeas.

6. The Mysteries of God: The understanding of Judaism in terms of divine mystery which requires a revelation or mystical experience over and above the Mosaic Torah. The higher vision, again, can be conceived in various ways, ranging from the philosophical orientation of the Orphic fragments to the mythic mode of apocalypses such as 3 Baruch and 2 Enoch.

The division of the material proposed above is a practical means of organizing the various aspects of Jewish identity in the Diaspora. There is no implication that the different aspects are mutually exclusive. A text which retells Israelite history may also reflect political allegiance and may further attempt to propagate an ethical message. Accordingly, some of the major documents will be discussed, from different aspects, in more than one chapter. Our objective is not to impose any simple divisions on Diaspora Judaism, but rather to appreciate the variety and complexity of the factors which molded Jewish identity even in a single situation or in a single document.

Notes

1. See J. Bowker, *The Religious Imagination and the Sense of God* (Oxford: Clarendon, 1978) 17.

2. P. Berger, *The Sacred Canopy. Elements of a Sociological Theory of Religion* (Garden City: Doubleday, 1969) 16. See also P. Berger and T. Luckmann, *The Social Construction of Reality* (Garden City: Doubleday, 1967).

3. Berger, ibid.

4. Ibid., 13.

5. Ibid., 27: "Viewed historically, most of man's worlds have been sacred worlds."

6. Clifford Geertz, in his well-known definition of religion, speaks of "an aura of factuality" which makes its moods and motivations "seem uniquely realistic" ("Religion as a Cultural System," in Donald Cutler [ed.], *The Religious Situation: 1968* [Boston: Beacon, 1968] 643).

7. Josephus (*Ag Ap* 1.191) cites Hecataeus as saying that the Jews were subjected to religious persecution by the Persians. The authenticity of the passage is disputed.

8. Berger (*The Sacred Canopy*, 16) states: "The world is built up in the conscious-ness of the individual by conversation with significant others."

9. Jer 29:7. See W. Lee Humphreys, "A Life-Style for Diaspora: A Study of the Tales of Esther and Daniel," *JBL* 92 (1973) 211–23.

10. See J. Bright, *A History of Israel* (2nd ed.; Philadelphia: Westminster, 1972) 363. Josephus (*Ant* 11.1.3[8]) says that "many remained in Babylon, being unwilling to leave their possessions."

11. See J. Neusner, *A History of the Jews in Babylonia I* (Leiden: Brill, 1965); M. Stern, "The Jewish Diaspora," in *The Jewish People in the First Century* (Compendia Rerum Iudaicarum ad Novum Testamentum, vol. 1; ed. S. Safrai and M. Stern; Philadel-phia: Fortress, 1974) 170–80.

12. Jeremiah 41–44. Bright, *History*, 346; B. Oded, "Judah and the Exile," in *Israel-ite and Judaean History* (ed. J. H. Hayes and J. M. Miller; Philadelphia: Westminster, 1977) 486–88.

13. See A. Cowley, *Aramaic Papyri of the Fifth Century BC* (London: Oxford, 1923); E. G. Kraeling, *The Brooklyn Museum Aramaic Papyri* (New Haven: Yale, 1953); B. Porten, *Archives from Elephantine: The Life of an Ancient Jewish Military Colony* (Berkeley: University of California, 1968); P. Grelot, *Documents araméens d'Égypte: introduction, traduction, présentation* (Paris: Cerf, 1972). The Jews claimed to have lived at Elephantine prior to the Persian conquest of Egypt in 525 BCE. The garrison disappears from view shortly after 400 BCE.

14. See V. Tcherikover, *Hellenistic Civilization and the Jews* (New York: Atheneum, 1970) 269–73. The letter of Aristeas (12–14) tells of 100,000 Jewish captives brought to Egypt under Ptolemy I, of whom some 30,000 were placed in garrisons. The historical value of this evidence is questionable. At least the numbers are inflated. Tcherikover, however, accepts "that the Jewish diaspora in Hellenistic Egypt began under Ptolemy I, and that the vast majority of the Jews left their native country not of their free will but under compulsion." Josephus cites Hecataeus for the view that Jews (including a high priest Hezekiah) followed Ptolemy willingly, but the authenticity of the passage is disputed (*Ag Ap* 1.186–87). Josephus's own claim that the Jews came to Egypt under Alexander and were given equal rights with the Greeks (*Ag Ap* 2.35; *JW* 2.487) is widely rejected.

15. V. A. Tcherikover and A. Fuks (eds.), *Corpus Papyrorum Iudaicarum* (Cam-bridge, Mass.: Harvard, 1957) 1:1–3 (henceforth *CPJ*). Tcherikover notes that Jewish migration was part of a wider phenomenon of Syrian migration and also notes that there was an active trade in slaves.

16. Josephus, *JW* 7.3.3 (44–45). C. H. Kraeling, "The Jewish Community at Antioch," *JBL* 51 (1932) 130–60; W. A. Meeks and R. L. Wilken, *Jews and Christians in Antioch in the First Four Centuries of the Common Era* (Sources for Biblical Study 13; Chico: Scholars Press, 1978) 2–5. For an overview of the history of Jewish communities in the Diaspora see Stern, "The Jewish Diaspora," 117–83. Noteworthy studies of particular areas include H. J. Leon, *The Jews of Ancient Rome* (Philadelphia: Jewish Publication Society, 1960); A. T. Kraabel, *Judaism in Western Asia Minor under the Roman Empire* (Diss. Harvard, 1968); and S. Applebaum, *Jews and Greeks in Ancient Cyrene* (SJLA 28; Leiden: Brill, 1979).

17. Jerome (*In Daniel* 11:13–14, *Patrologia Latina* 25.562): "Onias sacerdos, as-sumptis Judaeorum plurimis, fugit in Aegyptum"; ibid., 563: "sub occasione ergo Oniae pontificis, infinita examina Judaeorum Aegyptum confugerunt." Tcherikover comments on the "infinita examina": "even taking into consideration the usual tendency of an-cient authors to exaggerate numbers . . . we may infer that the number of new immi-grants from Judaea was certainly considerable" (*CPJ* 1:2).

18. 1 Mac 15:16–21 cites a letter from a Roman consul to the reigning Ptolemy, which asks that "if any pestilent men have fled to you from their country hand them over to Simon, the high priest, that he may punish them according to their law." If the letter is genuine, the consul is Lucius Calpurnius Piso in 140–139 BCE and the Ptolemy is Euergetes II Physcon. See Tcherikover, *CPJ* 1:3. Tcherikover also notes a Talmudic tale concerning a Pharisaic leader who fled to Egypt from a Sadducean king.

19. Philo, *In Flaccum*, 43, 45. Cf. *De Vita Mosis*, 2.232; *Legatio ad Gaium*, 214, 245. Also Hecataeus in Diodorus Siculus, 40.3, 8 and Strabo, *Geography*, 16.2, 28. See Stern, "The Jewish Diaspora," 117.

20. There was no enumeration of Jews until the introduction of the Jewish tax in 71–72 CE, so there were no exact figures available to Philo.

21. Tcherikover, *CPJ* 1:19. For an overview see S. Applebaum, "The Social and Economic Status of Jews in the Diaspora," *Compendia* 2:701–27. There was apparently a very large class of Jewish slaves in Rome, and the Roman satirists repeatedly mock Jewish poverty, but even there many Jews were well-to-do.

22. Tcherikover, *CPJ* 1:38–39. In the Ptolemaic period the gymnasia were in private hands and it would seem that no special qualifications were needed for entry. In Tcherikover's view, Jewish access to the gymnasia was a major point of contention in the time of Caligula. On the other hand, A. Kasher ("The Jewish Attitude to the Alexandrian Gymnasium in the First Century A.D.," *American Journal of Ancient History* 1 [1976] 148–61) denies that Jews even wanted access to the gymnasium and holds that they were hostile to it. See also Kasher, *The Jews in Hellenistic and Roman Egypt* (Tel Aviv: Tel Aviv University, 1978, in Hebrew) chap. 9.

23. Tcherikover, *CPJ* 1:27–36. The recourse to Hellenistic law is noteworthy because there was an autonomous Jewish tribunal in Alexandria.

24. A. Momigliano, *Alien Wisdom* (Cambridge: Cambridge University, 1975) 74–96 ("The Hellenistic Discovery of Judaism").

25. M. Stern, *Greek and Latin Authors on Jews and Judaism* (2 vols.; Jerusalem: Israel Academy of Sciences and Humanities, 1974, 1981); "The Jews in Greek and Latin Literature," *Compendia* 2: 1101–59; J. N. Sevenster, *The Roots of Pagan Anti-Semitism in the Ancient World* (Nov T Sup 41; Leiden: Brill, 1975); J. L. Daniel, "Anti-Semitism in the Hellenistic Roman Period," *JBL* 98 (1979) 45–65 and the literature there cited.

26. *Ag Ap* 1.209–12; *Ant* 12.1.1 (5–6).

27. *Ag Ap* 2.112–14.

28. See E. Bickermann, "Ritualmord und Eselskult," *Studies in Jewish and Christian History* (AGJU 9; Leiden: Brill, 1980) 225–55 (originally published in *Monatsschrift für Geschichte und Wissenschaft des Judentums* 71 [1927]).

29. *Ag Ap* 2.79.

30. Stern, "The Jews in Greek and Latin Literature," 1123–25. For the fragments of Posidonius, see L. Edelstein and I. G. Kidd, *Posidonius I, The Fragments* (Cambridge: Cambridge University, 1972).

31. *Ag Ap* 2.147.

32. Eusebius, PE 9.19.1–3.

33. Stern, "The Jews in Greek and Latin Literature," 1144–45; B. Wardy, "Jewish Religion in Pagan Literature during the Late Republic and Early Empire," *ANRW* 19/1 (1979) 592–613.

34. Horace, *Satires* 1.5.100. See further Daniel, "Anti-Semitism," 54–57.

35. Stern, "The Jews in Greek and Latin Literature," 1150–59.

36. See further Wardy, "Jewish Religion in Pagan Literature," 613–35.

37. *Ag Ap* 1.227–87. See P. M. Fraser, *Ptolemaic Alexandria* (Oxford: Clarendon, 1972) 1:508–9. Jews in Egypt encountered hostility long before the Hellenistic period as can be seen from the case of Elephantine.

38. *Ag Ap* 1.288–320.

39. Josephus (*Ag Ap* 2.48) says that Apion derides the names of the Jewish generals Onias and Dositheus for taking the side of Philometor's widow against Ptolemy Euergetes II. The rivalry between Jews and Greeks in the Ptolemaic court may be reflected in the Greek translation of Esther which makes Haman a Macedonian (see *CPJ* 1:24).

40. For a concise summary of this history see *CPJ* 1:48–93. Also E. M. Smallwood, *Philonis Alexandrini Legatio ad Gaium* (2nd ed.; Leiden: Brill, 1970) 3–36. For further bibliography see J. J. Collins, *The Sibylline Oracles of Egyptian Judaism* (SBLDS 13; Missoula: Scholars Press, 1974) 184–86.

41. Sevenster, *The Roots of Pagan Anti-Semitism*, 89–144; Daniel, "Anti-Semitism," 51–54.

42. See Bowker, *The Religious Imagination*, 31–45. The insistence on clear boundary markers and distinctive observances is typical of a beleaguered community, struggling to retain its identity in a hostile environment.

43. For references see Daniel, "Anti-Semitism," 55–56.

44. For the following see Stern, "The Jews in Greek and Latin Literature," passim; J. G. Gager, *Moses in Greco-Roman Paganism* (SBLMS 16; New York: Abingdon, 1972).

45. M. Friedländer, *Geschichte der jüdischen Apologetik* (Zurich: Schmidt, 1903); P. Dalbert, *Die Theologie der Hellenistisch-Jüdischen Missionsliteratur unter Ausschluss von Philo und Josephus* (Hamburg: Reich, 1954); D. Georgi, *Die Gegner des Paulus im 2 Korintherbrief* (WMANT 11; Neukirchen-Vluyn: Neukirchener Verlag, 1964) 51–53.

46. V. Tcherikover, "Jewish Apologetic Literature Reconsidered," *Eos* 48 (1956) 169–93.

47. I take the term *dissonance* from L. Festinger, *A Theory of Cognitive Dissonance* (Evanston, Ill., and White Plains, N.Y.: Row, Peterson & Co., 1957). A useful summary of the theory and of the subsequent critical literature can be found in R. P. Carroll, *When Prophecy Failed: Cognitive Dissonance in the Prophetic Traditions of the Old Testament* (New York: Seabury, 1979) 86–128.

48. Festinger, *A Theory of Cognitive Dissonance*, 18. For various ways in which this may be done, see ibid, 182.

49. Another example is Dositheus, son of Drimylus, whose apostasy is recorded in 3 Mac 1:3 and who is also known from the papyri (*CPJ* 1:230–36). At the end of the first revolt against Rome an apostate Antiochus, son of the archon of the Antiochene Jews, incited a pogrom against the Jews of Antioch (*JW* 7:47). On the phenomenon of apostasy see further H. A. Wolfson, *Philo* (Cambridge: Harvard, 1948) 1:73–78.

50. "If more and more people can be persuaded that a system of belief is correct, then clearly it must after all be correct" (L. Festinger, H. W. Riecken, and S. Schachter, *When Prophecy Fails* [New York: Harper, 1956] 28). See also J. G. Gager, *Kingdom and Community* (Englewood Cliffs: Prentice-Hall, 1975) 39. Compare Festinger, *A Theory of Cognitive Dissonance*, 200–202.

51. See esp. M. Hengel, *Judaism and Hellenism* (2 vols.; Philadelphia: Fortress, 1974): *Juden, Griechen und Barbaren, Aspekte der Hellenisierung des Judentums in vorchristlicher Zeit* (SBS 76; Stuttgart: KBW, 1976) (ET, *Jews, Greeks and Barbarians* [Philadelphia: Fortress, 1980]); Tcherikover, *Hellenistic Civilization*, 39–265; E. Schürer, *The History of the Jewish People in the Age of Jesus Christ* (rev. and ed. G. Vermes, F. Millar, and M. Black; Edinburgh: Clark, 1979):2:29–80. On the Greek language in Palestine see G. Mussies, "Greek in Palestine and the Diaspora," *Compendia* 2:1040–64 and the literature there cited. See also D. Flusser, "Paganism in Palestine," ibid., 1065–100.

52. For the Zeno papyri see *CPJ* 1:115–46; for the Tobiads, Josephus, *Ant* 12.4.1–11 (154–234).

53. Schürer, *History*, 2:85–183.

54. Tcherikover, *Hellenistic Civilization*, 253.

55. Josephus, *Ant* 13.11.3 (318).

56. See chap. 4 below.

57. C. A. Moore, *Daniel, Esther and Jeremiah: The Additions* (AB 44; Garden City: Doubleday, 1977) 250–51. The reliability of the ascription is questionable.

58. H. W. Attridge, *The Interpretation of Biblical History in the Antiquitates Iudaicae of Flavius Josephus* (HDR 7; Missoula: Scholars Press, 1976) and the articles by L. H. Feldman noted in Attridge's bibliography. H. R. Moehring, "The Acta pro Judaeis in the *Antiquities* of Flavius Josephus. A Study in Hellenistic and Modern Apologetic Historiography," in J. Neusner (ed.), *Christianity, Judaism and other Greco-Roman Cults: Studies for Morton Smith at Sixty* (Leiden: Brill, 1975) 3:124–58. Josephus, unlike the Diaspora apologists, addressed his work explicitly to the gentiles.

59. C. Rabin, "Hebrew and Aramaic in the First Century," *Compendia* 2:1007–39; Schürer, *History*, 2:20–28.

60. M. Hengel, "Qumran und der Hellenismus," in M. Delcor (ed.), *Qumrân. Sa piété, sa théologie et son milieu* (BETL 46; Paris/Gembloux: Duculot/Louvain University, 1978) 333–72.

61. On the development of the idea of a canon see S. Z. Leiman (*The Canonization of Hebrew Scripture* [Transactions of the Connecticut Academy of Arts and Sciences 47; Hamden, Conn.: Archon, 1976] 16–26), who concludes that "the Torah in its present form was certainly canonical during the lifetime of Ezra and his associates (fifth–fourth centuries B.C.)."

62. See S. Jellicoe (*The Septuagint and Modern Study* [Oxford: Clarendon, 1968] 55): "Association direct or indirect with Philadelphus places the undertaking well before the middle of the third century B.C. Apart from the Aristeas tradition this is borne out by the available external evidence." So also Fraser, *Ptolemaic Alexandria,* 1:690. Jellicoe discusses the various modern theories of origin on pp. 59–73. A good sample of modern views on the LXX can be found in S. Jellicoe (ed.), *Studies in the Septuagint: Origins Recensions and Interpretations* (New York: Ktav, 1974). The main opponent of the view that the LXX was translated in the time of Philadelphus was Paul Kahle, who argued that the Greek Bible developed in the form of unofficial targumlike translations and that the Letter of Aristeas was promoting a revised translation about 100 BCE. Kahle's view can be found in *The Cairo Geniza* (Oxford: Blackwell, 1959). It has been widely rejected in the light of the Qumran discoveries. See Jellicoe, *The Septuagint,* 59–63.

63. Hengel, *Juden, Griechen und Barbaren,* 131–32; E. J. Bickermann, "The Septuagint as a Translation," *Studies in Jewish and Christian History* 1:167–200. Since the discovery of the Qumran scrolls it has become apparent that in many cases where the LXX differs from the MT it had a different Hebrew prototype. See F. M. Cross and S. Talmon (eds.), *Qumran and the History of the Biblical Text* (Cambridge: Harvard, 1975). It should be noted that the divergence from the Hebrew is more significant in later books such as Job and Proverbs than it is in the Pentateuch. See Jellicoe, *The Septuagint,* 316–18.

64. See H. M. Orlinsky, "The Septuagint as Holy Writ and the Philosophy of the Translators," *HUCA* 46 (1975) 89–114. "It is the literal word-for-word rendering that prevailed in the Septuagint rendering of the Torah" (ibid., p. 103). There is widespread agreement that "the translation was made for Jews, undoubtedly for use in synagogue worship and instruction. To this its style bears witness, and is against its being a translation executed for purely literary effect" (Jellicoe, *The Septuagint,* 55).

65. Philo, *De Migratione Abrahami,* 89–93. See the discussion by Wolfson, *Philo* 1:66–71. Wolfson contends that while Philo "blamed" the allegorists, he did not blame the literalists, citing *De Confusione Linguarum,* 38, 190, where he says that he would "not blame such persons, for perhaps the truth is with them also." However, it does not follow that Philo would never "blame" the literalists, but only that he did not in this particular case.

66. See O. Betz, *Offenbarung und Schriftforschung in der Qumransekte* (WUNT 6; Tübingen: Mohr, 1960).

67. See, e.g., P. D. Hanson, "The Theological Significance of Contradiction within the Book of the Covenant," *Canon and Authority* (ed. G. W. Coats and B. O. Long; Philadelphia: Fortress, 1977) 110–31.

68. E. P. Sanders, *Paul and Palestinian Judaism* (Philadelphia: Fortress, 1977) 17.

69. Ibid., 426.

70. E. P. Sanders, "The Covenant as a Soteriological Category and the Nature of Salvation in Palestinian and Hellenistic Judaism," in R. Hamerton-Kelly and R. Scroggs (eds.), *Jews, Greeks and Christians: Essays in Honor of William David Davies* (SJLA 21; Leiden: Brill, 1976) 41; *Paul and Palestinian Judaism,* 75, 235–36. Sanders does not claim that this was the only pattern of religion in Judaism. In Palestinian Judaism he finds 4 Ezra exceptional in that salvation is strictly according to an individual's works, while in Hellenistic Judaism he recognizes another view of "realized salvation through a mystic rite or vision."

71. Ibid.

72. I am not convinced that this view is justified, but 4 Ezra's understanding of the covenant is in any case somewhat different from, say, 2 Baruch.

73. Sanders, "The Covenant as a Soteriological Category," 42.

74. Ibid., 34.

75. Mendenhall, *Law and Covenant in Israel and the Ancient Near East* (Pittsburgh: Presbyterian Board of Colportage, 1954); K. Baltzer, *The Covenant Formulary* (Philadelphia: Fortress, 1971); D. Hillers, *Covenant, The History of a Biblical Idea* (Baltimore: Johns Hopkins, 1969).

76. O. H. Steck, *Israel und das gewaltsame Geschick der Propheten* (WMANT 23; Neukirchen-Vluyn: Neukirchener Verlag, 1967).

77. J. J. Collins, "Cosmos and Salvation: Jewish Wisdom and Apocalyptic in the Hellenistic Age," *HR* 17 (1977) 121–42; *Apocalypse. The Morphology of a Genre* (Semeia 14; Missoula: Scholars Press, 1979) 9–12; U. Luck, "Das Weltverständnis in der jüdischen Apokalyptik, dargestellt am äthiopischen Henoch und am 4 Ezra," *ZTK* 73 (1976) 283–305.

78. J. J. Collins, "The Biblical Precedent for Natural Theology," *JAAR* 45/1 (1977) Supp B:35–67.

79. Cf. the remarks of J. Bowker, *The Religious Imagination*, 17–18.

80. Martial 12.57.13.

81. On the social stratification of Jews in the Diaspora, see esp. S. Applebaum, "The Social and Economic Status of the Jews in the Diaspora," *Compendia* 2:701–27.

Part One

NATIONAL AND POLITICAL IDENTITY

Chapter 1

THE USES OF THE PAST

The expression of Jewish identity in national and political terms is found in a wide range of writings and literary genres. The form which lent itself most readily to this purpose was undoubtedly history writing, not in the modern critical sense but broadly construed to embrace the myths and legends of the people. History, as the story of the people's past and origin, had always been highly valued in Judaism. Much of the biblical material has a "historylike" character in the sense that it tells the story of the people within a chronological framework.[1] In the Hellenistic age the Jews had new reason to retell the story of their past.

The spread of Hellenism under Alexander and his successors was accompanied, at least initially, by considerable Greek curiosity about the strange peoples of the East. A number of writers, such as Megasthenes and Hecataeus of Abdera attempted to satisfy it.[2] While these writers were "important and responsible persons,"[3] they had only a superficial knowledge of the cultures they described and were hampered by their ignorance of the relevant languages. They did, however, have a tradition of ethnography dating back to the histories of Herodotus and the geographical writings of Hecataeus of Miletus, and they tended to cast the eastern peoples in molds prepared by the Greek imagination. So, for example, the early Hellenistic writers tended to depict the Jews as "priestly sages of the type the East was expected to produce."[4] Romance and legend were blended with factual reporting. Hecataeus of Abdera preserves a detailed description of the Ramasseum, the mortuary chapel of Rameses II, but also a lengthy and highly legendary account of the conquests and deeds of Sesostris.[5] Other factors besides simple curiosity undoubtedly influ-

25

enced these writers. Hecataeus's tendency to assert the superiority and greater antiquity of Egyptian culture may well have been motivated by a desire to establish the superiority of the Ptolemaic kingdom.[6]

The writings of the Greeks about the East prompted some of the native peoples to explain their own culture to the Greek world. Their attempts were inevitably influenced by Greek prototypes, but they were diverse in kind. Some "wanted to replace the romantic tales of Herodotus, Ctesias, Megasthenes, and other Greek authorities on the orient by a dry but authentic recapitulation of native records."[7] Such, essentially, were Berossus of Babylon[8] and Manetho of Egypt.[9] Yet their free inclusion of myths and legends could not satisfy the more scientific of the Greeks, who had grown skeptical of the historical value of myths. Bickermann has observed the implausibility of the primeval history of Berossus, or of the Bible, for those who questioned the historicity of Homer's epics.[10] On the other hand, some gave free rein to the romantic and legendary elements, and tales about Semiramis and Nebuchadnezzar, Sesostris and Nektanebo circulated widely.[11] The writers of the various nations were also aware of each other and their writings often had a competitive aspect, as each laid claim to the greatest antiquity and most impressive culture heroes.[12] They also engaged in polemics. Already Manetho incorporated a derogatory account of Jewish origins in his Egyptian history[13] and thereby initiated a long line of Jewish-Egyptian polemics, which is recorded and continued in Josephus's tract against Apion at the end of the first century CE.

The earliest literature of the Hellenistic Diaspora developed in the context of this initial mutual discovery by the Greeks and their subjects. The Septuagint itself could be viewed in part as a contribution to this process but it was singularly unsuited to catch the attention of the Greeks.[14] In fact, the Greeks paid little attention to any of the writings of the native orientals,[15] but many Jewish writers did express themselves in forms which might have been accessible to the Greeks. Even if they failed to make any significant impact on the gentile audience they surely helped satisfy the self-understanding of the increasingly Hellenized Jewish community.

The earliest writings of the Hellenistic Diaspora have survived only in fragments. Their survival was due to the industry of Alexander

Polyhistor of Miletus, who was brought to Rome as a prisoner of war and given his freedom by Sulla about 80 BCE, and wrote in the following decades.[16] While he may have "lacked taste and originality,"[17] his compilations of excerpts from other authors preserved samples of much literature that would otherwise have been lost. It is noteworthy that the work of Berossus, also, was known to posterity only through Alexander.[18] Alexander's own work has not survived, but substantial fragments have been preserved by other authors.[19] His work on the Jews was cited at length by Eusebius in the ninth book of his Praeparatio Evangelica, and this is our chief source for the fragments of the early Hellenistic Jewish authors.[20] Fragments are also preserved by Clement of Alexandria and by Josephus.[21] Both Eusebius and Alexander repeated their sources accurately, insofar as we can judge.[22] While the preserved fragments are less than we should wish they attest a rich variety in Jewish Hellenistic literature which has seldom been given its due by modern scholars.[23]

We may distinguish three main approaches to the past in the Jewish Hellenistic literature:

1. The faithful chroniclers, whose main representative is Demetrius.
2. The historical romances, represented by, e.g., Artapanus.
3. The epic poets, Philo and Theodotus.

THE FAITHFUL CHRONICLERS

DEMETRIUS

The earliest known Hellenistic Jewish author, Demetrius, often called the Chronographer,[24] has been aptly classified by Bickermann with those oriental historians like Berossus and Manetho who sought to produce "a dry but authentic recapitulation of native records."[25] His date is indicated by the passage in Clement (*Stromateis*, 1.141.8), where he reckons the time from the fall of Samaria to the fourth Ptolemy. The numbers given are problematic but we may agree with Fraser that the reference to Ptolemy IV is less likely to be corrupt than the numbers, and so accept the usual dating to the time of Philopator (222–205 BCE), approximately half a century after Manetho.[26]

The rather scanty fragments have been variously characterized. Freudenthal regards Demetrius as a forerunner of midrashic literature; Walter classifies him as an exegete, while Fraser insists that he is more historian than exegete. There is some basis for each of these opinions. Demetrius is concerned to resolve problems in the biblical text, but the problems on which he focuses are primarily matters of chronology and genealogy.[27] By resolving the apparent historical problems he sought to establish the reliability of the tradition. His picture of Judaism, such as it is, is then allowed to emerge from the retelling of history. The approach to Jewish identity is through the record of the people's past.

The concerns of Demetrius may be illustrated by the passage (PE 9.29.1–3) on the marriage of Moses and Zipporah, the daughter of Jethro.[28] Demetrius postulates, on the basis of "the similarity of the names," that Zipporah was descended from Abraham and Khettourah. He then fills out her genealogy by following the LXX Gen 25:1–3 (against the Hebrew) in saying that Raguel was a descendant of Abraham in the fourth generation.[29] He goes beyond the LXX in saying that Raguel is the father of Jethro. (The two are identified both in the Hebrew and in the Greek Bible). Zipporah is thus in the sixth generation from Abraham. Demetrius next sets himself to show how Moses in the seventh generation could be contemporary with Zipporah in the sixth. He points out that "Abraham married Khettourah at the age of one hundred and forty, when Isaac, from whom Moses was descended, was already married." Hence the gap of one generation. He goes on to assert on the basis of Gen 25:6 that Abraham had sent the children of his concubines to the east and concludes that this is how Moses was said to marry an Ethiopian woman—i.e., Zipporah and the Ethiopian woman were one and the same.

On the one hand, this passage shows that Demetrius was sensitive to "the requirements of scientific historical writing"[30] in attempting to resolve chronological problems. On the other hand, the passage also reflects a typically Jewish concern by showing that Moses was not polygamous and did not marry outside his own people. The historical record can then lend its support to a legal view of Judaism on an issue which must have been highly relevant for Diaspora Judaism.

Demetrius's method was certainly influenced by Hellenistic standards. Fraser and Wacholder have pointed out a general similarity to Eratosthenes in the critical attitude towards his sources.[31] The entire work reflects the common Alexandrian procedure of *aporiai kai luseis* ("problems and solutions").[32] Not all his *aporiai* are chronological. He also addresses such questions as why Joseph delayed to bring his relatives to Egypt and how the Israelites got their weapons at the time of the Exodus.

Demetrius provides a good illustration of the difficulty in determining whether the Hellenistic Jewish literature was designed for Jewish or gentile readers. The issues he discusses would scarcely be of interest to anyone other than Jews. Against this, Fraser contends that "the Jews of Alexandria did not need a chronological study of the book of Genesis."[33] We have seen that there is some concern to satisfy the requirements of Greek scientific historiography. Demetrius evidently assumed a readership which used the Greek language and was aware of Hellenistic critical standards. It may well be, however, that the Jews of Alexandria constituted such an audience, and that Fraser is mistaken when he asserts that they did not need a chronological study of Genesis. The credibility of the biblical record had to be established in face of the growing critical awareness of the Hellenistic Jews themselves. Fraser tentatively suggests that Demetrius wished to refute Manetho's hostile account of the Exodus, but there is no trace of polemic in Demetrius, so such a refutation would be very indirect. On the other hand, the demonstration that Moses did not marry outside his people had very direct relevance for the Hellenistic Jews. Demetrius would surely have welcomed, and perhaps hoped for, gentile readers, but his work can be most fully understood as an attempt to shape the self-understanding of the Jewish community.

What survives of Demetrius's history is too fragmentary to permit a full grasp of his understanding of Judaism. He was obviously attached to the Torah and was concerned to establish its credibility. He dealt with it as history, which might be compared with the histories of other peoples. The surviving fragments do not explicitly discuss the Jewish law, but the identification of the Cushite woman as a descendant of Abraham makes it probable that he saw Judaism as a "covenantal nomism" where it was important to remain within the bounds of the chosen people by keeping its laws. He lacks the tendencies to syncretism and to symbolism which are common in other Jewish Hellenistic writers, and gives an impression of narrow concentration on the Torah, which is quite rare. Yet in attempting to establish the credibility of the Torah for gentile or Hellenized Jew, he accepted Hellenistic

forms of thought as the framework for his presentation and helped lay
the foundation for the fusion of Jewish tradition and Hellenistic culture.

THE FOLLOWERS OF DEMETRIUS

Demetrius had few followers in his detailed exegetical approach to
Jewish history. Aristeas, sometimes called "the exegete," may have
been a kindred spirit, but his work "On the Jews" survives only in a
single fragment.[34]

This fragment is entirely devoted to Job. Its dependence on the
LXX of Job is evident from several factors. Job is identified with Iobab
of Gen 36:33. The Hebrew forms of the names would not suggest the
identification. Job's homeland is given as Ausitis, as in the LXX. The
statement that Job's mother was Bassara is most easily explained from
the LXX of Gen 36:33, *Iobab huios Zara ek Bosorras,* where Bosorra
represents the place name Bozra of the Hebrew. The friends of Job are
called *basileus, tyrannos,* and *basileus* as in the LXX, and there are
further verbal correspondences.[35]

There are also striking correspondences between Aristeas and the
addition to the LXX Job in 42:17. Both assert that Job is descended
from Esau and from Bassara. Ausitis is located on the borders of Edom
and Arabia, and Job is identified with Iobab. Freudenthal argued that
the addition to the LXX was dependent on Aristeas and this position is
accepted by Walter, but the relationship may be more complex. LXX
Job 42:17 claims to be derived from "a Syriac book" and there are
minor differences between the two.[36] Both may depend on an exegetical tradition.

None of this is of much help for dating Aristeas since we cannot date
the translation of LXX Job. The possible time period is approximately
250–60 BCE (the time of Polyhistor). Whether this Aristeas is at all
related to the pseudonymous Aristeas of the Letter to Philocrates is
doubtful. Walter categorically rejects any relation.[37] It is conceivable
that this work of Aristeas is the referent in the Letter of Aristeas 6: "On
a previous occasion also I transmitted to you an exposition of matters I
deemed worthy of record concerning the race of the Jews which I
received from the most erudite High Priests in the most erudite land
of Egypt." In view of the lack of anything that could be construed as
propaganda in the fragment of Aristeas's "On the Jews," it is most

unlikely that the two authors were the same. If the pseudonymous writer of the Letter did mean to take the name of this Aristeas, he would presumably have taken him for a Greek, gentile, author.

The affinity of Aristeas with Demetrius lies in his exegetical interest. While he lacked the latter's complicated chronological calculations (insofar as we can tell from the surviving fragment), he too was not content to repeat the biblical story. He wanted to tie up loose ends and resolve the historical and geographical problems. So he identified Job with Iobab, and thereby provided a specific location for Ausitis. In theology, Aristeas appears quite Deuteronomic. Job is tested, suffers patiently, and is rewarded. Aristeas avoids the perplexing divine speech to Job in Job 38–41 and takes no note of Job's complaints. The supernatural element is minimized (in strong contrast to the later Testament of Job). The reference to Job's resurrection, which is found in LXX Job 42:17a, is absent here, but this was possibly a later addition to the LXX. In view of the brevity of the fragment we cannot be sure whether the "prologue in heaven" was omitted by Aristeas or by Polyhistor. Aristeas does, however, go beyond the tradition in one respect. The striking formulation that "God admired his courage" has no biblical basis and puts the emphasis on the virtue in a way that is Hellenistic rather than Hebraic. (We shall find analogies to this development in Part Two below when we discuss the approaches to Jewish identity through ethics and piety.)

The fragment of Aristeas is too brief to permit any definite conclusions but the impression we are given is that a traditional Deuteronomic theology is being adapted for a Hellenized audience through a retelling of history which still endeavors to be faithful to the biblical account.

One other name may be associated with Demetrius, that of a historian Philo, called "Philo the Elder" by Josephus. He is mentioned twice, by Clement (*Stromateis*, 1.141) and Josephus (*Ag Ap* 1.218) in the sequence Demetrius, Philo, and Eupolemus. Clement says that he (like Demetrius) wrote on the kings of the Jews but that he did not agree with Demetrius. Josephus seems to regard all three as pagan authors and to have no direct knowledge of them. In short, we know nothing whatever about the nature of this author's history. Some scholars have even wondered whether he is not identical with Philo the epic poet. His separate existence has been defended by Walter.[38]

HISTORY AND ROMANCE

ARTAPANUS

Demetrius and (insofar as we can judge) Aristeas represent sober attempts to present the Jewish tradition to the Hellenistic world. They depart from the biblical text only to clarify it and resolve its problems. A very different use of the tradition is found in Artapanus, who was possibly the most colorful of all the Hellenistic Jewish writers.[39]

The date of Artapanus is far from certain. Since he depended on the LXX[40] and was used by Polyhistor, he must have written somewhere between 250–60 BCE.[41] Three considerations may help to specify the date further. Lucien Cerfaux has argued that certain passages in Artapanus reflect an attempt by Ptolemy IV Philopator (222–205 BCE) to assimilate Jews to the worship of Dionysus.[42] Such an attempt is explicitly alleged in 3 Mac 2:29–30, but 3 Maccabees is of questionable value as historical evidence.[43] An enigmatic passage in Artapanus (PE 9.27.24–27) tells how the king bids Moses speak the name of his God and then writes the name on a tablet and seals it. Cerfaux relates this to the evidence of the Schubart Papyrus that Philopator attempted to organize the cult of Dionysus by requiring those who practiced initiation to deposit their sacred doctrine (*hieros logos*) sealed and signed with their names.[44] According to PE 9.27.20 the Egyptian Chenephres required the Jews to wear linen garments. Cerfaux takes this also as an allusion to the attempted assimilation to the cult of Dionysus. If Artapanus is indeed referring indirectly to measures taken by Philopator, then we must emphasize that he regards them negatively, as an imposition on Judaism. In no case is he promoting a Jewish Dionysiac cult. Whether in fact Philopator did take such measures against the Jews is still uncertain, but Cerfaux's theory would provide an explanation for these passages in Artapanus, which are otherwise very puzzling. On Cerfaux's theory, Artapanus would have written during the time of Philopator or shortly thereafter.

A second possible clue to the date arises from the mention of the disease elephantiasis in PE 9.27.20. Despite a statement in Plutarch that this disease was first identified in the time of Asclepiades of Prusa, who flourished in the first century BCE,[45] it had already been the subject of a treatise falsely ascribed to Democritus and believed to be the work of Bolus of Mendes in Egypt, who was a contemporary of Callimachus in the third century BCE.[46] Artapanus could have referred to it at any later time, but he would have had more reason to single it out for mention if it were newly identified when he wrote.

The third consideration is provided by the statement in PE 9.27.7 that Moses included Egyptian farmers in his army. Ptolemy IV Philopator was the first Ptolemy to permit the Egyptian peasantry to bear arms in his service, before the battle of Raphia in 217 BCE.[47] The allusion by Artapanus to peasant participation in Moses' army is not prompted by the biblical account, nor by the polemics of Egyptians such as Manetho. It may be taken to reflect the historical development in the time of Philopator.

None of these considerations is conclusive. Artapanus may have written at any time in the period 250–100 BCE. However, all the specific clues that have been suggested point to a date at the end of the third century BCE and there is nothing against such a date. Accordingly, we may tentatively assign Artapanus to this period. That he wrote in Egypt cannot be doubted. All the fragments, including the one on Abraham, are set in Egypt. Within Egypt we need not necessarily think of Alexandria. Artapanus has little in common with the known Jewish literature of Alexandria and may well have lived in another settlement.[48]

While Demetrius had been content to wrestle with the internal problems of the biblical text, Artapanus is engaged in what might be called "competitive historiography" (with the understanding that historiography here can include a liberal component of legend and romance).[49] Abraham, Joseph, and Moses are each presented as founders of culture. Abraham taught the Egyptians to study the stars. Joseph organized the division of the land and discovered measurements. Moses is described at greatest length. He is identified with Mousaeus, teacher of Orpheus, and also with the god Hermes. He is credited with a wide variety of discoveries and with establishing the Egyptian animal cults. He is also credited with a great military success in a campaign against Ethiopia and with supernatural powers in his encounter with the pharaoh to secure the release of the Hebrews.

The competitive aspect of his presentation can be seen most directly by comparison with the hostile account of the Jews which Manetho had included in his history.[50] Manetho had alleged that Moses forbade his people to worship the gods or abstain from the flesh of the sacred animals (Ag Ap 1.239). Artapanus claimed that it was Moses who established these cults. Manetho alleged that Moses had invaded Egypt (*Ag Ap* 1.241). Artapanus claimed that Moses restrained Raguel and the Arabs from invading. According to Manetho, the pharaoh had to protect the sacred animals from Moses (*Ag Ap* 1.244). Artapanus claims that the pharaoh buried the animals which Moses had made sacred, since he wished to conceal Moses' inventions. In Manetho's account, the pharaoh sought refuge in Ethiopia when Moses invaded (*Ag Ap* 1.246). In Artapanus, Moses conducted a campaign against Ethiopia on behalf of the pharaoh. In view of these correspondences, it seems highly probable that Artapanus intended, inter alia, to refute Manetho's version of Jewish origins. How far that version represented a wider Egyptian polemic is not clear, but at least some of Manetho's charges were derived from an older tradition.[51] Unlike Josephus, Artapanus does not set out the material he wishes to refute. His polemic is carried on implicitly in the course of his own account.

The refutation of writers such as Manetho is only the negative side of Artapanus's work. More positively he portrays each of his subjects, especially Moses, as a founder of culture and attributes to each inventions which are beneficial to humanity. Here again the claim was competitive. While the romantic legends of the Egyptians extolled the greatness of Sesostris and Nektanebo, and others recounted the glorified exploits of Semiramis, Nebuchadnezzar, or even Alexander, Artapanus claims for Moses accomplishments elsewhere attributed to others, so that "not only does he surpass each one individually, but also all of them combined."[52] The correspondences with Sesostris are especially striking.[53] Sesostris was credited with being the first Egyptian to build warships, with dividing Egypt into thirty-six nomes and with organizing Egyptian religion. All of these accomplishments are claimed for Moses by Artapanus. The motif of a campaign against Ethiopia was widespread. Semiramis was said to have subdued it. Cambyses failed. Sesostris was said to have been the first man to conquer Ethiopia and the only Egyptian to rule over it. The Moses of Artapanus conquers it with a nonprofessional army.

Not only does Moses outshine the heroes of other peoples and especially of the Egyptians. He also outshines their gods. The Egyptian goddess Isis was taught by Hermes.[54] Moses "was deemed worthy of divine honor by the priests and called Hermes." The subordination is explicit in PE 9.27.32, where Moses strikes the earth with his rod and Artapanus adds that "the earth is Isis."[55] He was also called Mousaeus by the Greeks and "this Mousaeus was the teacher of Orpheus."[56]

Artapanus's zeal to exalt his national heroes above those of other nations not only led him beyond the traditional history. It also led to a view of Judaism sharply at variance with the Deuteronomic tradition. While other Jewish writings use the story of Abraham to denounce astrology, Artapanus has Abraham teach it to the Egyptians.[57] More strikingly, he says that Moses established the animal cults,[58] which were so frequently the objects of derisive polemic at the hands of other writers,[59] and even claims with apparent approval that the Egyptian priests identified Moses with the god Hermes. While all of these views must be considered syncretistic, Artapanus still contends that the god of the Jews is "the master of the universe." The pagan gods, including the animals worshipped by the Egyptians are explained euhemeristically as inventions which were useful to mankind.[60] This involves a positive evaluation of the pagan cults, which flies in the face of all Jewish tradition, but it also undermines their divinity. The animals worshipped by the Egyptians are "only" animals which Moses judged to be useful. Hermes, though he is superior to Isis, is really only the man Moses, and great though he is, Moses is still human. It is crucial to the theology of Artapanus that the god of the Jews is never demythologized in this euhemeristic way. On the contrary, the very endorsement of the pagan divinities as useful for humanity shows their inferiority not only to the god of the Jews but even to Moses.

The piety of Artapanus is conspicuously similar to that of Hellenistic paganism. He is especially interested in the miraculous, and even in the magical. While the Egyptian magicians might seem to be disparaged for their reliance on tricks and charms, great emphasis is placed on Moses' rod and on the mysterious power of the divine name.[61] In the events related to the Exodus, even when they are not based on the biblical account, Moses is clearly subordinate to his god. Yet for much of the narrative, the emphasis is on the human achievements of the Jewish heroes, in which God plays no explicit role. Even in the Exodus, God acts through Moses and is in effect the guarantor of his own people's superiority.

A few passages suggest the traditional biblical theme of divine retribution in history. Chenephres contracts elephantiasis because of his treatment of the Jews. A priest who disparages the divine name which Moses wrote on a tablet is stricken with a convulsion. This kind of retribution is found in every religion that believes in a god (or gods) who is at all capable of showing displeasure, but at least the first case posits a special bond between God and the Jews. This bond, however, is the nearest Artapanus comes to anything that could be called covenantal. While Moses is credited with all kinds of inventions from waterworks to philosophy, he is conspicuously not presented as a lawgiver.[62] The fact that the biblical story locates the giving of the law outside Egypt and after the Exodus cannot account for the omission, since Artapanus does refer to Moses' later life. The omission is all the more surprising in view of the focus on Moses as lawgiver in Hecataeus of Abdera, who was apparently one of Artapanus's sources.[63]

Artapanus evidently thinks of Moses as national hero rather than as lawgiver. The purpose of the work is evidently to bolster the ethnic pride of Jews in a foreign land, partly by refuting their detractors, such as Manetho, and partly by fabricating a more glorious history than that of other peoples. Such propaganda is directed to both gentile and Jew, with the complementary objectives of inspiring respect from without and self-respect from within. The portraits of Abraham, Joseph, and especially Moses are determined, not by the biblical story, but by the demands of competitive historiography, which draws on the biblical material (among other sources) for its own purpose. Holladay concludes his analysis of Artapanus by claiming "that he was not totally without scruples, and that his faith imposed some restrictions on what he would allow. Indeed, his faith is the only plausible explanation of why he attempted what he did."[64] This assessment is valid only if faith is understood not as fidelity to the Mosaic law, or even a strict avoidance of other gods, but as faith in the superiority of the Jewish people, with its God and its heroes. The restrictions on what Artapanus would allow are quite simply determined by whatever would augment the glory of the Jews. He is not an assimilationist but he is not devoted to holiness by separation either. He is concerned with the identity of the Jewish people. That identity must remain rooted in the tradition, but not necessarily in the articulation of that tradition in the book of the Torah. It is enough that people be able to define their own identity in terms they can relate (however imaginatively) to the traditional heroes, just as Egyptians in the Hellenistic age could relate their identity to Sesostris, or Babylonians to Semiramis. The only fidelity required is that Jews maintain a distinct identity and affirm their superiority over against other peoples.[65]

Artapanus's theology is an offshoot of his politics. In this respect his attitude to the Egyptians is significant. Holladay has underlined the strongly pro-Egyptian cast of the fragments, in the sense that the Jewish heroes are consistently benevolent and beneficent to Egypt. Abraham, Joseph, and Moses are all consistently portrayed as introducing things that are beneficial for Egyptian life. Even the animal cults fall under this heading. Yet there is also considerable destruction of Egyptians not all required by the biblical account. Chenephres is smitten with elephantiasis, Egypt is ravaged by plagues and most of the temples are destroyed, and the Egyptians, apparently with their sacred animals, are killed at the Red Sea. In part, the benevolence of the Jews to the Egyptians is meant as a refutation of Manetho, but it also expresses Artapanus's attitude in his situation of exile. The Jews bear the Egyptians no ill will. If friction arises, it is because of the envy of individual Egyptians such as Chenephres, or their abuse of the Jews. In this respect we may compare the attitudes towards the gentiles in the stories of the eastern Diaspora, Esther and Daniel 1–6.[66] In each case, friction arises when a Jew (or Jews) has risen to a position of prominence. In each case, the Jews are benevolent and loyal subjects and do nothing to warrant the antagonism. But when conflict arises through the gentiles' fault the Jews prevail. The tales in Daniel emphasize the role of God in the triumph of the Jews. Those in Esther do not. In Artapanus the issue is not true religion. Moses does not even attempt to convert the gentiles to the worship of the God of the Jews, and when the Jews are persecuted or treated badly (PE 9.27.2, 20) no reason is given. While Artapanus does not acknowledge the divinity of the Egyptian gods, and rather demythologizes them, his attitude towards them is still positive. They are useful. There is no reason to oppose their cults. In fact, Jews encourage their cults. Problems arise only through the misguided opposition of some leaders to the Jews.

From all of this we may wonder whether Artapanus wrote in a time of conflict. The generally positive attitude to the Egyptians makes it unlikely that there was any severe persecution in his time. Undoubtedly there were occasional local conflicts from the earliest settlement of Jews in Egypt. The writings of Manetho show that there was some anti-Jewish sentiment at the beginning of the Hellenistic age. The setting of Artapanus is adequately explained by this general background. On the other hand, the fact that the Egyptian rulers in Artapanus are consistently portrayed in a negative light makes it improbable that Artapanus wrote under a ruler who was particularly favorable to the Jews, such as Philometor. A date around the end of the third century BCE remains plausible.

In all, then, Artapanus reflects an understanding of Judaism which is based on pride in the national tradition, but is prepared to treat that tradition in a rather plastic manner to bolster the identity of the Jews as a distinctive people worthy of respect in Hellenistic Egypt.

PSEUDO-EUPOLEMUS

Artapanus provides the most elaborate example of "competitive historiography" which has survived from the Egyptian Diaspora. While he is extreme in his imaginative elaboration of the tradition, he represents a phenomenon which was widespread in Hellenistic Judaism, as can be seen from the wide distribution of the fragments of the genre which have survived.

Closest to Artapanus is the anonymous Samaritan work, of which a fragment is erroneously ascribed to Eupolemus in Eusebius, whence the name "Pseudo-Eupolemus," although there is nothing to indicate pseudonymity.[67] The Samaritan origin of the work is indicated by the location of Abraham's encounter with Melchizedek at Argarizim,[68] translated as "the mount of the Most High God," and perhaps also by the interest in Phoenicians, since the Samaritans were known to refer to themselves as Sidonians.[69] It is probable however that Pseudo-Eupolemus wrote before the schism between the Samaritans and the Jews reached its final and irreparable stage. Recent research has shown that the sectarian redaction of the Samaritan Pentateuch should be dated to the Hasmonean period and that the final break was most probably a result of the destruction of Shechem and ravaging of Gerizim by John Hyrcanus.[70] While the Samaritans were certainly distinct from the Jews throughout the postexilic period, and relations between the two communities were often strained, especially after the building of the temple on Mt. Gerizim in the early Greek period and the Hellenizing of Shechem under Antiochus IV,[71] the identity of both groups was still grounded in the same biblical tradition. We need not be surprised then to find that Pseudo-Eupolemus was dependent on the LXX.[72] There is no clear evidence as to whether he wrote in Samaria or in Egypt.[73] His use of the LXX, which might be taken to favor an Egyptian origin, must be balanced against the parallels with the Enoch traditions and the Genesis Apocryphon from Qumran, and, in any case, neither the LXX nor the supposedly Palestinian traditions can be restricted to a single geographical location.

Pseudo-Eupolemus drew not only on the biblical tradition. There are also indications of influence by Berossus.[74] The work is marked by a euhemeristic attitude to pagan gods (the first giant was Belus, who is Kronos, who begat Belus and Cham) and by an attempt to correlate the figures of various mythologies. Belus is Kronos, Atlas is the same as Enoch. The discovery of astrology is traced ultimately to Enoch, indicating a familiarity with the traditions reflected in 1 Enoch. The main focus of the narrative is on Abraham, "who surpassed all men in mobility and wisdom, who also discovered the Chaldean science, and who, on account of his piety was well-pleasing to God." Abraham teaches the Phoenicians "the changes of the sun and the moon and all things of that kind" and also teaches the priests at Heliopolis astrology and other sciences.[75] Pseudo-Eupolemus seems to draw on more of the biblical framework than Artapanus did. Abraham's sojourn in Phoenicia involves the exploits recorded in Genesis 14, while his sojourn in Egypt is occasioned by a famine and involves the wife/sister episode of Genesis 12. However, Pseudo-Eupolemus is no exegete. He adds freely to the biblical story. His conception of his religion is closely similar to that of Artapanus. It finds its identity in a glorified tradition, but one that is placed in a cosmopolitan, syncretistic setting.

THALLUS AND CLEODEMUS

Two other historical writers, Thallus and Cleodemus Malchas, were thought by Freudenthal to be Samaritans.[76] Thallus wrote later than Alexander Polyhistor and his work is lost except for eight scattered fragments which have been collected by Jacoby.[77] His history apparently extended from the fall of Troy to the time of Christ,[78] but the surviving fragments deal mainly with the mythological *Urzeit* and refer to Bel, Kronos, and Ogygus. References to the time of Cyrus also survive. The supposition that he was a Samaritan rests on the identification of the historian with the Thallus mentioned by Josephus in *Ant* 18.6.4 (167), who was a Samaritan by birth and was a freedman of Tiberius. It has also been suggested that he is identical with the figure named in an inscription, Tiberius Claudius Thallus, and even with the secretary of Augustus mentioned by Suetonius, in *Augustus* 67,2.[79]

Whether the writer was in fact identical with any of these figures remains hypothetical and has been disputed.[80] Insofar as one may judge from such scanty evidence, his work has some affinity with that of Pseudo-Eupolemus and the identification with the Samaritan mentioned in Josephus is plausible.

There is no reason to regard Cleodemus as a Samaritan. He is even more poorly attested than Thallus. He is cited briefly by Josephus, and again, from Josephus, by Eusebius.[81] He is called a "prophet" but the fragment makes it clear that he wrote a propagandistic history which endeavored to derive various peoples from the children of Abraham. Abraham's sons Apher and Aphras are said to have given their names to the continent Africa and the city Aphras, and another son, Assurim, to Assyria. The first two join Heracles in a battle against Libya and Antaeus, and Heracles marries the daughter of Aphras. From their son Diodorus a barbarian people, the Sophacians, are descended.

It is generally assumed that Cleodemus wrote in Libya about the second century BCE. He is probably dependent on the LXX and wrote early enough to be used by Polyhistor, but otherwise there is no specific indication of date. The fragment, despite its brevity, is of considerable interest. Not only does Cleodemus attempt to relate the history of Libya and its populace to Abraham. He also treats Heracles as an historical human being who can be integrated into the line of Abraham. This fits well with the euhemeristic tendencies of the other writers we have considered.

Cleodemus refers briefly to Moses the lawgiver as his source. It is not likely however that he understood his identity in terms of the Mosaic law. While we cannot say anything with certainty on the basis of so brief a fragment, it would seem that descent from Abraham is more important to him than fidelity to the law.[82] There is no reason to see his syncretism as peculiarly Samaritan, despite Fraser's argument that "Heracles, no doubt, is Melkart, to whom the Samaritans dedicated the temple of Zeus Xenios on Mt. Gerizim."[83] The identification with Melkart is not suggested in the surviving fragment. Kippenberg is probably right that he was a Hellenized Jew.[84]

EUPOLEMUS

One of the most striking examples of "competitive historiography" comes neither from the Hellenized Diaspora nor from the Samaritans but from the heart of Judea in the wake of the Maccabean revolt. The

authentic Eupolemus[85] is almost certainly the Eupolemus named in
1 Mac 8:17f who was entrusted with a mission to Rome by Judas Maccabee about 160 BCE.[86] The fact that he wrote his propagandistic history in Greek[87] is highly significant for our understanding of Judaism
in this period. The *Tendenz* of the work bears a general similarity to
Artapanus. "Moses was the first wise man; and he handed over the
letters to the Jews first, the Phoenicians received them from the Jews,
the Greeks from the Phoenicians." Moses is also noted as "the first
who wrote laws for the Jews." The most lengthy fragment concerns
the building of the temple. The detailed account of the building lends
plausibility to the view that Eupolemus was inspired by the Maccabean purification of the temple.[88] However, the account is embellished by the insertion of the purported letters of Solomon to the kings
of Egypt and of Tyre and Sidon and their replies. The tone of the
correspondence implies the superiority of Solomon. Indeed the very
choice of Solomon as the focal figure suggests a measure of triumphal-
ism. Eupolemus details the conquests of David and Solomon in the
Seleucid territory, but emphasizes their good relations with Egypt.
Hengel has rightly seen here a reflection of Maccabean politics.[89] The
concluding verse of this fragment contains the striking information
that Solomon gave the king of Tyre "a pillar of gold which was set up
in Tyre in the Temple of Zeus." Apparently Eupolemus was not em-
barrassed by this contribution to a foreign God.[90] Yet in another fragment he explains the Babylonian exile as a punishment for sacrificing
to a golden idol named Baal. Even in this passage there is no hostility
to gentiles. Nebuchadnezzar only decides to campaign against Jerusalem when he hears of the prophecy of Jeremiah. The Jews are apparently forbidden to engage in idol worship but the gentiles are not
criticized for having their own religions and Solomon is not criticized
for indirectly contributing to them.

The Jewish Eupolemus and the Samaritan Pseudo-Eupolemus
would obviously disagree sharply over their respective temples. Apart
from that, Hengel claims that a further essential difference can be
found between "the universalist breadth of the Abraham narratives in
the anonymous Samaritan and the Judean nationalistic narrowness of
the fragments of Eupolemus, where even the international relationships of Solomon only serve to the greater glory of the Jewish king
and the sanctuary built by him." He further claims that it makes a
significant difference whether Abraham or Moses appears as the first

wise man for "in one case the universalist tendency predominates, and in the other the nationalist."[91] Abraham had come from Chaldaea and lived among the Phoenicians and Egyptians. Unlike Moses he was not associated with the restrictive aspects of the Jewish law. He was a favorite figure in the syncretistic literature of the Diaspora, as can be seen most clearly in the genealogical fictions of Cleodemus Malchas.[92] Yet, both writers were concerned to assert the superiority of their tradition and to build a cosmopolitan platform on which that superiority could be displayed. Eupolemus may be a nationalist, but he is no isolationist. His vision of Judaism includes alliances with other peoples and a tolerance of their religion. On the other hand, the more obviously syncretistic Pseudo-Eupolemus and Artapanus are universalistic only in a limited way. They are not assimilationists. They retain the sense of the value of their distinct identity, and bolster it with a claim of superiority. Again, as is surely apparent from Artapanus, the figure of Moses could be used in a highly syncretistic way. Eupolemus mentions the law only in passing, despite its major role in the Maccabean movement, as recorded in the books of Maccabees, and even despite its potential for propaganda in the Hellenistic world. The identity of Judaism for Eupolemus is not rooted in the law. He takes the biblical record as a point of departure but adds to it freely.[93] The identity of Judaism for Eupolemus is not rooted in the law. He which can be defined by association with Moses, Solomon, and the major figures of the tradition. One gets in, presumably, by birth, and stays in by not denying one's heritage. The ideals of Judaism are the popular ideals of the Hellenistic world: to be first in everything that is beneficial to mankind. The primacy of Judaism is never abandoned, but it is seen in the context of a common human enterprise.

PSEUDO-HECATAEUS

In view of the Palestinian provenance of Eupolemus, Wacholder has raised the possibility that much of the Jewish-Greek literature preserved by Alexander Polyhistor originated in Jerusalem and that it was primarily the work of priests. He claims that the tradition of such writing in Jerusalem can be traced back to "an eye-witness report intended for Ptolemy I, the founder of the Macedonian dynasty in Egypt," by a native priest who wanted to explain Judaism to the Greeks just as the gentile priests Berossus and Manetho explained their cultures. This report was subsequently attributed to Hecataeus of Abdera.[94] Since the allegedly "pseudo-" Hecataeus was not concerned with the ancient past but with the contemporary structure of Judaism and its regard for the laws, it will be discussed below in Part Two. For the present it must suffice to say that it is quite possible that the fragment was actually written by Hecataeus, and not the work of a Jewish writer at all. There was, however, another work attributed to Hecataeus, which was definitely the work of a Jewish author. This was the book "On Abraham and the Egyptians" which is cited by Josephus and Clement.[95] It is not certain how far Josephus drew on this source but it is likely that Abraham's discovery of God through nature and his instruction of the Egyptians in astronomy derives from Pseudo-Hecataeus. The fragment in Clement cites verses on monotheism which are spuriously attributed to Sophocles and says they were transmitted in (Pseudo-) Hecataeus's book. Presumably Pseudo-Hecataeus claimed that the Greek poet had derived his idea of monotheism from Abraham. In all of this we recognize the familiar motifs of competitive historiography, designed to establish the antiquity and superiority of Jewish culture over against other traditions. Since the work was on Abraham and the Egyptians, it is reasonable to suppose that it was written in Egypt. The date cannot be specified except that it was prior to Josephus.[96]

In the case of other writers listed by Wacholder such as Demetrius and Philo the epic poet, Palestinian provenance is a mere possibility and there is no positive evidence of priestly authorship. In the single case of Theophilus Palestinian provenance may be supported because of a close parallel to Eupolemus, but the single surviving fragment is insufficient to permit any definite conclusion.[97] The existence of an ongoing tradition of Graeco-Palestinian historiography is, however, supported by the emergence of Josephus and Justus of Tiberias at the end of the first century CE.

THE EPIC POETS

PHILO

Not all the attempts to glorify the tradition were in the form of prose history writing. At least one poet, Philo, was engaged in the same general enterprise as Artapanus and Eupolemus.[98] We have nothing to indicate his date except that he was earlier than Alexander Polyhistor.

Philo's epic appears to have consisted chiefly of a recitation of the biblical history. His presentation of it as *Peri Hierosolyma* already indicates his affinity with the literature of the Hellenistic age, which had strong geographical interests and was often concerned with the foundation of cities.[99] Hellenistic epics also show a predilection for obscure and recherché language.[100] In Philo's case this tendency results in some scarcely intelligible passages, since he did not in fact have a great command of the Greek language. The fragment on Joseph is said to be from the fourteenth book. Freudenthal may be right in emending this to the fourth; even so, the poem must have been lengthy, since it presumably continued down to the Israelite occupation of Jerusalem.

The three fragments deal with Abraham, Joseph, and the water supply of Jerusalem. The last one is evidently a simple praise of the loveliness of the city in summer when the streams are flowing. The theme is reminiscent of the biblical psalms: "there is a stream which gladdens the city of God."[101] Joseph is the lord of dreams who sat on the throne of Egypt. The final line is striking: *dineusas lathraia chronou plēmmyridi moirēs* ("spinning secrets of time in a flood of fate"). The reference to *moira*, "fate," may be included only for its bombastic resonance, but it shows that Philo had no great aversion to heathen concepts.

The most controversial fragment is that on Abraham. The passage is extremely obscure. Wacholder claims that "the first book depicted God's covenant with Abraham (circumcision)"[102] but there is no reference to circumcision here. The passage might be taken to suggest that the blessing of Abraham's descendants results from the sacrifice of Isaac, but the text is too cryptic to allow certainty. The most elaborate interpretation of the passage has been offered by Gutman. Gutman argues that Philo's style finds its parallel in the Orphic hymns "in so far as there too the author's motive is apparent to shroud himself in a cloud of mystical obscurities."[103] He translates:

> A thousand times have I heard how once (the spirit of) Abraham abounded in primeval doctrines, the far-echoing lofty and radiant link of chains; how (his spirit abounded) with wisdom of great praise, the ecstasy beloved of God. For when he left the goodly abode of the blessed born, the great-voiced Blessed One prevented the immolation, and made immortal His word, from which day much-sung glory fell to the lot of the son of the blessed-born.[104]

On the basis of this rendering he proceeds to expound Philo's intention:

> The Law of Israel is in his view one of the principal and basic elements in the cosmic process. This Law existed before the creation, but when the word came into existence the Law and its commandments served as that force of harmony which created order and rule, and fused the isolated parts of the cosmos into a process of unity, as they could not be fused without it. Men had no conception of the chains of this harmony in the cosmos—law and its regulations—till Abraham came and revealed them to humanity.[105]

This interpretation depends heavily on three elements, all of them doubtful:

First, it is said that Abraham "abounded in primeval doctrines" (*archegonoisi thesmois*). Gutman argues that this expression must refer to "codes or doctrines which preceded all things and anticipated all creation, even the creation of the world," and infers the Jewish idea of preexistent wisdom and the preexistent law.[106] However, it is not apparent that *archegonoisi* necessarily implies existence before creation. In accordance with Philo's generally bombastic style it may simply connote extreme antiquity. Again, *thesmois* is not automatically to be identified as the law of Israel. The parallel with *logismois* suggests traditional wisdom. True, the Jewish law is identified with wisdom in other texts, but there is no clear reference to the Jewish law here, certainly not to the "book of the law of Moses."[107] The point is simply that Abraham is informed by the most ancient wisdom.

Second, *hamma ti desmōn* is understood as "link of chains" in the light of Plato's use of *desmos* in the Timaeus, where the heavenly bodies are linked by *desmois empsychois*.[108] Philo of Alexandria evidently drew on the Platonic tradition when he said that God was the *desmos* of the universe.[109] However, the cosmic sense of *desmos* depends on its context. In itself the word simply means bond. Since the immediate context here concerns the binding of Isaac, the *desmoi* in question may simply refer to that. There is no explicit cosmic reference here.

Third, Gutman translates *theiophilē thelgeitra* as "ecstasy beloved of God." However, *thelgeitra* means "charm" or "spell," not an experience such as ecstasy, but something one does to stimulate the experience. If the *desmōn* refers to the binding of Isaac, Philo is saying that the binding was an act pleasing to God.[110] The allusion to the binding as a charm or spell is a striking conception, but it does not support Gutman's interpretation.

We may then propose an alternative translation for the first sentence:

> Ten thousand times have I heard how once Abraham abounded in ancient doctrines, glorious reasonings, in respect of the famous, surpassing, splendid cord of bonds, spells pleasing to God.

Admittedly the passage abounds in problems, but Gutman's interpretation strains probability. The Abraham fragment, like the others, should be read as a bombastic glorification of Jerusalem and its history.

Philo lacks the direct comparison with the heroes and traditions of other peoples which we find in Artapanus. The only indications of syncretism might be dismissed as loose use of terms such as *thelgeitra* or *moira*. This language is not insignificant, however, as it reflects the author's desire to express his tradition in an idiom familiar to the Hellenistic world. The adaptation of terms which were laden with significance in Hellenistic religion is essentially syncretistic, as it results in a mixture of the ideas of both traditions. Further, the appeal to primeval *thesmoi* points to a wisdom older than Abraham and certainly older than Moses. Even if the law of Israel is regarded as the supreme embodiment of this wisdom, it is not the exclusive expression of it. The possibility that truth and wisdom can be gained through other traditions too is fundamental to the entire apologetic of Hellenistic Judaism. Whether we regard that apologetic as an outward-directed attempt to persuade the gentiles or an inward-directed attempt to boost self-respect, the underlying assumption is that there are universal norms by which the different traditions can be compared. The desire to find a common cross-cultural basis underlies the experimentation with Greek literary forms such as the epic. This kind of cosmopolitan Judaism may have been fostered in Judea as well as Alexandria, but the similarities between Philo's work and other Hellenistic epics favors Alexandrian authorship.[111]

THEODOTUS

The only other biblically inspired epic which has survived is that of Theodotus.[112] Since it is usually linked with that of Philo, we may discuss it here for convenience, but in fact it is animated by a very different spirit. The title of the work is given in Eusebius as *Peri Ioudaiōn*, but most scholars have assumed that it was in fact a poem on Shechem, which would only have been written by a Samaritan, and that the title merely reflects Polyhistor's inability to distinguish between Hebrews (which would include Samaritans) and Jews.[113] The scholarly consensus, however, is not well founded.[114] The fact that the single surviving fragment concerns Shechem does not prove that the whole poem was on that subject. Apart from the opening verses, which praise the beauty of Shechem and refer to it as a sacred town, *hieron asty*, the content weighs heavily against the theory of Samaritan authorship. We are told that God prompted Simeon and Levi to destroy Shechem because the people in Shechem were impious, *dia to tous en Sikimois asebeis einai*,[115] and another passage calls on God to destroy the inhabitants of Shechem.[116] Even though the Samaritans claimed descent from the sons of Jacob rather than from Emmor, it is surely unlikely that a Samaritan author would choose to depict "the inhabitants of Shechem" in such a negative light. By contrast the passage would make excellent sense as a Jewish work from the time of John Hyrcanus. The poem has a strongly legalistic bent, insisting on the prohibition of intermarriage with gentiles and the necessity of circumcision. Circumcision is especially emphasized "for God himself said it." A paraphrasing statement in PE 9.22.5 says that Jacob required the inhabitants of Shechem to be circumcised and convert to Judaism, *peritemnomenous ioudaïsai*. While the terminology here is Polyhistor's rather than Theodotus's, circumcision was widely associated with conversion to Judaism in the Hasmonean period. By contrast, the Samaritans had gone along with the policies of Antiochus Epiphanes, even renaming their temple and referring to themselves as "Sidonians."[117] This episode undoubtedly contributed to the tensions between Jews and Samaritans which came to a climax in the reign of John Hyrcanus.

After the death of Antiochus VII Sidetes in 129 BCE, John Hyrcanus began a campaign against the neighbors of the Jews. He compelled the Idumeans to be circumcised and accept the laws of the Jews. He ravaged Shechem, destroyed the temple of Mt. Gerizim and later, about 107 BCE, besieged and destroyed Samaria.[118] The poem of Theodotus could easily be read as a paradigmatic justification for the actions and policies of Hyrcanus. The laudatory description of the appearance of Shechem may be only the conventional style of the epic. The accuracy of the description is not surprising in a Jewish author.[119] The statement that Shechem is a *hieron asty* is not surprising, since Shechem was a traditional holy site in biblical history. Theodotus conspicuously does not refer to a holy mountain at Gerizim. The problem with Shechem was not with the site but with the inhabitants.

Despite his use of the epic form, and a Greek style far superior to that of Philo the epic poet, Theodotus lacks the universalism which characterizes most Hellenistic Jewish writers. His vision of Judaism is covenantal nomism of the narrowest variety. The children of Abraham are defined by circumcision and marriage within their own race. There is no attempt at correlation with universal history. The one apparent piece of syncretism, in PE 9.22.1, which states that Sikimos was son of Hermes, must be regarded as a blunder by Polyhistor, since the father's name is otherwise given consistently as Emmor. The work is a striking instance of the fusion of a Greek form with an exclusive view of the Hebraic tradition. The epic form here could scarcely be intended to appeal to gentiles. It presupposes a degree of Hellenization in its audience, despite the insistence on Jewish distinctiveness. Of course the epic form lent itself admirably to nationalistic propaganda, but it is striking that Jewish nationalism is comfortably clad in such an obviously Hellenistic dress. If this poem was written in support of John Hyrcanus it offers a remarkable illustration of the Hasmonean blend of nationalism and Hellenization. It supports the contention of Tcherikover that the Judaizing policies of the Hasmoneans were not religious in intent but political and that their struggle with the Greek towns "was not for or against culture, but the rivalry between two political powers."[120]

THE CONTINUING DEVELOPMENT OF
THE HISTORIOGRAPHICAL TRADITION

Our review of the propagandistic use of ancient history in Hellenistic Judaism would be incomplete without some reference to the two

Palestinian historians from the late first century CE, Justus of Tiberias and Josephus. The work of Justus is lost except for three fragments. Its nature is described by Photius, the ninth-century patriarch of Constantinople:

> I have read the Chronicle of Justus of Tiberias, which is entitled: *The Jewish Kings Arranged in Genealogical Tables*. He was a native of Tiberias in the Galilee. Beginning his history with Moses, he concluded it with the death of Agrippa, the seventh of the Herodian dynasty, the last king of the Jews.[121]

One of the surviving fragments tells an unhistorical anecdote about Plato at the trial of Socrates. The other two synchronize the date of the Exodus with Attic and Egyptian kings. It would seem that much of Justus's work was devoted to chronography. He is thought to have influenced Africanus and through him Christian chronography, but he is known chiefly through the polemical references of Josephus in his *Vita*.[122] The remains of Justus's work are too scanty to give any clear impression of its character but he evidently stood in the tradition of the Hellenistic Jewish historians in his endeavor to correlate Jewish and universal history.

Josephus, by contrast, stands with Philo as one of the two Hellenistic Jewish writers whose work has survived in substantial quantity. Unlike the earlier Jewish historians, Josephus wrote with an explicitly apologetic purpose.[123] His *Antiquities* were designed, in his own words, to demonstrate "the extreme antiquity of our Jewish race, the purity of the original stock, and the manner in which it established itself in the country which we occupy to-day" (*Ag Ap* 1.1). While he usually stays close to the biblical text he includes some of the characteristic motifs of Hellenistic Jewish propaganda. The account of Abraham borrows from Pseudo-Hecataeus the motifs of instructing the Egyptians and of philosophical speculation (*Ant* 1.7.1–8.2 [154–168]). The account of Moses includes a legendary campaign against Ethiopia, a variant of the tradition found in Artapanus (*Ant* 2.10.1–2 [238–253]). More significantly, the whole genre of the *Antiquities* conforms to the model of patriotic and apologetic history provided by Dionysius of Halicarnassus, as has been demonstrated by H. W. Attridge.[125] So, while the instances of direct dependence on the Jewish historiographical tradition are limited, the whole work is informed by a basic principle of that tradition—the assimilation to Hellenistic models.[126]

Josephus only rarely mentions his predecessors, and then he seems to think that many of them were gentiles.[127] He throws invaluable light on their work, however, by his review of the Graeco-Egyptian polemical literature to which they often implicitly responded. The tract against Apion, by its explicit apologetic, throws much light on the issues in the conflicting propaganda between Jews and gentiles, but we should remember that the intensity of the anti-Jewish propaganda only developed in the period after Alexander Polyhistor. Despite the hostility of Josephus towards the Graeco-Egyptian writings, he still appears eager to impress the Greeks and Romans by the antiquity and the philosophy of the Jews.

The apologetic of Josephus was far more complex than that of the earlier Jewish historians. It included a significant philosophical component,[128] and attached great importance to the Jewish law, which he compared with the *Laws* of Plato in *Ag Ap* 2.255–258 (36). (Josephus claimed that Plato followed the example of Moses.) He was even capable of allegorical exegesis on occasion.[129] In all of this he had other precedents in Hellenistic Jewish literature, as we shall see. What is noteworthy is the fusion of competitive historiography with the philosophical approach to the law. Yet the "moral lesson" with which he begins his *Antiquities* is the doctrine of retribution in history which is squarely in the tradition of the Deuteronomic historians of the Hebrew Bible: "men who conform to the will of God, and do not venture to transgress laws that have been excellently laid down, prosper in all things beyond belief, and for their reward are offered by God felicity; whereas in proportion as they depart from the strict observance of these laws . . . whatever good thing they strive to do ends in irretrievable disasters" (*Ant* Proem. 3 [14]).

Detailed analysis of Josephus does not fall within the scope of this study. It is noteworthy however that the last and greatest Hellenistic Jewish historian was a Judean. The distinction between Judea and the Diaspora has perhaps its least value in the tradition of nationalistic historiography.

CONCLUSION

In this chapter we have been concerned with the propagandistic rewriting of history which is characteristic of the earliest Hellenistic-

Jewish literature. In a few cases such as Demetrius and Aristeas the use of history reflects a Deuteronomic theology, by showing how Moses' wife was not really an alien or how Job was rewarded for his patience.[130] This theology is also reflected in the exegetical concern to resolve apparent problems in the biblical text. In the greater number of these writers, however, the dominant focus is not on the law but on the glory of the Jewish people. Jewish identity is viewed in terms of ethnic and national solidarity. To be Jewish is to belong to the same people as Abraham and Moses and the other heroes of the past. The exploits of these heroes show the preeminence of the Jews by outshining the heroes of the other peoples. At the same time the criteria for excellence are those commonly accepted in the Hellenistic world. The distinctively Jewish virtues of the Torah are thrust into the background. In this way the dissonance between Jewish tradition and Hellenistic environment is decreased. Jews and gentiles have common values, and so far from being witless barbarians, the Jewish people have produced the greatest culture heroes of all.

We can see from the epic of Theodotus that insistence on detailed observance of the law was compatible with the glorification of Jewish tradition in Hellenistic categories. In fact, however, the law is seldom emphasized in this literature. Josephus is exceptional among the historical writers for his explicit interest in the law. This fact is remarkable in view of the attention paid to the lawgiver by gentile authors beginning with Hecataeus of Abdera.[131] We will find in Part Two of this study that extensive use was made of the law for apologetic purposes. For the present we must emphasize that a significant segment of Hellenistic Judaism did not think primarily in terms of the law or ethical practices, but found its identity in the often fantastic stories of ancestral heroes who outshone the best of the Greeks, Babylonians, and Egyptians.

Notes

1. J. Barr, "Story and History in Biblical Theology," *JR* 56 (1976) 6; J. J. Collins, "The 'Historical' Character of the Old Testament in Recent Biblical Theology," *CBQ* 41 (1979) 185–204.

2. A. Momigliano, *Alien Wisdom: The Limits of Hellenization* (Cambridge: Cambridge University, 1975) 7–8, 82–87; B. Z. Wacholder, *Eupolemus: A Study of Judaeo-Greek Literature* (Cincinnati: Hebrew Union College, 1974) 261–62. On Hecataeus of Abdera see P. M. Fraser, *Ptolemaic Alexandria* (Oxford: Clarendon, 1972) 1:496–504.

On Greek accounts of the East see further R. Drews, *The Greek Accounts of Eastern History* (Center for Hellenic Studies; Cambridge, Mass: Harvard, 1973).

3. Momigliano, *Alien Wisdom*, 86.

4. Ibid.

5. See Fraser, *Ptolemaic Alexandria*, 1:500.

6. Ibid., 1:504.

7. E. J. Bickermann, "The Jewish Historian Demetrios," in J. Neusner (ed.), *Christianity, Judaism and other Greco-Roman Cults: Studies for Morton Smith at Sixty* (Leiden: Brill, 1975) 3:72–84 (77); reprinted in *Studies in Jewish and Christian History* (AGJU 9; Leiden: Brill, 1980) 2:347–58.

8. S. M. Burstein, *The Babyloniaca of Berossus* (SANE 1/5; Malibu: Undena, 1978).

9. Fraser, *Ptolemaic Alexandria*, 1:505–11.

10. Bickermann ("The Jewish Historian Demetrios," 79–80): "since Ephorus (ca. 340), Greek scholarship had given up the pretension to be able to discover the historical facts underlying the myths. The realm of the legend began beyond ca. 1200 B.C. In the days when Eratosthenes refused to discover history in the Homeric tale of Odysseus' wanderings, Berossus asserted that in his land the kings reigned for more than 30,000 years before Alexander the Great."

11. For this literature see M. Braun, *History and Romance in Graeco-Oriental Literature* (Oxford: Blackwell, 1938) and S. K. Eddy, *The King is Dead: Studies in the Near Eastern Resistance to Hellenism* (Lincoln: University of Nebraska, 1961). Also Fraser, *Ptolemaic Alexandria* 1:675–87, and the literature there cited, esp. for the Alexander Romance which derives from the third century CE in its present form but contains material dating back to the early Hellenistic age.

12. See esp. Braun, *History and Romance*. Syncellus states that Manetho wrote "in imitation of Berossus" (Fraser, *Ptolemaic Alexandria*, 1:505; 2:728 n. 95).

13. See Fraser, *Ptolemaic Alexandria*, 1:508–9.

14. See Momigliano, *Alien Wisdom*, 91–92. Despite the account of the Letter of Aristeas, there is little doubt that the LXX was primarily designed for the internal needs of the Jewish community.

15. See Bickermann, "The Jewish Historian Demetrios," 79.

16. J. Freudenthal, *Hellenistische Studien, 1-2, Alexander Polyhistor und die von ihm erhaltenen Reste judäischer und samaritanischer Geschichtswerke* (Breslau: Skutsch, 1875); E. Schwartz, "Alexandros von Milet," *PWRE* 1/2 (1894) 1449; F. Jacoby, *FGH* IIIa 96–126; F. W. Walbank, "Alexander(11) 'Polyhistor,'" *OCD* 35; A. M. Denis, *Introduction aux Pseudépigraphes Grecs d'Ancien Testament* (SVTP 1; Leiden: Brill, 1970) 244–46; Wacholder, *Eupolemus*, 44–52.

17. Walbank, "Alexander," 35.

18. Bickermann, "The Jewish Historian Demetrios," 79.

19. Apart from the transmission of the Jewish authors, Alexander was an important source for Diogenes Laertius and Stephanus of Byzantium. See Wacholder, *Eupolemus*, 45.

20. K. Mras, *Eusebius' Werke, 8, Die Praeparatio Evangelica* (GCS 43; 2 vols.; Berlin: Akademie, 1954). The texts are reprinted in W. N. Stearns, *Fragments from Graeco-Jewish Writers* (Chicago: University of Chicago, 1908) and A. M. Denis, *Fragmenta Pseudepigraphorum quae supersunt Graeca* (PVTG 3; Leiden: Brill, 1970) 175–228. The historical and quasi-historical texts can also be found in Jacoby, *FGH* III C (1958) 666–713.

21. Wacholder, *Eupolemus*, 52–70. It is possible that Clement also had independent knowledge of the Hellenistic Jewish authors.

22. Ibid., 48–49; Denis, *Introduction*, 242–43.

23. The classic study is still Freudenthal's *Hellenistische Studien*. Other significant treatments are E. Schürer, *Geschichte des jüdischen Volkes im Zeitalter Jesu Christi* (4 ed.; Leipzig: Hinrichs, 1909) vol. 3, sec. 33; P. Dalbert, *Die Theologie der hellenistisch-jüdischen Missionsliteratur unter Ausschluss von Philo und Josephus* (Hamburg: Reich, 1954); Y. Gutman, *The Beginnings of Jewish-Hellenistic Literature* (Jerusalem: Bialik, 1958, in Hebrew); N. Walter, *Fragmente jüdisch-hellenistischer Historiker* (JSHRZ 1/2; Gütersloh: Mohn, 1976); *Fragmente jüdisch-hellenistischer Exegeten* (JSHRZ III/2; 1975);

M. Hengel, "Anonymität, Pseudepigraphie und 'Literarische Fälschung' in der jüdisch-hellenistischen Literatur," *Entretiens sur l'Antiquité Classique XVIII* (Pseudepigrapha I) (1972) 231–309; Denis, *Introduction*, 239–83; Fraser, *Ptolemaic Alexandria* 1:687–716. Translations with introductions and notes are forthcoming in J. H. Charlesworth (ed.), *The Pseudepigrapha* (Garden City: Doubleday).

24. There is no ancient warrant for this label. The fragments were preserved by Alexander Polyhistor and are found in Eusebius, PE 9.19.4 (where the attribution to Demetrius is conjectural); PE 9.21.1–19; PE 9.29.1–3; PE 9.29.15; PE 9.29.16c and Clement, *Stromateis*, 1.141.1–2. See Freudenthal, *Hellenistische Studien*, 219–23; Fraser, *Ptolemaic Alexandria*, 1:690–94; Wacholder, *Eupolemus*, 98–104; Walter, "Demetrios," in *Fragmente . . . Exegeten*, 280–92, and the literature there cited. Demetrius's work is called "On the Kings of the Jews" by Clement, although most of what survives is concerned with the Pentateuch.

25. Bickermann, "The Jewish Historian Demetrios," 77.

26. Fraser, *Ptolemaic Alexandria* 2:960–61 n. 94.

27. We cannot be sure how fully the preserved fragments represent the work of Demetrius. See Fraser, *Ptolemaic Alexandria* 1:691.

28. Ibid., 1:692; Wacholder, *Eupolemus* 100–101.

29. We may accept the general view that Demetrius is the earliest witness to the LXX (with Ezekiel the tragedian, who was roughly contemporary). For further evidence of his use of the LXX, see Fraser, *Ptolemaic Alexandria* 2:961 n. 98.

30. Fraser, *Ptolemaic Alexandria*, 1:692. Also 1:509–10 on the importance of chronology in the work of Manetho. Wacholder, *Eupolemus*, 103, points out that Demetrius is more restrained than Manetho on the mythical period.

31. Ibid., 692–94; Wacholder, *Eupolemus*, 104.

32. Hengel, "Anonymität," 236; Walter, "Demetrios," 281.

33. Fraser, *Ptolemaic Alexandria*, 1:693.

34. PE 9.25.1–4. See Freudenthal, *Hellenistische Studien*, 136–43; Walter, *Fragmente . . . Exegeten*, 293–96.

35. Walter, *Fragmente . . . Exegeten*, 293.

36. In Aristeas Job is a son of Esau, in LXX Job, a great-grandson. LXX Job also says that Eliphaz was among the sons of Esau. Aristeas may have known this tradition and changed Job's genealogy to make them contemporary.

37. Walter, *Fragmente . . . Exegeten*, 294.

38. Ibid., 295.

39. Three fragments of Artapanus are preserved in PE 9.18, 23, and 27, dealing respectively with Abraham, Joseph, and Moses. The Moses fragment is partially paralleled in Clement, *Stromateis*, 1.23.154, 2–3. See Freudenthal, *Hellenistische Studien*, 143–74; K. I. Merentitis, *Ho Ioudaios Logios Artapanos kaito Ergonautou* (Athens: Murtidos, 1961); D. L. Tiede, *The Charismatic Figure as Miracle Worker* (SBLDS 1; Missoula: Scholars, 1972) 146–77; Walter, *Fragmente . . . Historiker* (JSHRZ 1/2; Gütersloh: Mohn, 1976) 121–43; C. R. Holladay, *Theios Anēr in Hellenistic Judaism* (SBLDS 40; Missoula: Scholars, 1977) 199–232.

40. Freudenthal, *Hellenistische Studien*, 216. The verbal correspondences are closest in the account of the plagues.

41. A. M. Denis (*Introduction*, 257) suggests a date in the time of Philopator (221–204 BCE), following a suggestion of L. Cerfaux ("Influence des Mystères sur le Judaïsme Alexandrin avant Philon," *Receuil L. Cerfaux* [BETL 6; Gembloux: Duculot, 1954] 1:81–85); Wacholder (*Eupolemus*, 106 n. 40) suggests the early second century; Hengel ("Anonymität," 24) suggests the second century; Walter (*Fragmente . . . Historiker*, 125) and Merentites (*Ho Ioudaios Logis*, 9) propose a date about 100 BCE.

42. Cerfaux, "Influence des Mystères," 1:81–85. Philopator's interest in the Dionysus cult is well attested (Fraser, *Ptolemaic Alexandria*, 1:202).

43. Philopator is said to require that the Jews be registered and "branded on their bodies by fire with the ivy-leaf symbol of Dionysus." Cf. 2 Mac 6:7–8 which says that in the persecution of Antiochus Epiphanes Jews in Jerusalem were compelled "to wear ivy wreaths and walk in the Dionysiac procession." Judaism was occasionally confused

with the cult of Dionysus because of the nature of the celebration of Tabernacles (see Plutarch, *Quaestiones Convivales* 4.6 [671–72]).

44. For the text of the papyrus, see Fraser, *Ptolemaic Alexandria*, 2:345–46 n. 114. It is debated whether the decree was intended to promote or arrest the growth of the Dionysus cult.

45. Plutarch, *Quaestiones Convivales*, 8.9.1.

46. Wacholder, *Eupolemus*, 106, n. 40. On Bolus see H. Diels, *Die Fragmente der Vorsokratiker*[8] (Berlin: Weidmann, 1956) 2:216.

47. See W. W. Tarn, *Hellenistic Civilization* (New York: World, 1961) 179. I owe this suggestion to Prof. John Strugnell.

48. Fraser argues that Artapanus "is familiar with the native life of Egypt and the purely priestly traditions" and suggests that, as his Persian name might suggest, he was "a Jew of mixed descent, possibly resident in another centre such as Memphis" (*Ptolemaic Alexandria*, 1:706; 2:985 n. 199). Fraser notes the occurrence of related Persian names in Egypt and the village of Artapatou, near Oxyrhyncus, attested from the third century CE. Hengel ("Anonymität," 239) tentatively suggests that Artapanus's work "könnte auf Grund ihrer politische Ansprüche und ihrer synkretistischen Tendenz aus der Militärkolonie um den jüdischen Tempel von Leontopolis stammen" (cf. also Holladay, *Theios Anēr*, 217). There is nothing to tie Artapanus specifically to either Memphis or Leontopolis (Leontopolis would require a later date than we have suggested), but there is nothing to tie him to Alexandria either. In qualification of Fraser, it should be said that Artapanus appears to have derived his knowledge of Egyptian customs primarily from Greek sources, such as Hecataeus, rather than from Egyptian priests. (See Wacholder, *Eupolemus*, 80).

49. See esp. Braun, *History and Romance*, followed by Tiede, *The Charismatic Figure*, 149–50. Holladay (*Theios Anēr*, 215) categorizes it as "national romantic history" and classifies it with Hecataeus's work "On the Egyptians."

50. Fraser, *Ptolemaic Alexandria*, 1:705–6; Holladay, *Theios Anēr*, 213.

51. Fraser, *Ptolemaic Alexandria*, 1:508–9. Hecataeus already had the story that the Jews were descended from foreigners expelled by the Egyptians during a plague. Manetho goes further in claiming that Moses was leader of a group of "lepers and other polluted persons."

52. Braun, *History and Romance*, 26. See also Tiede, *The Charistmatic Figure*, 151–77. Cf. Plutarch (*Isis and Osiris* 24 [360 B]): "Mighty deeds of Semiramis are celebrated among the Assyrians; and mighty deeds of Sesostris in Egypt, and the Phrygians even to this day call brilliant and marvellous exploits 'manic' because Manes, one of their early kings, proved himself a good man and exercised a vast influence among them."

53. Tiede, *The Charismatic Figure*, 153–59. For Sesostris see Diodorus 1.54–57; Herodotus 2.102–109.

54. Diodorus 1.17.3; 1.27.4. Tiede, *The Charismatic Figure*, 155.

55. The identification is also found in Diodorus 1.12.4; Plutarch, *Isis and Osiris* 32 and 38.

56. In Greek tradition Orpheus is usually the teacher, not the pupil of Mousaeus. According to Hecataeus (Diodorus 1.96.4–9), Orpheus brought back cultural and religious lore to Greece from his travels in Egypt. Artapanus is here claiming that Moses was the ultimate source also of Greek culture. See Walter, *Fragmente . . . Historiker*, 123; Tiede, *The Charismatic Figure*, 152.

57. Abraham is also a teacher of astrology in Pseudo-Eupolemus (PE 9.17.3). Cf. *Ant* 1.8.2 (167–68), a passage which may be derived from Pseudo-Hecataeus. Contrast Abraham's rejection of astrology in Philo, *De Abrahamo*, 69–71, 77, and Jub 12:60. Also Sib Or 3:218–30 (where the reference is to the descendants of Abraham). See in general J.H. Charlesworth, "Jewish Astrology in the Talmud, Pseudepigrapha, the Dead Sea Scrolls and Early Palestinian Synagogues," *HTR* 70 (1977) 183–200. The most striking endorsement of astrology by a Jewish author is found in the Treatise of Shem, Charlesworth, "Rylands Syriac Ms. 44 and a new Addition to the Pseudepigrapha: The Treatise of Shem, Discussed and Translated," *BJRL* 60 (1978) 376–403.

58. This is apparent from PE 9.27.12: "the creatures which Moses had made sacred." Holladay (*Theios Anēr*, 229–31) emphasizes that the ibis is not consecrated by Moses but by his associates and that Chenephres institutes the Apis cult, while Moses only explains that the bull is useful to mankind. Nonetheless, Moses has a causal role in both these cases.

59. E.g., Wis 13:10; Philo, *De Decalogo*, 16; Sib Or 3:218–36.

60. Euhemerism is the theory that the gods were originally kings and conquerors who brought benefits to mankind and that their worship arose as an expression of gratitude. The term is derived from Euhemerus of Messene who put forward this theory about 300 BCE.

61. See Tiede, *The Charismatic Figure*, 166–74. This aspect of Artapanus was emphasized by Otto Weinreich, *Gebet und Wunder* (Stuttgart: Kohlhammer, 1929). The most spectacular example is Moses' escape from prison in PE 9.27.23–26, but also the prominence given to the plagues. It is noteworthy that the citation in Clement plays down the miraculous element in Moses' escape from prison. According to the text in Eusebius, the doors opened *automatōs*. In Clement they open "in accordance with the will of God." Also Moses pronounces the divine name in pharaoh's ear and causes him to fall speechless. The name of the god of the Jews was noted for its potency in Hellenistic magic (M. Hengel, *Judaism and Hellenism* [Philadelphia: Fortress, 1974] 1:260).

62. He is identified with Hermes "on account of the interpretation of the sacred letters" (PE 9.27.6), but the letters in question are the Egyptian hieroglyphs (cf. PE 9.27.4) and associate Moses with Thoth (see Holladay, *Theios Anēr*, 226).

63. For Artapanus's dependence on Hecataeus, see Freudenthal, *Hellenistische Studien*, 160–61; H. Willrich, *Judaica* (Göttingen: Vandenhoeck & Ruprecht, 1900) 111–16. Artapanus has numerous parallels with Diodorus Siculus and Hecataeus is the most likely common source.

64. Holladay, *Theios Anēr*, 232.

65. That Jewish solidarity is a virtue may also be implied: when Raguel wants to campaign against Egypt, Moses restrains him "taking thought of his compatriots." The reference here is almost certainly to the Jews in Egypt, not to the Egyptians. A similar moral is found in Greek Esther and 3 Maccabees.

66. See W. L. Humphreys, "A Life-Style for Diaspora: A Study of the Tales of Esther and Daniel," *JBL* 92 (1973) 211–23; J. J. Collins, *The Apocalyptic Vision of the Book of Daniel* (HSM 16; Missoula: Scholars, 1977) chap. 2; S. Berg, *The Book of Esther* (SBLDS 44; Chico: Scholars, 1979) 72–82.

67. Eusebius (PE 9.17), which is said to be from Eupolemus "On the Jews," but the title is certainly mistaken. Another fragment (PE 9.18.2) appears to be a briefer summary of the same source, but is said to be from an anonymous work. See Wacholder, *Eupolemus*, 287–93; Walter, *Fragmente . . . Historiker*, 137–40; Hengel, *Judaism and Hellenism*, 1:88–92; H. G. Kippenberg, *Garizim und Synagoge* (Berlin: de Gruyter, 1971) 80–83.

68. In Genesis, Melchizedek is king of Salem. LXX Gen 33:18 reads *kai ēlthen Iakob eis Salēm polin Sikimōn.* Here Salem is "a city of Shechem." (The Hebrew *šalēm,* "safely," is construed as a place name). The translation may be only a misunderstanding of the Hebrew. In any case, even if there was a tradition that located Salem in Samaritan territory, the mention of the incident and the specific association with Gerizim would only have been made by a Samaritan. Jewish tradition identified Salem with Jerusalem (e.g., Josephus, *Ant* 1.10.2 [180]). See B. Z. Wacholder, "Pseudo-Eupolemus' Two Greek Fragments on the Life of Abraham," *HUCA* 34 (1963) 107.

69. According to Josephus, the Shechemites at the time of Alexander "were Hebrews but were called the Sidonians of Shechem" (*Ant* 11.8.6 [344]). Again in *Ant* 12.5.5 (257–64) the Samaritans who appeal to Antiochus Epiphanes refer to themselves as "Sidonians in Shechem" and protest that they are Sidonians by origin." Sidonians were, of course, Phoenicians.

70. J. D. Purvis, *The Samaritan Pentateuch and the Origin of the Samaritan Sect* (HSM 2; Cambridge: Harvard, 1968) 86–118. On the history of the Samaritan schism, see further Kippenberg, *Garizim und Synagoge*, 33–93.

71. Purvis, *The Samaritan Pentateuch*, 98–112.

72. Hengel, *Judaism and Hellenism*, 1:89; Walter, *Fragmente . . . Historiker*, 138–39. The forms of the names provide the decisive evidence.

73. Hengel (*Judaism and Hellenism*, 1:88), Wacholder (*Eupolemus*, 289), and Walter (*Fragmente . . . Historiker*, 139) all favor Palestinian origin. G. Vermes (*Scripture and Tradition in Juaism* [Leiden: Brill, 1961] 124) assumes Alexandrian provenance. On the Samaritans in Alexandria, see Josephus, *Ant* 13.3.4 (74–79) and in Egypt generally, *Ant* 12.1.1 (7–10).

74. Hengel, *Judaism and Hellenism*, 1:89; Wacholder, *Eupolemus*, 288; P. Schnabel, *Berossos und die babylonisch-hellenistische Literatur* (Berlin: Teubner, 1923) 67–69. The influence of Berossus is apparent in the foundation of Babylon by Bel (Belus). It is possible that the claim that the builders of the tower were giants reflects the influence of Hesiod's Theogony.

75. Cf. Artapanus, above, for Abraham as a teacher of astrology. Many scholars have held that Sib Or 3:218–36 is a direct criticism of Pseudo-Eupolemus; so J. Geffcken, *Komposition und Entstehungszeit der Oracula Sibyllina* (TU 8/1; Leipzig: Hinrichs, 1902) 7; A. Peretti, *La Sibilla Babilonese nella Propaganda Ellenistica* (Biblioteca di Cultura 21; Firenze: La Nuova Italia Editrice, 1943) 131; Wacholder, *Eupolemus*, 290–91. The evidence for direct dependence is not, however, sufficient. See V. Nikiprowetzky, *La Troisième Sibylle* (Etudes Juives 9; Paris: Mouton, 1970) 127–33; J. J. Collins, *The Sibylline Oracles of Egyptian Judaism* (SBLDS 13; Missoula: Scholars, 1974) 164.

76. Freudenthal, *Hellenistische Studien*, 100. The epic poet Theodotus, who was also thought to be Samaritan will be discussed below.

77. Jacoby, *FGH* 2B (1929) 1156–58. See Schürer, *Geschichte* 3:368–69; R. Laqueur, "Thallos," *PWRE* 2 Reihe A 9 (1934) cols. 1225–26; Denis, *Introduction*, 267–68; J. H. Charlesworth, *The Pseudepigrapha and Modern Research* (SCS 7; Chico: Scholars, 1976) 209–10.

78. Schürer, *Geschichte*, 3:369. Africanus (in Syncellus) says that an eclipse which he mentions in his third book was the eclipse at the crucifixion of Christ.

79. See Denis, *Introduction*, 267–68.

80. Wacholder("Thallus," *EncJud* 15col. 1045) regards Thallus as a gentile, Kippenberg (*Garizim und Synagoge*, 84) regards him as a Hellenized Jew.

81. Josephus, *Ant* 1.15 (239–41); PE 9.20.2–4. See Walter, *Fragmente . . . Historiker*, 115–20; Hengel, "Anonymität," 241–42.

82. The tendency to derive various peoples from Abraham was widespread. The most striking example was the Spartans in the forged letter of Areus to Onias (1 Mac 12:19–23; *Ant* 12.4.10 [226–227]). See B. Cardauns, "Juden und Spartaner, zur hellenistisch-jüdischen Literatur," *Hermes* 95 (1967) 317–24, Hengel, *Judaism and Hellenism* 2:62–63 n. 266.

83. Fraser, *Ptolemaic Alexandria*, 2:963.

84. Kippenberg, *Garizim und Synagoge*, 84.

85. PE 9.26.1 (Clement, *Stromateis*, 1.153.4); 9.30.1–34.8 (Clement *Stromateis*, 1.130.3); 9.34.20; 9.39.2–5; Clement, *Stromateis*, 1.141.4–5. See Wacholder, *Eupolemus*; Walter, *Fragmente . . . Historiker*, 93–108; Hengel, *Judaism and Hellenism*, 1:92–95; J. Giblet, "Eupolème et l'historiographie du Judaisme hellénistique," *ETL* 63 (1963) 539–54.

86. The mission is also recorded in Josephus, *Ant* 12.10.6 (415) and 2 Mac 4:11 (where the main reference is to Eupolemus's father John who obtained royal privileges for the Jews in the time of Antiochus III). The date of Eupolemus is indicated in Clement, *Stromateis*, 1.141.4, where he calculates the total number of years from Adam to the fifth year of king Demetrius, which is usually taken as 158 BCE, fifth year of Demetrius I.

87. That he also knew Hebrew is shown by the fact that he translates some terms in the passage on the temple which were not translated in the LXX (Walter, *Fragmente . . . Historiker*, 95). That he used both LXX and the Hebrew text has been established

since Freudenthal. Eupolemus's Greek style was pronounced "miserable" by Jacoby, *PW* 6.1229.

88. Walter, *Fragmente* . . . *Historiker*, 96; Dalbert, *Die Theologie der hellenistisch-jüdischen Missionsliteratur*, 42; Hengel, *Judaism and Hellenism*, 1:94.

89. Hengel, *Judaism and Hellenism*, 1:93.

90. Cf. the gold shield sent to Rome in 1 Mac 14:24, but contrast the sensitivity of 2 Mac 4:18–20. When Jason sent envoys to Tyre with 300 silver drachmas for the sacrifice of Hercules, the envoys diverted it to the construction of triremes. A parallel to this incident in Eupolemus is found in the lone fragment of Theophilus (PE 9.34.19) who says that Solomon gave the king of Tyre all the gold that was left over at the building of the temple, and the king used it on a statue of his daughter.

91. Hengel, *Judaism and Hellenism*, 1:95.

92. See further D. Georgi, *Die Gegner des Paulus im 2. Korintherbrief* (WMANT 11; Neukirchen-Vluyn: Neukirchener Verlag, 1964) 63–82.

93. As Hengel also notes, Eupolemus handles the biblical text with great freedom. Wacholder also points out that "Eupolemus' reports frequently contradict the traditions, creating more discord than do any differences found in the Bible" (*Eupolemus*, 70).

94. Wacholder, *Eupolemus*, 259–306. The passage is preserved in *Ag Ap* 1.183–205, 213–14. See M. Stern, *Greek and Latin Authors on Jews and Judaism* (Jerusalem: Israel Academy of Sciences and Humanities, 1974) 1:35–44; Walter, *Fragmente* . . . *Historiker*, 154–57.

95. Josephus, *Ant* 1.7.2 (159); Clement, *Stromateis*, 5.113.1–2.

96. Ibid., 151. Walter rightly points out that we cannot assume that Pseudo-Hecataeus composed the Pseudo-Sophocles verses or the other poetic forgeries which are transmitted with the fragments of Aristobulus (contrast Wacholder, *Eupolemus*, 264, who infers that Pseudo-Hecataeus must be prior to Aristobulus).

97. See above n. 90. Theophilus is preserved in PE 9.34. See Walter, *Fragmente* . . . *Historiker*, 109–11; Stern, *Greek and Latin Authors*, 1:126–27. Josephus mentions Theophilus in a list of Greek historians in *Ag Ap* 1.216. He mentions Demetrius, Philo the Elder, and Eupolemus in the same context, apparently on the assumption that all were pagan authors.

98. PE 9.20.1; 9.24.1; 9.37.1–3. See Wacholder, *Eupolemus*, 282–83; Y. Gutman, "Philo the Epic Poet," *Scripta Hierosolymitana* 1 (1954) 36–63.

99. Gutman ("Philo," 60–63) points esp. to the analogy of the *Messēniaka* of Rhianus of Crete, who wrote in the second half of the third century BCE. Apollonius of Rhodes, author of the *Argonautica*, also composed a *Ktiseis*, a series of poems concerning foundation legends. Fraser (*Ptolemaic Alexandria*, 1:626) comments on the geographical interests of Apollonius as a typically Alexandrian feature. On the Hellenistic epic, see further Fraser, 1:624–49.

100. See Fraser, *Ptolemaic Alexandria*, 1:633–38 on the scholarly language of Apollonius. The most obscure example of Hellenistic poetry was the Alexandra of Lycophron, which was deliberately difficult to decipher. Philo has often been compared to Lycophron, but Wacholder (*Eupolemus*, 283) is probably right that Philo wished to be understood, since the fragment on Joseph is quite clear.

101. Ps. 46:4. Note also Ps. 48:2, which claims that Zion is "the joy of all the earth," and cf. Philo's claim that it *deiknusin hypertata thambea laōn* ("shows forth the greatest wonders of the peoples").

102. Wacholder, *Eupolemus*, 283.

103. Gutman, "Philo," 37.

104. Ibid., 40. Gutman makes two emendations: *eplēmmyre* for *plēmmyre* and *hamma ti* for *hammati*. Then the two dative phrases, *archegonoisi thesmois* and *megauchetoisi logismois*, are in apposition and the two accusative phrases, *hamma ti desmōn* and *theiophilē thelgeitra*, are also in apposition.

105. Ibid., 53.

106. Ibid., 40–41. Aristobulus, who may have been roughly contemporary with Philo

identifies Torah with Wisdom and says that it existed before heaven and earth (PE 13.12.11). The preexistence of wisdom is found in Prov 8:22 and the identification with the Torah in Sir 24:23.

107. The phrase of Sir 24:23.

108. Gutman, "Philo," 44–45. Plato, *Timaeus* 38e.

109. Philo, *Quis Rerum Divinarum Heres*, 23.

110. Compare the cords which Job gives to his daughters in T Job 46–47.

111. Wacholder (*Eupolemus*, 282), following Karpeles, claims that Philo was a native of Jerusalem. The only element in the fragments which would tie him to the city is the reference to swimming in PE 9.37.1, but the passage is too obscure to bear any weight.

112. PE 9.22.1–11. Wacholder (*Eupolemus*, 283–85) sees Theodotus as a Samaritan counterpart of Philo the epic poet. See also A. Ludwich, *De Theodoti carmine graeco-judaico* (Königsberg University, 1899); Gutman, *Beginnings*, 1:245–61.

113. So Freudenthal, *Hellenistische Studien*, 99–100. Also Fraser, *Ptolemaic Alexandria*, 2:986; Hengel, "Anonymität," 242–43; Wacholder, *Eupolemus*, 285; Schürer, *Geschichte*, 3:499; Denis, *Introduction*, 272.

114. Kippenberg, *Garizim und Synagoge*, 84; Charlesworth, *The Pseudepigrapha*, 210. For full discussion, see J. J. Collins, "The Epic of Theodotus and the Hellenism of the Hasmoneans," *HTR* 73 (1980) 91–104.

115. Theodotus goes beyond the biblical account here. The fact that the men of Shechem were first circumcised and then attacked while they were still sore is not mentioned.

116. *Blapte theos Sikimōn oikētoras*. Because of the fragmentary nature of the text, the context and speaker are uncertain.

117. Josephus, *Ant* 12.5.5 (257–64). Cf. 2 Mac 6:1–6. Josephus preserves a letter from the "Sidonians of Shechem" to Antiochus Epiphanes. The authenticity of the letter has been defended by Bickermann ("Un document relatif à la persécution d'Antiochus IV Épiphane," *Studies in Jewish and Christian History* 2:105–35, first published in *RHR* 115 [1937] 118–223). See also Hengel, *Judaism and Hellenism*, 1:293–94. For different opinions, see M. Delcor ("Vom Sichem der hellenistischen Epoche zum Sychar des Neuen Testaments," *ZDPV* 78 [1962] 34–48) who argues that the letter came from a colony of actual Sidonians; and R. J. Coggins (*Samaritans and Jews* [Oxford; Blackwell, 1975] 99) who dismisses the title as a slighting reference by a Jewish author. On the name of the Samaritan temple see Kippenberg, *Garizim und Synagoge*, 74–80.

118. *Ant* 13. 254–58; 275–81; *JW* 1. 62–65; Purvis, *The Samaritan Pentateuch*, 113; Kippenberg, *Garizim und Synagoge*, 85–92.

119. On the accuracy of Theodotus's description of Shechem as shown by modern excavations, see R. J. Bull, "A Note on Theodotus' Description of Shechem," *HTR* 60 (1967) 221–28. Bull argues that Theodotus must have written before the mid-second century BCE because he refers to the wall of Shechem as a lofty defense enclosure (*aipythen herkos*). Archeological evidence shows that the wall had fallen into neglect in the second half of the first century. It is sufficient, however, that Theodotus remembered the wall as a substantial defense.

120. On the Hellenization of the Hasmoneans, see Tcherikover, *Hellenistic Civilization*, 248–53.

121. Photius, *Bibliotheca*, 31; *FGH* III C 695–99. See Wacholder, *Eupolemus*, 298–306.

122. Esp. *Vita* 336–67 (65).

123. See H. R. Moehring, "The Acta Pro Judaeis in the *Antiquities* of Flavius Josephus," in *Christianity, Judaism and other Greco-Roman Cults*, 124–58.

124. Whether Josephus depended directly on Artapanus, or drew on a variant tradition, is disputed. He omits some key points in Artapanus's account, such as the founding of Hermopolis and the introduction of circumcision, and has an entirely different explanation of the origin of the campaign. See T. Rajak, "Moses in Ethiopia: Legend and Literature," *JJS* 29 (1978) 111–22; A Shinan, "Moses and the Ethiopian Woman," *Scripta Hierosolymitana* 27 (1978) 66–78.

125. H. W. Attridge, *The Interpretation of Biblical History in the Antiquitates Judaicae of Flavius Josephus* (HDR 7; Missoula: Scholars, 1976) 29–70.

126. See further L. H. Feldman, "Abraham the Greek Philosopher in Josephus," *TAPA* 99 (1968) 143–56; "Hellenizations in Josephus' Portrayal of Man's Decline," *Religions in Antiquity: Festschrift E. R. Goodenough* (ed. J. Neusner; Leiden: Brill, 1968) 333–53; "Hellenizations in Josephus' Version of Esther (Ant. Jud. 11.185–295," *TAPA* 101 (1970) 143–70; Attridge (*The Interpretation*, 17–27) reviews scholarship on Hellenization in Josephus.

127. Attridge, *The Interpretation*, 33–35. See *Ag Ap* 1. 216–18 (23) which refers to Theophilus, Theodotus, Demetrius (of Phalerum !), Philo the Elder, and Eupolemus.

128. See Attridge's discussion of the idea of Providence and the moralizing character of the *Antiquities* (*The Interpretation*, 71–144). Note also Josephus's own claim in *Ant* 1.1.4 (18) that much of his work is devoted to natural philosophy.

129. Cf. *Ant* Proem 4(24), where Josephus acknowledges that some things are written in solemn allegory, but defers philosophical analysis for the present.

130. We may note in passing that the presentation of the history of the second century BCE in 2 Maccabees also has a strongly Deuteronomic flavor, despite its Hellenistic form. We shall return to 2 Maccabees in chap. 2 below.

131. See Gager, *Moses in Graeco-Roman Paganism*, 25–112.

Chapter 2

RELIGION AND POLITICS: THE PTOLEMAIC ERA

The political history of Egyptian Judaism falls into a number of distinct phases. The most obvious line of division is the transition from Ptolemaic to Roman rule. Within the Ptolemaic period it is generally recognized that the reign of Ptolemy VI Philometor (181–145 BCE) marks a major transition. In fact, our knowledge of Egyptian Judaism prior to the time of Philometor is very scanty, but the impression, in the words of Tcherikover, "is that of a slow settlement in a new place."[1] For much of that period Palestine also was ruled by the Ptolemies. This fact facilitated immigration of Jews to Egypt. It also simplified the political loyalties of Egyptian Jews. When Palestine passed to Seleucid control in 198 BCE, the political situation became more complex, but the complexity was greatly increased in the reign of Philometor by the Maccabean revolt. An independent Judea laid stronger claims than the Seleucid empire on the loyalty of Jewish exiles. Further, the revolt was the occasion of a significant influx to Egypt of Jews who fled from the new political situation, most notably Onias IV and his followers.[2] Some of these new exiles rose to prominence under the friendly rule of Philometor. From this period Egyptian Judaism has left more substantial literary remains and more information for the historian.

Little can be said of the political relations between Jews and gentiles in Egypt prior to the reign of Philometor. 3 Maccabees gives an account of a persecution of Jews by Ptolemy IV Philopator, which involved an attempt to have the Jews branded with the emblem of Dionysus.[3] Philopator was in fact devoted to Dionysus and may have made some attempt to assimilate the Jewish religion to the Dionysiac cult. 3 Maccabees, however, is a highly fantastic composition and cannot be regarded as an accurate historical account. It is more likely to reflect a crisis of the Roman period than the time of Philopator. Of the Jewish writings which can with any plausibility be dated prior to Philometor only Artapanus reflects a distinct political attitude. There Moses is depicted as a benefactor of the Egyptian people and is regarded by the priests as worthy of honor like a god. The king, however, is jealous of Moses and plots against him. It is the king who alienates the Egyptian people from Moses and plots against his life. The arrogance of the king further leads him to maltreat the Jews and so is responsible for the plagues which Moses brings upon the Egyptians, and for the destruction of the Egyptians at the Exodus. What is remarkable in all this is the degree to which the Egyptian people is exculpated and blame concentrated on the king. The political message of Artapanus to his own time would seem to be one of solidarity with the Egyptians and suspicion of the (Greek) king. Some later documents, such as 3 Maccabees, also depict the king as villain, but suggest solidarity with the Greeks, not with the native Egyptians.[4] In fact, most Jewish Hellenistic literature is very hostile towards the native Egyptians, which is not surprising in view of the Egyptian polemics against the Jews from the time of Manetho.[5] Artapanus may have been exceptional, even in his own day. Since his political attitudes are only implicit, no great weight can be placed on them.

THE SECOND CENTURY BCE

The Third Sibyl

The first major document of the Diaspora which explicitly addresses political relations is the Third Sibylline Oracle. The main part of this document dates from the mid-second century BCE, but it also includes material from the two following centuries. I will presuppose here my earlier discussion of the source-critical questions, which distinguished:

  a. the main corpus: vss. 93–349 and 489–829;
  b. oracles against various nations: vss. 350–488;
  c. vss. 1–96, which probably constitute the conclusion of a different book.[6]

The date of the main corpus is fixed by three references to the seventh king of Egypt in vss. 193, 318, and 608. While the number seven might be chosen as an ideal number, it would have lacked credibility after the reign of the seventh Ptolemy.[7] The enumeration of the Ptolemies is complicated by the question whether Alexander should be counted and by the overlapping reigns in the second century. There are three possible identifications: Ptolemy VI Philometor, who reigned from 180–164, 163–145; Ptolemy VII Neos Philopator, 145–144; Ptolemy VIII Physcon (also called Euergetes II), 170–164, 164–163, and 144–117.

The reign of Ptolemy VII was so brief that it might not be counted, especially as Physcon had already been king. Further, while the oracles could not have been written after the latest possible seventh Ptolemy, they could have been written before his reign: the seventh king may be anticipated as a future ruler. The strained relations of the Jews with Physcon make it unlikely that he was the "seventh king" in question, but it is conceivable that a Jewish sibyllist looked forward to a king who would succeed him. However, given the favorable attitude of Philometor to the Jews, a date in his reign is more probable.[8] The seventh king could then refer either to Philometor himself or to his son Neos Philopator.

A more specific indication of date may be found in vss. 162–95. This refers to the rise of Rome, which will fill many places with evils, but especially Macedonia. Macedonia was divided after the battle of Pydna in 168 BCE and was made a Roman province in 147 BCE. The references to Rome as a world power could not be earlier than the battle of Magnesia (190) where Rome defeated Antiochus III of Syria, and probably presupposes the intervention of Rome in Egypt in 168. In view of these considerations the period when Philometor was sole ruler in 163–145 is the most likely time of composition.

Virtually all scholars agree that the work was composed in Egypt.[9] Vs. 161 refers to a second world empire of Egypt after that of the Macedonians and the work is punctuated by references to the seventh king of Egypt. While it is conceivable that these references are the work of a Palestinian sympathizer of the Ptolemies, the lack of specific reference to Palestine makes an Egyptian origin almost certain.

The content of Sibylline Oracle 3

The main corpus of Sib Or 3 may be divided into five oracles: (1) vss. 97–161; (2) vss. 162–95; (3) vss. 196–294; (4) vss. 545–656, and (5) vss. 657–808.[10]

The first of these constitutes an introduction to world history. It includes (a) the fall of the tower of Babylon; (b) a euhemeristic account of the war of the Titans against Kronos and his sons (105–55), and (c) a list of world empires (156–61). This section establishes a universal framework for the rest of the book. It introduces the theme of world kingship and shows that it was a cause of strife from the beginning. Most significant here is the attempt to integrate Greek mythology into the overview of history. While the gods are demythologized in the euhemeristic fashion, they are not simply dismissed as unreal. This opening section shows most clearly the affinities of the sibyl with the Jewish historians discussed in Chapter 1.[11] More broadly the use of the sibylline form shows that the author, like his Hellenistic Jewish predecessors, was attempting to bridge two cultures. The sibylline form offered some affinities with the prophetic oracles of the Hebrew scriptures, but the more immediate analogy was with the use of oracles for political propaganda in the Hellenistic world.[12] Here again a Jewish writer was using a Hellenistic form to present his view of Judaism. The prototypes were not only the Greek and Roman sibyls and the Greek literary tradition represented by the Alexandra of Lycophron but also, more immediately, the Egyptian prophetic tradition which found expression in the Hellenistic age in such works as the Demotic Chronicle and the Potter's Oracle.[13]

The introduction to world history with which Sib Or 3 begins is followed by four other oracles which present a recurring pattern:

(i) sin, usually idolatry, leads to

(ii) disaster and tribulation, which is terminated by

(iii) the advent of a king or kingdom.[14]

Within these passages religious and ethical exhortation is supported by a political and eschatological framework. The hortatory sections may fairly be said to contain the view of Judaism which is presented to the Hellenistic world, and they are accordingly of the utmost importance. We will, however, defer the discussion of these passages to Part Two, where they can be compared with other presentations of Jewish ethical and religious requirements. For the present we will focus on the political view of Judaism, within which the exhortation is framed. The argument of Sib Or 3 is that those who keep the law of God will ultimately prosper, while those who do not will come to destruction. The prosperity of the righteous is envisaged in a peaceful world centered on the Jewish temple, but the manner in which this state is brought about is associated with the reign of an Egyptian king. The role assigned to this king is of crucial importance for understanding the Third Sibyl. Specifically, the question arises whether this king should be identified with the "king from the sun" of vs. 652 "who will stop the entire earth from evil war" and so usher in the messianic age, or, alternatively, is not the agent of transformation but merely the indicator of the date when the Jews will come to power.[15]

The seventh king

There are three explicit references to the seventh king. In vss. 175–95 we are told that the kingdom which will succeed the Macedonians will endure "until the seventh reign when a king who will be of the Greeks by race, will rule." Then "the people of the great God will again be strong, who will be guides in life for all mortals." The kingdom in question is described as "white and many-headed from the western sea" and is quite unambiguously Rome.

Many commentators have found such a denunciation of Rome by a Jew in the second century BCE problematic.[16] So Momigliano objects that the hostile allusions to Rome cannot be dated with the reference to the seventh king "since between 170 and 160 both Egypt and Judea were indebted to Rome, and in 161 Judea made an alliance with Rome."[17] Momigliano, like Peretti,[18] considers the allusion to Rome a later addition. Geffcken preferred to elide the reference to the seventh king.[19] Nikiprowetzky, who quite rightly protests that such procedures are unsupported by any textual arguments, dates the entire passage to the first century BCE and takes the seventh king, somewhat paradoxically, as Cleopatra VII.[20] However, the statement that Rome will "fill everything with evils . . . in many places, but especially in Macedonia" can only refer to the Roman conquest of Macedonia which took place precisely in the reign of Philometor, and so is fully compatible with a second-century "seventh king." The attempts to divorce the anti-Roman polemic from the date of the seventh king are only special pleading for particular interpretations. If we preserve the unity of the text, Momigliano's claim that "it will not be difficult to recognize a precise allusion to the Jewish rebellion in lines 194–5"[21] is difficult to maintain. The Maccabees looked on Rome as a friend. It is true that Egypt was also protected by Rome from Antiochus Epiphanes, but the role of Rome in Egypt was more complex, because of the civil strife between Philometor and Physcon. At first the Romans supported Philometor, but in 161 he incurred their displeasure by refusing to cede Cyprus to Physcon.[22] In view of Philometor's favor towards the Jews, an anti-Roman oracle by an Egyptian Jew is quite conceivable after 161. The friendship between Rome and the Maccabees would not have impressed all the Jews in Egypt favorably, especially those who had fled to Egypt in the wake of the revolt. The prophecy of the rise of the "people of the great God" in 194 is not necessarily *ex eventu*, any more than the destruction of the Romans. So, while this passage does not clarify the eschatological role of the Egyptian king, it provides no reference to the Maccabean revolt either.

The second reference to the seventh king in 318 concerns the cessation of civil strife in Egypt. The passage may be inspired by the relative calm in the later reign of Philometor, but more likely it is not *ex eventu* and simply expresses a hope for the future. Egypt continued to be torn by civil strife throughout the Ptolemaic period. The passage throws no light on the relation of this king to the Jews.

The third reference claims that men will cast away their idols when the "young seventh king of Egypt rules his own land, numbered from the dynasty of the Greeks" (vss. 608–9).[23] Again, the passage does not specify the role of the king. The passage goes on to tell how "a great king will come from Asia." The invasion by this king is seen as the prelude, and perhaps the indirect cause, of the conversion of the Egyptians to the one true God.

Most scholars have assumed that the king from Asia should be identified as Antiochus Epiphanes who invaded Egypt in 170 and again in 168.[24] This identification would require a very precise date for the passage. The king is said to depart in triumph. This would be appropriate for the first campaign of Antiochus but not for the second. The oracle would have to have been written immediately after the first campaign, before it became apparent that no conversion of Egypt would follow. The identification with Antiochus Epiphanes is not, however, as compelling as has generally been assumed. Taken as a whole the passage 601–18 is clearly not *ex eventu* but a real prophecy (which was never fulfilled). A king from Asia was a traditional threat to Egypt (we might compare a "king from the north" in biblical prophecy).[25] The invasion by the Hyksos was recalled by Manetho. More recently, the Persians, Cambyses and Artaxerxes Ochus were notorious invaders. In Egyptian prophecy the Potter's Oracle refers to a king who will come down from Syria and be hated by all, and the oracles of

Nechepso and Petosiris say that a great man will come from Asia to the land of the Egyptians, capture the ruler of Egypt, subject some of the people and kill others. It is gratuitous to assume that these oracular passages must refer specifically to Antiochus Epiphanes. The presentation in Sib Or 3 is in all probability colored by the invasion of Antiochus Epiphanes as the most recent king from Asia, but the passage cannot be taken as a historical reference. It is part of an eschatological oracle in which any historical reminiscences are used to project the future. Again, while the passage does not specify the role of the Egyptian king, it does not provide a reference to the Maccabean revolt or its setting.

The analogy with the Persian period

Two other passages are significant for the political context of Sib Or 3. The first concerns the restoration from the Babylonian exile, in vss. 286–94. The second is the reference to the "king from the sun" in vs. 652.

In 286–94 we read:

> And then the heavenly God will send a king and will judge each man in blood and the gleam of fire. There is a certain royal tribe whose race will never stumble. This too, as time pursues its cyclic course, will reign, and it will begin to raise up a new temple of God. All the kings of the Persians will bring to their aid gold and bronze and much-wrought iron. For God Himself will give a holy dream by night and then indeed the temple will again be as it was before.

This passage follows directly on the exile, when "for seven decades of times all your fruitful earth and the wonders of the temple will be desolate."

The reference to the kings of the Persians makes it clear enough that the reference is to the restoration in the sixth century. Yet a number of scholars have tried to find a messianic reference here.[26] Most recently J. Nolland has argued that the use of the second person in vss. 265–85 indicates an address to the present time. Further, the statement that the temple will again be as it was before ill fits the historical restoration of the sixth century and the judgment "in blood and fire" (287) has eschatological overtones and echoes Joel 3:3 and 4:2. Nolland concludes that the sibyllist is applying the sixth-century restoration to his own day and infers a situation where the temple was profaned. Analogies with Daniel 9 and Jubilees support a date in the time of Antiochus Epiphanes. Nolland then sees the restoration as eschatological and takes the reference to the "royal tribe whose race will never stumble" (288–89) as a reference to "the whole notion of the inviolability of the Davidic kingship (2 Sam vii etc.)"—and so to a Davidic messiah. Since such a hope is not easily applied to the Maccabees, he concludes that this oracle was composed "prior to significant Maccabean success . . . before the rise of popular hopes in the Maccabees."[27]

The argument for an application of the oracle to the author's own time is not a necessary one—not all Jews need have thought of the postexilic temple as inadequate. However, it is possible. At least the passage concludes a section of the book and one period of history, and so is functionally parallel to the eschatological oracles.[28] This does not necessarily mean that the book was written at a time when the temple was profaned but that there is a pattern in history—punishment for sin and restoration for the faithful, which will be repeated in the eschatological period. However, if we grant a parallel between the restoration under Cyrus and the author's time and/or the eschatological age, the passage still does not support either the messianic interpretation or the dating proposed by Nolland. The only individual mentioned (vs. 286) is not a Davidide, but Cyrus. If he is meant as a type of an eschatological messiah, he would suggest not a Davidide but a gentile king (a suggestion supported by other passages in Sib Or 3). It is doubtful whether the "certain royal tribe" can be identified as the Davidic house. The more natural interpretation is the Jewish race which attained a significant measure of self-rule after the exile.[29] Further, even if we suppose with Nolland that the author was awaiting a restoration of the temple (and this supposition is not clearly warranted by the text), the precise dating would not follow. Not all Jews recognized the Maccabean restoration. The lack of support for the Maccabean rebellion here was not necessarily due to an early date. It may have arisen from lack of sympathy with the Maccabees.

Since the primary reference in this passage is indisputably to the sixth-century restoration, inferences for the political context of the eschatological kingdom are only tentative. Insofar as such inferences can be drawn, the passage suggests that the Jewish state and its temple will be established through the mediation of a gentile monarch like Cyrus. It should of course be noted that Cyrus himself never set foot in Palestine. His role in the Jewish restoration was indirect in the sense that he enabled and permitted the Jews to reestablish their own state and rebuild their own temple. This analogy may be significant for the reticence of the Third Sibyl on the role of the seventh king in the messianic age.

The king from the sun

The final reference to an individual king is found in vss. 652–56: "And then God will send a king from the sun (*kai tot' ap' ēelioio theos pempsei basilea*) who will stop the entire earth from evil war, killing some, imposing oaths of loyalty on others; and he will not do all these things by his private plans but in obedience to the noble teachings of the great God."

The king in this passage is not said to act directly on the Jews, although the following verses go on to describe the prosperity of the temple.[30] His role is to put an end to war in the entire world. We may compare the historical role of Cyrus, who is also said to act in accordance with the purpose of God (Isa 44:28).

The expression "from the sun" has given rise to considerable controversy. It has commonly been translated as "from the east" on the analogy of Isa 41:2, 25 (where the phrases *apo anatolōn* and *aph hēliou anatolōn* refer to Cyrus), and presumed to refer to a Jewish messiah.[31] This position is riddled with difficulties. First, the actual phrase is different: Isaiah specifies the geographical connotation with the word *anatolōn*. The phrase *ap' ēelioio* does not mean "from the east," but "from the sun." Second, in Isaiah the reference is not to a Jewish messiah but quite clearly to the Persian Cyrus, who did in fact come from the east. Third, despite assertions to the contrary, there is no evidence that a Jewish messiah was ever referred to as a king from the east, or expected from the east. On the contrary, the king from the east is the destructive Nebuchadnezzar in the Testament of Moses (3:1) and the kings from the east are also destructive in Rev 16:12.[32] Fourth, given that the phrase was not a traditional title for a Jewish messiah, it is difficult to see why a Jew in the second century would have expected salvation from a king from the east. The Third Sibyl never indicates interest or hope in the east. On the contrary, the messianic age is always associated with the reign of a king of Egypt.

The closest parallel that we have to the phrase in Sib Or 3:652 is in fact found in an Egyptian document of the Hellenistic age, the Potter's Oracle: "and then Egypt will increase when the king from the sun, who is benevolent for fifty-five years, becomes present, appointed by the greatest goddess Isis."[33] In an Egyptian document the king from the sun has a clear meaning—it refers to the old pharaonic ideology. The Potter's Oracle is explicitly anti-Alexandrian and sees the king from the sun as a native Egyptian who would overthrow the Ptolemies. Momigliano admits the relevance of this text for Sib Or 3, but asserts "that the king from the sun is not a Ptolemy in either text."[34] Presumably, because the phrase does not refer to a Ptolemy in the Potter's Oracle it cannot in Sib Or 3 either. This argument is a non sequitur. There is ample evidence that the Ptolemies appropriated the ideology and titles of the pharaohs. Ptolemiac kings are elsewhere said to be "chosen by the sun" and "son of the sun, to whom the sun has given victory."[35] While the eschatological oracles of Hellenistic Egypt were anti-Ptolemaic, Sib Or 3 is evidently not anti-Ptolemaic but adapts the form and rhetoric of eschatological oracles. The phrase "king from the sun" in a document written in Egypt most naturally refers to an Egyptian king. At a time when the Palestinian Jews were locked in combat with the Seleucids, it was also natural for Jews, especially those in Egypt, to look to the Ptolemaic line to establish a world situation which would be favorable to Judaism.

Despite Momigliano's assertion that the seventh king is not identical with the king from the sun,[36] the identification is inevitable. While the passages which refer to the seventh king do not explicitly say that he will bring about the messianic age, it is surely implied that he will have something to do with it. In fact, the king from the sun is not directly said to bring about the messianic age either, but only to bring about the universal peace which is its precondition. The statements about the two are perfectly compatible, and there is no reference to any other individual king in the eschatological transformation.

Momigliano is unjustified in claiming that the oracles were written in support of the Maccabean revolt. As he notes, there is no reference to Judas, just as there is none in Daniel.[37] In Daniel silence does not mean tacit support. At most, Daniel considered the Maccabees "a little help" and it is doubtful whether he thought they were any help at all.[38] Sib Or 3 has a very different perspective from Daniel. It does not look for angelic intervention, but to the activity of a human king. Further, it contains no unambiguous reference to the Maccabean revolt at all. Such silence would scarcely be credible if the work were written in support of the rebellion as Momigliano claims.[39]

Jerusalem and the gentile kings

Two final passages require a brief mention. Vss. 657–68 describe how "the kings of the peoples" will be moved to envy against "the temple of the great God." The motif of the opulence of the temple and envy of the kings is reminiscent of the story of Heliodorus in 2 Maccabees 3. Yet the whole scene is evidently eschatological and has its biblical prototype in Psalms 2 and 48. The experience of the Maccabean era may have helped shape this scenario, but the reference is to a future eschatological attack.

However, in vss. 732–40 we have a clear address to the author's own situation: "But wretched Greece, desist from proud thoughts. Do not send against this city your planless people which is not from the holy land of the Great One." The Greeks who in fact sent armies against Jerusalem in this period were the Seleucids, and it is to them that the admonition is most directly addressed, but it could also apply to the Ptolemies or to anyone else if they sent forces against Jerusalem. The author does not expect or want the seventh king of Egypt to intervene in the internal affairs of Judea. He does not call on any Greek force either to assist or to oppose the Maccabees. The king from the sun should establish universal peace. Then, when the "sons of the great God" are allowed to "live peacefully around the temple" (702–3), God himself will shield them (705) and "the hand of the Holy One will be fighting for them" (708–9).

A Ptolemaic messiah

It appears then that Sib Or 3 looks for a Ptolemaic messiah in the same sense that Second Isaiah looks for a Persian one. In neither case is there any acceptance of a pagan religion. Rather, both look for the conversion of gentiles to Judaism. While the sibyl is definitely open to gentile conversion, she chides the gentiles, and especially gentile kings, quite severely, just as Second Isaiah does too. The Ptolemaic king, like Cyrus, has a crucial role to play but is ultimately at the service of Judaism in the designs of God.

We will return to the sibyl's ethical and religious conception of Judaism in Part Two below. For the present we must underline the political dimension of Jewish identity. The hopes of the sibyl are still

directed towards Jerusalem, but do not require the political independence of Judea. It is sufficient that a favorable international order be
provided by a Ptolemaic king. Ultimately, too, gentiles as well as Jews
will bring their gifts to the temple of Jerusalem.

The provenance of Sibylline Oracle 3

What circles in Judaism would have produced such a document? It
combines an insistence on the Jewish law, which we will examine in
Chapter 4 below, and a strong insistence on the temple cult with hope
in a Ptolemaic messiah and the ultimate conversion of the gentiles.
Prior to the Maccabean revolt such attitudes could plausibly be attributed to Onias III, the last high priest of the legitimate line of succession.[40] 2 Maccabees depicts him as a man of great piety, especially
devoted to the temple cult as befitted as high priest. The high priests
were inevitably political figures and Judean politics was heavily influenced by the rival claims of the Ptolemies and the Seleucids. The
father of Onias III, Simon the Just, was a supporter of the Seleucids,
but Onias himself inclined to the Ptolemies, as may be inferred from
the deposit of funds in the temple by the pro-Ptolemaic Hyrcanus, the
Tobiad, and Onias's displacement by Antiochus Epiphanes.[41] After
the revolt his son Onias IV sought refuge in Egypt, attained military
distinction in the service of Philometor and founded the temple at
Leontopolis.[42] I have suggested in previous publications that the
Third Sibyl originated in circles associated with the younger Onias.[43]
While this proposal is necessarily hypothetical, it accounts for all the
aspects of the work's *Tendenz*. It also explains why the Maccabean
rebellion is passed over in silence. Onias was evidently no supporter
of the Maccabees. Yet he never actively opposed them either, and his
sons actually interceded with Cleopatra III in defense of Alexander
Jannaeus.[44] Rather than engage in inner-Jewish polemics, which
could only impress a gentile audience negatively, the sibyl simply
ignores the Maccabees.

The strong insistence on the Jerusalem temple should not be
thought to weigh against an association with the founder of Leontopolis. To begin with, the Leontopolis temple was probably not founded
until several years after Onias arrived in Egypt[45] and the oracles may
come from the earlier period. Further Tcherikover has argued co-
gently that the temple at Leontopolis was never intended to rival that
of Jerusalem. Its remote location supports Tcherikover's thesis.[46] De-

spite the flagrant violation of Deuteronomic law, later Judaism stopped short of condemning the temple outright.[47] Onias was evidently a leading figure in Egyptian Judaism, and there is no record that his temple was ever a bone of contention. The example of his fellow Zadokites at Qumran shows clearly that rejection of the current temple and priesthood by no means excluded the continuing hope for an eschatological restoration of Jerusalem. Josephus repeatedly emphasizes that the temple at Leontopolis was modeled on that of Jerusalem,[48] and while this datum is inconclusive in itself, it is compatible with the view that Jerusalem was still regarded as the ideal temple.

THE LEONTOPOLIS INSCRIPTIONS

We have little information about the attitudes of Onias, apart from the tendentious and contradictory remarks of Josephus.[49] The epitaphs from Leontopolis are of little help, since they only reflect the attitudes of individuals to death, not the basic policies of the leaders, and are scattered over a period of two hundred years.[50] Much has been made of the syncretism of these epitaphs,[51] but we have no way of judging how far it affected the Jewish belief in monotheism or the practice of the law. Sib Or 3 provides ample evidence that a Judaism which was quite conservative on these central issues could be quite syncretistic in less fundamental matters.[52] One further point is worth noting. The Leontopolis epitaphs are distinguished among Jewish inscriptions for their lack of belief in a positive afterlife.[53] The Egyptian sibylline oracles are distinguished among the Jewish eschatological writings of the period for the same reason.[54] In this they continue the theological tradition attested in Ben Sira, who was an admirer of Onias's grandfather Simon the Just.[55]

THE ONIADS

Our knowledge of the attitudes of Onias IV rests on inferences from the careers of himself and his sons and from the background information of the activities of Oniads and Tobiads before the Maccabean revolt. Two documents are especially important in this context. The story of the Tobiads in Josephus (*Ant* 12.6.1 [265]–13.10.7 [300]) is widely believed to rest on an independent literary composition, from the middle or late second century BCE.[56] 2 Maccabees is an abridgment from the late second century of the five-volume history of Jason of Cyrene, which was probably composed not long after the Maccabean revolt.[57] Recently Jonathan Goldstein has attempted to reconstruct a propagandistic history, allegedly written by Onias IV, from the accounts of the Oniads and Tobiads in these two works.[58] Despite Goldstein's ingenuity, there is in fact no reason to believe that such a work by Onias IV ever existed, but the material is significant for the light it sheds on the Ptolemaic influence on Jewish political identity in the second century BCE.

THE TALE OF THE TOBIADS

The story of the Tobiads in Josephus has been described by Hengel as a "romance" and dated to the second half of the second century BCE since "on the one hand it contains such gross errors that one must assume that a considerable space of time had elapsed since the events described, but on the other hand it has such exact information that it is probable that it used good sources like a family chronicle of the Tobiads."[59] The errors involve a highly confused chronology. Tcherikover and others have shown that the emergence of Joseph, the son of Tobias, which is here set in the time of Ptolemy V Epiphanes, should be located in the reign of Ptolemy III Euergetes (246–221) and in fact the king is once referred to as Euergetes in *Ant* 12.4.1 (158).[60] The mistaken assertion in *Ant* 12.4.1 (154) that Antiochus III gave over Coele-Syria, Samaria, Judea, and Phoenicia to Ptolemy V Epiphanes as a dowry, is an attempt to explain why the Tobiads had their dealings with the Ptolemies in the time of Epiphanes, after the region had passed to the Seleucids. Despite its inaccuracies, the story paints a vivid picture of the Tobiad family before the Maccabean revolt, and of one unorthodox ideal of Jewish life.

Josephus praises Joseph the son of Tobias as "a good and generous man who brought the Jewish people from poverty and weakness to a brighter way of life" (*Ant* 12.4.10 [224]). Whether Josephus found this assessment in his source or added it himself, it reflects well the spirit of the story. While it is quite obvious that Joseph and his son Hyrcanus were motivated by self-interest with little concern for the Jewish people, they were in fact Jews who operated successfully in the international scene and often outwitted their gentile rivals. Their success and the friendship they enjoyed with the Ptolemies are a source of pride for the Jewish people. The name of Joseph, in a context of dealings with Egypt, and the rivalry between Hyrcanus and his brothers inevitably recall the biblical Joseph story. There is no attempt however to attribute to these heroes the moral character of Joseph. Joseph the Tobiad becomes a successful tax collector by killing those who resist his demands and by large-scale bribery of the Ptolemaic court.[61] He indulges in drunkenness and falls "in love" with a dancing girl. His son Hyrcanus outdoes even his father by giving the Ptolemy a present of two hundred slaves—a hundred boys and a hundred virgin girls. We know from the Zeno papyri that the Tobiads had engaged in slave trading before the middle of the third century BCE.[62] Only at one point does a concern for the Jewish law surface: Joseph wishes to have his affair with the dancing girl in secret because of the violation of Jewish law, and his brother substitutes his own daughter to prevent Joseph from having intercourse with a foreigner. It is possible that even this detail was added by Josephus, but in any case it relates to the ethnic purity of the Jewish people rather than to any moral concern. It is interesting to note that avoidance of exogamy does not imply a concern for the whole Jewish law. At no point does the story disapprove of Joseph or of Hyrcanus. Rather they are presented as heroes, and the positive presentation is mirrored in the sustained approval of the Ptolemaic king. The story maintains the distinctiveness of the Jews, but as a matter of ethnic pride, not religious or moral principle. In all of this it is rather reminiscent of Artapanus's syncretistic treatment of Moses, which still insists on his superiority to the gentiles.

There is no doubt that the story has a strongly pro-Ptolemaic bias. The rights of the Ptolemies to exact tribute are not questioned. Those who oppose the Ptolemies (the high priest Onias in the time of Joseph) and those who oppose the pro-Ptolemaic Hyrcanus (his brothers, and by association, the high priest Simon who is lauded by Ben Sira (*Ant* 12.4.11 [229]) are depicted as villains. Hyrcanus is driven to suicide by the rise of Antiochus Epiphanes. The approval of the Ptolemies for Joseph and Hyrcanus is regarded as definitive. Further, the ambitions of Joseph and Hyrcanus are clearly circumscribed by the sovereignty of the Ptolemies. They succeed by ingratiating the Ptolemies. There is no aspiration to independence. As Stern and Goldstein have observed, the story uses the Ptolemaic terminology "Syria and Phoenicia" or "Syria" rather than the Seleucid "Coele-Syria."[63]

While the tale is definitely pro-Ptolemaic, it is not especially pro-Oniad, and there is no reason to conclude with Goldstein that it must be the work of the pro-Ptolemaic Onias IV. Against such a conclusion we must note that the story begins with a very negative portrayal of

Onias II, ancestor and namesake of the founder of Leontopolis. This Onias was anti-Ptolemaic and pro-Seleucid, and it is difficult to see why Onias IV should have chosen to emphasize this. Further, Onias III, who is known from 2 Maccabees to have been friendly to Hyrcanus, is not mentioned here in connection with the Tobiads at all. The story of the Tobiads pays minimal attention to the priestly Oniad line and depicts Onias II and Simon in a negatve light. Tcherikover's suggestion, that the tale was composed by a descendant of Hyrcanus in Trans-Jordan is far more plausible.[64]

The tale of the Tobiads was probably composed about the same time as the earliest stage of Sib Or 3. It displays a similar pro-Ptolemaic leaning, but completely lacks the ethical and religious interests of the oracles. While it does not reflect the attitudes of Onias IV, it provides valuable background information for his career. The Tobiads, like Onias, found the way to fame and fortune in the service of the Ptolemies. The "land of Tobias" in Trans-Jordan anticipates the "land of Onias" in Egypt by a century.[65] Further, we know from the archeological excavations of the site that a temple was built there in the early second century BCE, apparently at the time when Hyrcanus was repulsed from Jerusalem by his brothers and the high priest Simon, after the death of his father.[66] Josephus tells us that at this time Hyrcanus "gave up his intention of returning to Jerusalem."[67] Yet Hengel is not justified in assuming that he intended to build "a temple to compete with Jerusalem."[68] If this were so, he would scarcely have deposited funds in the temple at Jerusalem in the time of Onias III.[69] Rather, the temple was for his own convenience, since he appears to have had a self-sufficient domain in Trans-Jordan. His continued relationship with the temple in the time of Onias III shows that he did not see any incompatibility between the two temples. Significantly, Onias III did not find the Tobiad temple objectionable either. All of this casts much light on the actions of Onias IV. While he inevitably rejected the Hasmonean priesthood, there is no reason to believe that he would have definitively rejected the Jerusalem temple. He would also naturally have seen that his future role in Jewish affairs was dependent on the actions and attitudes of the Ptolemies.[70]

2 MACCABEES AND THE ONIADS

Our second source for the history of the Oniads is 2 Maccabees. Unlike the story of the Tobiads in Josephus, 2 Maccabees does deal at length with Onias III, who is described in glowing terms as "the benefactor of the city, the guardian of his fellow countrymen and zealot for the laws" (2 Mac 4:2). 2 Maccabees records only good and no evil of Onias III. Because of his piety, the city enjoyed peace and the laws were observed (3:1). He received Heliodorus (the delegate of the Seleucid king) graciously, and it was through his intercession that the life of Heliodorus was spared by the angels sent to chastise him (3:33). When he appealed to the king against the intrigues of Simon, it was not to accuse his fellow citizens but to preserve the welfare of all the people (4:5). Finally, he was murdered because he rebuked Menelaus for his abuse of the temple vessels (4:34). In all Onias III is a major figure in 2 Maccabees, in sharp contrast to 1 Maccabees, which ignores him entirely.

The prominence which Onias enjoys in 2 Maccabees has led Goldstein to suggest that the hypothetical "propagandistic work of Onias IV" served as a source here too,[71] but his arguments do not warrant the conclusion. There is nothing to suggest that the piety of Onias III is the *exclusive* cause of the city's welfare in 2 Mac 3:1, or that this passage is in any tension with the rest of 2 Maccabees. The association of Onias III with the pro-Ptolemaic Hyrcanus in 2 Mac 3:11, which Goldstein takes as "conclusive proof" of an Oniad source, may be simply historical fact. The hypothesis of a document written by Onias IV is unnecessary.[72]

Goldstein is on firmer ground when he argues that the neglect of Onias III in 1 Maccabees and in Josephus arises from a pro-Hasmonean *Tendenz*.[73] The account in 2 Maccabees, despite its penchant for the miraculous, fills in an important area of the history of this period and supplies the most immediate background we have to Onias IV. To be sure, 2 Maccabees exaggerates the pietistic character of Onias III. His involvement in political intrigue may fairly be deduced from his association with Hyrcanus and should in any case be expected from his family history. The fact that he took refuge in the sanctuary near Daphne (presumably the temple of Apollo) just before his death shows that he did not have a great aversion to pagan religion. The idealized portrayal which we find in 2 Maccabees is undoubtedly influenced by reaction to the extreme corruption of the priesthood which followed his displacement.

2 MACCABEES AND THE DIASPORA

The importance of 2 Maccabees for our purpose does not lie only in the background history of the Oniads. It also provides significant insight into relations between Jerusalem and the Egyptian Diaspora in the second century BCE. Jason of Cyrene, whose five-volume work is abridged in 2 Maccabees, "either came from the Jewish Diaspora in Cyrenaica or at least spent a good part of his life there"[74] as his name indicates. Yet the content of his work deals entirely with events in Palestine. Hengel has plausibly suggested that the intention of Jason's work "was to gain some understanding and support in the Greek-speaking Diaspora and the Greek world in general for the Jews who were fighting for the integrity of their sanctuary and their piety."[75] We should not be surprised that a work which supports the Maccabean rebellion was composed in Greek, following Hellenistic conventions and style.[76] The Maccabees were not xenophobic, as can be seen from their delegations to Rome and Sparta.[77] Jason stands with Eupolemus as a supporter of the Maccabees who was still concerned to build bridges with the Hellenistic world.

The view of Judaism presented in 2 Maccabees may reasonably be described as covenantal nomism. When the laws were well observed, because of the piety of Onias III, the city was inhabited in unbroken peace (3:1). The sufferings of the persecution were not designed to destroy but to discipline the people (5:12). Even the martyrs suffered for the sins of the people, but they helped to bring an end to the wrath of God (7:38). In a typical prayer in 8:15, the Jews call upon God to rescue them "if not for their own sake, at least for the sake of the covenants made with their fathers" (8:15). The primary emphasis, then, is on God's covenant with the people, but individuals can fall from the covenant relationship by their sins. So in 2 Mac 12:40 all the Jews killed in the battle against Gorgias are found to have idols under their tunics. The temple plays a pivotal role in 2 Maccabees, but nonetheless it is clear that "the Lord did not choose the nation for the sake of the holy place, but the place for the sake of the nation" (5:19). The covenantal relationship between the people and God provides the underpinning for the political and geographical factors in Jewish identity.

The attitude of 2 Maccabees to the gentiles is ambiguous. On the one hand, throughout the book, the gentiles are the adversaries of the Jews, the "blasphemous and barbarous nations" (10:4). On the other hand, 2 Maccabees suggests that gentiles are impressed by Jewish piety. Even Antiochus Epiphanes "was grieved at heart and filled with pity" at the death of Onias III because of his moderation and good conduct (2 Mac 4:37) and Nicanor was warmly attached to Judas

(2 Mac 14:24). There is also a persistent hope for the conversion of the gentiles, which is fantasized in the confession of Heliodorus (2 Mac 3:35–40) and the deathbed conversion of Antiochus Epiphanes (2 Mac 9:13–18).

The relation of the Diaspora to Jerusalem is directly brought into question by the two letters which are prefixed to the abridgment of Jason's history. The first, 1:1–9, is dated to the year 188 of the Seleucid era, or 124/3 BCE, and contains a reference to an earlier letter from 143/2 BCE.[78] The second letter is undated and its provenance is disputed. Some scholars hold that it is a late composition from approximately 60 BCE.[79] Others distinguish an interpolation in the legend about the temple fire and allow that the rest of the letter may be old.[80] Both letters invite the Jews of Egypt to join their Judean brethren in celebrating the purification of the temple by observing the festival of Hanukkah "like the feast of Tabernacles" in the month of Kislev. The relation of these letters to the rest of 2 Maccabees is problematic. It is unlikely that either letter was composed by the epitomator, in view of the lack of cross-references. The second letter actually contradicts the main text of 2 Maccabees on the manner of the death of Antiochus Epiphanes.[81] Yet there is a measure of congruity between the invitation of the letters and the history itself. Glorification of the Jerusalem temple is undeniably a major theme of 2 Maccabees.[82] It is possible that the abridgment of Jason's history was undertaken to provide support for the promotion of the festival, as Momigliano suggests,[83] or that the author of the letter seized on 2 Maccabees as a convenient and suitable account which supported his general enthusiasm for the temple. In any case, the question arises what message 2 Maccabees would bear for the Jews of the Egyptian Diaspora. Momigliano has proposed that "like the introductory letters, the epitome would try to keep the Jews of Egypt within the influence of the temple of Jerusalem against the competition of the temple of Leontopolis," and so help to avoid the fragmentation of Judaism and the secession of the Egyptian Jews."[84] This view is an elaboration of a widespread scholarly opinion that 2 Maccabees contains an implicit polemic against the temple of Leontopolis.[85] In fact, the presence of such polemic is highly dubious. The relations between Judaism and the Diaspora reflected in 2 Maccabees are far more complex than Momigliano suggests.

The claim that either 2 Maccabees or the letters prefixed to it contain a polemic against the temple of Leontopolis has been soundly refuted by Arenhoevel and Doran.[86] Nowhere in the book is there any explicit reference to Leontopolis, nor even any insistence on the unique validity of Jerusalem as a place of worship. The complete lack of reference to Leontopolis may have a simple enough explanation: it is quite possible that Jason wrote his history before the temple of Onias was built. There is no doubt that the temple was in existence by the time the first letter was written, but here again it is simply ignored. The letter does not command the Jews to desist from worshipping at other places but only to observe the festival of Hanukkah. The second letter concludes with the hope that God "will soon have mercy on us and will gather us together from under heaven to the Holy Place" (2:18). This passage reflects the hope for a definitive Jewish restoration around the temple in Jerusalem—a hope which we have also found in Sib Or 3. There is no reason, however, why Onias IV and his followers should not have shared that hope, or why it should be considered incompatible with an interim sanctuary at Leontopolis. In short, the silence of the letters on the subject of Leontopolis is not necessarily an indication of polemic. It may simply indicate that the temple in Egypt was never seriously considered as a rival to that of Jerusalem.

Yet the view that 2 Maccabees in its present form was designed to maintain the unity of Judaism is not entirely without basis. It is noteworthy that at least two letters were sent from Jerusalem to Egypt, urging the observance of the festival. The earlier (the former letter referred to in 1:7) must have gone unheeded if a second (the present first letter) was necessary. In fact, we should not be surprised if Egyptian Judaism hesitated to celebrate the revolt. At least Onias IV and his followers were estranged from the Jerusalem temple and its illegitimate priesthood. The letters which call on the Diaspora Jews to celebrate the purification of the temple are attempting to overcome that estrangement, even though they are not necessarily condemning Leontopolis. The letters do this merely by asserting that the purification of the temple was an act of divine deliverance. The abridgment of Jason's history may also be seen to contribute to this goal by its presentation of the story of the revolt.

Two aspects of 2 Maccabees are especially significant for the relation between Palestinian and Egyptian Judaism. The first is the glorification of Onias III. It is difficult to see how the entirely positive portrayal of the father of Onias IV could serve as a polemic against Leontopolis, especially when there is no hint that his son departed from his father's ways. Rather, the virtue of the father creates the presumption of virtue in the son. 2 Maccabees makes amply clear that the misfortunes which befell Jerusalem stemmed from the overthrow of Onias. While the book does not argue for the restoration of the Oniad line, the portrayal of the history leading up to the revolt would surely be acceptable to the supporters of Onias IV in Egypt.

Scholars have often noted the relative lack of attention to the Hasmonean house in 2 Maccabees.[87] Judas is indeed the hero, but Mattathias is overlooked and the brothers have a subsidiary role. We are indeed told that Judas placed his brothers "Simon, Joseph, and Jonathan" in charge of divisions (8:22),[88] but Jonathan is never mentioned again. The heroic death of Eleazar (1 Mac 6:43–46) is ignored, although the occasion is mentioned in 2 Mac 13:15. Simon is mentioned in 10:19–20, where some of his men take bribes and let some of their enemies escape from a siege. Judas has to intervene to punish the offenders. Again in 14:15–18, Simon is checked until Nicanor hears of the valor of Judas. Neither reference is flattering to Simon. The fact that 2 Maccabees concludes before the death of Judas and does not pursue the careers of Simon and Jonathan may be simply due to the early date at which Jason's history was written. At the time of the abridgment, or of the composition of the first letter, the omission of the history of Simon and Jonathan was significant. Judas had never claimed the high priesthood. He had no part in supplanting the house of Onias. On the contrary, he was the instrument of God's wrath against the sinners who had disrupted the priesthood. 2 Maccabees even claims the support of Onias III for Judas by having him appear in a vision in 2 Mac 15:11–16.

The story of Judas then might be acceptable to the followers of Onias in Egypt as part of the common Jewish heritage, while the story of his brothers would not. A history which in effect separated the temple and the story of the revolt from the Hasmonean priest-kings could avoid party dissensions and enable the Jews of the Diaspora to affirm both the temple and the independent Jewish state without acknowledging the authority of the Hasmoneans. In fact, neither the introductory letters nor the text of 2 Maccabees makes any attempt to subordinate the Diaspora to Jerusalem. The implications of the book for Egyptian Judaism are highly conciliatory. There is no polemic, but rather an affirmation of the acceptable common ground and an avoidance of those issues which might prove to be divisive. The ideal of Judaism which is held forth is not primarily political but is based on the pious observance of the law, and includes the hope of the martyrs for resurrection. The law-abiding Jew is content to live in peace and give no offense to his neighbor, as can be seen in the concern of Onias III for Heliodorus in 2 Maccabees 3.[89]

How far 2 Maccabees had an effect on the Egyptian Diaspora is difficult to say. In the following centuries the Jerusalem temple was certainly held in high honor in the Diaspora, even while Egyptian Judaism showed little deference to Judea. Whatever ill feeling originally existed between Onias IV and the Hasmoneans had apparently been dissipated by the next generation. Ananias, the son of Onias IV, is known to have used his influence with queen Cleopatra III on behalf of Alexander Jannaeus. The words attributed to Ananias by Josephus are significant: "For I would have you know that an injustice done to this man will make all us Jews your enemies" (*Ant* 13.13.2 [354]). Whatever regional diversity existed in Judaism and whatever the relation of the Oniad temple to Jerusalem, ethnic solidarity prevailed.

THE LETTER OF ARISTEAS

Our view of the political stance of Diaspora Judaism after the Maccabean revolt can be filled out from a few documents which are not primarily historical or political in nature. The so-called "Letter of Aristeas to Philocrates"[90] is one of the very best known compositions of Hellenistic Judaism.[91] It has been studied mainly in connection with the problem of the origins of the LXX. Much of the interest of the work lies in its understanding of the Torah, which is its primary expression of Judaism and which will be discussed in Part Two below. The Letter is also significant, however, for the light it throws on the relations of Diaspora Judaism both with the Ptolemies and with Jerusalem.

The date of Pseudo-Aristeas is set in the reign of Ptolemy II Philadelphus (283–246 BCE) but this is universally recognized as a fiction.[92] The termini post and ante were established by Bickermann at 160 and 125 BCE (approximately) on the basis of the salutations and other linguistic usage.[93] He argued that the terminus post quem could be lowered to 145 by the geographical allusions, yielding a date in the reign of Ptolemy VIII Euergetes II (Physcon). The latter argument is questionable since it rests on a particular interpretation of the "some parts, those in Samaria so-called" of section 107, as the districts of Lydda, Aphairema and Ramathain, which came under Judean control in 145 BCE.[94] This interpretation is not specified in the text and rests on the assumption that Pseudo-Aristeas is geographically precise—an assumption which few scholars are willing to share. Yet, a date in the reign of Physcon is plausible for other reasons.

Arguments for an earlier date have been based in part on the alleged dependence of Aristobulus on Pseudo-Aristeas for the story of the translation of the LXX.[95] However, the actual story of the translation, while it frames the work of Pseudo-Aristeas, occupies only a small part of the Letter and would seem to be derived from tradition rather than the fresh composition of the author.[96] We shall see below (Part Two) that the other parallels between the two works favor the priority of Aristobulus. The lack of any explicit reference to the Maccabean revolt raises the complex problem of the attitude of Pseudo-Aristeas to the Maccabees, but does not require a pre-Maccabean date.[97]

Considerations which might support a date under Philometor are indecisive. Ptolemy's letter to Eleazar says that "when he judged their chief men to be loyal, he gave them fortresses which he built" (36). The best known endowment of a Jewish leader in Egypt was the grant of Leontopolis to Onias by Philometor. However, the statement in Pseudo-Aristeas may simply refer to the garrisons of Jewish mercenaries which were already attested by the Elephantine papyri.[98] The further claim in the letter, that some Jews were elevated to offices of state (37) points less ambiguously to the reign of Philometor or later. A date under Philometor is supported by Fraser, because of the author's "use, in the correct context, of the technical language of the Ptolemaic court and administration, which is parallel to his knowledge of court protocol, and reveals an intimate knowledge of the whole administrative system."[99] Fraser concludes that the author was "a Jew of high rank at the Ptolemaic Court, and no member of that house was more likely to elevate a Jew than Philometor."[100] All this is true, but a Jew who acquired his experience at court under Philometor could still have written under Physcon, or continued in the service of Queen Cleopatra when she was reconciled with Physcon and became his co-ruler.

A possible indication of the author's date may be found in the atten-

tion given at the beginning of the Letter to the question of the liberation of Jewish slaves. The incident is evidently fictional and is designed to illustrate the generosity of the Ptolemy. Yet it has the
peculiar disadvantage of drawing attention to the fact (if fact it was)
that the Ptolemaic house had held Jews in slavery.[101] The prominence
which is quite unnecessarily given to this incident suggests that the
author had some reason to illustrate Ptolemaic generosity especially
in the form of clemency to the Jews. Now we know from Josephus that
after the death of Philometor the Jews from the land of Onias continued to support his widow Cleopatra II against Physcon.[102] Since Physcon triumphed, the Jews were in a difficult situation. Josephus makes
this the occasion for the legendary story of an attempted persecution
of the Jews which appears in a different form in 3 Maccabees. Tcherikover has argued that the story may well reflect, in an exaggerated
way, historical events in the time of Physcon.[103] Physcon would naturally have considered some reprisals against the Jews, and the danger,
or some actual persecution, may be reflected in the legendary account
of 3 Maccabees. The entire reign of Physcon was extremely turbulent,
but there were periods of reconciliation with Cleopatra, and finally in
118, a decree of amnesty was issued.[104] We have no clear documentation of the fortunes of the Jews during this period, but two dedications
of synagogues "on behalf of the king" survive from the reign of Physcon,[105] and the sons of Onias survived to play a prominent role under
Cleopatra III.[106] It would seem that Jewish life in Egypt was not
disrupted in any lasting way. The account of the liberation of slaves in
Pseudo-Aristeas may have been designed as a subtle appeal to the
king by praising the clemency of his ancestor, or it may have been
designed to reassure Jews of the basic good will of the monarchy and
suggest that the threat to the Jews was due either to the greed of
soldiers (14) or to the impulses of the mob (37). Two other items in the
Letter might be illuminated by this context. In 166–67 the high priest
singles out informers (*emphanistae*) for special condemnation and
praises the king for putting such people to death.[107] Diodorus 33.6
reports that Physcon exiled many people and seized their property on
the false allegations of sycophants.[108] Aristeas may be subtly suggesting how such informers should be treated. In 148 the high priest
interprets some of the dietary laws as symbols "that they may be just
and achieve nothing by violence, nor confiding in their own strength
oppress others." This statement would seem to distance the Judaism

of Pseudo-Aristeas from the military followers of Onias, on the one hand, and from the Hasmoneans on the other, and to advocate a non-militant stance which would be inoffensive to Physcon. By contrast, the prominence of Jews under Philometor was due in no small part to their military activities. In view of these considerations, Bickermann's dating to the time of Physcon would seem to be most probable.

Pseudo-Aristeas makes no reference to Leontopolis, but scholars have inevitably speculated on his implicit attitude to the temple of Onias. So Jellicoe has proposed that Pseudo-Aristeas's endorsement of the LXX translation which originated in Jerusalem was intended to counter an otherwise unknown translation from Leontopolis.[109] Meisner has accepted this proposal and further suggested that Pseudo-Aristeas is polemicizing against the Leontopolis settlement for its military role against Physcon.[110] However, Pseudo-Aristeas shows little sign of a polemic against Leontopolis. While it presents an idealized picture of Jerusalem, it is supposed to be a pre-Maccabean Jerusalem, presided over by a high priest who was an ancestor of Onias.[111] The references in Ptolemy's letter to Jews who were given fortresses and exalted to offices of state presume that these things are for the glory of Judaism. There is no evidence whatever that Leontopolis had its own translation of the Torah or that there is any polemic in this regard. This is not to say that Pseudo-Aristeas was pro-Leontopolis. The claim that Judaism is nonviolent fits as ill with the aspirations of a military colony as it does with the policies of the Hasmoneans. Pseudo-Aristeas distances himself from the military colony without thereby carrying out any polemic against it.

Again, the attitude of the Letter to Jerusalem is by no means clearcut. The manner of the description of the cult and city has been taken to suggest that Pseudo-Aristeas had visited Jerusalem as a pilgrim.[112] This is far from certain. The description of Jerusalem is based on biblical sources,[113] and some of the details, such as the alleged flooding of the Jordan (section 116), suggest an ignorance of the actual conditions of the land.[114] Pseudo-Aristeas never claims that it was customary for Diaspora Jews to visit Jerusalem on pilgrimage, although such a statement could have fitted in very well with his narrative. The bold assertions that Ptolemy's prodigious gifts were deposited in the temple could hardly withstand the possibility that some of his readers would actually check.[115] In all, the description of Jerusalem is of a utopian, rather fantastic and remote city, not one with which the author or his readers had any great personal familiarity.[116] Jerusalem and its cult are brought in to embellish the portrayal of Judaism. It is important for the author that Diaspora Judaism has an illustrious source. It does not follow that Jewish life in the Diaspora is in any sense directed from or towards Jerusalem.[117]

A similar point must be made on the entire issue of the translation of the Torah. As we have seen Pseudo-Aristeas regards the Torah as indispensable. It is also true that he tells of an official translation made by duly appointed authorities from Jerusalem. The purpose of this account has given rise to endless debate. Much of it has centered on the memorandum of Demetrius to the king in 29–32, which says that the books of the law of the Jews "are written in Hebrew characters and in the Hebrew tongue, and they have been committed to writing somewhat carelessly and not adequately, according to the testimony of experts, for they have never benefited from a king's forethought." Despite the contentions of Kahle,[118] it is now widely agreed that this passage does not refer to pre-Septuagint Greek translations but to inadequate copies of the *Hebrew* text.[119] We may assume with Good-ing,[120] that the texts in question are those available in Alexandria. If there were no adequate Hebrew text, there could be no translation. However, the net effect is to say that the Greek translation is more reliable than the Hebrew available in Alexandria. Further, it is formally canonized by the acclaim of the people and so established as a self-sufficient biblical text.[121] Pseudo-Aristeas is not polemicizing against any other Greek translation, but is proclaiming the adequacy of the LXX over against the Hebrew.[122] (In fact, in at least one case, the table of pure gold in 57, Pseudo-Aristeas follows the LXX against the Hebrew). There is no reason for Egyptian Jewry to rely on the Hebrew text or to correct their translations on the basis of the Hebrew.[123]

Tcherikover has suggested that the disavowal of "a crude and un-couth disposition" (122) is a polemic against the literalism (and He-braism) especially characteristic of Palestinian Jews.[124] The Letter as a whole is not characterized by any polemic against Judea, but it does not present a view of Judaism centered on Jerusalem either. It is rather a manifesto of the self-sufficiency of Diaspora Judaism, which respects Jerusalem as its source, but speaks of an idealized biblical Judea rather than of the actual state of the Hasmoneans. Its lack of reference to Leontopolis is most easily explained by the character of that establishment. Tcherikover is surely right in arguing that it never was a rival to Jerusalem, or intended as a center for all Egyptian Jews but only a chapel for the land of Onias.[125] Pseudo-Aristeas would have respected Onias insofar as he added to the glory of the Jews but was careful to distance himself from his military policies.

The Judaism of Pseudo-Aristeas seeks a cautious political course. It reassures gentiles of its loyalty to the Ptolemaic house. It seeks to confirm Jews in that loyalty. Judaism is not defined in national terms. The law is the vehicle of a philosophy which is potentially universal.[126] Accordingly we will defer our main discussion of the view of Judaism in Pseudo-Aristeas to Part Two, where we discuss philosophical Judaism.

THE FIRST CENTURY BCE

The literature of the Egyptian Diaspora in the second century is characterized on the whole by a positive attitude towards the gentile authorities. On the one hand, the sibylline oracles reflect a wholehearted participation in the political arena which was characteristic of Onias IV and his followers. On the other hand, the Letter of Aristeas reflects a withdrawal from the political arena and presents Judaism more as a philosophy. Neither the sibyl nor the Letter questions the loyalty of the Jews to the Ptolemies or envisages any significant friction between Jew and gentile. Even a document like 2 Maccabees, for all its enthusiasm for the Maccabean revolt, presents Judaism in strongly religious terms, and does not suggest that the Jews initiate hostilities against their neighbors. The solicitude of Onias, that he not be suspected of foul play against Heliodorus (3:32) is indicative of the attitude of 2 Maccabees. While the documents of the second century cover a wide spectrum of attitudes, they are remarkably void of aggressive hostility towards the gentiles. The dissonance between Jewish tradition and Hellenistic environment is reduced by shared political loyalty and by emphasizing common aspirations.

We cannot conclude that there were no tensions between the Jews and their neighbors in this period. The literary polemic had been initiated as early as Manetho. We know that the Jewish community incurred the wrath of Ptolemy Physcon, but this was a matter of internal Egyptian politics since the Oniad Jews were actively supporting Cleopatra II. In the first century BCE we hear of the first Greek pamphlet against the Jews, by Apollonius Molon, and there is some evidence of a persecution of Jews in Alexandria about 88 BCE.[127] Yet these tensions are scarcely reflected in the Jewish literature of the Ptolemaic era, in sharp contrast to the subsequent Roman period. We are not given the impression that antagonism to the gentiles was a significant factor in Jewish identity.

GREEK ESTHER

Tension between Jew and gentile in the Diaspora was not, of course, a new phenomenon. Perhaps the most characteristic product of the eastern Diaspora in the Hellenistic age was the so-called *Diasporanovelle* represented by Esther and Daniel 1–6.[128] These tales envisaged situations in which exiled Jews were threatened with mortal danger, but in the end were dramatically delivered. Like many other Hebrew and Aramaic writings these stories were translated into Greek in the Ptolemaic period and so were available as models for Egyptian Judaism. The case of Esther is especially significant since the expanded Greek translation was already tailored in some respects for the Egyptian milieu.[129]

According to the colophon appended to the Greek translation of Esther the book was brought to Egypt by one Dositheus "in the fourth year of Ptolemy and Cleopatra" and was the work of "Lysimachus son of Ptolemy, a member of the Jerusalem community." Bickermann has shown decisively that the date in question was the fourth year of Ptolemy XII Auletes and Cleopatra V, i.e., 78/77 BCE.[130] There is no good reason to doubt the reliability of the colophon on the question of provenance.[131] It appears then that Greek Esther is not a product of Egyptian Judaism, but like 2 Maccabees was sent to Egypt from Jerusalem, and may have been modified in the light of its destination.

The Greek version of Esther contains six extended additions to the text now found in the MT: Mordecai's dream (Addition A) and its interpretation (F); a royal letter commanding the extermination of the Jews (B) and a second letter countermanding it (E); the prayers of Mordecai and Esther (C) and a description of Esther's going before the king unsummoned (D). In addition to these there are various scattered alterations of the Hebrew text.[132] The expansions and changes serve two main purposes.[133] They clarify the Hebrew text—e.g., by having Mordecai explain in his prayer why he refused to bow to Haman. They also provide the explicit piety which is strikingly lacking in the Hebrew. So Esther professes in her prayer that she has not partaken of the king's table, although this is most implausible in the context of the story. Two other modifications are more significant for our present study. First, in the dream of Mordecai and again in its interpretation there is a simple antithesis between Israel and "every nation" which "got itself ready for battle that it might fight against the righteous nation" (A 6). God "made two lots, one for the people of God and one for all the nations."[134] Second, Haman is said to be a Macedonian who was plotting to gain control for the Macedonians over the Persians.

The rigid division between Israel and the nations and the exaggerated emphasis on the separatist piety of Esther may be taken to reflect the Hasmonean milieu in which the translation was made. It is noteworthy that such an exclusive and nationalist view of Judaism was quite compatible with the use of the Greek language and mastery of Greek style,[135] as we have found earlier in the epic of Theodotus.[136]

The identification of Haman as a Macedonian is especially apt for the situation of Alexandrian Judaism.[137] The story of Esther was centered on the rivalry between a Jewish and a pagan courtier. In Alexandria, the relevant courtiers who were rivals to the Jews were the Macedonians. Greek Esther goes beyond the Hebrew in accusing Haman of plotting against the state. The issue between the courtiers is no longer simple ambition, but devotion to the state. The accusations against the Jews in the first decree are parallel to those against Haman in the second. In the first, the Jews are accused of obstructing government by their peculiar customs. In the second, Haman is accused of conspiring against the king, while the Jews are vindicated and recognized (in the person of Mordecai) as benefactors. Even more clearly than in the Hebrew original, the triumph of the Jews takes place within the context of the undisputed rule of the gentile king. If the Jews slaughter their enemies, they do so by the king's permission and are none the less his excellent servants.

The Greek translation of Esther may, in a sense, be regarded as Hasmonean propaganda.[138] It urged the Jews of the Egyptian Diaspora to celebrate the feast of Purim like the rest of their brethren. It propagated separatist attitudes towards the gentiles in religious observance. Yet it did not interfere with the political allegiance of Diaspora Jews. It provided them rather with moral support in their efforts to rise within the service of the kingdom.

The antagonism of Jew and gentile and the fantasy of vengeance with which Greek Esther concludes are atypical of the literature of the Ptolemaic period, but they anticipate ominously the events of the Roman era. The advent of Rome introduced a new factor which could only complicate the relationships of the Jews. The increasing dissonance of Diaspora life in the first century is reflected in a *Diasporanovelle* of Egyptian Jewish origin in 3 Maccabees, and would ultimately erupt in the great Diaspora revolt in the time of Trajan.

THE POLITICS OF RECONCILIATION

An attitude closer to that of Pseudo-Aristeas is found in a document which may derive from the later decades of Ptolemaic Egypt, Joseph and Aseneth. The date is far from certain. Linguistic dependence on the LXX, including the prophets, and on some apocryphal writings, makes a date before the first century BCE unlikely.[139] This terminus a quo is also supported by the general linguistic character of the book, which has several words only attested in the NT and later.[140] The place of composition was evidently Egypt, in view of the Egyptian setting of the entire story, the polemic against specifically Egyptian idolatry and the Egyptian coloring of some of the symbolism (especially the points of contact between Aseneth and the goddess Neith).[141]

The positive tone of Joseph and Aseneth and its focus on proselytism make a date before the revolt under Trajan highly probable. Within these limits, more specific indications are hard to find. Burchard favors a date in the late first century BCE because of the lack of any reference to proselyte baptism,[142] but this criterion is worthless since there is no clear allusion to proselyte baptism anywhere in Hellenistic Jewish literature. Claims that the practice was known before the rise of Christianity are unsupported.[143] Philonenko prefers a date at the beginning of the second century CE on the basis of parallels with the Gospel of John and Ignatius, and also with the Greek romances,[144] but parallels can also be adduced from Philo and the date of the early romances is uncertain. Kilpatrick and Jeremias favored a date between 100 and 30 BCE, since there is no hint of Roman presence and the independence of Egypt is apparently assumed.[145] These considerations are not decisive either, since they may be dictated by the fictional setting of the story.

Joseph and Aseneth consists of two distinct but related stories, the conversion of Aseneth (chaps. 1–21) and the jealousy of pharaoh's son (chaps. 22–29). The first story, which is the greater part of the whole, is a presentation of Judaism as a nonethnic, monotheistic religion. We will discuss it in some detail in Part Two below. The political dimension of Joseph and Aseneth is found mainly in the second story.

The second story in chapters 22–29 concerns the jealousy of pharaoh's son and his attempts against Joseph and Aseneth. By contrast with the pharaoh and Pentephres, pharaoh's son has no sympathy for Joseph and is portrayed as utterly ruthless. The opposition however is not simply between Israelite and Egyptian. Pharaoh's son plots not only against Joseph but also against the pharaoh, his own father, because he is like a father to Joseph (24:13). The strategy against Joseph is to recruit some of his brothers to betray him. Levi and Simeon refuse, although they are threatened with death, but Gad and Dan agree. These two (both sons of servant maids, Gen 30:6, 11) are singled out as the black sheep in the famiy of Jacob and are blamed exclusively for selling Joseph into slavery (24:9; 25:6; 28:13). On the other hand, Levi assumes the leading role in this story. His prophetic knowledge is repeatedly emphasized—he sees Aseneth's resting place in heaven and foresees the danger of the ambush. More importantly, he restrains the anger of Simeon against pharaoh's son since "it does not befit a pious man to return evil for evil" (23:9). This does not mean that he is a pacifist. He boasts of the destruction of Shechem, which is viewed here as a fully justified act, and warns pharaoh's son that his sword is ready if there is further plotting against Joseph (23:12). Levi is not an aggressor, but he is willing and able to defend himself and his brethren. Again, when Benjamin is about to strike down pharaoh's son with the sword, Levi intervenes, saying that a pious man should not return evil for evil nor afflict his enemy unto death. Instead they should heal his wound and make him their friend. Even though pharaoh's son dies from the wound, relations with pharaoh are not strained. In the case of Dan and Gad, however, it is Aseneth who intervenes to save their lives by invoking the principle of nonretaliation. We are given, then, a nicely complex picture, in which the proselyte Aseneth understands what is fitting better than Simeon does, and even the pagan pharaoh comes off better than Dan and Gad.

The story of chapters 22–29 is evidently paradigmatic of Jewish-gentile relations in the Egyptian Diaspora, although it is by no means a simple historical allegory. The benevolence of the sovereign is assumed. The enemy of the Jews is the enemy of the pharaoh too. This pattern is reminiscent of Esther. Even in 3 Maccabees, the ultimate benevolence of the sovereign is assumed. If he acts against the Jews for a time it is due to madness. Yet there are also powerful forces, high at court, which are hostile to the Jews and which are represented here by pharaoh's son. Those Jews who side with pharaoh's son against their own people stand self-convicted, but the pious do not seek vengeance against either them or the hostile gentiles. Reconciliation is best. In all of this the pious, represented by Levi and Simeon, retain a self-sufficiency based on their strength of arms and the help of God. Their conciliatory attitude comes from strength, not from weakness.

Is this political background of the book of any help in dating it? Some features seem especially appropriate for the Ptolemaic age. The treachery of pharaoh's son towards his father recalls the internecine strife of the late Ptolemaic dynasty. The armed prowess of Levi and Simeon recalls the heyday of Jewish mercenaries in Egypt, which virtually disappeared after the Roman conquest. The rise of Joseph to supreme power recalls the days when Onias and Dositheus were allegedly given power over the land of Egypt, without suggesting that Joseph is a direct allegory for any historical individual. The offer of pharaoh's son to enlist his accomplices among his *hetairoi* is a throwback to the old Macedonian terminology.[146] There is nothing in the story which clearly reflects the presence of Rome. In view of all these considerations I am inclined to date Joseph and Aseneth in the early first century BCE. Yet it must be admitted that the story is compatible with a Roman date, taking pharaoh as representative of the Romans and his son of the Macedonians and other courtiers who resented favors to the Jews. The details of the story do not have precise historical equivalents. The attitudes towards the gentiles are not greatly different from those of 3 Maccabees. Such conciliatory attitudes become somewhat less probable after 70 CE, but prior to that they are typical of the Egyptian Diaspora.

CLEOPATRA AND THE SIBYL

The ongoing tradition of political involvement is attested in three sibylline oracles from about the time of Cleopatra VII, which reflect the contrasting attitudes of Egyptian Jewry to the last great monarch of the Ptolemaic line.

Sib Or 3:350–80 is a later addition to the Third Sibyl, and is dated by all critics to the first century BCE.[147] It predicts the vengeance of Asia on Rome, which will be exacted by a *despoina*. The "mistress" in question should be identified as Cleopatra, who also represented Egypt, as its queen, and Isis whom she claimed to incarnate.[148] The oracle looks beyond the anticipated triumph of Cleopatra to an age of harmony (*homonoia*) when peace and prosperity would be shared by both Europea and Asia. The oracle makes no reference to the Jewish people and contains none of the ethical or religious exhortation characteristic of the Jewish sibylline tradition. Yet it stands in continuity with the enthusiasm of the earlier Jewish sibyl for the Ptolemaic house. Whether it was composed by a Jew or taken over from a gentile source, its presence in the sibylline collection attests the support of some strand of Judaism for Cleopatra. We cannot assume that this support was typical of all Jews. We know that the relations of King Herod with Cleopatra were less than friendly.[149] Josephus reports a charge by Apion that Cleopatra withheld corn from Jews in time of famine, but the historical reliability of this report is questionable.[150] Whatever the predominant attitude of the Jews to Cleopatra may have been, Sib Or 3:350–80 shows the survival of a tradition which hoped for a utopian age of peace and reconciliation through the agency of the Ptolemaic line.

Sib Or 3:350–80 must have been written before the battle of Actium. Two other oracles in the sibylline collection reflect the aftermath of that battle. Sib Or 3:75–92 predicts cosmic destruction "when a widow rules the whole world." The "widow" here should be identified as Cleopatra, who no longer brings harmony to the world, but desolation.[151] The radical change of attitude from Sib Or 3:350–80 is probably due to disillusionment with her after Actium. She had proved to be a false messiah.

Cleopatra also figures prominently in Sib Or 11. This book has been variously dated to the first or third century CE.[152] The case for the later date rests on the assumption that the reference to the Roman conquest of the Parthians and Mesopotamia (vss. 160–61) must be a *vaticinium ex eventu*. This assumption is not justified since the Parthians were a menace to Roman power in the East in the first century BCE and their subjection could have been prophesied by anyone sympathetic to Rome. The oracle concludes with the time of Cleopatra and the conquest of Egypt by Rome, and may be presumed to have been written shortly after that time.[153] Further, the summary passage which is found in Sib Or 5:1–11[154] contains details which do not occur in any earlier sibyl except Sib Or 11, and may in fact be regarded as a summary of Sib Or 11. This consideration supports an early date for the eleventh book.

Sib Or 11 consists of a review of history from the flood to the death of Cleopatra. Its focus is political. It is remarkably void of the theological and hortatory interests of the other sibylline books.

Two aspects of Sib Or 11 reflect its political attitudes. Cleopatra is an "ill-wed maiden" who "will make amends for all you formerly did in wars of men" (285–87). This passage is a direct reversal of the taunts against Rome in Sib Or 3:350–58. Sib Or 11 may be seen as a rebuttal of the earlier sibyl. As in Sib Or 3:75–92, the word *chērē*, widow, recurs as a leitmotiv (Sib Or 11:279, 290). Even more explicitly, Cleopatra is condemned as "a female destructive of mortals, betrayer of her own kingdom" (247).

By contrast with all the earlier Egyptian sibylline writings, Sib Or 11 lacks any criticism of Rome. On the contrary it dwells at length on the story of Romulus and Remus (109–17), the Trojan war (122–43), Aeneas (144–62) and Virgil (163–71), and prophesies the victory of Rome over the Parthians. There is no trace of hostility to Rome. We must infer that the author of this book welcomed the advent of Roman rule. In fact, the initial relations between Romans and Jews in Egypt were friendly, and it is probable that Sib Or 11 is representative of a far wider segment of Egyptian Judaism than the pro-Cleopatran oracle in Sib Or 3:350–80.

The reign of Cleopatra marked the end of the Ptolemaic line and of whatever hopes the Jews may have pinned on it. Never again in the literature of the Egyptian Diaspora do we find such enthusiastic endorsement of a gentile ruler as we have seen in the earlier stage of Sib Or 3 or in the pro-Cleopatran oracle. With the breakup of the Ptolemaic administration, the Jews lost two of their most prominent occupations—the army and the civil service.[155] Consequently, the class of Jews which was most likely to exert some influence in political life was disbanded. In the first century CE the Jews of Egypt seems to have been preoccupied with defending their own status. This was usually done within a context of loyalty to Rome, but eventually the tensions would break into open rebellion in the early second century CE.

Notes

1. Tcherikover and A. Fuks (eds.), *Corpus Papyrorum Iudaicarum* (Cambridge, Mass.: Harvard, 1957) 1:19 (hereafter *CPJ*). See also Fraser, *Ptolemaic Alexandria* (Oxford: Clarendon, 1972) 1:54–58; Kasher, *The Jews in Hellenistic and Roman Egypt* (Tel Aviv: Tel Aviv University, 1978) chaps. 1 and 3.

2. Tcherikover, *CPJ* 1:2.

3. 3 Mac 2:29–30. See Tcherikover, "The Third Book of Maccabees as a historical source," *Scripta Hierosolymitana* 7 (1961) 4–5. Cf. above chap. 1 on a possible reference to an incident involving the Dionysiac cult in Artapanus. On Philopator's interest in Dionysus, see Fraser, *Ptolemaic Alexandria* 1:202. Cf. 2 Mac 6:7–8, which says that Jews were compelled to participate in the cult of Dionysus by Antiochus Epiphanes. Plutarch (*Quaestiones Convivales*, 4.6 [671–72]) says that the feast of Tabernacles resembles the cult of Dionysus. 3 Maccabees will be discussed at length in chap. 3 below.

4. E.g., 3 Mac 3:8–10 stresses that the Greeks of Alexandria were sympathetic to the Jews.

5. The most obvious illustrations of the mutual abuse by Jews and Egyptians are found in Josephus's tract *Against Apion*.

6. Collins, *The Sibylline Oracles of Egyptian Judaism* (SBLDS 13; Missoula: Scholars, 1974) 21–34. See also my introduction to the sibylline oracles in J. H. Charlesworth (ed.), *The Pseudepigrapha* (Garden City: Doubleday, forthcoming).

7. This is disputed only by V. Nikiprowetzky, *La Troisième Sibylle* (Etudes Juives 9; Paris: Mouton, 1970) 215, who dates the entire work to the reign of Cleopatra VII.

8. In addition to the bibliography in Collins, *The Sibylline Oracles*, 144, see now Fraser, *Ptolemaic Alexandria*, 1:709–13; 2:989–99.

9. The exception is Fergus Millar, in his review of Nikiprowetzky in *JTS* 23 (1972) 223–24, who asserts the possibility of a Palestinian origin, but does not show that it is more probable.

10. Collins, *The Sibylline Oracles*, 35–39.

11. Nikiprowetzky, *La Troisième Sibylle*, 112–33.

12. Collins, *The Sibylline Oracles*, 1–19.

13. Ibid. See further, L. Koenen, "The Prophecies of the Potter: A Prophecy of World Renewal Becomes an Apocalypse," *Proceedings of the Twelfth International Congress of Papyrology* (Ann Arbor: University of Michigan, 1970) 249–54; J. Z. Smith, "Wisdom and Apocalyptic," *Religious Syncretism in Antiquity* (ed. B. Pearson; Missoula: Scholars, 1975) 131–56; F. Dunand, "L'Oracle du Potier et la formation de l'apocalyptique en Egypte," *L'Apocalyptique* (Etudes d'Histoire des Religions 3; Paris: Geuthner, 1977) 39–67.

14. Collins, *The Sibylline Oracles*, 37.

15. The latter view has been defended by A. Momigliano, "La Portata Storica dei Vaticini sul Settimo Re nel Terzo Libro degli Oracoli Sibillini," *Forma Futuri* (Studi in Onore del Cardinale Michele Pellegrino; Torino: Bottega d'Erasmo, 1975) 1077–84, and is implied in the interpretation of Nikiprowetzky.

16. Collins, *The Sibylline Oracles*, 31.

17. Momigliano, "La Portata Storica," 1082.

18. A. Peretti, *La Sibilla Babilonese nella Propaganda Ellenistica* (Biblioteca di Cultura 21; Firenze: La Nuova Italia Editrice, 1943) 190.

19. J. Geffcken, *Die Oracula Sibyllina* (GCS 8; Leipzig: Hinrichs, 1902) 58, apparatus to vs. 192.

20. Nikiprowetzky, *La Troisième Sibylle*, 208–16. The numeral seven was not part of Cleopatra's title in antiquity and it is doubtful that she could be referred to as a "king."

21. Momigliano, "La Portata Storica," 1081.

22. Polybius 31.20 and 18. Fraser, *Ptolemaic Alexandria*, 1:120; 2:214 n. 225 and the references in Collins, *The Sibylline Oracles*, 147 n. 70.

23. On the significance of the epithet *neos* see Collins, *The Sibylline Oracles*, 30. Both Philometor and Physcon first came to the throne at an early age. The epithet was

part of the title of Neos Philopator. Moreover, it was commonly applied to Horus, the divine king.

24. On the invasions, see Fraser, *Ptolemaic Alexandria*, 1:119. On the identification of the king from Asia, Collins, *The Sibylline Oracles*, 39–40. Momigliano ("La Portata Storica," 1081) accepts the identification with Antiochus.

25. For the following, Collins, *The Sibylline Oracles*, 39–40.

26. Nikiprowetzky, *La Troisième Sibylle*, 133–35. See Collins, *The Sibylline Oracles*, 38–39.

27. J. Nolland, "Sib Or III.265–94, An Early Maccabean Messianic Oracle," *JTS* 30 (1979) 158–67.

28. Collins, *The Sibylline Oracles*, 39.

29. So also H. C. O. Lanchester, *APOT* 2.384.

30. The text is disputed. Nikiprowetzky reads "people."

31. So again Momigliano, "La Portata Storica," 1081.

32. Collins, *The Sibylline Oracles*, 152 n. 29. The famous passage in Tacitus 5.13 ("Many were convinced that it was said in the ancient writings of the priests that at that very time the East would grow strong and men coming from Judea would come to power") is written from a Roman point of view from which Judea was east. Josephus (*JW* 6.5.4 [312]) omits the reference to the East in reporting this prophecy. The opposition of East and West, which plays a prominent role in later Sibylline prophecies (Collins, chap. 4), has no role in the earliest stratum of the Third Sibyl, but only emerges when Rome becomes the archenemy.

33. Collins, *The Sibylline Oracles*, 41. On the Potter's Oracle, see above n. 13.

34. Momigliano, "La Portata Storica," 1081–82.

35. Collins, *The Sibylline Oracles*, 41, and the literature there cited.

36. Momigliano, "La Portata Storica," 1081.

37. Ibid.

38. Collins, *The Apocalyptic Vision of the Book of Daniel* (HSM 16; Missoula: Scholars, 1977) 168.

39. Momigliano, *Alien Wisdom* (Cambridge: Cambridge University, 1975) 119.

40. V. Tcherikover, *Hellenistic Civilization and the Jews* (New York: Atheneum, 1970) 156.

41. Josephus (*JW* 1.1.1 [31–33]) claims that the outbreak of hostilities which led to the Maccabean revolt was directly related to the struggle between the Seleucids and the Ptolemies for Palestine and that Onias was on the Ptolemaic side. Unfortunately, Josephus's entire account is confused. He identifies Onias III as the founder of Leontopolis, but in *Ant* 12.9.7 (387) and 13.3.1 (62) he says it was his son, who had the same name. 2 Mac 4:34 records that Onias III was murdered near Antioch and this is confirmed by Dan 9:26.

42. This is the most probable reconstruction of events despite the contradictory accounts in Josephus. See Collins, *The Sibylline Oracles*, 49–51; Tcherikover, *Hellenistic Civilization*, 276–81, and Fraser, *Ptolemaic Alexandria*, 1:83.

43. Collins, *The Sibylline Oracles*, 52–53; also "The Provenance of the Third Sibylline Oracle," *Bulletin of the Institute of Jewish Studies* 2 (1974) 1–18.

44. *Ant* 13.13.2 (354); Tcherikover, *Hellenistic Civilization*, 283.

45. M. Delcor, "Le Temple d'Onias en Egypte," *RB* 75 (1968) 188–205. Josephus (*Ant* 13.3.1 [64]) says that Onias lived at first in Alexandria and had fought for Philometor in Coele-Syria and Phoenicia. For the archeological evidence, see Collins, *The Sibylline Oracles*, 162, esp. Flinders Petrie, *Hyksos and Israelite Cities* (Cairo: British School of Archeology in Egypt and Egyptian Research Account, 1906) 19–27.

46. Tcherikover, *Hellenistic Civilization*, 280.

47. Collins, *The Sibylline Oracles*, 52.

48. *JW* 1.1.1 (33); *Ant* 12.9.7 (388); 13.3.1–3 (62–73). In *JW* 7.10.2 (427) Josephus says that the temple was not like the one in Jerusalem but resembled a tower. The altar was modelled on that in Jerusalem.

49. Josephus (*JW* 7.10.3 [431]) alleges that Onias bore a grudge against the Jews in

Jerusalem and hoped that the masses would leave them for his temple. In view of the location of his temple this motivation is implausible and may be attributed to the bias of Josephus. In *Ant* 13.3.1 (62–73) he says only that Onias "was encouraged chiefly by the words of the prophet Isaiah" (Isa 19:19), a factor which he also mentions in *JW*.

50. *CIJ* 2.1451–1530; *CPJ* 3:145–63; H. Lietzmann, "Jüdisch-griechische Inschriften aus Tell-el-Yehudieh," *ZNW* 22 (1923) 280–86.

51. Fraser, *Ptolemaic Alexandria*, 1:83: "In the course of a century and a half its religious beliefs, under the impact of the surrounding Greco-Egyptian population, became a curious mixture of Greek, Egyptian and Jewish elements." Compare U. Fischer, *Eschatologie und Jenseitserwartung im Hellenistischen Diasporajudentum* (BZNW 44; Berlin: de Gruyter, 1978) 237–42.

52. Fischer, *Eschatologie*, 238, illustrates the syncretism of the epitaphs as follows: "So wird beispielsweise als allgemeiner Todesort mehrfach der Hades genannt oder die Unterwelt als finsteres Gebiet der Lethe bezeichnet; so wird einmal die Moira, ein anderes Mal der "Alleszähmer" (Chronos) für den Tod eines Menschen verantwortlich gemacht."

We may compare the frequent use of *moira* in Sib Or 3 (also *chronos* in vs. 117). Hades is a reasonable equivalent for Sheol. Sib Or 3 displays an ample familiarity with Greek mythology in vss. 97–161.

53. Fischer (*Eschatologie*, 238): "Jenseitshoffnungen spielen so gut wie keine Rolle." There are only two or three exceptions. The contrast with other Jewish epitaphs is striking (Fischer, 226–36).

54. Collins, *The Sibylline Oracles*, 110. The Egyptian Jewish sibyllina are 3, 5, and 11. Books 12–14 are also Jewish and Egyptian but come from a later date. Book 4, which clearly professes a resurrection, cannot be assigned to Egypt. See Collins, "The Place of the Fourth Sibyl in the Development of the Jewish Sibyllina," *JSJ* 25 (1974) 365–80.

55. See J. A. Goldstein ("The Tales of the Tobiads," in J. Neusner [ed.], *Christianity, Judaism and other Greco-Roman Cults: Studies for Morton Smith at Sixty* (Leiden: Brill, 1975] 3:112), who speculates that Ben Sira represents an Oniad, proto-Sadducean theology which Onias IV would have shared.

56. Tcherikover, *Hellenistic Civilization*, 140–42; M. Hengel, *Judaism and Hellenism* (Philadelphia: Fortress, 1974) 1:269.

57. So C. Habicht, *2 Makkabäerbuch* (JSHRZ 1/3; Gütersloh: Mohn, 1976) 175; J. G. Bunge, *Untersuchungen zum zweiten Makkabäerbuch. Quellenkritische, literarische, chronologische und historische Untersuchungen zum zweiten Makkabäerbuch als Quelle syrisch-palästinensischer Geschichte im 2. Jh. v. Chr.* (Diss. Bonn, 1971) 203; U. Kellermann, *Auferstanden in den Himmel. 2 Makkabäer 7 und die Auferstehung der Märtyrer* (SBS 95; Stuttgart: KBW, 1979) 13; Hengel, *Judaism and Hellenism*, 1:96–98. Hengel summarizes the conflicting opinions of older scholarship.

58. Goldstein, "The Tales of the Tobiads," 85–123; *1 Maccabees* (AB 41; Garden City: Doubleday, 1976) 55–61; 90–103.

59. Hengel, *Judaism and Hellenism*, 1:269.

60. Tcherikover, *Hellenistic Civilization*, 128–30; see further Goldstein, "The Tales of the Tobiads," 85–102.

61. *Ant* 12.4.5 (180–85). Joseph put to death the leading citizens of Ascalon and Scythopolis when they refused to comply with his demands.

62. *CPJ* 1:118–21. See Hengel, *Judaism and Hellenism*, 268.

63. Goldstein, "The Tales of the Tobiads," 107–8; M. Stern, "Notes on the Story of Joseph the Tobiad," *Tarbiz* 32 (1962) 35–47 (Heb.).

64. Tcherikover, *Hellenistic Civilization*, 141–42. Hengel (*Judaism and Hellenism*, 2:179 n. 78) approves Willrich's suggestion that work was composed in Egypt, but without supporting argument. Goldstein ("The Tales of the Tobiads," 103) denies that the work can be a family history because it ignores the earlier glories of the Tobiads, but we simply do not know whether the original document recorded the earlier history of the family or was only concerned with its relations to the Ptolemies.

65. *CPJ* 1:116.

66. *Ant* 12.4.11 (228–34). For the archeological evidence, see P. W. Lapp, "The Second and Third Campaigns at ʿAraq el-Emir," *BASOR* 171 (1963) 8–39. Lapp concluded that "The Qasr emerges as a unique example of the old Syrian temple type in the Hellenistic period."

67. *Ant* 12.4.11 (229).

68. Hengel, *Judaism and Hellenism*, 1:274. Hengel suggests a parallel to the sanctuaries of Elephantine, Leontopolis, and Gerizim, but Elephantine was definitely not in competition with Jerusalem, Leontopolis is disputed and there is nothing to suggest that either Hyrcanus or Onias led a movement as distinct as the Samaritans.

69. 2 Mac 3:11. See Tcherikover (*Hellenistic Civilization*, 138), who asserts that Hyrcanus did not give up his desire to return to Jerusalem and suggests that he may have lived there for a time.

70. The suicide of Hyrcanus was prompted not only by the accession of Antiochus Epiphanes but by the weakness of Egypt after the death of Ptolemy Epiphanes. Hyrcanus did not have a patron to protect him (*Ant* 12.4.11 [234–236]).

71. Goldstein, *1 Maccabees*, 58–61, 90; "The Tales of the Tobiads," 112–13.

72. See further the critique of Goldstein by R. Doran, *Temple Propaganda: The Purpose and Character of 2 Maccabees* (CBQMS 12; Washington: CBA, 1981) 17–19.

73. *1 Maccabees*, 56–57. Note also the tendentious criticism of Philometor in 1 Mac 11:8–19 and contrast *Ant* 13.4.5–9 (103–20). It is not necessary to assume with Goldstein ("The Tales of the Tobiads," 111) that Josephus derived his account from a work by Onias IV. He may have drawn on a non-Jewish source.

74. Hengel, *Judaism and Hellenism*, 1:95. Hengel reviews the spectrum of scholarly opinion as to whether Jason was an eye-witness of the events he describes and rightly concludes that Jason probably spent some time in Judea in those years.

75. Ibid., 97.

76. On the Hellenistic form of 2 Maccabees and of Jason's work, see most recently Doran, *Temple Propaganda* and "2 Maccabees and 'Tragic History,'" *HUCA* 50 (1979) 107–14. Also W. Richnow, "Untersuchungen zu Sprache und Stil des 2 Makkabäerbuches. Ein Beitrag zur hellenistischen Historiographie" (Diss. Göttingen, 1967).

77. 1 Mac 8; 12. 2 Mac 4:11.

78. The authenticity of this letter was established by E. Bickermann, "Ein jüdischer Festbrief vom Jahre 124 v. Chr. (II Macc 1.1–9)," *ZNW* 32 (1933) 233–54 (reprinted in *Studies in Jewish and Christian History* [AGJU 9; Leiden: Brill, 1980] 2:136–58). See Habicht, *2 Makkabäerbuch*, 199–201.

79. So Bickermann, *Studies*, 137; Habicht, *2 Makkabäerbuch*, 199.

80. A. Momigliano ("The Second Book of Maccabees," *Classical Philology* 70 [1975] 84) expresses doubts about the authenticity of the second letter but "should like to leave open the possibility that the writer of the first letter was misled by what he considered an authentic letter of Judas" and so that the second letter was composed before 124 BCE.

81. See Doran, "Studies," 16, 35; Momigliano, "The Second Book," 81–82.

82. Habicht, *2 Makkabäerbuch*, 186–87. The importance of the temple in 2 Maccabees has been stressed by virtually all commentators. Recently Doran has characterized the book as "Temple Propaganda" and emphasized its affinity with Hellenistic accounts of the epiphanic defense of cities ("2 Maccabees and Tragic History," 113–14).

83. Momigliano, "The Second Book," 83.

84. Momigliano, ibid.; compare *Alien Wisdom*, 119.

85. Habicht, *2 Makkabäerbuch*, 186; Bickermann, "Ein jüdischer Festbrief," 154–55; F. M. Abel, *Les Livres des Maccabées* (Paris: Gabalda, 1949) XLIV.

86. D. Arenhoevel, *Die Theokratie nach dem 1. und 2. Makkabäerbuch* (Mainz: Matthias-Grünewald, 1967) 100–102; Doran, *Temple Propaganda*, 11–12.

87. See G. W. E. Nickelsburg, "1 and 2 Maccabees—Same Story, Different Meaning," *CTM* 42 (1971) 515–26 (esp. 524). In this respect 2 Maccabees is in sharp contrast to 1 Maccabees.

88. Joseph is apparently an error for John (cf. 1 Mac 2:2).

89. Cf. Doran, *Temple Propaganda*, 76.

90. M. Hadas (*Aristeas to Philocrates* [Dropsie College Edition; New York: Harper, 1951] 56–59) has pointed out that the work is not a letter, but a *diēgēsis*, a genre defined by the rhetorician Theon as "a discourse expository of things which happened or might have happened." By the canons of ancient rhetoric, the work of Pseudo-Aristeas could be considered a *plasma* or "an imaginative treatment of history" which should however preserve historical verisimilitude and present a higher "poetical" truth.

91. In addition to Hadas's useful edition, which is cited here, see the commentaries of R. Tramontano, *La lettera di Aristeo* (Naples: Ufficio Succursale della Civiltà Cattolica, 1931); H. G. Meecham, *The Letter of Aristeas* (Manchester: Manchester University, 1935); A. Pelletier, *La Lettre d'Aristée à Philocrate* (SC 89; Paris: Cerf, 1962), and N. Meisner, *Aristeasbrief* (JSHRZ 2/1; Gütersloh: Mohn, 1973); and also Meisner's two-volume dissertation *Untersuchungen zum Aristeasbrief* (Berlin: Kirchliche Hochschule, 1973).

92. For a concise review of the objections to the purported date, see Hadas, *Aristeas*, 5–9. The classic demonstration was made by Humphrey Hody in 1685. Among the more conspicuous "giveaways" are: (1) The claim that Demetrius of Phalerum was in charge of the Alexandrian library under Philadelphus (he was never librarian, and he was banished from Alexandria by Philadelphus for supporting Ptolemy Geraunus instead of Philadelphus as successor of Ptolemy I Soter). (2) The introduction of the philosopher Menedemus of Eretria (201) who had died about 287 BCE. (3) The statement that "these kings used to administer all their business through decrees and with great precaution" (28). Philadelphus had only one predecessor.

93. E. Bickermann, "Zur Datierung des Pseudo-Aristeas," *Studies in Jewish and Christian History* 1:108–36, esp. 128 (first published in ZNW 29 (1930). On the linguistic evidence see further Fraser, *Ptolemaic Alexandria*, 2:970–71.

94. Bickermann, *Studies*, 128–32. See 1 Mac 10:30, 38; 11:28, 34, for the acquisition of these territories from Samaria.

95. A pre-Maccabean date was endorsed by Schürer, Tramontano, Vincent, Wellhausen, Pelletier, and Orlinsky. See Jellicoe, *The Septuagint and Modern Study*, 48–49, with a summary of Orlinsky's arguments in his review of Hadas in the *Crozer Quarterly* 29 (April, 1952) 201–5. Orlinsky notes, but does not commit himself to the possible dependence of Aristobulus on Pseudo-Aristeas. Fraser, *Ptolemaic Alexandria*, 1:696, uses the supposed relation to Aristobulus as an argument for a date about 160 BCE.

96. So also Meisner, *Aristeasbrief*, 39; M. Hengel, "Anonymität, Pseudepigraphie und 'Literarische Fälschung' in der jüdisch-hellenistischen Literatur," *Entretiens sur l'Antiquité Classique XVIII* (1972) 298.

97. Much of Orlinsky's argument centers on the silence of the letter on Leontopolis and the Jewish struggle against Syria.

98. For Jewish military garrisons in Ptolemaic Egypt in the third century BCE, see A. Kasher, "Three Jewish Communities of Lower Egypt in the Ptolemaic Period," *Scripta Classica Israelica* 2 (1975) 113–23; "First Jewish Military Units in Ptolemaic Egypt," *JSJ* 9 (1978) 57–67. The word *pro-ontas* ("leaders") could also be translated "those who were there before."

99. Fraser, *Ptolemaic Alexandria*, 1:703.

100. Ibid., 699.

101. Tcherikover (*Hellenistic Civilization*, 273) finds "no grounds for doubting the historical trustworthiness of this tale" except for the inflated number of 100,000.

102. Ag Ap 2.51–56.

103. Tcherikover, *Hellenistic Civilization*, 274–75; "The Third Book of Maccabees," 1–26.

104. Fraser, *Ptolemaic Alexandria*, 1:119–23. Physcon married Cleopatra II after his return to Egypt in 145 and she bore him a son, whom he later murdered. However, he later married her daughter Cleopatra III, without divorcing her mother. He was expelled from Alexandria in 131 BCE by "a rising of the population, supported or spon-

sored by Cleopatra II," but he returned in 127. He was reconciled with Cleopatra II in 124 and reigned with both queens until his death in 116 BCE.

105. Fraser, *Ptolemaic Alexandria*, 2:215 n. 232; Tcherikover, *CPJ* 1:23 n.8.

106. Tcherikover, *Hellenistic Civilization*, 283. Josephus (*Ant* 13.10.4 [287]), citing Strabo, says that they "were held in very high esteem by the queen."

107. This passage has been used as a basis for dating the letter to the time of Tiberius, assuming a reference to the Roman *delatores* put to death in 33 CE. See Hadas, *Aristeas*, 15.

108. Fraser, *Ptolemaic Alexandria*, 2:215 n. 232.

109. S. Jellicoe, "The Occasion and Purpose of the Letter of Aristeas: A Re-examination," *NTS* 12 (1965–66) 144–50; *The Septuagint and Modern Study* (Oxford: Clarendon, 1968) 50.

110. Meisner, *Aristeasbrief*, 43. He also dates Pseudo-Aristeas to the reign of Physcon but specifies the later period of his reign.

111. It is noteworthy that the Greek translation of Ben Sira 50:24 omits the Hebrew verse which ascribes to Simon's house the eternal priesthood promised to Phineas (Bickermann, "Zur Datierung," 132). There is no such evidence of polemic here.

112. Hadas, *Aristeas*, 6, 136–37.

113. V. Tcherikover, "The Ideology of the Letter of Aristeas," *HTR* 51 (1958) 77–79; Hadas, *Aristeas*, 64.

114. The assertion is based on Joshua 3:15 but is explicitly offered as a parallel to the Nile.

115. One could perhaps suppose that these objects had been pillaged by Antiochus Epiphanes but the Letter contains no hint that would prepare for such an assumption.

116. Hadas (*Aristeas*, 64): "All references to that country in Aristeas envisage a remote and idealized Biblical Palestine and seem purposely to ignore contemporary reality."

117. Tcherikover, "Ideology," 83.

118. Jellicoe, *The Septuagint and Modern Study*, 59–63.

119. H. M. Orlinsky, "The Septuagint as Holy Writ and the Philosophy of the Translators," *HUCA* 46 (1975) 92 n. 4; D. W. Gooding, "Aristeas and Septuagint Origins: a Review of Recent Studies," *VT* 13 (1963) 158–80.

120. Ibid., 165–74.

121. Orlinsky, "The Septuagint as Holy Writ," 94–103.

122. Hadas, *Aristeas*, 122–23.

123. Hengel ("Anonymität," 300–301) suggests a possible polemic against Palestinian revisions of the LXX, such as the later ones of Aquila and Theodotion.

124. Tcherikover, "Ideology," 67–68. Also G. Howard, "The Letter of Aristeas and Diaspora Judaism," *JTS* 22 (1971) 337–48.

125. Tcherikover, *Hellenistic Civilization*, 277–78. The remote location of Leontopolis is decisive here.

126. Tcherikover ("Ideology," 71): "Judaism is a combination of a universal philosophy with the idea of monotheism."

127. Tcherikover, *CPJ* 1:25. The evidence consists of an obscure reference in Iordanis, *Roman History*, 81. A few obscure passages in the papyri might also reflect hostility to the Jews in the Ptolemaic period, but the evidence is far from clear. There was also conflict in Cyrene about this time: see S. Applebaum, *Jews and Greeks in Ancient Cyrene* (SJLA 28; Leiden: Brill, 1979) 201–2.

128. A. Meinhold, "Die Gattung der Josephgeschichte und des Estherbuches: Diasporanovelle, I, II," *ZAW* 87 (1975) 306–24; 88 (1976) 79–93; W. L. Humphreys, "A Life-Style for Diaspora: A Study of the Tales of Esther and Daniel," *JBL* 92 (1973) 211–23; Collins, *The Apocalyptic Vision of the Book of Daniel* (HSM 16; Missoula: Scholars, 1977) 27–66; S. B. Berg, *The Book of Esther*, (SBLDS 44; Chico: Scholars, 1979) 123–45.

129. On the additions to Esther and Daniel, see C. A. Moore, *Daniel, Esther and Jeremiah. The Additions* (AB 44; Garden City: Doubleday, 1977). At least some of the

additions to Esther were composed in Greek. This does not seem to be the case with Daniel. The additions to Daniel show no special links to Egyptian Judaism.

130. E. J. Bickermann, "The Colophon of the Greek Book of Esther," *Studies in Jewish and Christian History* (AGJU 9; Leiden: Brill, 1976) 1:225–45 (originally published in *JBL* 63 [1944]). The decisive points are the use of the singular *basileuontos* for the reign of king and queen and the fact that the name of the king precedes that of the queen. This usage is incompatible with the reigns of Ptolemy IX (114/113) and XIII (49–48) since the queen was regent in the fourth year of each of their reigns, and so her name preceded the king's. Moore (*The Additions*, 250), following B. Jacob ("Das Buch Esther bei dem LXX," *ZAW* 10 [1890] 241–98), regards 114/113 as the more probable date. H. Bardtke (*Zusätze zu Esther* (JSHRZ 1/1; Gütersloh: Mohn, 1973) 27) dates the translation to the time of the Maccabean revolt but provides no objective evidence.

131. E. Bickermann ("Notes on the Greek Book of Esther," *Studies in Jewish and Christian History*, 1:258 n. 41 [originally published in *Proceedings of the American Academy for Jewish Research* 20 (1951)] refutes the contention of Jacob and others that the translation has an Egyptian flavor.

132. Bickermann, "Notes," 246–56; Moore, *Additions*, 153–68. Both provide discussion of the complex textual transmission.

133. Bickermann, "Notes," 256–68.

134. Bickermann, "Notes," 268–74. The term *lots* is presumably used because of the association with Purim, but it recalls the deterministic language of the Qumran scrolls. The imagery of the dream, though not its interpretation, is reminiscent of the apocalyptic literature, which became popular in Palestine in the second century BCE.

135. On the elements of Greek style in Greek Esther see Bickermann, "Notes," 256–65. He comments on the (initially) unexplained dream as a Hellenistic device.

136. Above chap. 1. See further, Collins, "The Epic of Theodotus."

137. E 10,14. See Tcherikover, *CPJ* 1:24.

138. Bickermann ("The Colophon," 244): "The historical background of this literature is the violent and implacable war between the Maccabees and the Greek cities in Palestine."

139. C. Burchard, *Untersuchungen zu Joseph und Asenath* (Tübingen: Mohr, 1965) 144; M. Philonenko, *Joseph et Aséneth. Introduction, Texte Critique et Notes* (Studia Post-Biblica 13; Leiden: Brill, 1968) 27–32; G. Delling, "Einwirkungen der Septuaginta in 'Joseph und Aseneth,'" *JSJ* 9 (1978) 29–56.

140. Philonenko, *Joseph et Aséneth*, 29.

141. Ibid., 61–78.

142. Burchard, *Untersuchungen*, 146.

143. G. Delling (*Die Taufe im Neuen Testament* [Berlin: Evangelische Verlagsanstalt, 1963] 30–38) contra J. Jeremias (*Die Kindertaufe in den ersten vier Jahrhunderten* [Göttingen: Vandenhoeck & Ruprecht, 1958] 29–34). Jeremias takes T Levi 14:6 as the earliest allusion to proselyte baptism (Levi's sons will marry gentile women and purify them with an unlawful purification), but it is far from evident that the "unlawful purification" is a polemical reference to proselyte baptism. Sib Or 4:165, which is frequently adduced as an example, must be distinguished from proselyte baptism because of its eschatological setting. Proselyte baptism is not attested in Philo or Josephus and there is no indication that it was current in the Diaspora before the end of the first century CE.

144. Philonenko, *Joseph et Aséneth*, 109.

145. G. D. Kilpatrick, "The Last Supper," *ET* 64 (1952/53) 4–8; J. Jeremias, "The Last Supper," *ET* 64 (1952/53) 91–92.

146. Fraser, *Ptolemaic Alexandria*, 2:184 n. 63.

147. For full discussion, see Collins, *The Sibylline Oracles*, 57–62.

148. This identification was first proposed by W. W. Tarn, "Alexander Helios and the Golden Age," *JRS* 22 (1932) 135–59.

149. *Ant* 15.4.2 (96–103). Cleopatra wished to restore Ptolemaic rule in Syria and Palestine and tried to persuade Antony to hand over to her the territory of the Jews.

Antony in fact gave her the coastal strip and the oasis of Jericho. See M. Avi-Yonah, *A History of the Holy Land* (New York: Macmillan, 1969) 88–89.

150. *Ag Ap* 2:56–61. Doubts arise because of the bias of Apion and the pro-Roman (and therefore anti-Cleopatran) leanings of Josephus.

151. See Collins, *The Sibylline Oracles*, 66–69. Another oracle from this time which does not refer to Cleopatra but predicts cosmic destruction after Actium, is found in Sib Or 3:46–62.

152. For full discussion, see my introduction to Sib Or 11 in J. H. Charlesworth (ed), *The Pseudepigrapha*. The later date was defended by Geffcken and Rzach. The earlier date was defended by W. Bousset, "Sibyllen und Sibyllinische Bücher," *Real-Encyclopedie der Protestantischen Theologie und Kirche* 18 (1906) 276, and A. Kurfess, *Sibyllinische Weissagungen* (Berlin: Heimeran, 1951) 333–41 and "Oracula Sibyllina XI(IX)–XIV(XII), Nicht Christlich sondern Jüdisch," *ZRGG* 7 (1955) 270–72.

153. So Bousset, "Sibyllen," 278.

154. This summary passage is repeated in Sib Or 12:1–11.

155. E. M. Smallwood, *The Jews under Roman Rule* (SJLA 20; Leiden: Brill, 1976) 231.

Chapter 3

RELIGION AND POLITICS: THE ROMAN PERIOD

The initial relations between Egyptian Jewry and the Romans were friendly.[1] The Jews had supported the attempt of Gabinius to reestablish Ptolemy XII Auletes in 55 BCE and Julius Caesar's intervention on behalf of Cleopatra in 47 BCE.[2] Josephus refers to a "slab which stands in Alexandria recording the rights bestowed upon the Jews by Caesar the Great" (*Ag Ap* 2.37) and asserts that he declared them citizens of Alexandria (*Ant* 14.10.1[188]). This report is certainly incorrect. There is a scholarly consensus that the Jews as a class were never full citizens of Alexandria;[3] in any case, Julius Caesar was never official ruler of Egypt and could not have granted rights there. However, since the stele in question must be presumed to have existed, Tcherikover plausibly suggests that it carried an edict of Augustus, not Julius Caesar, confirming the rights which the Jews had hitherto enjoyed.[4] Such confirmation was in accordance with Roman policy and lent stability to the Jewish community at the time of the transition from Ptolemaic to Roman rule.

The Roman conquest of Egypt did however make the status of the Jews more problematic than it had previously been. While the Jews were not citizens of Alexandria (with few exceptions),[5] they were *politai* of their own Jewish *politeuma,* and in practice their status may not have been very different from that of citizens.[6] The Romans, however, introduced the *laographia* or poll-tax on the Egyptians. The Greek citizens of Alexandria, and probably those of Ptolemais and Naucratis, were exempted, and Greeks in the provincial towns payed at a reduced rate. Since the Jews were not exempted from this tax, their status was lowered. They were classified with the Egyptians as opposed to the Greeks. In short, the line between citizens and noncitizens was more sharply drawn.[7]

In fact, the question of citizenship was an ambiguous one for the Jews, since it involved pagan religious observances and practices such as nudity in the gymnasium, which were objectionable to Jewish tradition. Whether the Jews as a group sought full citizenship is disputed.[8] It is at least apparent that they sought equal rights with the Alexandrian citizens, although the issue may have been the status of the Jewish *politeuma* rather than integration into the Alexandrian *polis*. The aspirations of the Jews were resented by the Greeks, especially when the Jews were not prepared to accept the full religious implications of citizenship. The complaint of Apion reflects one cause of Greek resentment: "why, then, if they are citizens, do they not worship the same gods as the Alexandrians?" (*Ag Ap* 2:66). There were other reasons. The Greeks presumably feared that the extension of their privileges to other groups would lead to the erosion of these privileges and diminish their own status. It is also possible that the Alexandrian Greeks used the Jews as an outlet for anti-Roman resentment since the Jews could be seen as Roman protegés because of the special status they still enjoyed.[9]

We know of no disturbances involving the Egyptian Jews under Augustus and Tiberius, but matters came to a head under Gaius (Caligula). The Roman prefect Flaccus had been a protegé of Tiberius and felt his position and life were in jeopardy under the new emperor. Accordingly, his authority deteriorated and he became subject to the influence of the Alexandrian nationalists, Lampo and Isidorus. These inclined him against the Jews, and the situation was exacerbated by the untimely visit of King Agrippa which provoked the mockery of the Greeks and was perceived as a threat to the authority of Flaccus. The ensuing riots and the subsequent delegations to Gaius are described in Philo's treatises *In Flaccum* and *Legatio ad Gaium*. They have often been discussed in modern scholarship and need not be dealt with in detail here.[10] At the heart of the crisis was Flaccus's attack on the rights of the Jewish *politeuma* by a proclamation in which he declared that the Jews were "aliens and foreigners" in Alexandria. By this measure he lowered their status from "resident aliens" (*katoikoi*). As foreigners (*xenoi*) the Jews would now be confined to only one of the five sections of Alexandria and so in effect to a ghetto.[11] The

Alexandrians eagerly attempted to enforce this proclamation. In the end, however, the measures against the Jews failed. When Claudius came to power he reaffirmed the traditional status of the Jews. At the same time, he firmly rejected the Jewish claims to citizenship, bidding them not to aim at more than they had previously had.[12] The execution of the Alexandrian leaders Lampo and Isidorus when they attempted to impeach the Jewish king Agrippa helped defuse the situation, at least for a period of time.[13]

THE THIRD BOOK OF MACCABEES

The turbulent Roman period lent itself to the literature of confrontation, exemplified in Esther, more readily than the Ptolemaic era had. Third Maccabees, the product of the Egyptian Diaspora which most closely resembles Esther is now generally dated to this period. The work is a melodramatic account of two alleged episodes in the career of Ptolemy IV Philopator (222–203 BCE). The first concerns an attempt by the Ptolemy to enter the temple of Jerusalem, and his miraculous prevention. The second concerns the persecution of the Egyptian Jews by reducing them "to the popular census and slave condition" (*eis laographian kai oiketikēn diathesin*, 2:28) and branding them with the emblem of Dionysus. When the majority of the Jews resisted, the king is said to have rounded them up and ordered them to be trampled by elephants. The execution of this order is thwarted first by lapses of the king's memory, then by the miraculous intervention of two angels. Finally, the king is brought to repentance and becomes benevolent to the Jews.

The stories in 3 Maccabees are stereotypical. There are numerous points of contact with 2 Maccabees.[14] The attempt of Philopator to enter the temple is clearly based on the incident involving Heliodorus in 2 Maccabees. The general situation in the persecution story is reminiscent of Esther, especially in its conclusion, when the Jews are permitted to take revenge on their enemies and institute an annual festival.[15] There are verbal parallels between 3 Maccabees and Greek Esther, which are so close as to require us to assume literary influence.[16] Moreover, the style of the work shows many similarities to the Greek romances.[17] Yet there is general agreement that it reflects some historical episodes, however obliquely. The opening account of the battle of Raphia resembles that given by Polybius in several details and the references to the cult of Dionysus (2:29–30) may draw on a real inscription from the time of Philopator.[18] Kasher, following Y. Gutman, has even claimed "that its contents can be corroborated as genuinely historical without departing from its own chronological framework,"[19] but at most we can speak of historical reminiscences. The fantastic genre of the story should warn against any attempt to treat it as "genuinely historical." The account of the persecution of the Jews may also reflect a historical tradition. Josephus, *Ag Ap* 2.53–55, preserves a variant of this story but sets it in the reign of Ptolemy VIII Euergetes II (Physcon).[20] In view of Physcon's notorious cruelty and the opposition of the Jews in his civil war with Cleopatra II (the widow of Philometor),[21] Tcherikover and others have argued that the story is a melodramatic dramatization of the real threat to the Jews in his reign.[22] Since Physcon gave an amnesty to his enemies when he was reconciled with Cleopatra, the miraculous deliverance of the story may reflect the unexpected reprieve of the Jews. Here again we can only speak of partially historical reminiscences which are used as building blocks in a fictional composition.

In its present form, 3 Maccabees must be dated to Roman times.[23] Bickermann showed that the opening formulae in the letters at 3:12 and 7:1 can be no earlier than the first century BCE.[24] A more specific indication of date is provided by the statement in 2:28 that the Jews should be reduced to the popular census (*laographia*) and slave condition. While the word *laographia* simply means "census," and censuses had been taken in Ptolemaic times, the word took on a special connotation in Roman times. It referred to the poll-tax introduced by Augustus in 24/23 BCE. This was the only *laographia* which involved a reduction of status for the Jews, because of the clear distinction between Greeks and non-Greeks as we have noted above. So Tcherikover and Hadas conclude that 3 Maccabees was written shortly after the introduction of this *laographia*. The fact that "political parity with the Alexandrians" is an issue in 3 Maccabees (2:30) further fits a setting in the Roman era.[25] We should also note that the price of this parity is religious apostasy, as was also true for Jews who became full citizens in the Roman era.

Yet the reference to the *laographia* only provides a terminus a quo for 3 Maccabees. If we assume that the author picked up and recast the traditional stories because they were appropriate to his time, then it seems unlikely that he wrote in the reign of Augustus. Not only was there no threat to the Jerusalem temple in his time, but Philo recounts that "he and almost all his family enriched our Temple with expensive dedications" (*Leg* 157). Again, there is no record of any persecution of the Jews of Alexandria under Augustus. While the *laographia* was surely unwelcome to the Jews, there is no evidence that they resisted it, or that they regarded Augustus as a persecutor. On the contrary, Philo affirmed that Augustus deserved the title "averter of evil" and was "the first and greatest universal benefactor" (*Leg* 144–49). Because of his insistence on the traditional rights of the Jews, "the whole population of the empire, even if not instinctively well-disposed towards the Jews, was afraid to tamper with any Jewish practice in the hope of destroying it" (*Leg* 159). Josephus (*Ag Ap* 2.61) also refers to "the letters of Caesar Augustus which attest our services." The intervention of Augustus in the administration of the Jewish *politeuma* to replace the office of ethnarch by a council of elders was recalled by Philo as a gracious act by "the savior and benefactor Augustus" (*Flac* 74). Tiberius was also remembered as a benevolent ruler, and even Flaccus was praiseworthy while Tiberius was alive. In short, there was no occasion before the reign of Caligula when 3 Maccabees would appear to be an appropriate expression of the situation of the Egyptian Jews.

The similarities between the situation envisaged in 3 Maccabees and that which existed in the time of Caligula are obvious, and did not escape the older generation of scholars, although they have been overlooked in more recent works.[26] First is the juxtaposition of an attempt to violate the Jerusalem temple and the persecution of Egyptian Jewry. The only time when Judaism endured this particular combination of dangers was under Caligula. Since the apparent models for these two sections of 3 Maccabees—the episode of Heliodorus and the legend about Physcon preserved in Josephus—were unrelated to each other, their combination is a significant clue to the setting of the composition. It is true that 3 Maccabees inverts the order in which Philo treats the persecution and the temple episode,[27] but this may be explained by the dramatic conception of 3 Maccabees. The climax of the story is the attempt to annihilate Egyptian Jewry and this is what leads to the definitive deliverance. Accordingly, it must conclude the book. Some details of the story seem applicable to Caligula, especially the hubris of the king and his periodic loss of rational control. These details are not found in Josephus's version of the story. We should not of course expect to find in 3 Maccabees a detailed allegory with reference to the crisis under Caligula at every point. As we have seen, the stories are woven from traditional material, and the author is content with the general correspondence. It should be obvious, however, that the correspondence is far closer than any that can be found with the reign of Augustus.

Only one aspect of 3 Maccabees may seem at first anomalous in relation to the situation of 38–41 CE. The author is at pains to exculpate "the Greeks": "The Greeks in the city, who were in no way injured, when they saw the unforeseen tumult . . . were not strong enough, indeed, to help them, for they lived under a tyranny, but they did try to comfort them and were distressed for them" (3:8–10). In fact, the Alexandrian Greeks were the most immediate and bitter enemies of the Jews. This was so not only in the time of Caligula but throughout the Roman period, and is problematic on any dating. It is unlikely that the author was unaware of the enmity of the Greeks. Rather, it would seem that he deliberately chose to portray them in the most positive light possible, choosing to refer the name Greeks to the "friends and business associates" who were well disposed to the Jews, rather than to the hostile mass. 3 Maccabees does not pretend that all the gentiles were well disposed to the Jews. It refers to "the hatred which had long grown inveterate in their hearts" and was now given free expression. He does not, however, specify just who those gentiles were who hated the Jews.

The usage of 3 Maccabees, which distinguishes between "the Greeks" and the Alexandrian enemies of the Jews, is in accordance with that of Philo and Josephus. Philo refers scathingly to the "promiscuous and unruly Alexandrian mob" (*Leg* 120) but he does not call them "Greeks."[28] On the contrary he attributes their malice explicitly to the Egyptian character (*Flac* 29; cf. *Flac* 17) and ridicules them for the Egyptian animal cults which he regards simply as their religion (*Leg* 139, 162, 165). Caligula's friend and adviser Helicon, who is said to be "from the most garrulous section of the Alexandrian population," is also leader of a band of "Egyptians, a worthless breed, whose souls were infected with the poison and bad temper alike of the crocodiles and asps of their country" (*Leg* 166–70). The Jewish position on the conflict of the races in Alexandria is most clearly stated by Josephus (*Ag Ap* 2.68–70):

> The real promoters of sedition, as anyone can discover, have been
> the citizens of Alexandria of the type of Apion. The Greeks and
> Macedonians, so long as the citizenship was confined to them,
> never rose against us, but left us free to enjoy our ancient worship.
> But when, owing to the prevailing disorders, their numbers were
> swelled by a host of Egyptians, sedition became chronic. Our race,
> on the contrary, remained unadulterated. It is they, then, who
> originated these disturbances, because the populace, possessing
> neither the Macedonians' strength of character nor the Greeks'
> sagacity, universally adopted the evil habits of the Egyptians and
> indulged their long-standing hatred of us.

Accordingly, Josephus is at pains to establish that Apion and his ilk
should be regarded as Egyptians rather than Greeks (*Ag Ap* 2.29–32,
34, 41, 66). The distinction of 3 Maccabees between "the Greeks" and
those who hate the Jews is part of the standard Jewish apologetic.

The attempt to exculpate "the Greeks" is highly significant for our
understanding of the ideology of the work as it shows that the author
perceives no intrinsic enmity between the Jews and the gentiles as
such. It is true that the prayers of Eleazar make a simple antithesis
between Jews and gentiles and speak of "the abominable and lawless
nations" (6:9). Yet, it is not assumed that all nations are lawless, only
those who attack the Jews. Tcherikover, while recognizing the lack of
hostility towards the Greeks, still refers to it as "hating the gentiles in
general" and takes the book as a particular example of Jewish hatred
against Rome, mainly because of the portrayal of the king.[29] This view
is ill founded. Far from hating the Roman government and supporting
a nationalist cause, 3 Maccabees insists that "the Jews continued to
preserve their good will toward the royal house and their unswerving
fidelity" (3:3), and in the end the king admits that he has no complaint
against the Jews "who have shown me and my ancestors full and firm
loyalty in extraordinary measure" (5:31). The king's final change of
heart and patronage of the Jews cannot simply be dismissed as a
traditional ending which the author could not change.[30] The traditional motif was retained because it expressed the Jews' enduring
hope for good relations with their rulers, as they had enjoyed in the
past. The reaffirmation of Jewish rights by Claudius gave substantial
confirmation to this hope, and provides a plausible background for the
ideology of 3 Maccabees. The extremely negative portrayal of the king
which predominates in 3 Maccabees does not reflect Jewish attitudes

to all Roman rulers but to the exceptional case of Caligula. By portraying the king as the instigator and prime cause of the Jewish troubles, 3 Maccabees is in fact isolating and restricting the enmity between Jews and gentiles. Despite the inveterate hatred of some gentiles for the Jews (4:1), they are not held responsible for the persecution, and the Jews express no desire for vengeance on them, in marked contrast to the earlier story of Esther. The crisis is ascribed to the mad insolence of an individual ruler and can be resolved when he passes away or comes to his senses. This construction of the situation is not an accurate analysis of the crisis in Alexandria in 38–41 CE, but it is remarkably similar to that offered by Philo in his *Legatio ad Gaium*. There (in contrast to his *In Flaccum*), Philo attributes the disturbances to Caligula's self-deification. His religious demands lead to a confrontation with the Jews, and this provides an occasion for the hostility of the Alexandrians.[31] 3 Maccabees does not accuse Philopator of self-deification[32] but traces the disturbance to his hubris, nonetheless. Again, religious demands are at the heart of the confrontation and the Jews' enemies in Egypt are relegated to a secondary role. There is no reason to think that either the *Legatio* or 3 Maccabees was influenced by the other, but there is close similarity between their constructions. In each case, the focus on the individual monarch permits the full expression of outrage while restricting the hostility towards the gentiles and maintaining loyalty towards Rome.

Not all the hostility of 3 Maccabees is directed towards the monarch. The Jews who voluntarily abandon the law are singled out for contempt (2:33) and eventual vengeance (7:10–16). Where the Jews in the story of Esther slaughter their gentile enemies, in 3 Maccabees they kill more than three hundred apostates "with ignominy." There is no doubt that 3 Maccabees supports the strict observance of the Jewish law. No apology is made for the distinctive dietary observances even if they appear odious to some. If Greek citizenship is offered in return for the worship of pagan gods, the choice is clearcut. Those who accept are despised. The strict allegiance to the law is not based on any philosophical or strictly religious reasoning, but is rather a matter of ethnic solidarity as is also the case in Esther: "they despised those who separated themselves from them, accounting them as enemies of their people and excluding them from social intercourse and the rendering of any service" (3:33). Yet this fidelity to the law and to distinctive Jewish identity is not seen as being in conflict with loyalty to the pagan rulers, even though it was so represented by their enemies (3:3–7). On the contrary, the king agrees that "those who had transgressed the divine commandments for their belly's sake would never be well disposed to the king's estate either" (7:11–12). Consequently we cannot accept Tcherikover's view that 3 Maccabees opposed "the official representatives of Alexandrian Judaism" by rejecting the aspiration to Greek citizenship as an avenue to apostasy.[33] The official representatives may not have sought citizenship but parity for the Jewish *politeuma* with the *polis*. What is rejected is citizenship at the price of apostasy. The author contends throughout that full observance of Jewish law is not only compatible with loyal service to gentile rulers but, in the end, will win more respect than a compromising attitude. There is nothing to indicate that the position of 3 Maccabees was any different from that of Philo on this matter. We may recognize here the attitude which provoked Apion's frustration: "why then, if they are citizens, do they not worship the same gods as the Alexandrians?" (*Ag Ap* 2.65).

It is also apparent that 3 Maccabees finds no incompatibility between loyalty to a gentile ruler and its links with Jerusalem. In the time of Caligula, as in the time of Philopator, Egyptian and Palestinian Jews were subject to the same sovereign. The political scene was admittedly more complex in the Roman period since an Alexandrian Jew had potentially three claims on his loyalty—Rome, Jerusalem, and Alexandria itself. 3 Maccabees, like the other Jewish writings of the period, has no place for Alexandrian nationalism. In this sense, Tcherikover is right to suggest that 3 Maccabees is not deeply rooted in its Egyptian setting.[34] Loyalty to the sovereign is affirmed, but it is subordinated to the religious demands of the Jewish law. How far Jewish identity involves a link with Jerusalem is less clear. The prayer of Eleazar repeatedly refers to the present residence as a place of exile and says that the Jews are "strangers in a strange land" (6:3).[35] He does not, however, pray for an end to his exile but asks God to remember them "in the land of their enemies" (6:15). The emphasis on the situation of exile reflects the realization that it was indeed the land of their enemies or, as Claudius put it in his letter, "a city which is not their own," but does not express either a desire or an obligation to return to Jerusalem. Rather, what is needed is effective protection from the Ptolemy or emperor. Again, there is no doubt that the author holds the Jerusalem temple in high esteem. The threat to the temple is a threat to Judaism itself since it symbolizes the special bond between God and Israel. The horror of 3 Maccabees at the prospect of profanation is paralleled by Philo's reaction in the *Legatio ad Gaium*. The book does not, however, give any indication of the actual relations of Egyptian Jews to the temple. Inevitably, it could not play a great role in the practical religion of the Diaspora, despite the sending of offerings and the pilgrimages which were undoubtedly common, although they are not noted here.[36] The practical allegiance of the Jews of Alexandria was to the law, which regulated their daily lives. Jerusalem and its temple had a less immediate role which was largely symbolic. The deliverance of the temple does not save Egyptian Jewry and, important though it is, it is not the climax of the story.

Despite its greater emphasis on literal observance of the distinctive laws, the attitudes of 3 Maccabees are not very different from the so-called "apologetic" writings of Egyptian Judaism. The main differences are due to the crisis situation reflected in this book, but the manner in which the crisis is handled is designed to keep open a door to good relations with the gentile world. 3 Maccabees also lacks the philosophical interests of Philo or even Pseudo-Aristeas, but on the other hand it is not so crude in its conceptions as Artapanus. In its own genre it is well informed in Greek style and linguistic usage.[37] It is not so obvious that the author must have come from the "common people" as Tcherikover held. Not all educated Alexandrian Jews were necessarily inclined to philosophy. The most striking features of the book are ultimately the willingness to excuse "the Greeks" and the merciless vengeance on the Jews who betrayed the solidarity with their people. The latter point was undoubtedly more conspicuous in the crises of the Roman era than it had ever been before in Egyptian Judaism.

PHILO'S POLITICS

Much of our knowledge of Egyptian Judaism in the early Roman period comes from Philo of Alexandria. Philo's view of Judaism lies outside the scope of the present study, but we must briefly consider the light he throws on the political/ethnic understanding of Judaism in the Hellenistic Diaspora. There is no doubt that his own approach to

Judaism was primarily philosophical and mystical. Political considerations have a subordinate place. Yet, they too are important and may
be significant indicators of the common opinions of Alexandrian Jews
who were less rarified in their philosophy.

Philo's interest in political affairs is evident from his participation in
the embassy to Caligula.[38] Moreover, his brother, Alexander, and his
nephew, Tiberius Julius Alexander, played leading roles in the political life of Alexandria.[39] His political interests were not unrelated to his
philosophy. In the famous passage in *De Migratione Abrahami* 89-90
where he addresses the relation between allegorical and literal meaning, he criticizes those who overlook "all that the mass of men regard," and concern themselves only with allegorical meaning "as if
they were disembodied souls." Instead, he insists that "we should
look on all these outward observances as resembling the body, and
their inner meaning as resembling the soul. It follows that, exactly as
we have to take thought for the body, because it is the abode of the
soul, so we must pay heed to the letter of the laws. If we keep and
observe these, we shall gain a clearer conception of those things of
which these are the symbols; and besides that we shall not incur the
censure of the many and the charges they are sure to bring against us"
(*De Migr Abr* 93). The "letter of the laws" includes the distinctive
Jewish rituals, but also the sanctity of the temple (which is mentioned
explicitly in 92) and the eschatological promises of the scriptures.
Philo's respect for the letter of the law is obviously not a result of his
philosophy as such. Philo was an apologist for Judaism more profoundly than he was a philosopher. The entire structure of his writings
is designed as an explanation of the Jewish scriptures, not as an independent philosophical quest. His loyalty to the letter of the law is
partly due to an instinctive respect for tradition, partly to an appreciation of the need for concrete symbols on the part of the mass of humanity. It is, however, integrated into his philosophy as part of a sacramental thought structure whereby spiritual truths are mediated by
visible entities and practices.

Philo's application of his philosophical principles to the political
realm is clearly evident in the *Legatio ad Gaium*. The survival of
Judaism through the crises in Alexandria and Jerusalem is taken as
proof of God's providential care for all mankind, but especially for
"the race of suppliants" which is his particular concern. Israel is,
symbolically, the race of those "who see God." Its fate then symbol-

izes, and illustrates for the mass of humanity, God's care for those who lead spiritual lives. Philo's indignation at the attacks on the Jewish people and on its temple is no less than that of 3 Maccabees, but the motivation is quite different. For 3 Maccabees, as for the great majority of Jewish writers, the survival of the people and the glory of its temple are in themselves adequate goals of providential design. For Philo they are symbols of a deeper spiritual concern which is the real focus of attention.

The main question, then, which arises in connection with Philo's politics, is how far his symbolism requires an exclusive exaltation of Judaism and its actual triumph over the gentiles. The majority of scholars have tended to discount his interest in practical nationalism. While there is no doubt that he was concerned to ensure the survival of Judaism and its visible symbols, he did not necessarily share the aspirations to dominion, or even political independence, typical of Palestinian Judaism of the time. On the other hand, both Goodenough and Wolfson, the most influential students of Philo in this century, have argued, from different perspectives, that he fully shared the nationalistic hopes of Judaism, whatever significance he may have attached to them.[40]

Goodenough's interpretation of Philo's politics is based on his interpretation of the portrayal of Joseph in *De Somniis*, which he reads as a veiled attack on Roman rule. Since Philo presents a positive assessment of Joseph in the *De Iosepho*, the negative critique in *De Somniis* is not simply the product of exegesis. It is indeed likely that Philo's portrayal is motivated by the excesses of Roman rule. In the *Legatio ad Gaium* and *In Flaccum* he is outspoken in condemning the "measureless excesses" of Rome's "lawless iniquities." Goodenough, however, claims more: that Philo passionately hated Roman rule as such and hoped for a militant messiah who would put an end to it. The key passage is *De Somniis*, 2.63–64:

> And therefore the Holy Word did well in giving the name of Addition to one who was the enemy of simplicity and the friend of vanity. For just as we find on trees, to the great damage of the genuine growth, superfluities which the husbandmen purge and cut away to provide for their necessities, so the true and simple life has for its parasite the life of falsity and vanity, for which no husbandman has hitherto been found to excise the mischievous growth root and all.

If this is an expression of messianic hope, it is indeed an indirect one, but Goodenough finds a clue to the indirectness of Philo's allegory in *De Somniis*, 2.91–92:

> Do not we too, when we are spending time in the market-place, make a practice of standing out of the path of our rulers, and also of beasts of carriage, though our motive in the two cases is entirely different? With the rulers it is done to show them honor, with the animals from fear and to save us from suffering serious injury from them. And if ever occasions permit it is good to subdue the violence of enemies by attack, but if they do not permit, the safe course is to keep quiet, and if we wish to gain any help from them the fitting course is to soften and tame them.

Goodenough concludes that Philo "was no fanatic, and knew that so long as the Messiah had not yet come one must get on with the Romans in the most conciliating spirit possible. So Philo kept his messianism to himself. But one could secretly think, hope, and hate. And Philo seems to me to be assuring his Jewish friends that he was passionately doing all three."[41]

Despite Philo's animated opposition to Roman oppression, the evidence does not indicate that he was opposed to Roman rule as such, or imbued with any hatred of Rome. Even in his most polemical treatises, the *Legatio* and *In Flaccum*, Philo contrasts the abuses of power with the excellent administration of the past. Augustus is described as a virtual savior of the human race (*Leg* 143–47) and the beginning of Caligula's reign as an "age of Cronos" (*Leg* 13). Admittedly the quotation from *De Somniis*, 2.91–92 may make any positive statements suspect as an attempt to "soften and tame" the Romans, but the fact that these praises are found in works which are so outspoken in criticism of Roman rulers tells against such a view. In a manner somewhat similar to 3 Maccabees, Philo seeks to contain the criticism of Roman rule by presenting the abuses as aberrations due to particular individuals.

The reference in *De Somniis*, 2.64 to a husbandman who will destroy the corruption "root and all" has often been taken as a reference to the messiah.[42] The passage is brief and ambiguous. Philo says only that "no husbandman has hitherto been found." We may infer that he expects one, but he does not actually say so. Such a "husbandman" could be a messianic figure who would put an end to Roman rule, or he might be a reformer who would put an end to corruption. In view of the unclarity of this passage we must turn to the treatise. *De Praemiis et Poenis* where Philo addresses the subject of the future in far greater detail.

In *De Praemiis et Poenis*, 79–172 Philo presents an elaborate eschatological tableau which reaches its climax in 165–72. The eschatological blessings will include the reunion of the exiles, the prosperity of the land, the establishment of peace not only among men but also between men and beasts, and a sudden reversal of fortunes which will bring about the ruin of the enemies of the Jews. Wolfson concluded from this passage that "the solution found by Philo for the Jewish problem of his time was the revival of the old prophetic promises of the ultimate disappearance of the Diaspora."[43] The "ideal polity" was to exist only in Palestine, because of the Deuteronomic insistence on a single temple.[44] While Philo envisaged the conversion of the gentiles,[45] the eschatological utopia is definitely Jewish. More clearly than in *De Somniis*, Philo here assigns a role to a messianic figure. "For 'there shall come forth a man' says the oracle, and leading his host to war he will subdue great and populous nations, because God has sent to his aid the reinforcement which befits the godly" (*Praem* 95).[46]

Wolfson's interpretation, which seeks to assimilate Philo to what he regards as "native Judaism,"[47] must be modified at several points. First, the dramatic reversal is contingent upon the repentance of the Jews, and their "conversion in a body to virtue," which will "strike awe into their masters, who will set them free, ashamed to rule over men better than themselves" (*Praem* 164). Philo is interested in the spiritual triumph of virtue rather than in the physical victory of a messianic king. Second, in most of the treatise Philo does not contrast Jews and gentiles but the virtuous and the wicked. So the messianic "man" does battle not with the gentiles but with "some fanatics whose lust for war defies restraint or remonstrance" (*Praem* 94). Third, the distinction between the virtuous and the wicked does not fall exactly along ethnic lines. In *Praem* 152 Philo contrasts the proselyte who "came over to the camp of God" with "the nobly born who has falsified the sterling of his high lineage." God "welcomes the virtue which springs from ignoble birth" and "takes no account of the roots but accepts the full-grown stem." Finally, the physical rewards and punishments are only symbols of the spiritual. The "wild beasts in the soul" must be tamed before those of the forest (*Praem* 88). Those who "possess stored up in heaven the true wealth whose adornment is wisdom and godliness have also wealth of earthly riches in abundance" (*Praem* 104). For Philo the "matter" of earthly kingdoms is "nothing," only "a shadow or a breath which flits past."[48] Its importance lies in its symbolic power to indicate another realm.[49]

In short, Philo's eschatological tableau is viewed from a very different perspective from the concrete nationalism of Wolfson's "native Judaism." Yet he does speak of a gathering in of the exiles and overthrow of the enemies of Judaism, and the virtuous, while not simply the Jews by birth, are at least the Jews by practice of the law. In view of Philo's insistence on the value of concrete entities and the letter of the law as a basis for symbolism, we may ask whether he did not, after all, expect a visible triumph of Judaism.

The political dimension in Philo's eschatology cannot be completely dismissed. He does in fact read the blessings and curses of Deuteronomy and Leviticus as predictions of a definitive eschatological upheaval, when they could have been taken in a less final sense. This fact at least indicates that he was familiar with political eschatology and assumed that some scriptural passages should be read that way. In his desire to be faithful to the letter of the law he did in fact maintain the belief in the eventual disappearance of the Diaspora.

Where Philo differs from the eschatology of many apocalyptic writers and from most of the sibylline books, is not so much in the actual concepts as in the degree of urgency. The paucity of references to national eschatology shows that it was not at the heart of his thought. Philo speaks of Jerusalem as the metropolis of the Jews but he admits that "they severally hold that land as their fatherland . . . in which they were born and reared" (*Flac* 46). Philo is eager to establish the rights of the Jews in the lands in which they are "settlers and friends, eagerly seeking equality of privilege with burgesses and already being near in status to citizens, differing but little from natives" (*De Vita Mosis* 1.35). Attainment of rights in Alexandria is far higher on Philo's agenda than return to Jerusalem. Again, the temple is of vital importance, and any threat to it is a threat to Judaism itself. There is some evidence that Philo may have made the pilgrimage to Jerusalem.[50] Yet the real significance of the temple is allegorical, in its symbolism of cosmic worship.[51] It is necessary that there be a temple as a visible sign, to convey the symbolism to the masses, but it is not necessary that Philo, or other spiritually minded Jews, live in proximity to it or go there frequently. The urgent needs of the religion lie elsewhere. Jerusalem and the homeland remain very much in the background of Philo's thought. They are essential to Jewish identity, but they do not normally interfere with the life of the Diaspora Jew in his own environment.

The Popular Attitudes in Egyptian Judaism

Political and national considerations are then a minor component in Philo's understanding of Judaism. The fact that he still finds some place for national eschatology indicates that messianic beliefs must have been widespread in his time, even in Egyptian Judaism.[52] In the case of Num 24:7, the oracle of Balaam used by Philo in *De Praemiis*, the messianic note had already been introduced by the LXX translators.[53] To say that messianic ideas were widespread is not, however, to suggest that they were held with intensity or that there was significant messianic agitation. While one of the messianic pretenders mentioned by Josephus was from Egypt,[54] we hear of no messianic movement in Egypt until the Diaspora revolt under Trajan.

A few incidents reflect the attitudes of the Egyptian Jews in the first century. One of the factors which led to the riots of 38 CE was the visit of King Agrippa to Alexandria. The Greeks reacted to this by holding a demonstration in mockery in which they dressed up a madman named Carabas and hailed him as *Marin*, "the name by which it is said that kings are called in Syria."[55] The point at issue was that Agrippa was a Jewish king. If the Alexandrian mockery is assumed to reflect the claims of the Jews, we might suspect that the king's visit had kindled a flame of Jewish messianism. In fact, there is no doubt that the Jews were proud that Agrippa was a Jewish king. They did not, however, look for him to overthrow the Romans or liberate the Jews but only to intercede with Gaius for the protection of Jewish rights.[56] The friction with the Greeks was not due to any desire to end the Diaspora, but to the determination to maintain Jewish identity even in exile.

The Events of 66–73 CE

The Jews of the Diaspora did not join in the revolt of 66–70, but there was trouble in Alexandria in 66 CE.[57] When the Greek population was holding a meeting concerning an embassy to Nero, some Jews mingled with them in the amphitheater. They were detected, and three of them were captured and burned alive. This outraged the Jewish population which proceeded to riot. The outbreak was brought to an end when Tiberius Alexander, Philo's nephew, who was governor of the city "let loose upon them the two Roman legions stationed in the city together with two thousand soldiers, who by chance had just arrived from Libya to complete the ruin of the Jews; permission was given them not merely to kill the rioters but to plunder their property and burn down their houses." The Jews "offered a prolonged resistance," but "wholesale carnage ensued" (*JW* 2.18.8 [494–95]). Josephus relates this incident to the earlier tensions between Jews and Greeks in the city. While the purpose of the embassy to Nero is not stated, it was presumably concerned with the status of the Jews in some way, whence the interest of the Jews in infiltrating the meeting. But while the incident may have begun as a conflict between Jews and Greeks, the primary agents of destruction were the Romans. Despite the fact that the governor himself was of Jewish stock, it was at this juncture that the Roman army was first "let loose" on the Jews of Alexandria. Josephus is at some pains to present Tiberius as reasonable and moderate. At first he "attempted to recall them to reason without recourse to arms," and at the end he was moved to compassion and ordered the Romans to retire. The Romans withdrew at once, but the Alexandrians were not so easily called off. Yet Josephus cannot hide the brutality with which the revolt was suppressed. It is possible that Tiberius protected some of the upper-class Jews such as the members of the *gerousia* since we find this body still in control of the Jewish community in the events of 73 CE.[58] The governor's handling of the situation may of course have been influenced by the contemporary events in Palestine, although there is nothing to indicate that the Egyptian Jews intended to revolt against Rome.

The severe blow dealt to the Jewish community in 66 CE was not fatal. When Titus visited Alexandria in 71 CE the Greeks requested that he disband the Jewish *politeuma* but he refused and reaffirmed Jewish rights.[59] The *gerousia,* or council of the elders, continued to function and played a decisive role in averting another outbreak in 73 CE. A group of Sicarii who had fled to Egypt "sought to induce many of their hosts to assert their independence, to look upon the Romans as no better than themselves and to esteem God alone as their lord."[60] They murdered some of the leading Jews who opposed them, but the *gerousia* prevailed on the Jewish population to hand them over to the

Romans. According to Josephus, six hundred were captured on the spot and others who had fled into Egypt were arrested and brought back. They were then tortured and executed.

From the episode of 73 CE we may infer that the more prominent members of the Jewish community were more loyal to the Romans than the lower classes. This is only to be expected, since they obviously had more to lose in a rebellion. Yet the Sicarii could not find enough popular support to withstand the *gerousia*. Perhaps chastened by the events of 66 and the outcome of the war in Judea, the Jewish community of Alexandria had no appetite for rebellion. Despite the collaboration of the Jewish leaders to an extreme and shameful degree on this occasion, the Romans were not impressed with their loyalty. Rather, "suspicious of the interminable tendency of the Jews to revolution" they proceeded to close up the temple at Leontopolis.[61] The Jews of the Diaspora were all liable for the *fiscus Judaicus*. The didrachmon or half-shekel previously paid to the temple of Jerusalem was now paid to Rome, initially to defray the expenses of rebuilding the temple of Jupiter Capitolinus. Since this tax was levied on both sexes, three years and over, including slaves, and was added to the various other taxes of Roman Egypt, it amounted to a considerable burden.[62]

The betrayal of the Sicarii in Alexandria is the first overt division in the Egyptian Jewish community for reasons of social class. A similar class conflict is reflected in an episode at Cyrene about the same time.[63] A weaver named Jonathan, who had taken refuge in the town "won the ear of not a few of the indigent class, and led them forth into the desert, promising them a display of signs and apparitions." Although Josephus refers to Jonathan and his followers as Sicarii, his conduct resembles rather that of the messianic prophets such as Theudas or the prophet from Egypt, who were not militant revolutionaries but visionaries hoping for miracles. His exodus to the desert escaped notice, but "the men of rank among the Jews of Cyrene" reported his activities to the governor, Catullus. Catullus overpowered the crowd, slaughtered many, and took Jonathan prisoner. Now, with a fine irony, Jonathan claimed he had received instructions from the wealthiest of the Jews. Catullus exploited the situation and had Jonathan accuse all the well-to-do Jews, three thousand in all, according to Josephus. He confiscated their property to the imperial exchequer and had them killed. The scheme came to an end when the

accusations were extended to prominent Jews in Rome and elsewhere, including Josephus. Vespasian then made an inquiry. Jonathan was tortured and burned alive but Catullus was only reprimanded.

The division between the Jewish upper and lower classes emerges
in the context of the revolt against Rome. The upper classes had too
much to lose and inevitably incurred the resentment of the revolutionaries. The episode in Cyrene especially shows the vulnerability of the
Jews. No matter how either Jonathan or the wealthy Jews cooperated
with the Romans, they were not safe. Since Vespasian was concerned
to consolidate his empire, the governor could act with virtual impu-
nity. As a result, both the upper class and the revolutionary element
were wiped out. The latter was the more easily replaced. The removal
of the Jewish upper class in Cyrene may have contributed eventually
to the spread of the revolt under Trajan, since there was now no
restraining element within the Jewish community.

THE BACKGROUND OF THE GREAT REVOLT

We have little direct evidence of the relations between Jews,
Greeks, and Romans between 73 and 115 CE. The Acta Hermaisci, in
the Acts of the Alexandrian Martyrs, tells of a confrontation between
Greek and Jewish embassies before Trajan.[64] In accordance with the
genre of the Alexandrian acts, the emperor is represented as heavily
biased in favor of the Jews. The account is highly fictional, but may be
taken to indicate the persistence of the old conflicts between Greeks
and Jews. This traditional animosity is hardly sufficient to account for
the revolt which spread through the Diaspora in 115–17 CE.

This crucial chapter in the history of the Jewish Diaspora is very
poorly documented.[65] Even the sequence of events is not entirely
clear. There was an outbreak of fighting in Alexandria in 115 CE which
is known from a papyrus containing what appears to be an edict of the
governor of Egypt.[66] The papyrus says that a judge came from Rome to
investigate this incident, and the governor warns the Jews not to dis-
turb the peace. It would seem that this incident followed the traditional pattern of friction between Jews and Greeks in Alexandria. It
also appears, however, that this incident was isolated and was not the
spark of the wider revolt, which broke out in Cyrene and Cyprus. The
main conflict in Egypt developed when the rebels from Cyrene invaded the Egyptian countryside. The Alexandrian Jews were then
drawn into the conflict when the Greeks who had fled from the

countryside attacked them, and a particularly destructive struggle ensued. According to some medieval sources, the Jews of Cyrene eventually penetrated Judea and were crushed by Lusius Quietus, but this stage of the revolt is extremely obscure.[67] There was some fighting in Palestine, known as the "War of Quietus" in Jewish tradition.[68]

The revolt was especially destructive, and the wrath of the Jews was directed against pagan temples in particular. Casualties of the violence included the Ptolemaic Sarapeum and the largest Jewish synagogue in Alexandria. The terror inspired by the revolt is aptly expressed in the prayer of a Greek mother for her son "that they may not roast you."[69] In the end, the Jewish population was decimated, and some of those who survived lost their property. The Jews were no longer allowed to live in Alexandria but were given a settlement just outside it, although even this drew objections from the Greeks.[70] It appears from the Acts of the Alexandrian Martyrs that Jewish and Greek deputations appeared before Hadrian after the end of the revolt and traded charges about the whole series of disturbances, but the Acts, as always, are unreliable in their details.[71]

The surviving accounts of the revolt give no rational explanation of why it started. The Jews rose "as if mad" according to Orosius or "as if in the grip of some terrible spirit of rebellion" (Eusebius). Modern authors have often suggested that the revolt had no more specific cause than the intensity of messianic expectation.[72] The emergence of a "king," whose name is variously given as Lukuas (Eusebius) or Andreas (Dio)[73] lends some support to such an idea. The revolt had evidently a strong religious dimension as can be seen from the destruction of the pagan temples. We have seen above that messianic ideas were current in the time of Philo. Yet there was little support for messianic or nationalistic movements before 115, as can be seen from the treatment of the Sicarii in Alexandria and Cyrene. A number of factors may have inclined the Diaspora Jews more strongly towards messianism in the period after 70 than had previously been the case. One was the *fiscus Judaicus* which not only branded all Jews as seditious people but also imposed a considerable financial burden. Applebaum considers "agrarian factors," including excessive taxation, as a factor in the revolt.[74] The acknowledged abuses of the tax, especially under Domitian,[75] could not fail to arouse resentment against Rome. The destruction of the temple was itself an event of great symbolic significance. There was an influx of Jewish prisoners to Egypt, for compulsory work or for sale as slaves.[76] These people had ample reason for anti-Roman feeling. The role of the Roman legion in the Alexandrian disturbances of 66 was surely remembered. Tcherikover cites the "steady increase in the use of Hebrew names from the Ptolemaic to the Roman period" as evidence for "the gradual increase of national spirit among the Egyptian Jews."[77] The involvement of Trajan in a Parthian war, and the transfer of some forces from Egypt to the east, provided an occasion for revolt against Rome.[78]

The increase in messianic fervor went hand in hand with the deterioration of Jewish life in Egypt, because of taxation among other things, and with the influx of prisoners and refugees from Judea. Only now do we find a real attempt to abandon the Diaspora and return to the land of Israel. The progress of Lukuas and his followers through Egypt, and if the late reports are correct, into Judea, has eschatological overtones of the return of the exiles. The far-reaching destruction is indicative of the abandonment of the Diaspora. It is significant that the Jews of Alexandria were drawn into the revolt late and even then were not firm allies of the rebels. Eusebius says that the rebels "lost the alliance" of the Alexandrian Jews.[79] The spirit which motivated the revolt was very different from that of the Jews who had struggled for status in the mid-first century CE, and drew its vigor from a different social class.

THE FIFTH SIBYL

We have only one document which may reflect the attitudes of Egyptian Judaism in the period leading up to the revolt. The Fifth Sibylline Oracle is made up of six oracles or collections of oracles.[80] The first, vss. 1–51, reviews history from Alexander to Hadrian (or, if vs. 51 be original, Marcus Aurelius) and constitutes an introduction to the book. The next four oracles, vss. 52–110, 111–78, 179–285, and 286–434 show a common pattern of (a) oracles against various nations, (b) the return of Nero as an eschatological adversary, (c) the advent of a savior figure, and (d) destruction (usually by fire). Vss. 435–530 constitute a concluding oracle which is largely concerned with Egypt and which concludes with an elaborate battle of the stars (512–31). Only one passage, 256–59, reflects Christian redaction, and even there it is probable that an original Jewish passage has only been modified by an allusion to the crucifixion.

It is unlikely that all of Sib Or 5 was composed at the same time.

The prominence of the Nero legend requires a date no earlier than 70 CE but more probably later than 80. At the other extreme, the favorable reference to Hadrian in vss. 46–50 must have been written before the revolt of 132 CE. The bitterness of complaint about the destruction of the temple, especially in vss. 398–413, suggests that at least the central oracles were not too far removed in time from that event. It seems likely that the greater part of Sib Or 5 comes from the period between 70 and 115 CE, although the introduction, and possibly the conclusion, is later. It is significant that the sibyl speaks more than once of the destruction or dereliction of pagan temples (52–59, 484–91).[81] Destruction of temples was a noteworthy feature of the revolt. The allusion to the overthrow of Sarapis in the concluding oracle (vs. 487) may reflect the destruction of the Ptolemaic Sarapeum.

The attitude of Sib Or 5 to the gentile nations is far more negative than anything in the earlier sibylline tradition. Only in the introductory oracle does the sibyl find something positive to say about any gentile ruler. Two of the four central oracles (52–110 and 179–285) are dominated by prophecies of the destruction of Egypt. Not only does the sibyl repeat the familiar denunciations of Egyptian idolatry and theriolatry (Sib Or 5:77–85; cf. Sib Or 3:30–33; Wis 13–15), but she also denounces Egypt "because you have raged against my children . . . and incited evil against good men" (67–68). Undoubtedly, the Alexandrians, who were the most immediate adversaries of the Jews, are included in the Egyptians here. The most bitter words of the sibyl however are directed against Rome. Like Babylon in the OT (which is invoked in Sib Or 5 as a type of Rome),[82] Rome had said, "I alone am and no one will ravage me."[83] This blasphemous pretension to divinity is typified by Nero and is the ultimate sin in the biblical tradition. In more specific terms, Rome is denounced for immorality (166), a charge familiar from the earliest strata of the sibylline oracles. More significantly, it was Rome which destroyed Jerusalem (160–61) and was thereby established as the new Babylon.

Rome is raised to a mythological level in the sibyl's use of Nero as an eschatological adversary.[84] Drawing on the popular legend that Nero had not died but had fled to Parthia and would one day return, the sibyl presents him both as king of Rome (vs. 139) and as leading an attack on Rome in the eschatological period (vs. 367). He is not yet identified with Belial, as he is in Sib Or 3:63–74 and Asc Isa 4:1, or said to return from the dead as in Revelation,[85] but he still approximates to the scale of an Antichrist figure. His evil character corresponds directly to that of Rome: he is morally evil, responsible for the destruction of Jerusalem (since the Jewish war began in his reign), and he claims to be god (34, 139–40).

The hostility of the sibyl to Rome does not entail any endorsement of Rome's enemies. Unlike the earlier pro-Cleopatran sibyl in Sib Or 3:350–80 which had enthusiastically looked for the subjection of Rome to Asia, Sib Or 5 has no positive counterpart to Rome. Prophecies of destruction against Asia alternate with those against Egypt (111–36, 286–327). The main enemies of Rome in this period, the Parthians, are closely linked with Nero. In fact, Nero would seem to be "the Persian" or "the one who obtained the land of the Persians" (93, 101; in vs. 147 he is said to have gone to the Persians), and Nero is the only human or quasi-human who is said to prevail over Rome (367). Both Rome and the Parthians are seen as near-diabolical powers in Sib Or 5, irrespective of their mutual relations.[86] The general xenophobia of the sibyl is perhaps best illustrated in its strange allusions to the "Ethiopians." In 206–13 the Indians and Ethiopians are warned of a coming conflagration. Since only the land of the Ethiopians is said to be destroyed, the Indians and the Ethiopians appear to be identified here, a confusion that is also attested elsewhere in ancient geographers.[87] Then in the concluding oracle, the final conflagration is precipitated by the Ethiopians who "leave the shameless tribes of the Triballi," launch on a course of wickedness and destroy the (mysterious) temple which will have been erected to the true God in the land of Egypt. Then God will rain on them a terrible wrath. This passage makes even less geographical sense than 206–13. The Triballi were a tribe in Thrace. Sib Or 5 may be influenced by Sib Or 3:319–20 where Gog and Magog are located between the Ethiopian rivers, so that the Ethiopians now become a general and vaguely conceived eschatological adversary. What is noteworthy is the willingness of the sibyl to regard a remote nation, whose location was not even known clearly, in such a hostile way.

The bitterness of the sibyl against Rome does not displace the enmity towards Egypt. Two of the four central oracles are devoted to Egypt, and the sibyl complains of Egyptian hostility to the Jews. Again, the final oracle prophesies the overthrow of Isis and Sarapis. Yet, the final oracle also holds out the prospect of the conversion of Egypt to the one true god, even though this is brought to nought by the invasion of the Ethiopians. No such prospect is ever held out for Rome. Rome clearly supersedes Egypt and the Egyptian Greeks as the primary enemy of the Jews.

The hatred for Rome that pervades Sib Or 5 is of interest as background to the Diaspora revolt. As we have seen above, the disturbances in the Diaspora in the first century CE appear to have been local conflicts with the Greeks, and the involvement of the Alexandrian Jews in the revolt under Trajan seems to have been initially a defensive reaction to the attack of the Greeks. Yet in Sib Or 5 hostility towards Rome seems more deeply rooted than the traditional ethnic conflict with the Greeks.

The final oracle of the book is especially intriguing in this regard. The allusions to the overthrow of Isis and Sarapis in 484–88 provide the clearest echoes of the revolt. Yet, they are followed by the fantasy of a temple to the true God in the land of Egypt. While this is definitely a fantasy, it had a precedent in the temple of Leontopolis. If, as we have suggested, the Egyptian sibyllina originated in the circles of the Oniads and their descendants, the dream of a Jewish temple in Egype is more understandable. Yet the sibyl anticipates the destruction of this fantasized temple too. The temple of Leontopolis had been closed by the Romans in 73 CE, and we may suspect here the basis for the sibyl's pessimism on the fate of the future temple. The "Ethiopians" take the place of the Romans in the eschatological tableau and may conceivably, because of their association with Gog and Magog, be no more than a symbolic name for Rome. The final battle of the stars vividly expresses the desolation brought about by the failure of the revolt, a desolation which was ultimately the work of Rome.

Sib Or 5 is exceptional in placing the major share of blame on Rome rather than on Egypt. It is difficult to judge how far it was typical of the Jews who joined in the revolt. On the one hand, hostility towards Rome was a characteristic of the sibylline tradition,[88] and it may be that those Jews who had benefited most from Ptolemaic patronage, such as the soldiers of the land of Onias, were always more resentful towards Rome than their compatriots in Egypt. On the other hand, it may be that hatred for Rome was a greater factor in the revolt than the fragmentary sources indicate. Finally, it is possible that all the oracles of Sib Or 5 were written during or after the actual revolt, when the conflict had developed into a war against Rome, although this seems unlikely in view of the prominence of the temple and the Nero legend. In any case, it is striking that Sib Or 5, the only document which reflects even in part the attitudes behind the revolt, holds out a modified hope for the conversion of Egypt and directs its wrath primarily against Rome.

While the earlier sibyls had hoped for the overthrow of Rome through the agency of a Ptolemy or Cleopatra, Sib Or 5 looks for an intervention of God himself (vs. 174) or, more typically, of a "king sent from God" (108) or a "man from heaven" (414).[89] The reference in vs. 108 could apply to a human, earthly king, as was envisaged in Sib Or 3, but could also be a heavenly figure. Vs. 414 clearly refers to a heavenly figure. The other allusions to a savior figure also suggest a heavenly origin. In 256, where the issue is confused by the Christian interpolation in vs. 257, he is said to come "from the sky." In 158–59 "a great star" comes from heaven and burns the sea and Babylon (i.e., Rome). Stars were frequently associated with savior figures in the Hellenistic world.[90] Messsianic figures in Judaism could be designated as stars by application of the oracle of Balaam. The name given to the leader of the revolt of 132 CE, Bar Kochba, son of the star, is significant in this regard. Since stars were frequently identified with angels in the Jewish tradition, Sib Or 5:158–59 must be seen in the context of such heavenly saviors as the archangel Michael in the book of Daniel and 1QM, Melchizedek in 11QMelchizedek, and the "son of man" figure in Daniel and the Similitudes of Enoch.[91] The man from heaven in vs. 414 has traditionally been associated with the "son of man" figure.[92] The parallel with Bar Kochba should warn us, however, against a sharp dichotomy between heavenly and earthly savior figures. Already in the Similitudes of Enoch the heavenly "son of man" figure is identified as the messiah,[93] and 4 Ezra, which was roughly contemporaneous with Sib Or 5, speaks of a "man from the sea" who comes on the clouds, as well as of a messiah who is subject to death.[94] The traditional conceptions of an earthly messiah and a heavenly savior appear to have been confused by the late first century CE.[95] The savior figure of Sib Or 5 is then quite compatible with the messianic expectations of the Jewish revolt, although the oracles do not indicate a specific figure like Lukuas.[96]

The role of the savior figure in the first two references (Sib Or 5:108 and 156) is purely destructive. In the other cases, however, he is associated with a restoration of Jerusalem. The restoration of the temple is explicit in vs. 422 and is implied in 268 by the offering of sacrifices. In both cases, Jerusalem is enlarged by a wall, which in 252 extends as far as Joppa and reaches to the clouds (251, 425).[97] Not only will the restored Judea enjoy peace. It will be freed from "the unclean foot of the Greeks" (264) and sexual immorality (430). More clearly than in any previous document of the Egyptian Diaspora, the exaltation of Jerusalem is accompanied by the destruction of other nations. In 414–19 the man from heaven "destroyed every city from its foundations with much fire, and burned nations of mortals who were formerly evildoers." In 264–85 all the earth will be desolate, unsown and unploughed, except for the "holy land of the pious" which will flow with milk and honey. This passage allows for an eventual reprieve, if men "pay attention to the immortal eternal God" and desist from idol worship. Both passages, however, would seem to presuppose the end of the Diaspora and abandon the hope for Jewish prosperity under gentile powers. Judaism is here identified more closely with the ancestral land than in any of the earlier Diaspora documents. Yet this conception is modified in the concluding oracle, which envisages a temple to the true God in the land of Egypt. When this fails there is no restoration of Judea but a cosmic conflict, resulting in a conflagration of the earth and a starless sky. It is possible that the concluding oracle comes from a different hand than the rest of the book and probable that it reflects the desolation after the revolt had failed. In the end, it allows no more hope for the diaspora than the other oracles, but it sees none for Judea either. Sib Or 5 is not fully consistent in its expectations. It reflects two attitudes, both of which had probably some currency at the beginning of the second century: the hope for salvation in Judea, and the sense that if the Diaspora failed, all failed. It is remarkable that Sib Or 5 never entertains the hope for salvation beyond death which was commonplace in the apocalyptic literature of the day.[98]

The introduction to Sib Or 5 (vss. 1–51), which consists of a list of emperors, does not share the animation of the rest of the book. While vs. 51 continues the list down to Marcus Aurelius, this verse is probably an addition, since the sibyl does not comment on any emperor after Hadrian, and the favorable remarks on him could scarcely have been written after the Jewish revolt of 132. It would seem then that this introduction was written within a decade or so after the Diaspora revolt. Yet it lacks the seething hatred of Rome characteristic of Sib Or 5 and is rather in the tradition of Sib Or 11, which in part it summarizes. While the sibyl here is scathing in the portrayal of Nero ("a terrible snake"), the odium is not extended to Rome as such. The attitude is that of a Roman provincial. Some emperors may be criticized but others are praised. So Vespasian is "a destroyer of pious men" but there is no reference to Trajan's suppression of the revolt. Hadrian, who was evidently the current emperor, is "a most excellent man." It is somewhat paradoxical that such a benign preface should introduce the vehemently anti-Roman Sib Or 5. We should probably understand its role as a modification of the attack on Rome, though not a complete disavowal. As was the case in Philo and 3 Maccabees, the message is that Rome itself is not the problem, but only certain evil emperors. The Jews after the revolt had learned again the art of accommodation, since for better or worse their destiny lay within the Roman empire.

THE LATER SIBYLLINES

Both the vehement anti-Roman rhetoric of Sib Or 5 and the more submissive stance of the introduction are echoed in the later sibylline tradition. Sib Or 8 preserves an extensive Jewish oracle in vss. 1–216, although the remainder of the book is clearly Christian. The Jewish oracle can be dated with some precision to the reign of Marcus Aurelius, about 175 CE, since the return of Nero is expected in his reign (8:65–74). Its provenance is uncertain, but an extraneous oracle in vss. 131–38 is obviously from Egypt.[99] In view of their general familiarity with the sibylline tradition, the Jewish parts of Sib Or 8 are quite probably from Egypt too. The vehemence of their anti-Roman invective surpasses even Sib Or 5. It focuses on social injustices rather than any specific acts against the Jews, and may be an accumulation of anti-Roman oracles over a period of time.

The last three books of the sibylline collection are essentially lists of emperors in continuity with Sib Or 11 and 5:1–51.[100] The first eleven verses of Sib Or 12 correspond exactly to Sib Or 5:1–11. Books 12–14 are continuous with each other, although the ends and beginnings of the books are punctuated by prayers of the sibyl and introductory formulae. It would appear that the material was constantly updated and the eschatological conclusion of book 14 was retained as the end of the entire sequence. The locus of the tradition was Alexandria. The latest identifiable event in Sib Or 14 is the Arab conquest of Egypt in the seventh century.[101] Sib Or 12 is the most significant part of this material. Its interest lies chiefly in its collection of opinions and traditions about emperors down to the mid-third century. Some emperors, Caligula, Nero, Nerva, Commodus, Septimius Severus, are negatively presented, but the general tone is positive. Augustus, Domitian, Hadrian, and Marcus Aurelius are praised. Vespasian is "noble" and "excellent" despite his suppression of the Jewish revolt. Trajan's suppression of the Diaspora revolt is passed over in a single verse. The passage on Hadrian makes no reference to a revolt, although it is based on a hostile passage in Sib Or 8:52–59. In all, Geffcken's opinion that the sibyllist placed his loyalty to Rome above his Judaism seems well founded.

CONCLUSION

Looking back over the four hundred odd years from the early Ptolemaic period to the Diaspora Revolt, we may say that the dominant tendency of Diaspora Jewry was to live as loyal subjects of their gentile masters and participate in the culture and society as fully as possible within the constraints of their religious tradition. In the early period, we found some cases, such as Artapanus and the tale of the Tobiads, where the main element of Jewish identity was ethnic and national pride, but even there loyalty to the gentile rulers was not in doubt. In the early sibylline oracles there is an apparent hope for the restoration of Jerusalem and the Jewish homeland through the agency of the Ptolemies. In Sib Or 5 there is, finally, a sharp rejection of all gentile power, and here we might legitimately speak of a nationalistic hope centered on the land of Israel. There is little evidence for such hope in Egyptian Judaism before 70 CE. Even in Sib Or 5, in its final form, the rejection of the gentiles is muted in the introduction and the hope for the land of Israel is abandoned in the final oracle of destruction.

The early sibyllines reflect the most energetic attempt of the Jews to participate actively in Egyptian politics. We know that Onias IV and his sons were indeed activists in this way. Their hopes for the glory of Judaism were evidently centered on the Ptolemaic line. Such hopes, however, died with Cleopatra. Even in the second century BCE not all Jews shared this active approach to politics. The Letter of Aristeas carefully avoided political alignment and suggested that Judaism was essentially a religious philosophy. 2 Maccabees, despite its revolutionary subject matter, presented Judaism as devotion to the law and was at pains to suggest that there was no necessary hostility between gentiles and pious Jews. In the Roman period, Philo evidently regarded Judaism as primarily a religious philosophy. Even 3 Maccabees, which is scarcely a philosophical document, locates Jewish identity in observance of the law rather than in political allegiance. In short, the great bulk of the literature of Egyptian Judaism disregarded political allegiance as a factor in Jewish identity. By presenting Judaism as a religious philosophy or as the piety of Torah observance, the Hellenistic Jews left themselves free to be loyal subjects of the state in which they lived.

Despite the persistent concern with matters of political allegiance and civil status, the dominant locus of Jewish identity was in the area of ethics and piety. Even the politically oriented sibylline oracles still present a code of behavior which is distinctively Jewish. In Part Two below we will consider several works which pay no attention to political matters but present Judaism as an ethical or religious system in which political identity plays virtually no part.

Notes

1. On the relations between Jews and Romans, see, in general, J. Juster, *Les Juifs dans l'empire Romain* (2 vols.; Paris: Geuthner, 1914); Smallwood, *The Jews under Roman Rule* (SJLA 20; Leiden: Brill, 1976).

2. H. I. Bell, *Juden und Griechen im Römischen Alexandreia* (Leipzig: Hinrichs, 1926) 9; V. Tcherikover and A. Fuks (eds.), *Corpus Papyrorum Iudaicarum* (Cambridge, Mass.: Harvard, 1957) 1:55 (hereafter *CPJ*).

3. Smallwood, *The Jews*, 224–30. See also A. Kasher, *The Jews in Hellenistic and Roman Egypt* (Tel Aviv: Tel Aviv University, 1978, in Hebrew).

4. Tcherikover, *CPJ* 1:56 n. 20. In the *Antiquities* Josephus refers explicitly to Julius Caesar but in *Ag Ap* he refers ambiguously to Caesar the Great.

5. Smallwood (*The Jews*, 227): "It is beyond dispute that some individual Jews in Alexandria obtained Greek citizenship." She mentions two specific cases: Philo's brother Alexander, who was alabarch (customs official) in the thirties, and another Jew Demetrius, who held the same position under Claudius. See *Ant* 18.6.3 (159); 20.5.2 (100); 20.7.3 (147).

6. Smallwood, *The Jews*, 229–30; Tcherikover, *CPJ* 1:62–63; Kasher, *The Jews*, XI-XII.

7. Smallwood, *The Jews*, 231–32; Tcherikover, *CPJ* 1:60–62.

8. The view that the Jews tried to obtain Alexandrian citizenship by infiltrating the gymnasium has been vigorously disputed by A. Kasher, "The Jewish Attitude to the Alexandrian Gymnasium in the First Century A. D.," *The American Journal of Ancient History* 1 (1976) 148–61; and *The Jews*, chap. 9. Yet both the letter of Claudius (*CPJ* 2:36–55) and the Boule Papyrus (ibid., 25–29) indicate that infiltration of the ranks of citizens was a problem in Alexandria, and, as we have seen, at least some individual Jews became citizens. Kasher argues that the issue was equal polity between two distinct bodies, the *polis* and the Jewish *politeuma*.

9. Smallwood, *The Jews*, 233–35.

10. See H. Box, *Philonis Alexandrini In Flaccum* (Oxford: Oxford University, 1939); E. M. Smallwood, *Philonis Alexandrini Legatio ad Gaium* (2d ed.; Leiden: Brill, 1970); Smallwood, *The Jews*, 235–50; Tcherikover, *CPJ* 1:65–74.

11. Philo, *In Flaccum*, 53–54. See Smallwood, *Legatio*, 20–21.

12. The famous letter of Claudius, together with other related papyri can be found in *CPJ* 2:25–43. See Tcherikover's introductory comments in *CPJ* 1:69–74 and Smallwood, *Legatio*, 6–7, where extensive bibliography can be found. See also the edict of Claudius in Josephus, *Ant* 19.5.2–3 (280–91) and the comments of A. Kasher, "Les Circonstances de la Promulgation de l'Edit de l'Empereur Claude et de sa Lettre aux Alexandrins (41 ap. J.C.)" *Semitica* 26 (1976) 99–108.

13. The fate of Isidorus and Lampo is described in the imaginative "Acts of the Alexandrian Martyrs." The relevant texts can be found in *CPJ* 2:55–81 and Tcherikover's comments in *CPJ* 1:72. See also H. Musurillo, *The Acts of the Pagan Martyrs* (Oxford: Clarendon, 1954) and Smallwood, *The Jews*, 250–55. The Agrippa in question was Agrippa I and the trial should be dated about 41 CE. The downfall of Isidorus and his companions was due to their role in the deaths of some friends of Claudius under Caligula.

14. C. W. Emmet, "The Third Book of Maccabees," *APOT* 1:156; M. Hadas, *The Third and Fourth Books of Maccabees* (Dropsie College Edition; New York: Harper, 1953) 11–12; V. A. Tcherikover, "The Third Book of Maccabees as a Historical Source," *Scripta Hierosolymitana* 7 (1961) 5–6.

15. Hadas, *The Third and Fourth Books*, 6–7.

16. Ibid., 7–8; Moore, *The Additions*, 195–99. The direction of the influence is disputed, but in view of the independent evidence for dating both works, the priority of Greek Esther must be assumed. It is significant that the parallels are not confined to the Greek additions to Esther, as we might expect if 3 Maccabees were prior.

17. M. Hadas, "III Maccabees and the Tradition of the Patriotic Romance," *Chronique d'Egypte* 47 (1949) 97–104.

18. Tcherikover, "The Third Book," 2–5. On Philopator's promotion of the cult of Dionysus see the discussion of Artapanus in chap. 1 above.

19. A. Kasher, "Anti-Jewish Persecutions in Alexandria in the Reign of Ptolemy Philopator according to III Maccabees," in *Studies in the History of the Jewish People and the Land of Israel* (vol. 4; ed. U. Rappaport; Haifa: Haifa University, 1978, Heb. with English summary) 59–76.

20. Since Josephus says that Physcon's concubine, who interceded for the Jews, was variously called Ithaca or Irene, it would seem that he knew more than one version of the story.

21. See Fraser, *Ptolemaic Alexandria* (Oxford: Clarendon, 1972) 1:119–23.

22. Tcherikover, "The Third Book," 6–9; Hadas, *The Third and Fourth Books*, 11.

23. Emmet ("The Third Book of Maccabees," 158) argues for a date at the end of the second century BCE because of general similarities with 2 Maccabees and Pseudo-Aristeas. B. Motzo ("Il Rifacimento Greco di Ester e il III Mac.," *Saggi di Storia e Letteratura Giudeo-Ellenistica* [Firenze: Le Monnier, 1924] 272–90) argued that it must antedate Greek Esther, and this argument was accepted by G. W. Nickelsburg, *Resurrection, Immortality and Eternal Life in Intertestamental Judaism* (HTS 26; Cambridge: Harvard, 1972) 90–91. Despite these positions, the arguments of Bickermann and Tcherikover noted below seem decisive.

24. E. Bickermann, "Makkabäerbücher (III)," *PWRE* 27 (1928) 797–800.

25. Tcherikover, "The Third Book," 11–18; Hadas, *The Third and Fourth Books*, 19–21.

26. A setting under Caligula was proposed by H. Ewald, *The History of Israel* (London: Longmans, Green & Co., 1880) 5:468–73. So also H. Willrich, "Der historische Kern des III. Makkabäerbuches," *Hermes* 39 (1904) 244–58.

27. Emmet, "The Third Book of Maccabees," 158.

28. Smallwood's translation of the *Legatio* is seriously misleading as it often introduces the word *Greeks* where Philo does not supply the subject.

29. Tcherikover, "The Third Book," 21; *CPJ* 1:68.

30. So Tcherikover, "The Third Book," 21.

31. Smallwood, *Legatio*, 3.

32. Emmet ("The Third Book of Maccabees," 158) sees this as an objection to a date under Caligula, since the Ptolemies were *theoi* and so the issue of self-deification could have been worked in. However, self-deification was not the issue in the traditional source adapted by 3 Maccabees, but the cult of Dionysus. The author was not obliged to provide an exact correspondence to Caligula.

33. Tcherikover, "The Third Book," 23.

34. Ibid., 25.

35. Ibid. Tcherikover also takes the word *paroikia* in 7:19 as "exile" ("they determined to celebrate these days also as festive for the duration of their *paroikia*"). Hadas translates "community."

36. S. Safrai, "Relations between the Diaspora and the Land of Israel," *The Jewish People in the First Century* 1:184–215; "Pilgrimage to Jerusalem at the End of the Second Temple Period," *Studies on the Jewish Background of the New Testament* (Assen: Van Gorcum, 1969) 12–21; *Wallfahrt in Zeitalter des Zweiten Tempels* (Neukirchen-Vluyn; Neukirchener Verlag, 1981).

37. Tcherikover, "The Third Book," 18–20.

38. Josephus, *Ant* 18.8.1 (257–60). Smallwood, *Legatio*, 24–27.

39. On his brother, see *Ant* 20.5.2 (100); 18.6.3 (159–60); 19.5.1 (276). Philo's nephew, Tiberius Julius Alexander, was Roman prefect in Egypt at the time of the Jewish revolt in 66 CE. See Tcherikover, *CPJ* 1:78–79 and V. Burr, *Tiberius Iulius Alexander* (Bonn: Habelt, 1955).

40. E. R. Goodenough, *The Politics of Philo Judaeus* (New Haven: Yale, 1938); *Introduction to Philo Judaeus* (New Haven: Yale, 1940) 52–74; H. A. Wolfson, *Philo* (Cambridge, Mass.: Harvard, 1947) 2:322–438.

41. Goodenough, *Politics*, 25.

42. Goodenough (ibid.) calls attention to parallels in the gospels: the announcement by John the Baptist that the axe is laid to the root of the tree (Matt 3:10; Luke 3:9) and the analogy of the vine in John 15.

43. Wolfson, *Philo* 2:407.

44. Ibid., 395.

45. *De Vita Mosis*, 2:44: "But if a fresh start should be made to brighter prospects, how great a change for the better might we expect to see! I believe that each nation would abandon its peculiar ways, and throwing overboard their ancestral customs, turn to honoring our laws alone."

46. See Wolfson, *Philo* 2:414–15. The scriptural quotation, from Num 24:7 (the prophecy of Balaam), follows the LXX, which is quite different from the Hebrew. The only doubt as to whether Philo has a messianic "man" in mind arises from the parallel passage in *Praem* 165 which says that the gathering of the exiles will be guided "by a vision divine and superhuman, unseen by others but manifest to them as they pass from exile to their home." If this passage refers to the Logos as seems probable, then Philo may have identified the messiah with the Logos and this identification may also be implicit in *Praem* 95. See J. de Savignac, "Le Messianisme de Philon d'Alexandrie," *NovT* 4 (1960) 319–24; U. Fischer, *Eschatologie und Jenseitserwartung im Hellenistischen Diasporajudentum* (BZNW 44; Berlin: de Gruyter, 1978) 184–213. F. Grégoire ("Le Messie chez Philon d'Alexandrie," *ETL* 12 [1935] 28–50) emphasizes that such interest in the messiah as we find in *De Praemiis et Poenis* is exceptional in Philo's works.

47. Wolfson, *Philo*, 2:415.

48. *Quod Deus Immutabilis Sit*, 172–77. This passage is remarkable for its review of world kingdoms, reminiscent of apocalyptic literature and the sibylline oracles. A similar passage is found in *De Iosepho*, 131–37.

49. Fischer, *Eschatologie*, 187–210 notes the limitations of Philo's interest in national and political eschatology and stresses the persistent emphasis on individual

virtue which he says is closer to Stoic than to Hebraic ethics. By stressing the individualized eschatology of *Praem* 152 as a focal point of the treatise, Fischer questions whether Philo is interested in national eschatology except as an allegory for individual psychology. While many of Fischer's observations are valid, he underestimates Philo's respect for the letter of the law.

50. J. Jeremias (*Jerusalem in the Time of Jesus* (Philadelphia: Fortress, 1969) 69 n. 13), who cites a fragment of *De Providentia* preserved in Eusebius PE 7.14.64. The authenticity of the fragment is not fully certain.

51. H. Wenschkewitz, *Die Spiritualisierung der Kultus Begriffe* (Leipzig: Pfeiffer, 1932); U. Fruchtel, *Die Kosmologischen Vorstellungen bei Philo von Alexandrien* (Leiden: Brill, 1968) 69–118.

52. So F. Dexinger, "Ein 'Messianisches Szenarium als Gemeingut des Judentums in nachherodianischer Zeit?" *Kairos* 17 (1975) 250–55.

53. On the question of eschatological references in the LXX see further P. Volz, *Die Eschatologie der jüdischen Gemeinde* (Tübingen: Mohr, 1934) 183; L. Prijs, *Jüdische Tradition in der LXX* (Leiden: Brill, 1948) 67–75.

54. Josephus, *Ant* 20.8.6 (167–72); *JW* 2.13.5 (261–63).

55. *In Flaccum*, 25–42. Smallwood, *Legatio*, 18–19; *The Jews*, 238–39.

56. Smallwood, ibid.

57. *JW* 2.18.7–8 (487–98); *CPJ* 1:78–79; Smallwood, *The Jews*, 364–66.

58. Tcherikover, *CPJ* 1:79.

59. *Ant* 12.3.1 (121). The people of Antioch made a similar request which was also denied. Smallwood, *The Jews*, 366.

60. *JW* 7.10.1 (409–19); *CPJ* 1:79–80; Smallwood, *The Jews*, 366–67.

61. *JW* 7.10.2–4 (420–36). The closing of the temple by Lupus had to be repeated by his successor Paulinus.

62. The Jewish tax had only been levied on men, between the ages of 20 and 50. It appears that women were exempted from the *fiscus Judaicus* at age 62, but we know of no age limit for men. See Smallwood, *The Jews*, 371–76; *CPJ* 1:80–82.

63. *JW* 7.11.1–4 (437–53). S. Applebaum, *Jews and Greeks in Ancient Cyrene* (SJLA 28; Leiden: Brill, 1979) 220–25.

64. *CPJ* 2:82–87 (no. 157); Musurillo, *The Acts of the Pagan Martyrs*, 44–48; Smallwood, *The Jews*, 389–92.

65. The main account is that of Eusebius, HE 4.2.1–4. Also Dio Cassius 68.32; Appian, *Bell Civ* 2.90 (Appian witnessed the revolt himself); Orosius 7.12; Syncellus 347d, 348d. There is also a brief notice in the Armenian version of Eusebius's chronicle. See *CPJ* 1:86–93; Smallwood, *The Jews*, 393–427; A. Fuks, "Aspects of the Jewish Revolt in A. D. 115–117," *JRS* 51 (1961) 98–104; Applebaum, *Greeks and Jews*, 242–344; E. Schürer, *The History of the Jewish People in the Age of Jesus Christ* (rev. and ed. G. Vermes and F. Millar; Edinburgh: Clark, 1973) 1:529–34; M. Hengel, "Messianische Hoffnung und politischer 'Radikalismus' in der jüdisch-hellenistischen Diaspora," *Apocalypticism in the Mediterranean World and the Near East* (D. Hellholm, ed.; Tübingen: Mohr, forthcoming); A. Kasher, "A Comment on the Jewish Uprising in Egypt during the days of Trajan," *JJS* 27 (1976) 147–58.

66. *CPJ* 2:228–33 (no. 435); Applebaum, *Jews and Greeks*, 266–67.

67. Applebaum, *Jews and Greeks*, 303. The authorities are Bar Hebraeus and Michael Syriacus.

68. Ibid., 300. Quietus had already suppressed the Jews in Mesopotamia.

69. *CPJ* 2:236 (no. 437). The papyri relevant to the revolt are collected in *CPJ* 2:225–60.

70. *CPJ* 2:95 (no. 158a col. 6).

71. *CPJ* 2:87–99 (The Acta Pauli et Antonini); Musurillo, *The Acts of the Pagan Martyrs*, 179–94; Smallwood, *The Jews*, 406–9.

72. So M. J. Lagrange, *Le Messianisme chez les Juifs* (Paris: Gabalda, 1909) 308; Fuks, "Aspects," 98–104; *CPJ* 1:90; Applebaum, *Jews and Greeks*, 260; Hengel, "Messianische Hoffnung."

73. It is not even certain that one individual is meant. *CPJ* 2:94 (no. 158a col. 1) refers enigmatically to "the king of the scene and the mime." It would appear that the Alexandrians had staged a mockery of the Jewish "king" as they had of Agrippa in the time of Caligula.

74. Applebaum, *Jews and Greeks*, 328–31.

75. Suetonius, Domitian 12.2. The elimination of these abuses under Nerva was commemorated by a Roman coin (*CPJ* 1:80).

76. *CPJ* 1:85. Josephus (*JW* 6.9.2 [418]) mentions that prisoners were sent in chains to the works in Egypt, while those under 17 were sold. Jerome (*Comm in Jerem*. 31.15 [PL 24.877]) says that "infinita millia captivorum" were sent to Rome via Gaza and Alexandria.

77. *CPJ* 1:84.

78. Smallwood, *The Jews*, 394.

79. HE 4.2.3. Applebaum, *Jews and Greeks*, 295.

80. Collins, *The Sibylline Oracles*, 73–76.

81. Ibid., 94–95. The point is also noted by Hengel, "Messianische Hoffnung."

82. Sib Or 5:143, 159. Cf. the use of Babylon for Rome in Rev 13; 17; 18; 2 Bar 36–40; 4 Ezra 11–12.

83. Sib Or 5:173; Isa 47:8. Collins, *The Sibylline Oracles*, 79.

84. Collins, ibid., 80–87.

85. A. Yarbro Collins, *The Combat Myth in the Book of Revelation* (HDR 9; Missoula: Scholars, 1976) 170–86.

86. Contrast the prediction of R. Simeon b. Yohai (mid-second century): "If you see a Persian horse tethered in Israel, look for the coming of the Messiah", Midr Song R. viii, 9 § 3; Lament. R. i, 13 § 41. See J. Neusner, *A History of the Jews in Babylonia* (2d ed. Leiden: Brill, 1965) 74–76; Smallwood, *The Jews*, 426. Smallwood's contention that "Palestinian Jews looked upon the Parthians . . . as potential saviors" lacks documentation for the first century.

87. Strabo 1.2. In Sib Or 11:61–79 the Indians/Ethiopians are said to rule over Media.

88. Sib Or 3:175–90 and esp. 350–80. Collins, *The Sibylline Oracles*, 57–64.

89. Collins, ibid., 87–92.

90. Ibid., 90. Stars or comets marked the births of Alexander, Mithridates, Augustus, Alexander Severus, and of course Jesus.

91. B. Lindars, "Re-enter the Apocalyptic Son of Man," *NTS* 22 (1975) 52–72; Collins, *The Apocalyptic Vision*, 145–46.

92. E.g., S. Mowinckel, *He That Cometh* (New York: Abingdon, 1954) 357.

93. 1 Enoch 48:10. J. Theisohn, *Der Auserwählte Richter* (SUNT 12; Göttingen: Vandenhoeck & Ruprecht, 1975) 53–99.

94. 4 Ezra 13:1–4; 7:29. M. E. Stone, "The Concept of the Messiah in 4 Ezra," in *Religions in Antiquity* (Goodenough Festschrift; ed. J. Neusner; Leiden: Brill, 1968) 295–312.

95. U. B. Mueller, *Messias und Menschensohn in jüdischen Apokalypsen und in der Offenbarung des Johannes* (Gütersloh: Mohn, 1972) 107–55.

96. So also Hengel, "Messianische Hoffnung."

97. In 424–25 it is a tower which covers many stadia.

98. Collins, *The Sibylline Oracles*, 110–11.

99. This passage is in praise of Hadrian, whom it calls the fifteenth king of Egypt.

100. J. Geffcken, "Römische Kaiser im Volksmunde der Provinz," *Nachrichten der königlichen Gesellschaft der Wissenschaften zu Göttingen* Phil-Hist Kl. (1901) 188–95; A. Kurfess, "Oracula Sibyllina XI(IX)–XIV(XII), nicht christlich sondern jüdisch," *ZRGG* 7 (1955) 270–72.

101. W. Scott, "The Last Sibylline Oracle of Alexandria," *Classical Quarterly* 9 (1915) 144–66; 207–28; 10 (1916) 7–16.

Part Two

IDENTITY THROUGH ETHICS AND PIETY

Chapter 4

THE COMMON ETHIC

The distinctiveness of Diaspora Judaism was never simply a matter of political allegiance. It was deeply rooted in customs and observances which ultimately derived from the Mosaic law. The strangeness of Judaism in the eyes of many gentiles sprang from the influence of Mosaic commandments, especially those which prohibited worship of pagan gods and restricted intercourse with neighboring peoples. Moses and his code drew the admiration of some philosophical Greeks and Romans but were the targets of the most vehement hostile polemic. Jewish apologists like Philo and Josephus could boast of the extent of Moses' fame but were also extended in their efforts to remove the scandal of his laws and reconcile them with Hellenistic culture. In fact, while the Mosaic law always retained an authoritative position in Jewish life in the Diaspora, its role was by no means a simple one. It could be treated selectively, by highlighting some laws and neglecting others, and it could be buttressed with philosophical and religious foundations, which were remote from the original Torah. The variety of Diaspora Judaism and its peculiar character can be appreciated in the light of the ways in which it adapted the traditional laws.

JUDAISM ACCORDING TO HECATAEUS

The simplest and most straightforward portrayal of Judaism as a religion of the law is found in the fragments attributed to Hecataeus of Abdera by Josephus. The historical import of these fragments is uncertain because of their disputed authenticity. If authentic they represent a view of Judaism by a distinguished Greek observer at the outset of the Hellenistic age. If they are forgeries, they tell us something of the self-identity of a Hellenistic Jew, most probably in the second century BCE.[1] In either case, they are of interest as an example of how a very traditional orientation to the law could be presented in terms that could be appreciated by a Hellenistic audience.

There is no doubt that Hecataeus wrote about the Jews in connection with his account of the Egyptians. A fragment is preserved in Diodorus, *Bibliotheca Historica*, 40.[2] Hecataeus follows the Egyptian account, of which a variant is found also in Manetho, according to which the Jews were foreigners expelled from Egypt, who settled in Palestine and founded Jerusalem. In accordance with Hecataeus's general interest in laws and lawgivers, the focus of the narrative is on Moses. While the way of life introduced by Moses is characterized as "unsocial and hostile to foreigners," the account on the whole is favorable. Hecataeus emphasizes the monotheism of the Jews and says that they rejected anthropomorphism: "He did not fabricate any image of the gods because he believed that god was not anthropomorphic; rather the heaven which encompassed the earth was the only god and lord of all." He notes the humanitarian aspects of the laws—the concern for the protection of the poor, and the insistence that children be raised and not exposed. He also notes favorably the prominent role of the priests. Judaism is portrayed as a religion of the law. In fact, traditional Judaism fitted well with Hecataeus's interest in laws and the regulation of society. His favorable attitude to Judaism resulted in part from the similarities between Jewish and Egyptian laws, and Hecataeus's preference for the latter over the Greeks.[3]

Two other works relating to Judaism are ascribed to Hecataeus. One of these, "On Abraham and the Egyptians," is universally agreed to be a forgery, as we have seen above in chapter one. The other work, "On the Jews," is preserved in a number of quotations in Josephus's *Against Apion*.[4] The authenticity of this work is widely disputed.[5] Herennius Philo expressed doubts about it in the second century CE, but his doubts are probably tendentious and can carry no weight as evidence.[6] Several items in the actual fragments have given rise to suspicion:

The statement that a "high priest of the Jews" named Hezekiah had gone to Egypt seemed to Hugo Willrich "ein Ding der Unmöglichkeit."[7] Willrich took the reference as a transparent allusion to Onias, founder of Leontopolis. The "impossibility," however, was put in question by the discovery of a coin at Beth-Zur bearing the name Hezekiah in Hebrew.[8] This evidence would seem to show "that there was an Ezechiah-Ezechias in late Persian or early Hellenistic times that was important enough to have his name stamped on a Jewish coin."[9] Since coins were usually stamped by the rulers, rather than by lesser officials, this Hezekiah would almost certainly have been a high priest.[10] It does not automatically follow that the Hezekiah of the coin is the individual to whom Hecataeus refers, but if Hezekiah was a name in the priestly family, the reference to a priest of the name gains plausibility. At the very least, the Hezekiah coin should remind us of the gaps in our knowledge of Jewish history in this period and warn us against hasty pronouncements of "impossibility." That a member of the high-priestly family should have gone down to Egypt is not at all implausible in view of the common entanglement of priests in politics.

A more recent objection to the authenticity of the *Peri Ioudaiōn* has been raised by B. Schaller.[11] In *Ag Ap* 188(22) we read of "the total number of Jewish priests who receive a tithe of the revenue." Schaller points out that the tithe was not given to the priests until the second century BCE. Previous to that it was given to the levites, who in turn gave a tithe of their income to the priests. However, it is surely unlikely that a Greek author would note the nuanced distinctions between priests and levites and between tithes and tithes of tithes. In fact, precision in such matters would be a stronger indication of Jewish authorship than the rough approximation in the actual text.

A further problem arises from the statement in *Ag Ap* 2.43(4) that Alexander gave to the Jews the land of Samaria free of tribute. We have no other record of this event and some scholars have seen here the reflection of the gift of some Samaritan territories tax-free by Demetrius II to Jonathan Maccabee in 145 BCE or of the conquest of Samaria by John Hyrcanus (128–107 BCE).[12] Yet Hecataeus's report is not implausible. There is a story in Curtius Rufus 4.8.9 that the Samaritans murdered Alexander's prefect in Syria and that Alexander in turn destroyed the murderers. Traditions in Eusebius and Syncellus report that Alexander destroyed Samaria and settled it with Macedonians. The archeological evidence is compatible with this report.[13] If the tradition of a Samaritan revolt is true, then the gift of the land to the Jews, who had not joined the revolt, would be quite plausible, though of course not proven.

Only one of the passages cited in *Ag Ap* (1.190–94[22]) directly attempts to categorize the Jews:

> In another passage, Hecataeus mentions our regard for our laws and how we deliberately choose and hold it a point of honour to endure anything rather than transgress them. "And so (he says) neither the slander of their neighbors and of foreign visitors, to which as a nation they are exposed, nor the frequent outrages of Persian kings and satraps can shake their determination; for these laws, naked and defenceless, they face death in its most terrible form rather than repudiate the faith of their forefathers."

Josephus goes on to paraphrase some examples: the refusal of Jewish workers to collaborate on the restoration of the temple of Bel in Babylon and "again when temples and altars were erected in the country by its invaders, the Jews razed them all to the ground, paying in some cases a fine to the satraps and in others obtaining pardon. For such conduct, he adds, they deserve admiration." Some scholars have questioned whether this uncritical praise of the Jews could have been written by the Hecataeus who found their way of life "unsocial and hostile to foreigners."[14] However, even the fragment in Diodorus attempts to explain the "unsocial" Jewish laws as a result of their being cast out of Egypt and praises Moses for requiring "the young men to practise courage, perseverance and in general endurance in the face of every adversity." The passage in Josephus goes on to say that "myriads of our race had already been deported to Babylon by the Persians." This statement is usually taken as a mistake for the Babylonians (a mistake which would be more readily comprehensible in a Greek than in a Jewish forger). However, there is a tradition in Eusebius and Syncellus that Artaxerxes III Ochus transported rebellious Jews to Hyrcania and Babylon.[15] Further, Josephus reports in *Ant* 11.7.1(297) that Bagoses, general of Artaxerxes, defiled the temple and put the Jews under tribute. The Bagoses in question was probably the notorious eunuch of Artaxerxes III who was active in Syria-Palestine after the Tennes rebellion of 350 BCE and who eventually murdered his king.[16] While we cannot prove that Jews had to die for their faith under the Persians, the statements of Hecataeus are plausible enough against this background.

The *Peri Ioudaiōn* of Hecataeus, then, is suspect for several reasons, but none of them is decisive. Stern has suggested that Josephus may have drawn on an authentic work of Hecataeus which had been re-touched by a Jew, since at least the statement that Hecataeus approved of the Jews for destroying foreign temples in their land strains credibility.[17] However, the statement of approval is not given as a quotation, and we cannot be sure how accurate Josephus's paraphrase is. Also the statement that the Jews were prepared to undergo torture and death is not supported by the actual examples cited, and is a favorite theme of Josephus himself.[18] Here again we may suspect some embellishment, but on the whole the *Peri Ioudaiōn* carries too much plausibility to be entirely dismissed as a forgery.[19]

The picture of Judaism in the *Peri Ioudaiōn* accords with that of the undisputed fragments of Hecataeus. The Jews are a people of the law and would endure anything rather than transgress it. The episode of Mosollamus, the archer, who killed the bird which was being observed by the seer,[20] adds a note of polemic against superstition, characteristic of the Jewish polemics against idolatry, but there is no attempt here to elaborate a philosophical basis for the law. The emphasis is on fidelity to ancestral customs. The traditional covenantal nomism is modified here only insofar as it is put in an international context and valued because of the importance of laws and fidelity in any culture. Yet this adaptation has its own significance, as it shows how easily traditional Judaism could find common ground with the Hellenistic world. The dominance of laws valued by Hecataeus was at the heart of traditional Judaism. The potential for rapprochement between Jewish and Greek traditions on the subject of law can be seen from Josephus's great eulogy of the law at the end of the treatise *Against Apion* (145–295 [14–41]), where he argues from the Greek respect for Sparta that "obedience to law is a proof of virtue." Yet such direct appeal to the category of law is found only rarely in the corpus of Jewish Hellenistic literature.

The Basis for a Common Ethic

The earliest literature of the Hellenistic Diaspora, which can be dated prior to the reign of Philometor, displays widely divergent attitudes towards the law. On the one hand, Demetrius the Chronographer shows a rather scrupulous attitude both in his concern for reconciling chronological data and in his demonstration that Moses did not marry outside his people. At the other extreme Artapanus shows no compunction in associating Moses with the Egyptian animal cults. We shall see later yet another distinct viewpoint in the *Exagōgē* of Eze-kiel. The fragmentary character of these early writings makes it diffi-cult to get a clear picture of their attitudes to the law. It is apparent however that those early writings which have in part survived were not primarily oriented to the law, and did not share any common underlying attitude towards it.

From the time of Philometor on, the Jewish documents have been more substantially preserved, but they also begin to reflect an emerg-ing common ethic. The characteristic feature of this ethic was that it emphasized those aspects of Jewish law which were likely to get a sympathetic hearing from enlightened gentiles—chiefly monotheism and the prohibition of idolatry, and various sexual laws such as the prohibition of homosexuality.[21] These matters had an important place in Jewish tradition but they could be embellished with further Helle-nistic features.

There had been a growing tendency towards monotheism in Greek philosophy since the fifth century BCE.[22] Antisthenes, a pupil of Socra-tes, had declared that there is only one god in nature.[23] The tendency was furthered by the natural theology of the Stoics and is vividly illustrated in Cleanthes' Hymn to Zeus. Critiques of idolatry were not uncommon in the philosophers, and they were often extended to the use of temples as well.[24] The philosophical critique of idolatry is found as early as Heraclitus,[25] and again in Zeno, the founder of Stoi-cism.[26] That attacks on idolatry could win the sympathy of enlight-ened observers is shown by the fact that Judaism is praised for the rejection of images in a passage in Strabo, which has often been thought to derive from Posidonius, and again in Varro.[27]

Jewish sexual ethics could also find support in the Hellenistic world. Greek attitudes towards adultery varied and, in general, were harsher on women than on men. There are numerous tales of individ-ual vengeance and public punishments.[28] Plutarch (*Lycurgus*, 15) re-counts a story in which adultery is said to have been unknown among the ancient Spartans. Plato, in the *Laws* (8.841–42) proposed "one or other of two standards of sexual conduct." Ideally, no one would dare to have relations with any woman or man other than his spouse. Alter-natively, if a man had an affair with another woman, he must keep it secret. If detected he would lose his citizen's rights. Later, Epictetus (*Dis* 2.22.28) even claimed that whatever produced incontinents adulterers, and seducers was not really human. Jewish strictness on the question of adultery, then, was not out of place in a Greek context.

No sin is denounced more frequently in Jewish writings than homosexuality. Despite the generally indulgent Greek tradition on this subject, there was also a long history of criticism. Plato conveys a positive attitude in the *Symposium,* but in the *Laws* (8.836) he condemns homosexuality unequivocally as contrary to natural law. Antisthenes and the Cynics likewise rejected it, and also the Epicureans.[29] Here again the Jewish writers were not simply at variance with Greek morality, but could be seen as taking sides in widespread Greek debate.

The Jewish law that children be reared, not aborted or exposed, had already been noted with approval by Hecataeus.[30] Greek and Roman moralists seldom concern themselves with this issue, but the Roman satirist Juvenal refers scathingly to the widespread practice of abortion.[31] In all these points, the sexual morality defended by the Jewish writers was indeed faithful to Jewish law, but could also expect to find some sympathy in a Greek audience.

By emphasizing those aspects of Jewish law which could command respect in a gentile context, the Hellenistic Jewish writers were able to project Judaism as a universal religion which was in accordance with the laws of nature.[32] Distinctive aspects of Judaism such as circumcision and dietary laws were played down. We need not conclude that the Jews of Egypt actually abandoned these practices—even such a Hellenized Jew as Philo was faithful to the letter of the law—but these elements were not up front or central in their formulations of Jewish ethics.

THE COMMON ETHIC: PSEUDO-PHOCYLIDES
The ethics of Hellenistic Judaism have been studied mainly with reference to the common material in Philo's *Hypothetica,* 7.1–9, Josephus's *Ag Ap* 2.190–219, and Pseudo-Phocylides.[33] While Philo and Josephus claim to be giving a summary of the Jewish laws, they are highly selective and they also include material which goes beyond the actual Torah but is derived from Greek sources or designed for a Hellenistic audience.[34] The poem of Pseudo-Phocylides is, of course, disguised as the work of a gentile, with no overt reference to the Jewish law at all. In addition to monotheism, all three place heavy emphasis on sexual matters—adultery (*Hyp* 7.1; *Ag Ap* 2.199; Ps.

Phoc 3, 177–78); homosexuality (*Hyp* 7.1; *Ag Ap* 2.199, 215; Ps. Phoc 3, 190–91); rape of a virgin (*Hyp* 7.1; *Ag Ap* 2.215; Ps. Phoc 198); abortion (*Hyp* 7.7; *Ag Ap* 2.202; Ps. Phoc 183). Josephus (*Ag Ap* 2.202) and Pseudo-Phocylides (185) forbid sexual relations with a pregnant woman. Philo (7.7) and Pseudo-Phocylides (186) forbid emasculation. The common material also extends to such duties as those of parents and children, husband and wife, the young and their elders, and the burial of the dead.[35]

Some of the offenses (e.g., abortion, abandoning children) are not explicitly noted in the OT. Philo and Josephus show influence from a group of laws which were known in antiquity as unwritten laws attributed to Buzyges, the legendary hero of an Attic priestly tribe.[36] The affinities of these codes with the Noachian laws have often been noted.[37] While the Noachian laws were fully developed in rabbinic literature, the underlying tradition is attested in the book of Jubilees in the second century BCE.[38] The relevance of the Noachian tradition for our purpose lies not so much in the content of the laws, but in the very idea of a code to which gentiles were responsible. Yet, while the Noachian laws provide a parallel for universalist ethics in rabbinic Judaism, there is no reason to suppose that the Hellenistic codes were actually derived from them. The crucial difference, as Crouch has noted, is that the rabbinic sources clearly differentiate between the laws that apply to Jews and those that apply to gentiles, while the Hellenistic Jewish codes do not.[39]

While the thesis of G. Klein that the common material in Philo, Josephus, and Pseudo-Phocylides reflected an actual catechism for proselytes is not sustained by the evidence,[40] there is no doubt that there was a well-established tradition in Diaspora Judaism, formed most probably in the synagogue service. An author such as Philo could elaborate this tradition and give it a philosophical basis in terms of the law of nature and the law of God, but it is reflected in a wide variety of Jewish writings from the second century BCE on. The sentences of Pseudo-Phocylides have rightly been regarded as the major repository of the ethics of Hellenistic Judaism before Philo, although they have too often been treated in isolation.

The sayings of Pseudo-Phocylides have obvious affinities with the Jewish wisdom literature, but the very choice of the pseudonym Phocylides emphasizes rather the relationship to the Greek genres of didactic poetry and gnomologies.[41] Since the composition is a collection of sentences rather than a coherent exposition, the affinities with the gnomologies are the most obvious. The original Phocylides was in fact a gnomic poet. Collections of *gnomai* had been made from the fifth century on and were promoted in the philosophical schools by such eminent figures as Epicurus and Chrysippus.[42] The choice of this genre already says much about the framework in which the ethical teachings are placed. The choice of a Greek pseudonym rules out any appeal to the revelatory status of Jewish law. The teachings claim their validity as natural law. Since the traditional sayings of Phocylides were regarded as useful for educational purposes,[43] it may be that the author wished to infiltrate Greek moral education. If so, we must assume that he was interested in spreading his values, not Judaism as such, since it is never explicitly mentioned.

As is typical of gnomic and of proverbial poetry, the content gives little indication of date. Pseudo-Phocylides knew the LXX and uses a number of word forms which were unknown before the Hellenistic age, some of which appear only in the first century CE. Parallels with such Stoic writers as Seneca and Musonius Rufus also point to the first century CE. Van der Horst, the best recent authority on Pseudo-Phocylides, tentatively suggests a date between 30 BCE and 40 CE, on the assumption that "an Alexandrian Jew could not have maintained such great openness towards pagan culture" after the pogroms of the time of Caligula.[44] It is by no means certain that this assumption is justified. The very difficulty of specifying the time of origin is due in part to the consistency of the ethical tradition and the lack of peculiar, distinguishing traits in Pseudo-Phocylides.

The character of the sentences has already been indicated in the comments above on the material shared with Philo and Josephus. Monotheism is implicit throughout, despite a few apparent polytheistic references. Vs. 98 (*metra de teuche theoisi*) is scarcely intelligible and must be emended.[45] Vss. 75 and 163 refer to the heavenly bodies as "blessed ones." Vs. 104 says that the dead become *theoi*. Neither the reference to the "blessed ones" nor that to the *theoi* in 104 is incompatible with monotheism. The latter case is simply a variant on the common Jewish idea that the righteous dead become angels or mingle with the angels.[46] Yet it must be said that monotheism is not an explicit issue in Pseudo-Phocylides as it is in Philo. Usually the author refers simply to "god" without qualification, a prodcedure which had ample precedent in philosophical and gnomic writings. Only once in vs. 54 does he specify that *heis theos esti sophos*. While the phrase *heis theos* often appears as "geradezu t erminus technicus der monotheistischen Missionspredigt"[47] the context here ("pride not yourself on wisdom") suggests that the phrase means "only God is wise." The unqualified references to "god" result in a practical monotheism. Yet no warning is given to the non-Jewish reader that vss. 98, 104, or 163 should not be read in a polytheistic sense. Evidently Pseudo-Phocylides was more concerned with the ethics one practiced than with the gods one worshipped. The poem is exceptional in Hellenistic Jewish literature in its failure to condemn idolatry. This apparent softness on polytheism and idolatry minimizes the disjunction from Hellenistic civil and social life required of the convert to Judaism, but also of the Jew who wished to participate fully in Hellenistic life, and the God-fearing pagan, who may not have broken with polytheism at all.[48]

The interest in sexual offenses is apparent already in vs. 3. Practical advice is added in 210–17: "Guard the youthful beauty of a comely boy, because many rage for intercourse with a man. Guard a virgin in firmly locked rooms . . ." The basis of the advice is natural law: "even animals are not pleased by intercourse of male with male (191) as Plato had also argued. Here the author indulges in a little uncharacteristic demythologizing: "eros is not a god but a passion destructive of all" (194). Yet Pseudo-Phocylides simply takes the keeping of concubines for granted, as indeed it was never strongly condemned in antiquity even in the OT or postbiblical Jewish writers.[49]

The greater part of Pseudo-Phocylides is taken up with the network of social relations, especially those within the family, but also those in society at large. The concern for the poor is conspicuous, though not distinctive in either Greek or Jewish traditions. Slavery is taken for granted, but a humane attitude is recommended. Money is the root of all evil (vs. 42)—a sentiment widely shared in antiquity. Most of the sentences are quite commonplace in both Jewish and Hellenistic ethics. Many have a distinctly Greek ring—e.g., "moderation is best of all" (69). There is scarcely any concern for cultic matters. Vs. 228 says that "purifications are for the purity of the soul, not of the body." This sentiment is significant as a widespread attitude of Hellenistic Judaism, which was in turn shaped by the spiritualizing philosophy of the Greeks.

The Jewish origin of the work is betrayed only by a few sayings which clearly echo the LXX (e.g., 140: "If a beast of your enemy falls on the way, help it to rise"—cf. Exod 23:5). The distinctive laws of Judaism, such as circumcision and sabbath observance are ignored. The admonition in vs. 31 ("Do not eat blood; abstain from food sacrificed to idols;") is an interpolation which is found in only one inferior manuscript).[50] There is only one element that is described by van der Horst as "typically Jewish and very un-Greek."[51] This is the formulation of the afterlife in vss. 103–4: "we hope that the remains of the departed will soon come to the light again out of the earth." This apparently physical notion of resurrection is juxtaposed with the assertion that the resurrected ones "will become gods" (104). Vss. 107–8 imply that the body dissolves after death while the spirit is released and vs. 115 states very explicitly that the soul is immortal. These variant formulations reflect the typical range of Jewish beliefs about the afterlife both in Judea and in the Diaspora. They cannot be neatly resolved into a coherent system. Needless to say, ideas of afterlife were widespread in the Hellenistic world. The particular suggestion of physical resurrection may be taken as a trace of the author's Judaism, but it is sufficiently counterbalanced with well-worn Greek formulations that the ideas could seem neither strange nor offensive to a Hellenistic audience.[52]

One final statement in Pseudo-Phocylides deserves comment. Vs. 39 states that "strangers should be held in equal honor with citizens."[53] The sentiment fits well enough with the general humanitarian attitudes of Pseudo-Phocylides, but takes on a special significance in the light of the Jewish struggle for recognition in Alexandria in the first century CE. Philo argued that "strangers, in my judgment, must be regarded as suppliants of those who receive them, and not only suppliants but settlers and friends who are anxious to obtain equal rights with the burgesses, and are near to being citizens because they differ little from the original inhabitants."[54] If Ps. Phoc 39 is indeed to be read in this context, it provides a rare confirmation of the date and setting of the work.

The purpose for which Pseudo-Phocylides was written has not been definitively established. Van der Horst leaves three possibilities open:[55] that the author wrote for his fellow Jews, that he wrote for a pagan public hoping to make them "sympathizers" of Judaism, and that he was actually a "God-fearer" who wished to promote his way of life. Whatever the primary audience envisaged by the author, his work is remarkable for its distillation of the ethical message of Judaism and suppression of the distinctive indicators of Judaism as a religion set apart. This was the kind of religion which could be embraced by a God-fearer without becoming a Jew. If the work was written by a Jew rather than by a God-fearer it provides a remarkable insight into the Hellenization of Diaspora Judaism.

The persistence of the attitude expressed in Pseudo-Phocylides is attested in the "Words of the Wise Menander," which have been preserved in Syriac but are thought to have been composed in Greek, in Egypt, towards the end of the second century CE.[56] The monotheism of Pseudo-Menander is not in doubt, but this, combined with allusions to Jewish wisdom tradition, is the only indication of the Jewish provenance of the work. Even the Mosaic laws are not reflected. Here again there is doubt as to the origin and purpose of the work. Audet suggested that it was the work of a God-fearer. This suggestion cannot be verified, but at least we can say that Pseudo-Menander illustrates the common ground between Jewish and Hellenistic ethical traditions and that such common ground could still be exploited in the late second century CE.

The Third Sibyl

The ethic of Pseudo-Phocylides, which emphasized what was common to Jews and gentiles, was representative of a wide spectrum of Hellenistic Judaism. The extent of this common ethic, combined with distinctive particular nuances, can be seen in two great corpora of Hellenistic Jewish writings, the sibylline tradition, which persists from the time of Philometor to the early second century CE, and the Testaments of the Twelve Patriarchs, whose provenance is disputed.

We have already seen that the Third Sibyl has its own distinctive political perspective. The ethical and religious requirements of that work are found in the hortatory passages, framed by the eschatological predictions. These passages specify the kinds of conduct that lead to destruction and those that lead to salvation and deliverance, and so identify the conduct required by true religion. Thus, the destruction of the Romans will be brought about through their "unjust haughtiness," homosexuality, and greed (182–90). The Greeks are condemned for idolatry (545–55), and several nations are denounced for homosexuality and idolatry and, in general, for "transgressing the holy law of immortal God, which they transgressed" (599–600). The conduct required by the sibyl is summarized in 762–66: "But urge on your minds in your breasts and shun unlawful worship. Worship the Living One. Avoid adultery and indiscriminate intercourse with males. Rear your own offspring and do not kill it, for the Immortal is angry at whoever commits these sins." Over against these denunciations stand the eulogies of the Jews—"a race of most righteous men" who avoid all forms of divination and "the astrological predictions of the Chaldeans,"[57] and are characterized by "righteousness and virtue and not love of money," helping the poor and sharing with them, "fulfilling the word of the great God, the hymn of the law,[58] for the Heavenly One gave the earth in common to all" (218–47). The future ideal is the restoration of "a sacred race of pious men who attend to the counsels and intention of the Most High" and "fully honor the temple of the great God" with all kinds of sacrifices. These, "sharing in the righteousness of the law of the Most High," will be "exalted as prophets by the Immortal and bring great joy to all mortals. For to them alone did the great God give wise counsel and faith and excellent understanding in their hearts. Hence they honor God, their parents and holy wedlock and avoid homosexuality" (573–600). In the final utopian state, "the sons of the great God will all live peacefully around the temple." The nations will be moved with admiration and resolve: "Let us send to the temple, since He alone is sovereign and let us all ponder the law of the Most High God" and avoid idolatry (702–31).

In all of this the Jewish law has a clear and pivotal place. The sibyl refers explicitly to the law given to Moses on Mt. Sinai (255–58). True worship is specifically located at the temple of Jerusalem, and only the Jews, in contrast with "Phoenicians, Egyptians and Romans, spacious Greece and many nations of others," observe the law (597–98). Jews do, indeed, fail on occasion, and can be punished like anyone else if they do not "obey in your heart the holy law of the immortal God" but "worship unseemly idols" (275–79). This is illustrated by the Babylonian exile. However, the exile also illustrates that they are restored "as immortal God decreed for you." What they must do is "remain trusting in the holy laws of the great God" (283–84). Yet it is not only to the Jews that the law applies. The other nations too can be condemned for failing to keep the law (599–600). The sibyl, like Romans 1 and Wisdom of Solomon 13, seems to presume that the essential law is known to everyone by nature. In fact the requirements of the sibyl could be seen to a great extent in terms of natural law.[59] The basic sin is idolatry.[60] Accordingly, the main requirement for the conversion of the Greeks is that they "revere the name of the one who has begotten all" (550) and bring their sacrifices to the temple of the one true God (545–72). Despite the implication of the superiority of Judaism, this demand is not alien to Greek sensibilities. The accusation of idolatry is based on a euhemeristic account of the origin of Greek religion, which was quite intelligible in a Greek context:[61] "it is a thousand years and five hundred more since the overbearing kings of the Greeks reigned, who began the first evils for mortals setting up many idols of dead gods" (551–54). The condemnation of idolatry in the sibyl was, in fact, far more typical of Hellenistic Judaism than the silence of Pseudo-Phocylides on this point.

The sibyl echoes the common Jewish position on sexual abuses. Her warnings against the dangers of arrogance and greed are also commonplace. The assertion that God gave the earth in common to all (247, 261) rings of Stoicism,[62] but the same sentiment is reflected in Pseudo-Phocylides (30), "Let all of life be in common." She takes a more distinctive position in her unequivocal condemnation of augury, divination, and "the astrological predictions of the Chaldeans" (220–28). Divination had philosophical respectability in the Hellenistic age, since it was defended by most Stoics. However, there were notable dissenters, such as Carneades, founder of the Third, or New, Academy (second century BCE) and the Epicureans, while the Stoic Panaetius had his doubts. Astrology was pervasive in the Hellenistic world, and one of the great astrological works, that of Nechepso and Petosiris, was composed in Egypt and roughly contemporary with the Third Sibyl.[63] Many Jewish writings from the period display a positive attitude on this subject, in sharp contrast to the sibyl. In addition to Pseudo-Eupolemus, who credited Abraham with inventing astrology, we should now note the Treatise of Shem, a full-fledged Jewish astrological work apparently composed in Egypt at some time in the Roman period.[64] Yet even here the sibyl's stand could probably be appreciated by the Greeks. Cicero could cite with approval the statement of Eudoxus, a pupil of Plato, that "no reliance whatever is to be placed in Chaldean astrologers," and he also listed false prophecies made to Pompey, Crassus, and Caesar.[65] Low-level astrology and Chaldaei were often assailed by Roman magistrates and satirists, and in 139 BCE the Chaldaei were expelled from Rome.[66] The sibyl was focusing attention on an issue of deep interest to the Hellenistic world, where debate was possible on the basis of one's understanding of nature.[67]

So, while the sibyl remains devoted to the law of Moses, she treats it in practice as natural law. There is no reference to the more peculiar dietary laws of Leviticus, or to the laws which separated Jew from gentile. There is no indication that circumcision was required of converts. At the end, God "will put in effect a common law for men throughout the whole earth" (757–58). It is evident that this law is not only concerned with Jewish traditions but with the fulfillment of human nature.

Yet, for all the universalism implied in the reduction of the law to ethical principles of broad human interest, the sibyl remains stubbornly particularistic. Unlike, for example, Pseudo-Aristeas, she does not say that those who worship Zeus are worshipping the same God; unlike Pseudo-Phocylides, she is unequivocal in her rejection of polytheism. Most significantly, she insists on the primacy of the Jerusalem temple.[68] This advocacy of the temple, as we have seen in chapter 2 above, is part of the particular political stance of the sibyl and reflects its provenance. It shows that the propaganda of the sibyl was in the service of concrete political and geographical ideals, not of a philosophy or mystical cult, as may have been the case in some other Jewish documents. The particularism of the sibyl arises from political considerations rather than from the conception of the Jewish law.

Sibylline Oracle 5

The ethical aspects of the sibylline tradition persist in Sib Or 5, at the beginning of the second century CE, despite the vastly different political climate of that book. Idolatry is repeatedly denounced (75–85; 278–80; 353–56; 403–5; 495–96) but with a new vehemence against Egyptian theriolatry: "They worship stones and brute beasts instead of God, revering very many things, one here, another there, which have no reason or mind or hearing, and things which it is not even lawful for me to mention" (75–79). Sexual offenses and homosexuality are again prominent, especially homosexuality. "Adulteries, illicit love of boys" are ranked with murder and din of battle as terrible things which will cease in the eschatological age (430). The Romans are "matricides . . . who formerly impiously catered for pederasty and set up in houses prostitutes who were pure before" and are also accused of incest and bestiality (386–97, cf. 166).[69] Most striking in Sib Or 5 is the emphasis on the temple and cultic piety. The sibyl bewails the destruction of the temple (150, 398–410) but also recalls how the Jews honored the great God with holy sacrifices and hecatombs (406–7). In the final section, a temple in Egypt is envisaged where sacrifices will be offered, though this too will be destroyed (500–507). Even after the temple was no more, this particular strand of the sibylline tradition remained bound to its concrete symbolism. Jewish identity in the sibyllines is derived mainly from this symbolism, and from the political attitudes implied. The ethics are not distinctive.

SIBYLLINE ORACLE 4

A different strand of the sibylline tradition is found in Sib Or 4, which, in its present form, was written towards the end of the first century CE. The date is established by references to the destruction of the Jerusalem temple (116), the legend of Nero's flight to the Parthians and future return (119–24; 138–39), and the eruption of Vesuvius in 79 CE (130–35). There is no clear indication of the place of origin, but the differences over against Sib Or 3 and 5 tell against an Egyptian provenance.[70] In view of the emphasis on baptism, a location in the Jordan valley has been proposed.[71]

The ethics of Sib Or 4 repeat the standard themes of the Diaspora literature. Monotheism and God's power as creator are emphasized. There is polemic against idolatry (6–7), adultery and homosexuality (33–34), as well as injustice and violence. But Sib Or 4 is distinguished from other Hellenistic Jewish writings in its outright rejection of temple worship: "For He has not, as house, stone set up as a temple, dumb and toothless, a bane which brings many woes to men, but one which it is not possible to see from earth nor to measure with mortal eyes, since it was not fashioned by mortal hand" (8–11). The righteous reject all temples, altars, and sacrifices (27–30). If the author intended an exception for the Jerusalem temple, he did not make it explicit. He mentions that a storm from Italy "will sack the great temple of God" (116). One of the marks of the occasion will be that they "commit repulsive murders in front of the temple" (118) suggesting that the temple will be defiled.[72] Disapproval of the Roman destruction, however, does not in itself imply a positive attitude towards the temple. Sib Or 4 is evidently at variance with Sib Or 3 and 5 on this point.

Even more striking is the attitude to conversion in Sib Or 4. In vs. 162, after describing the impiety of the last times, the sibyl appeals: "Ah, wretched mortals, change these things and do not lead the great God to all sorts of anger, but abandon daggers and groanings, murders and outrages, and wash your whole bodies in perennial rivers. Stretch out your hands to heaven and ask forgiveness for your previous deeds and make propitiation for bitter impiety with words of praise. God will grant repentance and will not destroy." This passage has been regarded as a reference to proselyte baptism. This is scarcely accurate. The appeal is addressed to humanity at large, and there is nothing to suggest that anyone is expected to convert to Judaism. Baptism is here a symbolic gesture of repentance, as it was with John the Baptist, not a rite of initiation.[73] It is noteworthy however that this is the only ritual action which is demanded. There is no question of circumcision or of any distinctively Jewish observance. Sib Or 4, like Pseudo-Phocylides, and indeed the other sibylline books, is quite open to God-fearers, who are not circumcised Jews. The oracle shows again the pervasiveness of the basic polemic against idolatry and sexual sins, but again it adds its own distinctive nuances.

THE SIBYLLINE FRAGMENTS

One other strand of the sibylline tradition must be noted briefly. Sib Or 3:1–45 and the fragments preserved by Theophilus and Lactantius attest a highly spiritual idea of God which goes far beyond anything else in the sibylline tradition and has its closest parallels in the Orphic fragments and in Philo. God is *one*, in the sense of both unity and uniqueness (3:11; F 1:7, 32; F 3:3; F 5:1). He is eternal (3:15) self-begotten and invisible (3:11). Great emphasis is laid on the contrast between perishable and imperishable (Fragments 1–3). Idolatry is the supreme sin because it is not in accordance with truth. Yet the highly spiritual fragments do not reject sacrificial cult as such, but only insist that it be offered to the true God (F 1:20–22). These passages evidently appealed to a more rarified audience than the main corpus of the sibyllina. Despite the characteristic Jewish polemic against idolatry, the Judaism of these fragments is indistinguishable from philosophical Hellenistic religion. Circumcision, sabbath observance, or such distinctive Jewish practices are not demanded by the sibyl in these passages. There is no clear distinction between the ethics of Judaism and those of a God-fearer, or even of a philosophically minded pagan.

THE TESTAMENTS OF THE TWELVE PATRIARCHS

Another possible window on the ethics of Hellenistic Judaism is provided by the Testaments of the Twelve Patriarchs. In this case, however, the evidence can be adduced only very tentatively since the provenance of the Testaments is notoriously problematic. Three main current views may be distinguished. The position which has been dominant since the late nineteenth century holds that the Testaments are Jewish but interpolated by a Christian. Variant forms of this view have been defended in recent years by J. Becker, A. Hultgård, and H. C. Kee, among others.[74] The theory of Christian authorship, which had been dominant before the late nineteenth century was revived in 1953 by M. de Jonge.[75] He has modified his position in recent years but continues to insist on the importance of the final stage of the Testaments and the difficulty of going behind it. The third position, that the Testaments are an Essene composition from Qumran, has been championed mainly by A. Dupont-Sommer and M. Philonenko.[76] Despite a number of important parallels between the Testaments and the scrolls, there are also far-reaching differences and this position has won little support in recent years. Much of the debate has centered on text-critical matters. Here it may be said that the attempts of Charles and others to remove Christian interpolations by text-critical arguments have been thoroughly undermined by the work of de Jonge and his students on the Greek text and of Burchard and Stone on the Armenian.[77] There is no longer room for doubt that the final text of the Testaments is a Christian document. It is also clear that attempts to go behind this stage are inevitably hypothetical. Yet the presence of much Jewish material is undeniable and even de Jonge admits that to speak of Christian composition is an oversimplification.

The most elaborate attempt to reconstruct the history of the Testaments is that of J. Becker. Becker distinguishes two Jewish stages and a Christian redaction.[78] The earliest stage was molded by the testament form. This was later expanded by the incorporation of traditional, usually hortatory, material. Becker reduces the Christian elements to the undeniable minimum, although, as de Jonge has repeatedly pointed out, much of the material could have been written by either Christian or Jew. It should also be said that the distinction between Becker's two Jewish stages rests on the assumption that different formal units may be ascribed to different sources. While an assumption of multiple stages is reasonable in itself, the distinction of Becker's two Jewish strata remains quite hypothetical.

Becker and others have argued that the Jewish stages of the Testaments originated in the Hellenistic Diaspora.[79] It is now widely agreed that Greek was the original language, and the ethics of the Testaments find many parallels in works of the Diaspora. Of course neither of these points is conclusive. Greek was widely known in Palestine and much of the ethical material is also paralleled in early Christian writing. A more specific indication of Egyptian origin may be found in the prominence of Joseph, not only in the Testament of Joseph but also in the Testaments of Reuben, Simeon, Dan, Gad, and Benjamin. This interest in Joseph is most readily comprehensible in an Egyptian document. Yet other explanations are also possible. J. Thomas suggested that the Testaments were written in Palestine for circulation in the Diaspora.[80] M. Küchler attributes them to Hellenized Palestinian Judaism.[81] In both cases, the scholars are trying to balance the Hellenistic elements against the parallels in Qumran and Palestinian Jewish literature. While there is a consensus that the Testaments are heavily Hellenized, there is no clarity on the more precise question of provenance.

The date of the Jewish strata of the Testaments is equally uncertain. E. J. Bickermann argued that the original Testaments were written before the Maccabean revolt, and he has been widely followed.[82] In T Levi 17:11 the priests of the seventh week, who immediately precede the "new priest" of the eschatological age, are denounced as "idolators, adulterers, lovers of money, proud, lawless, lascivious, abusers of children and beasts." This denunciation has been applied to the Hellenizers before the Maccabean revolt, although a polemic against the priesthood of the Hasmoneans cannot be absolutely excluded. T Naph 5:8 says that "Assyrians, Medes, Persians, Chaldeans, Syrians, shall possess in captivity the twelve tribes of Israel." Since no reference is made to the Romans, this passage must at least be dated before Pompey and it was probably written before the expulsion of the Syrians in 141 BCE. It cannot be earlier than 200 BCE since it presupposes Syrian, not Ptolemaic rule in Palestine. The lack of any reference to the Maccabean revolt has been taken as an argument for a pre-Maccabean dating, but this is unreliable, since the silence may be due to lack of sympathy. The prominence of the double messiahship of Levi and Judah, one of the more striking, if inexact, parallels with the Qumran scrolls, which also expect two messiahs, has often been taken as a criticism of the Hasmonean usurpation of the priesthood. It seems likely that there was a gradual process of growth in the formation of the Testaments, and so no one dating is valid for all the pre-Christian material. It also seems likely that some of the material was composed in circles opposed to the Hasmoneans in the second century BCE, and that these circles were Hellenized in language and ethics. These circles could have been located in Palestine or may have been part of the Jewish emigration to Egypt during the period after the revolt. Ultimately the ethics of the Testaments cannot be pinpointed as the product of a specific situation. They are of interest for our purpose as material which seems to have accumulated and circulated in Hellenized Jewish circles over two hundred years and was eventually taken over by Christianity.

The Testaments and the covenant form

The outline of the Testaments shows close similarity to the traditional covenant form, which would seem, prima facie, to bind them to the traditional covenantal ethic. The form may be set forth as follows:

A. *Preamble*, which gives the name of the patriarch, and the circumstances in which he delivered his testament shortly before his death.

B. A narrative section in which each of the patriarchs recounts stories from his life. T Ash is an exception on this point.

C. Ethical instruction follows.

D. A prediction of the future of the tribe, usually with an eschatological conclusion.

E. A conclusion which describes the death and burial of the patriarch. Points A and E are the distinctively testamentary elements in the outline.[83]

Becker has argued that the earliest stage of the Testaments is already shaped by the covenant form. So, for example, in T Reub we find a historical section, the example from the life of the patriarch in 3:11–15. Ethical instruction is found in the repeated warnings against adultery and again in 6:9: "I adjure you, by the God of heaven to do truth each one unto his neighbour, and to entertain love, each one for his brother." This is followed by a promise of blessing in 6:10–12. This outline provides a framework within which longer hortatory passages were later inserted. In T Jos the historical example is found in chapters 10–17. 18:1–2 contains an exhortation to follow the law and a promise of blessing. Both T Reub and T Jos are exceptional in the brevity of their predictions at the end. The majority of the Testaments included in their earliest stage a prophecy of the sin, punishment, and restoration of the people which illustrates the elements of curse and blessing in the covenant form.

A number of important differences between the testament form of the Testaments of the Twelve Patriarchs and the OT covenant form should be noted. In the OT covenant (e.g., Deuteronomy) the review of history served to remind the people of Yahweh's saving acts and therefore of their obligation to him. In the Testaments, the historical element consists of stories from the lives of the patriarchs which illustrate a virtue or vice. Baltzer emphasizes that the relationship between the patriarch and God is more important than the particular virtue or vice and notes the continuity with Jewish wisdom literature.[84] Nevertheless, history is used here as a source of moral examples to an extent which has no precedent in the Bible. The best parallels to the Testaments in this respect are found in writings of the Hellenistic Diaspora such as 4 Maccabees. The transformation of history into moral example is carried to an extreme in the allegorical commentaries of Philo, where, for example, in *De Abrahamo* 1–46 Enos symbolizes hope, Enoch repentance, and Noah justice. Similar symbolic meanings are elsewhere attached to the major figures of the Pentateuch.

Further, the emphasis on abstract, generalized virtues and vices which we find in the Testaments differs from the direct commands of the OT decalogue.[85] The interest in abstract virtues is characteristic of Greek philosophy rather than of the OT, although catalogues of virtues and vices are found at Qumran and some parallels can also be found in the biblical tradition.

The content of the exhortations

The ethical exhortations in the Testaments are expressed partly through the example of the patriarchs and partly through direct parenesis (often through lists of virtues and vices). The narrative section on each patriarch focuses on some virtue or vice. The story of Reuben illustrates the evil of fornication, that of Simeon envy, Judah inebriation and fornication. On the credit side, Issachar illustrates single-mindedness and Zebulon compassion. Joseph serves as a foil to many of the patriarchs by his chastity, despite the advances of the Egyptian woman, and by his forgiving love for the brothers who sold him into slavery. These two virtues are illustrated in T Jos 3–9 and 10:5–20:6 respectively.

The theme of brotherly love plays a prominent part in the Testaments. This love is extended not only to the people of Israel but to all mankind—e.g., T Issa 5:2; 7:6; T Zeb 5:1; 6:4; 6:7; 7:2; 8:1; T Ben 4:2. Such universalism is rare in Jewish writings of the Hellenistic period. Most of the parallels are found in Hellenized writings from the Diaspora.[86] It is not, of course, impossible that such sentiments should be expressed in Palestine, but the evidence may be taken to favor a setting in the Diaspora.

Homiletic material in the Testaments

In view of the strongly parenetic character of the Testaments it is only natural that they should draw on the homiletic practice of the synagogue. While we do not find in the Testaments any actual sermons we do find blocks of apparently traditional material which form units independent of their present context and which may well have been shaped by homiletic tradition. We may distinguish three types of homiletic material in the Testaments, all of them interrelated: First is the exposition of a particular vice or virtue, with the aid of biblical examples; second are lists of vices and/or virtues; and third are passages which put such lists in a dualistic context, e.g., by elaborating the contrast of the two ways.

1) *The exposition of particular virtues* with the aid of biblical examples is a typical feature of the Testaments. The discourse on fornication in T Reub 3:10–4:5; 4:6–6:5 provides a good example. First, the patriarch declares his theme: "Pay no heed to the face of a woman . . ." (3:10). He then provides as an illustration his misdemeanor with Bilhah (3:11–15) and concludes with the exhortation to "pay no heed to the beauty of women . . ." (4:1–5). This exhortation is complete in itself but is supplemented in 4:6–6:5 with another, similarly structured sermon, which may well be a redactional addition. Again, the patriarch begins by enunciating his theme: "For a pit unto the soul is the sin of fornication." This time the example adduced is that of Joseph: "how he guarded himself from a woman and purged his thoughts from all fornication" (4:8). The evil of women is further illustrated by the story of the Fall of the Watchers before the Flood (5:1–7). Finally, the exhortation concludes, "beware therefore of fornication."

The biblical incidents are included here specifically as illustrations of a vice or virtue and its effects. We should note that the form of T Reub 3:10–4:5 or 4:6–6:5 cannot be adequately explained by analogy with the covenant form. These passages do not simply recite history and then draw a moral from it. They begin with the declaration of a theme, illustrate it by historical (scriptural) example(s), and conclude with an exhortation. Therefore, they constitute a rounded self-contained homily within the Testament.[87] We may compare the list of examples of faith and the exhortation to perseverance in Hebrews 11–12. Similarly, in T Jos 2:4–10:3 we have a self-contained piece of exhortation. The patriarch begins by announcing his theme of *hypomonē* or endurance (2:7). He illustrates this at length from his adventures with the Egyptian woman (chaps. 3–9). The discourse concludes with the repetition of the moral: "ye see therefore my children how great things patience worketh" (10:1) and an exhortation, "So ye too if ye follow after chastity and purity with patience and prayer . . . the Lord will dwell among you . . ." (10:2–3). Similar homiletic passages are found in T Sim 2:5–5:3; T Jud 13–17. It should be noted that the theme of chastity/fornication enjoys special prominence in the parenetic passages of the Testaments.[88]

2) The second type of hortatory material included in the Testaments consists of *lists of vices and virtues*.[89] In Palestinian Judaism such lists are found in the Qumran texts where different virtues are assigned to the Spirit of Truth and vices to the Spirit of Perversity. The closest parallel to the scrolls in the Testaments is found in T Reub 2–3 which lists seven spirits which "are appointed against man": the spirits of fornication, insatiableness, fighting, obseqiousness, pride, lying, and injustice. Catalogues of vices and virtues also occur frequently in Stoic philosophy and in the popular diatribe.[90]

In a number of Testaments the consequences of a particular virtue or vice are elaborated in the form of a list. So in T Ben 6 we read:

> The inclination of the good man is not in the power of the deceit of the spirit of Beliar, for the angel of peace guideth his soul. And he gazeth not passionately upon corruptible things nor gathereth together riches through a desire of pleasure. He delighteth not in pleasure, he grieveth not his neighbour, he sateth not himself with luxuries, he erreth not in the uplifting of the eyes, for the Lord is his portion. The good inclination receiveth not glory nor dishonour from men, and it knoweth not any guile, or lie, or fighting or reviling. . . . The good mind hath not two tongues.

Again in T Issa 4:2–6 we read that

> the single-minded man coveteth not gold,
> he overreacheth not his neighbour.
> He longeth not after manifold dainties.
> He delighteth not in varied apparel.
> He doth not desire to live a long life
> but only waiteth for the will of God.

In both these passages a virtue, or a virtuous man, is described by a list of negatives. Precedents for lists of this type can be found in the "confessional" passages of the OT such as Deut 26:13b–14: "I have not transgressed any of thy commandments, neither have I forgotten them. I have not eaten of the tithe while I was mourning or removed any of it while I was unclean or offered any of it to the dead; I have obeyed the voice of the Lord my God." Further examples can be found in 1 Sam 12:3; Job 31:16–18; or in the Egyptian Book of the Dead. In each of these cases, a man declares himself innocent by enumerating the sins which he has not committed. The analogy with the Testaments is obvious, but also limited.[91] Here the speaker is no longer simply a man, but a man who embodies a particular virtue. The sharply increased interest in the virtues as such is a characteristic of the Hellenistic age. We may note again Philo's use of the patriarchs as allegories of virtues. Philo also makes frequent use of lists of vices and virtues. The influence of Greek popular philosophy is very probable in the catalogues of vices and virtues in Paul and Philo and cannot be discounted in the Testaments. These catalogues can also be viewed as an adaptation of an OT tradition, but we must allow for the possibility that Jewish preachers deliberately modelled their style on that of their Stoic and Cynic counterparts.[92]

3) *Dualistic framework:* It is typical of the Testaments that virtues and vices are contrasted in pairs—e.g., the fornication of Reuben with the chastity of Joseph or the envy of Simeon with the forgiving love of Joseph. Consequently, the catalogues of vices and virtues imply an ethical dualism in which two contrasting ways of life are set forth. This is most fully developed in the doctrine of the two ways in T Ash (1:3–8):

> Two ways hath God given to the sons of men, and two inclinations
> and two kinds of action and two modes (of action) and two issues.

> Therefore all things are by twos, one over against the other. For
> there are two ways of good and evil and with these are the two
> inclinations in our breasts discriminating them. Therefore if the
> soul taketh pleasure in the good (inclination) all its actions are in
> righteousness. . . . But if it incline to the evil inclination all its
> actions are in wickedness.

The doctrine of the two ways has roots in the ethics of the OT,
especially in the wisdom tradition.[93] Prov 4:10–14 sets out the contrast: "I have taught you the way of wisdom; I have led you in the
paths of uprightness. . . . Do not enter the path of the wicked and do
not walk in the way of evil men." The contrast between Dame Wisdom and Dame Folly in Proverbs 9 similarly implies the opposition of
two ways. Ps 1:6 says that "the Lord knows the way of the righteous,
but the way of the wicked will perish." The doctrine of the two ways
does not derive from the OT covenant but was obviously compatible
with it. We may compare Deut 30:15: "See I have set before you this
day life and good, death and evil." There is no implication of metaphysical dualism in any of these texts. They simply clarify basic op-
tions by formulating them in terms of binary oppositions. Such contrasts are probably found universally. In Hesiod's *Works and Days*
287–92 we read: "Badness can be got easily and in shoals: the road to
her is smooth, and she lives very near us. But between us and Good-
ness the gods have placed the sweat of our brows: long and steep is
the path that leads to her, and it is rough at first."[94]

The Testament of Asher goes beyond this purely ethical dualism
when it refers to the evil spirit and the angel of peace. In this respect,
it draws closer to the metaphysical dualism of the Qumran scrolls. It is
apparent however that the schema of the two ways was in itself quite
intelligible to a Hellenistic audience.

The ethic of the Testaments

The ethics of the Testaments resemble those of the Diaspora writings we have seen in their tendency to ignore the distinctive elements
of Judaism and emphasize those which would be acceptable to sophis-
ticated gentiles. Despite numerous references to the law (*nomos* and
entolē are used over sixty times), the ethics are presented in broad
moral terms.[95] There is no reference to the sabbath. Circumcision is
mentioned only in T Lev in connection with the destruction of She-

chem, not in the context of positive teaching. The Jewish cult is only discussed in connection with the eschatological priest. Purity laws are cited in T Ash 2:9 and 4:5 but are applied metaphorically to characterize types of sinners. The emphasis is on the virtues inculcated by the Testaments, not on specific commandments.

The most specific point of continuity with such documents as the sibyllines and Pseudo-Phocylides lies in the insistent polemic against fornication. The Testaments are closer to the sibyl than to Pseudo-Phocylides in their avoidance of any language which could be taken as polytheistic and in their political and eschatological interests. The sense of Jewish identity is reinforced by the choice of Jewish pseudonyms. The ethical teaching is safely within the bounds of Judaism but in itself is scarcely distinctive. It reflects the common tendency in Hellenistic Judaism to concentrate on these teachings which could be endorsed by any enlightened person of the Hellenistic age.

THE ROLE OF THE SYNAGOGUE

The common ethic which we have seen in such diverse writings as Pseudo-Phocylides, the sibyllines, and the Testaments was pervasive in Hellenistic Judaism. We will find it, with few exceptions, in the more philosophically and mystically inclined works which we shall discuss in the following chapters. Throughout, there is a tendency to bypass the distinctive laws of Judaism and concentrate on monotheism and matters of social and sexual morality. This tendency constitutes a unifying element among writings which are diverse in their political attitudes and in the details of their teaching.

Such unity as we find in the ethics of Hellenistic Judaism must be attributed to the influence of the synagogue preaching.[96] We have noted the formal traces of homilies in the Testaments of the Twelve Patriarchs. Other examples can be found in Philo.[97] We have little direct information about the preaching of the synagogue, but there is ample evidence that it played a central role in Diaspora life. An indication of the role of the synagogue may be taken from Philo, if due allowance is made for his tendency to portray Judaism as a philosophy:

> So each seventh day there stand wide open in every city thousands of schools of good sense, temperance, courage, justice and the other virtues in which the scholars sit in order, quietly, with

ears alert and with full attention, so much do they thirst for the draught which the teacher's words supply, while one of special experience rises and sets forth what is best and sure to be profitable and will make the whole of life grow to something better. But among the vast number of particular truths and principles there studied, there stand out practically high above the others two main heads: one of duty to God as shewn by piety and holiness, one of duty to men as shewn by humanity and justice.[98]

The reduction of the law to the "two main heads" (*dyo ta anōtatō kephalaia*) of duties towards God and humanity is especially significant and is characteristic of Hellenistic Judaism.[99]

The role of the synagogue also throws light on the recurring question as to whether this presentation of Judaism was designed primarily for the Jewish community or was addressed to the gentile world. The synagogue was evidently a major place of instruction for the Jewish community. Yet it was also open to gentiles and did in fact attract them. Josephus reports that the Jews of Antioch "were constantly attracting to their religious ceremonies multitudes of Greeks, and these they had in some measure incorporated with themselves."[100] This report accords well with the book of Acts where Paul is repeatedly said to encounter God-fearing gentiles in the synagogues.[101] We must assume then that the teaching of the synagogue was simultaneously designed to foster Jewish identity and to attract gentiles, or rather to attract gentiles by the Jewish self-identity which was developed and presented.

PROSELYTES AND GOD-FEARERS

There is no doubt that Hellenistic Judaism did attract gentiles in significant numbers. Many of these were full proselytes who had, in effect, become Jews, and, in the case of the males, were circumcised.[102] It is well known that Judaism was especially attractive to women, who, of course, did not have to undergo circumcision.[103] More interesting for our present purposes than the actual proselytes are the "God-fearers" and "sympathizers" who observed some Jewish laws and customs but stopped short of full conversion. Josephus boasts (*Ag Ap* 2.282 [39]) that "The masses have long since shown a keen desire to adopt our religious observances; and there is not one city, Greek or barbarian, nor a single nation, to which our custom of abstaining from work on the seventh day has not spread, and where fasts and the lighting of lamps and many of our prohibitions in the matter of food are not observed." The spread of Jewish customs is attested, reluctantly, by Roman writers such as Seneca and Dio Cassius.[104]

Some light is shed on the nature of Jewish proselytism by the famous conversion of the royal house of Adiabene, recounted in *Ant* 20.2.3–4 (34–38). The women of the royal house, including the queen, Helena, were converted to Judaism by a Jewish salesman named Hananias, and Helena's son, Izates, was persuaded that he too should convert. Helena, however, advised her son against circumcision lest his subjects refuse to be ruled by a Jew. Hananias concurred with this advice, saying that it was possible to worship God without circumcision, by observing the (other) ancestral laws of the Jews. Later, a Pharisee from Galilee, named Eleazar, contradicted this advice and persuaded Izates to be circumcised. By then Izates had succeeded to the throne, and many of his kindred followed his example. His successors also adhered to Judaism until the kingdom was conquered by Trajan in 116 CE.

The story of Izates is significant in several respects. Prior to his circumcision Izates conforms to the type usually designated as "Godfearers" in the scholarly literature. The advice of Hananias is remarkable and explains how such people were accepted by Judaism. Circumcision is not regarded as essential; one can worship God without it. We are reminded here of Philo's reduction of the law to the twofold commandment of service to God and neighbor—indeed, of the whole tendency of Hellenistic Judaism which we have seen in this chapter. It is noteworthy that the Pharisee from Galilee does not share this tolerant view. Evidently, there was a spectrum of different ways in which Judaism was presented to the gentiles. Finally, the high rank of the converts is notable. We know of several instances in first-century Rome where people of high station were attracted to Judaism. Josephus reports how a lady named Fulvia, in the time of Tiberius, had gone over to the customs of the Jews, and was persuaded by four Jews to send purple and gold to the temple of Jerusalem.[105] The four Jews appropriated the gifts, but the incident was reported to Tiberius and allegedly led to the expulsion of four thousand Jews, who were sent on military service to Sardinia. Josephus's account is not entirely reliable, but we need not doubt Fulvia's interest in Judaism. Poppaea, mistress and eventually second wife of Nero, was at least sympathetic to Judaism, although it is unlikely that she was a proselyte.[106] Under

Domitian, Flavius Clemens, cousin of the emperor, and consul, was executed, and his wife Flavia Domitilla was exiled. The charge against them was atheism, "a charge on which many others who were drifting into Jewish ways were condemned."[107] Presumably, the atheism of Flavius Clemens also consisted of drifting into Jewish ways, whether he was actually a proselyte or not. From these examples, we can see that Judaism made inroads into the upper classes, at least in the first century CE.[108] Against this background, we can appreciate Josephus's boast about the wealth of the Jerusalem temple: "for all the Jews throughout the habitable world and those who worshipped God, even those from Asia and Europe, had been contributing to it for a very long time" (*Ant* 14.7.2 [110]).

Further light is shed on the phenomenon of Jewish proselytizing by the satirical comments of Juvenal (*Satires*, 14:96–106):

> Some chance to have a father who fears the sabbaths,
> They adore nothing beside the clouds, and the deity of heaven
> Nor do they think swine's flesh to be different from human,
> From which the father abstained, and soon they lay aside
>   their foreskins;
> But used to despise the Roman laws
> They learn, and keep, and fear the Jewish law,
> Whatsoever Moses delivered in the secret volume:
> Not to show the ways, unless to one observing the same rites,
> To lead the circumcised only to a sought-for fountain;
> But the father is in fault, to whom every seventh day was
> Idle, and he did not meddle with any part of life.

This passage is of interest in the present context because of the clear contrast between the father "who fears sabbaths" (*metyentem sabbata*) and the son who is a proselyte and is circumcised. Despite the alleged secrecy of the book of Moses, Judaism evidently welcomed the sabbath fearers. Juvenal is not, of course, scrupulous about the accuracy of his portrayal of Judaism, but the very fact that he paints with broad strokes assures us that the "sabbath-fearing" father was a familiar figure in Rome in the late first century CE.

Much of the evidence for a class of God-fearers, who observed some of the Jewish laws but were not proselytes, comes from the book of Acts. The prime example is Cornelius, the centurion of Caesarea, in Acts 10. Two others are named: Titius Justus in 18:7 and Lydia in 16:14. Throughout Acts the phrases *phoboumenoi ton theon* (e.g.,

13:16, 26) and *sebomenos ton theon* (in various forms, e.g., Acts 17:4, 17) occur as technical terms for pious gentiles. Undoubtedly, this class serves a specific function in Luke's scheme of things: Paul is rejected by the Jews but accepted by the God-fearers and so makes his transition to the gentiles. Yet, the fact that Acts treats the God-fearers in a highly stylized way for its own purpose is no reason to question the existence of such God-fearing gentiles. Recently, their existence has been questioned by A. T. Kraabel, because the synagogue inscriptions never use the terms *phoboumenos* or *sebomenos* and there are no other references in the inscriptions which would suggest the presence of interested but nonconverted gentiles.[109] However, none of the synagogues surveyed by Kraabel is earlier than the second century CE and some are much later. Their relevance for the first century is therefore questionable. Kraabel has indeed highlighted the paucity of evidence for the God-fearers outside of Acts. The evidence for the technical use of *sebomenos* and *phoboumenos* is virtually confined to Acts, and so we must question how far the gentiles who inclined to Jewish ways constituted a well-defined class. Yet, evidence of Josephus and of the Latin authors which supports the existence of such people cannot be simply ignored. It is further supported by the Rabbinic references to the "heaven-fearers" (*yrʾê šmym*).[110] It is true that attempts to estimate the numbers of such people are unfounded,[111] but we must assume that the phenomenon caricatured by Juvenal was reasonably widespread.

We must reckon with a range of attitudes on both sides in the relations between Jews and gentiles. On the Jewish side, the story of Izates illustrates the contrast between the strict Eleazar and the more tolerant Hananias. On the gentile side, some were sympathetic to Judaism politically, without any necessary religious motivation. Others were attracted by superstitious curiosity.[112] Others, again, observed the Jewish law to varying degrees. Not all God-fearers were necessarily monotheistic. Indeed, strict monotheism would have been virtually impossible for anyone engaged in Roman public life.[113] The Jews, in turn, did not always demand strict monotheism from the gentiles. Sacrifices by gentiles (presumably polytheists) were accepted in the Jerusalem temple.[114] As we have seen above, Pseudo-Phocylides is far from clear on the question of monotheism. The Letter of Aristeas, which we will consider in the following chapter, suggested that the name *Zeus* refers to the same divinity as the God of the Jews.

Most of the evidence pertaining to God-fearers and to proselytizing comes from the first century CE or later. Yet the phenomena had roots in the second century BCE. The Third Sibyl had explicitly invited the Greeks to send gifts to the temple in Jerusalem (Sib Or 3:545–72) and Pseudo-Aristeas's identification of the God of the Jews with Zeus opened the way for gentile worshippers. In 139 BCE Jews were expelled from Rome for attempting "to infect the Roman manners with the worship of Iuppiter Sabazius."[115] Jewish influence had not yet penetrated the higher echelons of society in Rome as it would in the first century, but it is apparent that the spread of Jewish customs in the gentile world had already begun in the second century BCE.

JEWISH IDENTITY AND THE
APPEAL TO THE GENTILES

We have noted that the literature of the Hellenistic Diaspora consistently avoids the distinctive Jewish observances such as circumcision and concentrates on elements which would also be acceptable to enlightened gentiles. The question arises whether this literature was especially designed to attract gentiles and how far it reflects the practice of the Jewish community.

We must begin by recognizing that there was considerable diversity within the Jewish community. As is well known, Philo distinguishes his own position from the literalists on the one side and the extreme allegorists on the other. From the literature we have seen, it would seem that we should also reckon with a liberal strand of Judaism which was not characterized by allegory but by a reduction of the law to a few essential principles—monotheism (not always strictly defined), avoidance of idolatry, sexual ethics. We cannot, of course, assume that the Jews observed only those commandments which were mentioned in the literature. We have no reason to believe that any strand of Diaspora Judaism abandoned circumcision. Yet, the literature must be taken to reflect the priorities and emphases of the community. Just as Philo denied that the literal laws were dispensable but did not regard them as the most important dimension of religion, so the Jews who wrote the sibyllines and Testaments probably observed the distinctive commandments, but did not regard them as the heart of their religion. The understanding of the law in the terms of general principles entails a significant modification of the impression of covenantal nomism which one may get from a work like Sib Or 3.

The pattern of religion in the Hellenistic Diaspora is further modified by the attitude to proselytes and God-fearers. It is true that nearly
all the Diaspora literature assigns a special place to the covenantal
people. This is apparent in Sib Or 3 in the eschatological glorification
of the Jerusalem temple. Yet the gentiles are also invited to bring their
gifts to the temple and there is no suggestion that they must undergo
circumcision. We cannot say that the gentiles are excluded from salvation. Pseudo-Phocylides and, later, Pseudo-Menander attach no special significance to the covenant people at all and are distinguishable
as Jewish works only by their use of Jewish traditions. In this light,
the suggestion that Pseudo-Phocylides was a God-fearer can be appreciated, but, in fact, we have no sure way of distinguishing between a
God-fearer and the kind of Jew who welcomed God-fearers. If, as
Hananias told Izates, it is possible to serve God without circumcision,
then evidently membership of the covenant people was not required
for salvation, however salvation might be understood.[116] No doubt
there were differences of opinion on this point within Judaism, but,
on the whole, it appears that the Hellenistic Diaspora presented a soft
edge to the gentile world and was willing to recognize various degrees of attachment, and, by implication, of salvation.

Notes

1. B. Z. Wacholder (*Eupolemus: A Study of Judaeo-Greek Literature* [Cincinnati:
Hebrew Union College, 1974]) is exceptional in defending an early date (ca. 300 BCE)
but regarding the composition as the work of a Jerusalem priest.

2. Diodorus Siculus 40.3. The excerpt is preserved in the *Bibliotheca* of Photius, 244.
See M. Stern, *Green and Latin Authors on Jews and Judaism* (Jerusalem: Israel Academy of Sciences and Humanities, 1974) 1:20–44; "The Jews in Greek and Latin Literature," *Compendia* 2:1103–8; J. G. Gager, *Moses in Greco-Roman Paganism* (SBLMS
16; New York: Abingdon, 1972) 26–37. The fragment is attributed to Hecataeus of
Miletus, but this is universally taken for a simple mistake by Diodorus.

3. On the general *Tendenz* of Hecataeus, see P. M. Fraser (*Ptolemaic Alexandria*
[Oxford: Clarendon, 1972] 1:504): "The tendency being what it was—to prove the
superiority and greater antiquity of Egyptian culture—it seems very probable that
Hecataeus' ultimate aim was to establish the superiority of the kingdom ruled over by
Soter."

4. *Ag Ap* 1:183b–205a, 213b–14a; 2:43.

5. Against the authenticity of the *Peri Ioudaiōn* see H. Willrich, *Juden und Griechen
vor der makkabäischen Erhebung* (Göttingen: Vandenhoeck & Ruprecht, 1895) 20–
33; *Judaica. Forschungen zur hellenistisch-jüdischen Geschichte und Literatur* (Göttingen: Vandenhoeck & Ruprecht, 1900) 86–130; F. Jacobi, *FGH* IIIA, 61–74; B.
Schaller, "Hekataios von Abdera, Über den Juden. Zur Frage der Echtheit und der
Datierung," *ZNW* 54 (1963) 15–31; M. Hengel, "Anonymität, Pseudepigraphie und

'Literarische Fälschung' in der jüdisch-hellenistischen Literatur," *Entretiens sur l'Antiquité Classique XVIII* (1972) 302–3; N. Walter, "Pseudo-Hekataios I and II," *Fragmente jüdisch-hellenistischer Historiker* (JSHRZ 1/2; Gütersloh: Mohn, 1976) 144–48; Fraser, *Ptolemaic Alexandria*, 2:968–69; Wacholder, *Eupolemus*, 263–73. In defense of the authenticity, H. Lewy, "Hekataios von Abdera, peri Ioudaiōn," *ZNW* 31 (1932) 117–32; Tcherikover, *Hellenistic Civilization*, 426–27 n. 49; J. G. Gager, "Pseudo-Hecataeus Again," *ZNW* 60 (1969) 130–39.

6. Origen, *Contra Celsum*, 1.15. See Stern, "The Jews in Greek and Latin Literature," 1109.

7. Willrich, *Juden und Griechen*, 31. So also Jacobi, *FGH* III A, 62.

8. O. R. Sellers, *The Citadel of Beth-Zur* (Philadelphia: Westminster, 1933) 73 n. 9 and 74 fig. 9. A. T. Olmstead, "Intertestamental Studies," *JAOS* 56 (1936) 244.

9. Gager, "Pseudo-Hecataeus Again," 138. The coin bears a second word, which has been variously read as Yehohanan (possibly the high priest Onias I) and (more plausibly) Yehud. Sukenik had some doubt about the Hezekiah reading (see Fraser, *Ptolemaic Alexandria*, 2:969, n. 115).

10. F. M. Cross, "Aspects of Samaritan and Jewish History," *HTR* 59 (1966) 201–11.

11. Schaller, "Hekataios," 22–25. His argument is accepted by Walter, "Pseudo-Hekataios," 148.

12. See Walter, "Pseudo-Hekataios," 147–48.

13. See G. E. Wright, "The Samaritans at Shechem," *HTR* 55 (1962) 358; F. M. Cross, "Aspects of Samaritan and Jewish History," and "The Discovery of the Samaria Papyri," *BA* 36 (1963) 119.

14. E.g., Jacobi, *FGH* III A, 72.

15. Eusebius, *Chron* (ed. Schoene) II p. 112; Syncellus (ed. Dindorf) I. 486. N. L. Hirschy, *Artaxerxes III Ochus and his Reign* (Chicago: University of Chicago, 1909) 38–42.

16. On the Tennes rebellion see D. Barag, "The Effects of the Tennes Rebellion in Palestine," *BASOR* 163 (1966) 6–12.

17. Stern, "The Jews in Greek and Latin Literature," 1109.

18. Cf. his accounts of the Essenes, *JW* 2.8.10 (151–53) and of the persecution by Antiochus Epiphanes, *Ant* 12.5.4 (253–56).

19. Wacholder (*Eupolemus*, 267–73), while arguing for Jewish authorship, still concludes that "for the author of this fragment the Persian occupation was still a fresh experience, rather than, as scholarly consensus maintains, something remote as it would have been for someone who lived in the second or first century BCE" (269). In Wacholder's view, "A Jew, not a pagan, probably a priest of Jerusalem who flourished in the last decades of the fourth century, had authored this popular book" (273). However, it is as easy to believe that Hecataeus had a priestly source, Hezekiah, as to accept Wacholder's hypothesis.

20. *Ag Ap* 1.200–204 (22).

21. Compare K. Berger, *Die Gesetzauslegung Jesu* (WMANT 40; Neukirchen-Vluyn: Neukirchener Verlag, 1972) 39: "Für eine bestimmte Schicht des jüdischen Hellenismus ist *nomos* de facto nicht das atl. Gesetz, sondern lediglich ein Monotheismus, verbunden mit allgemeinen und sozialen Tugenden."

22. See M. Nilsson, *Geschichte der Griechischen Religion* (München: Beck, 1950) 2:546–52. See also the usage of the epithet *monos:* G. Delling, "Monos Theos," *Studien zum Neuen Testament und zum hellenistischen Judentum* (Göttingen: Vandenhoeck & Ruprecht, 1970) 391–400.

23. Cicero, *De Natura Deorum* 1.32.

24. H. W. Attridge, *First Century Cynicism in the Epistles of Heraclitus* (HTS 29; Missoula: Scholars, 1976) 13–23, and the material there cited.

25. H. Diels, W. Kranz, *Die Fragmente der Vorsokratiken* (7 ed.; Berlin: Weidmann, 1954) frag. 5. See also B. de Borries, *Quid veteres philosophi de idolatria senserint* (Göttingen: Dieterich, 1918) 72.

26. In his Republic, Zeno prohibited the building of temples, and also, according to

Clement, the erection of idols. Diogenes Laertius 7.33; Clement, *Stromateis*, 5.11.76, 1–3.

27. Strabo, *Geography*, 16.2.35–39; Gager, *Moses*, 38–47. Varro's comments are found in Augustine, *De civitate dei* 4.31.

28. For random anecdotes and references see H. Licht, *Sexual Life in Ancient Greece* (London: The Abbey Library, 1932) 61–63.

29. W. Kroll, "Knabenliebe," *PWRE* 11/1: 897–906. For a full treatment of the subject see K. J. Dover, *Greek Homosexuality* (Cambridge: Harvard, 1978). See also his *Greek Popular Morality in the Time of Plato and Aristotle* (Berkeley: University of California, 1974).

30. Diodorus 40.3. Gager, *Moses*, 27.

31. Sat 6.594–97. Attridge, *First Century Cynicism*, 28.

32. D. Georgi, *Die Gegner des Paulus in 2. Korintherbrief* (WMANT 11; Neukirchen-Vluyn: Neukirchener Verlag, 1964) 182–87.

33. Crouch, *The Origin and Intention of the Colossian Haustafel* (FRLANT 109; Göttingen: Vandenhoeck & Ruprecht, 1972) 84–101; M. Küchler, *Frühjüdische Weisheitstraditionen* (Orbis Biblicus et Orientalis 26; Freiburg: Universitätsverlag/ Göttingen: Vandenhoeck & Ruprecht, 1979) 207–318.

34. Cf. Berger (*Die Gesetzauslegung*, 151), who claims that Philo and Josephus derive their formulation of the twofold obligation to *eusebeia* and *dikaiosyne* from Greek rather than from biblical tradition.

35. Crouch, *The Origin and Intention*, 84–88.

36. Ibid., 87. On Buzyges, see L. Schmidt, *Die Ethik der alten Griechen* (Berlin: Hertz, 1882) 2:278–79; H. Bolkestein, *Wohltätigkeit und Armenpflege im vorchristlichen Altertum* (Utrecht: Oosthoek, 1939) 69–70.

37. M. Guttmann, *Das Judentum und seine Umwelt* (Berlin: Philo Verlag, 1927); Crouch, *The Origin and Intention*, 92–95. On the Noachian laws see L. Ginzberg, *The Legends of the Jews* (Philadelphia: Jewish Publication Society, 1955) 5.92 n. 55. The most frequently mentioned laws were against blasphemy, idolatry, incest, murder, robbery, eating meat torn from a living animal, and the commandment to establish civil law.

38. Jub 7:20, 28 lists the commandments of Noah to his sons. The actual commandments differ from the later Noachian laws. They include commands to observe righteousness, bless the creator, honor father and mother, love the neighbor, avoid fornication, uncleanliness, and bloodshed.

39. Crouch, *The Origin and Intention*, 95.

40. G. Klein, *Der älteste Christliche Katechismus und die Jüdische Propaganda-Literatur* (Berlin: Reimer, 1909).

41. P. W. van der Horst, *The Sentences of Pseudo-Phocylides* (SVTP 4; Leiden: Brill, 1978) 77–80.

42. K. Horna, "Gnome, Gnomendichtung, Gnomologien," *PWRE* Supp 6 (1935) 74–90; Küchler (*Frühjüdische Weisheitstraditionen*, 236–61) surveys the relevant Greek gnomologies.

43. Isocrates, *Ad Nicoclem*, 42–43 (cited by van der Horst, 60).

44. Van der Horst, *The Sentences of Pseudo-Phocylides*, 81–83. The Alexandrian provenance of the poem is indicated by vs. 102, which condemns the dissection of corpses. The study of anatomy by dissection is known only from Alexandria in the ancient world (F. Kudlien, "Anatomie," *PWRE* Supp 11 [1968] 38–48).

45. Van der Horst (*Sentences*, 180), translates Bernays's emendation *gooisi* for *theoisi*.

46. Ibid., 186–88.

47. Ibid., 151, citing R. Kerst, "1 Kor. 8,6—ein vorpaulinisches Taufbekenntnis?" *ZNW* 66 (1975) 130–39.

48. On the problem of monotheism for God-fearers, see F. Siegert, "Gottesfürchtige und Sympathisanten," *JSJ* 4 (1973) 140–47.

49. Van der Horst, *Sentences*, 231.

50. Ibid., 135.

51. Ibid., 185.

52. See further F. Christ, "Das Leben nach dem Tode bei Pseudo-Phokylides," *TZ* 31 (1975) 140–49; U. Fischer, *Eschatologie und Jenseitserwartung im Hellenistischen Diasporajudentum* (BZNW 44; Berlin: de Gruyter, 1978) 125–43.

53. Van der Horst, *Sentences*, 139. The word for strangers is *epēlydes*.

54. *De Vita Mosis*, 1.35. The term for strangers is *xenoi*.

55. Van der Horst, *Sentences*, 70–76.

56. J. P. Audet, "La sagesse de Ménandre l'Egyptien," *RB* 59 (1952) 55–81; Küchler, *Weisheitstraditionen*, 303–18.

57. The contrast with Pseudo-Eupolemus at this point has often been noted, but there is no adequate reason to suppose deliberate polemic.

58. I.e., *ennomon hymnon*. The adjective is a play on *nomos* as harmony and as law.

59. Cf. Berger, *Die Gesetzauslegung*, 41.

60. V. Nikiprowetzky, *La Troisième Sibylle* (Etudes Juives 9; Paris: Mouton, 1970) 82–83.

61. Euhemerism was the theory put forward by Euhemerus of Messene (ca. 300 BCE) that the gods of popular worship had been kings and conquerors to whom mankind had shown gratitude by worshipping them as gods (Diodorus Siculus 6.1; 5.41). On the theory and its predecessors, see Nilsson, *Geschichte*, 2:269–74. Sib Or 3 gives a euhemeristic account of early history in 3:110–55. Kronos and the Titans in that passage are presumably the "overbearing kings" referred to here.

62. Nikiprowetzky, *La Troisième Sibylle*, 81. Cf. Zeno in Plutarch, *De Alexandri Virtute* 1,6 (*SVF* 1,264).

63. See Nilsson, *Geschichte*, 261–67. For Nechepso and Petosiris, see E. Riess, "Nechepsonis et Petosiridis Fragmenta Magica," *Philologus* Supplementband 6 (1892–1893) 327–88.

64. See J. H. Charlesworth, "Jewish Astrology in the Talmud, Pseudepigrapha, The Dead Sea Scrolls, and early Palestinian Synagogues," *HTR* 70 (1977) 183–200; and "Rylands Syriac Ms. 44 and A New Addition to the Pseudepigrapha: The Treatise of Shem Discussed and Translated," *BJRL* 60 (1978) 376–403. Charlesworth suggests a date in the last third of the first century BCE, but the evidence is not clear and the document could be much later.

65. Cicero, *De Divinatione*, 87–99.

66. E. Bickermann, "The Altars of the Gentiles," *Studies in Jewish and Christian History* (AGJU 9; Leiden: Brill, 1980) 2:329; A. Baumstark, "Chaldaei," *PWRE* 3 (1899) 2059–60.

67. The Sibyl was not, of course, the only Jewish voice raised against astrology. See also Jub 12:17; Philo, *De Abrahamo*, 84; *De Migratione Abrahami*, 187–88. Astrology is part of the corrupting revelation of the Watchers in 1 Enoch 8.

68. In this regard, it is noteworthy that Sib Or 3, unlike Pseudo-Phocylides does not attach a spiritual significance to ablutions. The precise meaning of 591–93 ("at dawn they lift up holy arms towards heaven, from their beds, always sanctifying the flesh [or "hands"] with water") is unclear. (See Nikiprowetzky, *La Troisième Sibylle*, 238–40). These practices are said to be typical of Jews but are not required of gentiles. In any case neither prayer nor ablutions could be unfamiliar to a Hellenistic audience (See E. Pfister, "katharsis," *PWRE* Supp 6 (1935) 146–62.

69. The charge of matricide refers to Nero, a central figure in Sib Or 5 (Collins, *The Sibylline Oracles* [SBLDS 13; Missoula: Scholars, 1974] 80–87).

70. See J. J. Collins, "The Place of the Fourth Sibyl in the Development of the Jewish Sibyllina," *JJS* 25 (1974) 365–80, contra V. Nikiprowetzky, "Reflexions sur Quelques Problèmes du Quatrième et du Cinquième Livre des Oracles Sibyllins," *HUCA* 43 (1972) 29–76.

71. J. Thomas, *Le Mouvement Baptiste en Palestine et Syrie* (Gembloux: Duculot, 1938) 223.

72. Nikiprowetzky, "Reflexions," 68, argues plausibly that the "they" in question are the Romans, not the Zealots.

73. See Collins, "The Place of the Fourth Sibyl," 378–80. The biblical point of

departure was Isa 1:16. The closest parallels to Sib Or 4 can be found in the Ebionite and Elcasaite Christian sects, which also rejected both temple worship and bloody sacrifices.

74. J. Becker, *Untersuchungen zur Entstehungsgeschichte der Testamente der zwölf Patriarchen* (AGJU 8; Leiden: Brill, 1970); *Die Testamente der zwölf Patriarchen* (2 ed.; JSHRZ 3/1; Gütersloh: Mohn, 1980); A. Hultgård, *L'Eschatologie des Testaments des Douze Patriarches. 1. Interpretation des textes* (Uppsala: Almqvist & Wiksell, 1977); H. C. Kee, "Ethical Dimensions of the Testaments of the XII as a Clue to Provenance," *NTS* 24 (1978) 259–70.

75. M. de Jonge, *The Testaments of the Twelve Patriarchs: A Study of Their Text, Composition and Origin* (Assen: van Gorcum, 1953); *Studies on the Testaments of the Twelve Patriarchs. Text and Interpretation* (SVTP 3; Leiden: Brill, 1975).

76. A. Dupont-Sommer, *Nouveaux aperçus sur les manuscrits de la Mer Morte* (Paris: Maisonneuve, 1953). M. Philonenko, *Les Interpolations chrétiennes des Testaments des Douze Patriarches et les manuscrits de Qoumrân* (Paris: Presses universitaires de France, 1960). On the Qumran fragments relating to T Lev and T Naph, and other related Semitic material, see Becker, *Untersuchungen*, 69–128.

77. For a summary, see de Jonge, *Studies*, 120–39; H. J. de Jonge, ibid., 63–86.

78. Becker, *Die Testamente*, 23–27.

79. So also K. H. Rengstorff, "Herkunft und Sinn der Patriarchen Reden in den Testamenten der zwölf Patriarchen," *La Littérature Juive entre Tenach et Mischna* (ed. W. C. van Unnik; Leiden: Brill, 1974) 28–47. It is not disputed that older Semitic traditions, now attested at Qumran were incorporated.

80. J. Thomas, "Aktuelles in Zeugnis der zwölf Vater," *Studien zu den Testamenten der zwölf Patriarchen* (ed. W. Eltester; BZNW 36; Berlin: Töpelmann, 1969) 62–150.

81. Küchler, *Frühjüdische Weisheitstraditionen*, 431–545.

82. E. J. Bickermann, "The Date of the Testaments of the Twelve Patriarchs," *Studies* 2:1–23 (first published in *JBL* 69 [1950] 245–60).

83. K. Baltzer, *The Covenant Formulary* (Philadelphia: Fortress, 1971). On the form of the Testaments, see further E. von Nordheim, *Die Lehre der Alten. Das Testament als Gliedgattung im Judentum der Hellenistisch-Römischen Zeit* (Leiden: Brill, 1980); G. W. Nickelsburg, *Jewish Literature Between the Bible and Mishnah: A Historical and Literary Introduction* (Philadelphia: Fortress, 1981) 231–41.

84. Baltzer, *The Covenant Formulary*, 145.

85. Cf. Berger, *Die Gesetzauslegung*, 388.

86. E.g., 4 Mac 2:14; Philo, *De Virtutibus*, 109–24; Cf. Arist 225–30; Joseph and Aseneth, 28–29. See Becker, *Untersuchungen*, 377–401; Berger, *Die Gesetzauslegung*, 120; W. Harrelson, "Patient Love in the Testament of Joseph," *Studies on the Testament of Joseph* (ed. G. W. Nickelsburg; SCS 5; Missoula: Scholars, 1975) 29–35. On the role of Joseph, see H. W. Hollander, *Joseph as an Ethical Model in the Testaments of the Twelve Patriarchs* (SVTP 6; Leiden: Brill, 1981).

87. On the structure of homilies in the Hellenistic synagogue, see esp. P. Borgen, *Bread from Heaven* (Leiden: Brill, 1969) 28–58. Borgen stresses the use of scriptural quotations both as main text and as subordinate illustrations of the theme. His main examples are drawn from Philo.

88. The ascetic tendencies of the Testaments are noted by R. Eppel, *Le Piétisme Juif dans les Testaments des Douze Patriarches* (Paris: Alcan, 1930) 154–57.

89. A. Vögtle, *Die Tugend- und Lasterkataloge im Neuen Testament* (Münster: Aschendorff, 1936); S. Wibbing, *Die Tugend- und Lasterkataloge in Neuen Testament* (Tübingen: Mohr, 1964); H. Conzelmann, *1 Corinthians* (Hermeneia; Philadelphia; Fortress, 1975) 100.

90. For Stoic texts, see J. von Arnim, *Stoicorum Veterum Fragmenta* (Leipzig: Teubner, 1905) 3: nos. 377–490.

91. See esp. G. von Rad, "Die Vorgeschichte der Gattung von 1 Kor 13:4–7," *Geschichte und Altes Testament. Albrecht Alt zum siebsigsten Geburtstag* (Tübingen: Mohr, 1953) 153–68. Cf. also Ps 24; Ezek 18:5–9; Jer 17:5–8.

92. H. Thyen, *Der Stil der Jüdisch-Hellenistischen Homilie* (Göttingen: Vandenhoeck & Ruprecht, 1955), following the basic study of Bultmann, *Der Stil der paulinischen Predigt und die kynisch-stoische Diatribe* (Göttingen: Vandenhoeck & Ruprecht, 1910). Becker (*Untersuchungen*, 194) has shown how well Thyen's analysis can be applied to the parenetic passages in the Testaments.

93. W. Michaelis, "hodos," *TDNT* 5 (1967) 42–96, esp. 56–65, where he traces OT influence on the intertestamental writings.

94. Cf. also Heracles's choice between the ways of vice and virtue in Xenophon, *Memorabilia*, 2.1.21–34.

95. Kee, "Ethical Dimensions," 259–70; Berger, *Gesetzauslegung*, 42–45.

96. See esp. Georgi, *Die Gegner*, 83–100.

97. Borgen, *Bread from Heaven*, 28–58.

98. De Specialibus Legibus 2.62–63 (282). The term translated "thousands" (*myria*) may be taken as "numerous." See also Philo, *De Vita Mosis*, 2.216 (168).

99. See esp. Berger, *Die Gesetzauslegung*, 137–76. For comparison with rabbinic material, see A. Nissen, *Gott und der Nächste im antiken Judentum* (WUNT 15; Tübingen: Mohr, 1974).

100. *JW* 7.3.3 (45). Pagan authors were impressed by the openness of Judaism in this respect. (J. Juster, *Les Juifs dans l'Empire Romain* [Paris: Geuthner, 1914] 279, 413). It is debated whether part of the synagogue service was reserved for Jews.

101. Acts 13:16, 26, 43, 50; 17:4, 17. Note esp. 13:44, where "almost the whole city" came to the synagogue to hear Paul. See further E. Schürer, *Geschichte des jüdischen Volkes in Zeitalter Jesu Christi* (4 ed.; Leipzig: Hinrichs, 1909) 3:118.

102. G. F. Moore, *Judaism in the First Centuries of the Christian Era* (New York: Schocken, 1971, first published in 1927) 327–28; also Juster, *Les Juifs*, 254–74; Schürer, *Geschichte*, 3:133–35; K .G. Kuhn/H. Stegemann, "Proselyten," *PWRE* Supp 9 (1962) 1248–83; K. G. Kuhn, "Proselytos," *TDNT* 6 (1968) 727–44. The warning of Paul in Gal 5:3 is often cited in this context: "I testify again to every man who receives circumcision that he is bound to keep the whole law."

103. F. Siegert, "Gottesfürchtige und Sympathisanten," *JSJ* 4 (1973) 128.

104. Seneca in Augustine, *De civitate dei* 6.11; Dio Cassius 37.17. Schürer, *Geschichte*, 3:117; Compare also Josephus, *Ag Ap* 2.123 (10); Philo, *De Vita Mosis* 2:20–24 (137).

105. *Ant* 18.3.5 (81–84). For discussion, see Georgi, *Die Gegner*, 100–104; Smallwood, *The Jews under Roman Rule* (SJLA 20; Leiden: Brill, 1976) 201–8. This incident should be related to the report of Tacitus (*Annals* 2.85.4) that in 19 CE action was taken to expel Egyptian and Jewish rites and that 4,000 freedmen were sent to Sardinia on military duty. See also Suetonius, *Tiberius*, 36.

106. *Ant* 20.8.11 (195); *Vit* 3.16 (3). Josephus says she was *theosebēs*, but see Smallwood, *The Jews*, 278 n.79, who denies that she had any personal leanings towards Judaism.

107. Dio 67.14.1–3. Smallwood, *The Jews*, 378. Flavia Domitilla was almost certainly the niece of the emperor. Smallwood suggests that the rabbinic story of a senator Ketiah bar Shalom, who either was executed for interceding for the Jews or committed suicide, is based on the execution of Flavius Clemens (Smallwood, "Domitian's Attitudes Towards the Jews and Judaism," *Classical Philology* 51 [1956] 1–13).

108. For further contacts between the imperial household and the Jews see Siegert, "Gottesfürchtige," 150.

109. A. T. Kraabel, "The Disappearance of the God-fearers," *Numen* 28 (1981) 113–26. M. Wilcox ("The God-fearers in Acts—A Reconsideration," *JSNT* 13 [1981] 102–22) argues that the God-fearers in Acts include both Jews and gentiles.

110. See the thorough review by Siegert, "Gottesfürchtige," 109–64. Siegert is in agreement with Kraabel on the lack of inscriptional evidence and discounts the Latin "metuens" inscriptions.

111. E.g., *Encyclopedia Judaica*, 10:55, estimates that there may have been millions of *sebomenoi* in the first century.

112. Juvenal, *Satires*, 6:541–46: "For a small piece of money the Jews sell whatever dreams you may choose." Juvenal refers to a begging Jewess who is the vendor of dreams.

113. See Siegert, "Gottesfürchtige," 140–47.

114. See esp. Bickermann, "The Altars of the Gentiles," 324–46.

115. Valerius Maximus 1.3.3. See Bickermann, "The Altars of the Gentiles," 329–35.

116. Contrast the story of the Roman senator in Midrash Debarim Rabba 2.24, where circumcision is explicitly required for salvation (Siegert, "Gottesfürchtige," 111).

Chapter 5

PHILOSOPHICAL JUDAISM

The sibyl, Pseudo-Phocylides, and the Testaments represent some of the popular formulations of Jewish ethics. There was always a tradition in Hellenistic Judaism which attempted to provide a deeper philosophical basis for its teachings. Philo, of course, was the supreme example. However, Philo had his predecessors, even if they were less systematic in their approach. The first, and possibly most significant, of these was Aristobulus. Only fragments of his work survive, but they are sufficiently substantial to establish him as a major figure in the history of Hellenistic Judaism.[1]

ARISTOBULUS

The work of Aristobulus was dedicated to "Ptolemy the King." The Ptolemy in question was specified by Clement[2] as Philometor. Both Clement and Eusebius identify Aristobulus with the "Aristobulus . . . teacher of Ptolemy the king" who is addressed in 2 Mac 1:10. The identification and dating in Clement and Eusebius are probably inferred from 2 Maccabees and have accordingly been challenged. Bickermann has shown that the salutation form in 2 Mac 1:10 only became current about 60 BCE.[3] It seems probable that the forger of 2 Mac 1:10 knew the work of Aristobulus with the dedication to the king, and inferred that Aristobulus was the king's teacher. 2 Mac 1:10, then, only shows that Aristobulus's work was current in the mid-first century BCE. The reign of Philometor is, however, still the most likely period for a Jewish writer to dedicate his work to the king.

Walter has shown that the allegorical method of Aristobulus does not presuppose that of Philo[4] and has also argued that Aristobulus is not dependent on Pseudo-Aristeas. The issue here concerns Aristobulus's reference to the alleged translation of the LXX under Philadelphus, at the instigation of Demetrius of Phalerum (PE 13.12.2). Since at least the reference to Demetrius is unhistorical, some scholars have assumed that Aristobulus must be dependent on Aristeas. Walter, however, argues that both may have drawn on a common tradition. The priority of Aristobulus is supported by the other parallels between the two texts.[5] The scattered remarks of Pseudo-Aristeas on allegorical exegesis and the nature of God are not likely to have inspired the sustained exegesis of Aristobulus.[6] The similarities between the two writers suggest close proximity in date and provenance, although Pseudo-Aristeas seems to assume some methodological steps which Aristobulus feels obliged to justify. We can hardly assume that Aristobulus was the first to apply allegorical methods to the Torah. However, if there is influence in either direction between Aristobulus and Pseudo-Aristeas, Aristobulus would seem to be the prior. The relationship between Aristobulus and Pseudo-Aristeas, then, supports the dating to the time of Philometor.[7]

Both Clement and Eusebius refer to Aristobulus as a Peripatetic, but he was clearly eclectic and not restricted to any one system.[8] He is first and foremost a Jewish apologist.[9] His entire work is a defense of the Jewish Torah against interpretations that would make it seem crude or unsophisticated. The apologetic, as always, is addressed to two fronts. On the one hand, there is the explicit address to the gentile king and the attempt to use acceptable Hellenistic categories. On the other hand, this interpretation of Judaism is inevitably a challenge to more conservative Jews (the challenge is explicit in PE 8.10.5) and a reinforcement to those who thought in Hellenistic categories.

Aristobulus's allegorical interpretation springs directly from his apologetic interests. He exhorts the king to take the interpretations *physikōs* and not lapse into the mythical. *Physikōs* has a technical sense in Stoic exegesis. Aristobulus's usage does not conform to that sense, but he may well have borrowed the term from the Stoics. Walter has rightly remarked that Aristobulus's lack of a technical vocabulary is an indication that he was a pioneer in this kind of Jewish exegesis.[10] His conception, in any case, is clear. Moses uses language of outward appearance to express inward realities. So Aristobulus is led to criticize "those who have no share of power and understanding, but who are devoted to the letter alone." His criticism may, in part, be directed against gentile critics, but his primary reference is surely to the Jewish literalists, who were still a significant faction in the time of Philo. The issue between Aristobulus and the literalists was significant. If a religion is to function as any form of nomism, the meaning of the laws must be publicly accessible. The allegorical method shifts the basis of the religion from the actual text to the understanding which provides the hidden interpretation. There is obviously a relationship between this allegorical method and the visions of higher reality in Ezekiel the tragedian and the Orphic poem, which we will consider in chapter 6 below. There are differences too. Aristobulus does not rely on vision (even on a vision of Moses or Abraham) but on philosophical understanding, and he shows a critical self-consciousness which is lacking in the poetic works. Aristobulus is the first theologian of Hellenistic Judaism.

Aristobulus's use of allegorical interpretation is confined to the biblical anthropomorphisms—the hands, feet, "standing" and voice of God. His discussion of the Passover makes no reference to Jewish history but only to cosmic phenomena—the equinoxes of the sun and moon. The lengthy discussion of the holiness of the number seven involves no allegory but attempts to collect pagan witnesses too. The association between wisdom and light in PE 13.12.9–10 is not direct allegory but claims that what is said about light "might be said allegorically about wisdom also." Both in these cases and in the use of allegory, Aristobulus is guided by the underlying assumption of the unity of all truth. So the intention of the gentile poets refers to God, even when they call him Zeus or Dis. The poets also testify to the correlation of light and wisdom. The specific contribution of Judaism is that writers like Solomon "said more clearly and better that wisdom existed before heaven and earth." The common basis is that "it is agreed by all the philosophers that it is necessary to hold holy opinions concerning God," but this is "a point our philosophical school makes particularly well." Judaism is a "philosophical school" (*hairesis*) among others, though it claims to be the preeminent one. One of the ways in which Aristobulus makes his point about the superiority of Judaism is by claiming that Plato and the philosophers borrowed from Moses. (In this context, Aristobulus claims that there were translations of the Torah before Philadelphus, but this claim is obviously required if Plato were to have borrowed from Moses.) While the claim may seem ridiculously arrogant, it involved a recognition that truth was indeed to be found in the pagan writers; ultimately, in Philo, it meant that Moses could be interpreted in the light of Greek philosophy. This claim had its antecedents in the popular assertions of Jewish antiquity in the romantic historians, but Aristobulus goes further. The God of the Jews and the God of the gentiles are one. Judaism differs from the philosophical schools in degree. Judaism, in effect, is not a covenantal nomism, but a philosophy.

As part of his apologetic enterprise Aristobulus cites a number of verses from Greek poets to support the idea that the seventh day is holy. Only one of these verses (Hesiod, *Works and Days*, 770) is demonstrably authentic, although one of the Homer verses may be based on an authentic verse, and another may have been part of the Homeric tradition of the time.[11] The other verses are not necessarily Jewish in origin. Walter has argued that a Jewish forger would hardly have chosen such an obscure legendary figure as Linus,[12] and suggested that some of these verses may be of Pythagorean origin. The fact that these verses are cited in support of the sabbath is significant, since the sabbath was one of the more peculiar Jewish institutions. It reflects Aristobulus's desire to diminish the markers which would separate Judaism from its Hellenistic environment.

POETIC FORGERIES

Unrelated to these verses in Aristobulus is a series of verses attributed to Greek poets found in Pseudo-Justin and Clement.[13] The use of gnomologia was developed in the Hellenistic age by Greek writers, most notably Chrysippus (280–207 BCE), who succeeded Cleanthes as head of the Stoa. The method of using proof texts from respected writers was inherited by the Jewish apologists. The spurious verses in Pseudo-Justin and Clement are attributed to Aeschylus, Sophocles, Euripides, Pythagoras, Diphilus, Menander, and Hesiod. Clement (*Stromateis* 5.113.1) attributes one of the Sophocles quotations to (Pseudo-) Hecataeus in his book on Abraham and the Egyptians. Consequently, Schürer and others attributed all the poetic forgeries to Pseudo-Hecataeus.[14] This is unwarranted, in view of our lack of knowledge about Pseudo-Hecataeus. It is not possible to specify the sources of these fragments, except to say that they are before Clement. The content of the verses is mainly concerned to denounce idolatry and affirm monotheism. In this they resemble the J recension of the Orphic verses and Sib Or 3:1–45. The fragments of Pseudo-Menander are largely taken up with ethical issues and resemble Pseudo-

Phocylides. Pseudo-Diphilus discourses on the two ways and the question of justice after death. Pseudo-Sophocles, in one passage, describes a final conflagration in terms influenced by Stoicism. All of these focus attention on the aspects of Judaism with which Greek philosophers were sympathetic. The extent of the common ground may be illustrated by the epistles of Heraclitus. Since the work of Bernays it has been common to assume that some of these epistles were Jewish forgeries (at least epistles 4 and 7). However, Attridge has shown that even the most "Jewish" motifs in these epistles can be paralleled in the popular, especially Cynic, philosophers.[15] It is to this popular philosophy that the Jewish forgers appealed. Their appeal did not rest on any claim to revelation or to a special covenant of Judaism with God, but to the ethical and theistic convictions themselves, which were found to a higher degree in Judaism.

PSEUDO-ARISTEAS

A second representative of philosophical Judaism from the second century BCE is Pseudo-Aristeas. In considering the view of Judaism in the Letter of Aristeas two factors are of major importance. First, the prime expression of Judaism is the Mosaic law. This is what Demetrius wants for the library and this is the basis of the high priest's exposition. The sanctity of the law is emphasized in the passage which explains why it has not previously been known to the Greek world: when a historian or a tragic poet attempts to draw on it they are smitten with afflictions (312–16). We may contrast here the bold claim of Aristobulus that Plato, Pythagoras, and others had in fact drawn on Moses. Pseudo-Aristeas's comment would seem to cast doubt on the validity of the enterprise of Jewish writers such as Ezekiel the tragedian. The law is not to be paraphrased but is to be exactly translated and interpreted. This, of course, brings us to the second point. The law needs interpretation. Its sense is not plain or obvious. Further, it needs to be complemented with the wisdom provided by a Greek education.

Perhaps the most striking and fundamental assertion in the entire work is that put on the lips of Demetrius in section 16: "God, the overseer and creator of all things, whom they worship, is He whom all men worship, and we too, Your Majesty, though we address Him differently, as Zeus and Dis; by these names men of old not unsuitably signified that He through whom all creatures receive life and come into being is the guide and lord of all." The claim is not only that the God of the Jews is the creator of all, but that he is, in fact, the God worshipped by all. That the passage is attributed to a Greek does not change the fact that it is composed by a Jewish author and reflects the theology of the work as a whole. While the law is important, and Pseudo-Aristeas is concerned with the observation of the detailed dietary laws, Judaism is not a covenantal nomism. In the words of Hadas: "The theology premised is applicable to all mankind, not to the Jews alone, and God's providence is universal. It is not suggested that God will show special consideration for the Jews simply by virtue of their being Jews, nor is there any hint of proselytization. . . . The Jews follow their own traditional usage to attain a religious end; the same end may be attained by others by a different path."[16]

The understanding of the law is the subject of the high priest's discourse in 130–68. There are obvious affinities with Aristobulus. Nothing in the law has been set down heedlessly or in the spirit of myth (*mythōdōs*, 168), and the interpretation is based on the *physikē dianoia*. Moses, the lawgiver, is presented as a philosopher, proceeding from principles. The first principle is that God is one and his power is made manifest throughout creation. Thus, an evildoer cannot escape notice and the commandments are effectively enforced. This is followed by an attack on idolatry and polytheism, from an explicitly euhemeristic point of view. It should be noted that nothing in this attack could offend an enlightened pagan.[17] It does, however, provide a reason why Moses, "fenced us about with impregnable palisades and with walls of iron, to the end that we should mingle in no way with any of the other nations" (130). This statement has elicited comment, as it is indeed surprising that Pseudo-Aristeas should draw attention to this particular aspect of the Jewish law. Yet it becomes apparent that, while Pseudo-Aristeas is prepared to defend the full law, he does not understand it in a nationalistic sense. What the Jews really refuse to mingle with are "vain opinions," not other nations as such. Enlightened pagans, such as the Egyptian priests, can appreciate the Jewish position. The significant distinction is not between Jews and gentiles, but between "men of God, a title applicable to none others but only to him who reveres the true God" and "men of food and drink and raiment" (140). So the particular, concrete commandments are reinterpreted allegorically to apply to universal human virtues. The birds forbidden by the dietary laws symbolize oppression and violence, animals that part the hoof symbolize discrimination, those that chew the cud symbolize memory, and so forth. The law, in short, is one symbolic expression of the truth which can also be approached in other ways.

The universalism of Pseudo-Aristeas is further emphasized by the lengthy table-talk section. The answers of the sages, like the questions to which they respond are rather banal and commonplace wisdom. Many scholars have argued that it is adapted from a Hellenistic tract.[18] The constant references to God are the only distinguishing feature. The significant point is that the sages are expected to show a mastery of the common wisdom of the Hellenistic world. The Torah alone is not enough. The sages are expected to be proficient, not only in the literature of the Jews but also in that of the Greeks. They are distinguished in *paideia* (121). They "zealously cultivated the quality of the mean . . . and eschewing a crude and uncouth disposition they likewise avoided conceit and the assumption of superiority over others" (122). They did not, in short, regard themselves as a chosen people. The high priest himself is a *kalokagathos* or "a Greek gentleman" (3). The Torah, to be properly appreciated, must be complemented by Greek culture.

One other aspect of the Judaism of the letter requires comment. The description of Judea and Jerusalem includes a striking passage on the high priest (96–99): "We were struck with great astonishment when we beheld Eleazar at his ministration, and his apparel, and the visible glory conferred by his being garbed in the coat which he wears and the stones that adorn his person. . . . The total effect of the whole arouses awe and emotional excitement, so that one would think he had passed to some other sphere outside the world. I venture to affirm positively that any man who witnesses the spectacle I have recounted will experience amazement and astonishment indescribable, and his mind will be deeply moved at the sanctity attaching to every detail." No mention is made of the efficacy of the sacrifices or their effect on the relations between men and God. The liturgy is considered as a *spectacle,* and is admired for its emotional effect on onlookers. This is not how the cult functions in the context of covenantal nomism Rather, it is one specimen among others of the glory of Judaism— ranking with the description of the land and the order of the state. We are reminded of the praise of Simon the Just in Ben Sira, where, again, the *glory* of the priesthood is the issue. Pseudo-Aristeas goes beyond

Ben Sira in suggesting that the cult is an ecstatic experience because of the emotional effect of the solemn rituals. The concern is not with the mechanism of atonement but with the public impression of Judaism that is conveyed.

THE WISDOM OF SOLOMON

A third representative of philosophical Judaism is found in one of the major products of the Egyptian Diaspora, the Wisdom of Solomon. The Egyptian provenance of the work is not seriously in doubt in view of the prominence of Egypt in chapters 10–19, and the philosophical coloring of the work is most obviously compatible with an Alexandrian setting.[19] The book has been dated anywhere from the second century BCE to 40 CE.[20] The strongest arguments have been adduced by Winston, who sets the book in the time of Caligula.[21] The theory that idolatry arose from the desire of subjects to flatter a distant ruler (14:16–20) is most easily explained with reference to the early Roman period, and the term *kratēsis* in 6:3 may have a technical reference to the Roman conquest of Egypt. The atmosphere of persecution in the opening chapters suggests more specifically the time of Caligula. The genre of the book is the *logos protreptikos* or exhortatory discourse, which was "a union of philosophy and rhetoric" developed originally by the Sophists.[22]

Wisdom does not attempt to identify the god of the Jews with Zeus and so posit a common basis of religion for Jews and gentiles. Indeed, the central focus of the book is not on the divinity as such but on the figure of Wisdom. While Wisdom had a well-known prehistory in the Jewish wisdom literature, its presentation here is distinctly colored by Greek philosophy.[23] Wisdom is the principle of order which "stretches in might from pole to pole and effectively orders all things" (8:1). It can be expressed in physical terms: "manifold, subtle, agile, lucid, unsullied, clear, inviolable . . . more mobile than any motion, she pervades and permeates all things by reason of her pureness" (7:22–24). Wisdom is a spirit (*pneuma*) that loves humanity, which has "filled the inhabited earth" and "holds all things together." Much of this conception is evidently based on the Stoic Logos/Pneuma, although various nuances are derived from middle Platonism and from the aretalogies of Isis, in addition, of course, to the Jewish wisdom literature.[24] The author of Wis evidently found common basis for Judaism and Greek philosophy in this figure which carried less danger of polytheism than Zeus or Dis.

The figure of Wisdom has a pivotal role in determining the identity of the various parties in the book.[25] Wisdom "will not enter a fraudulent mind nor make her home in a body mortgaged to sin" (1:4). By implication, it will enter into a righteous soul and abide in a sinless body, or, in the formulation of Wis 7:27, "generation by generation she enters into holy souls and renders them friends of God and prophets."[26] While Wis 1:4 implies that the recipient of wisdom must already be righteous, Wis 7:27 suggests that it is wisdom which makes them righteous. We should not regard these statements as opposed. The point is that the presence of wisdom is an identifying mark of the righteous. The presence or absence of wisdom determines the eschatological fate of the individual. In the famous *sorites*[27] of 6:17–20:

> The true beginning of Wisdom is the desire to learn
> and a concern for learning is love of her;
> love for her means the keeping of her laws
> attention to the law is a surety of immortality
> and immortality makes one near to God.

The actual eschatological conceptions which are developed mainly in the "book of eschatology" (chaps. 1–5) are heavily dependent on Jewish apocalyptic traditions (especially in the judgment scene in 5:5: "How was he reckoned among the sons of God and how is his portion among the holy ones?").[28] Yet, it is combined with a distinctly Greek conception of the immortality of the soul, with a suggestion of preexistence, and avoids any reference to resurrection of the body.[29] The fate of both righteous and wicked is determined by their understanding of God and the world. The impious are those who "reasoned not rightly" (2:1) and "knew not the mysteries of God" (2:22). Consequently, they resolve to "let our strength be the rule of our righteousness for weakness is proved to be unprofitable" (2:11). When judgment comes they realize their mistake: "we erred from the path of truth . . . and we did not know the way of the Lord" (5:6–7). By contrast, the righteous individual "professes to have knowledge of God" and declares the end of the righteous blessed" (2:13, 16). Consequently, such people are not seduced by the short-term gains of wickedness, for their hope is full of immortality (3:4). Those who understand and appreciate the role of righteousness in the world order can benefit from its fruits: "the righteous live forever" (5:15). Even the cosmos joins in the rejection of the wicked, since God "will make all creation his weapons for the repulse of his foes" (5:17). The wisdom of the righteous is fully grounded in an understanding of the universe. It involves "unerring knowledge of existent being, to know the structure of the universe and the operation of the elements; the beginning, and end, and middle of times" (7:17–18).

The major illustration of the workings of wisdom is provided by the so-called "book of history" in chapters 10–19.[30] These chapters consist of a brief review of the history recorded in the book of Genesis (chap. 10) and a lengthy reflection on the Exodus (chaps. 11–19). The material is not treated as a recitation of "salvation history" as the unique and exceptional history of Israel. The events in question are not ascribed to the direct intervention of God but to the constant activity of wisdom in the world. The experience of Israel and its enemies is expressed as an experience of the cosmos rather than a direct encounter with God.[31] Idolators are punished "by means of those very creatures whom they esteemed as gods" (12:27). The plagues of Egypt and the crossing of the sea reveal that "nature fights for the righteous" (15:17) and that "creation, ministering to thee its maker, strains itself against the unrighteous for punishment and slackens for beneficence on behalf of those that trust in you [God]" (16:24). Even when "the whole creation in its particular nature was fashioned again anew complying with your commands so that your servants might be kept unharmed," this miraculous transformation does not require a direct intervention of God. Instead, it is brought about by an inner mutation of the universe, prompted only by God's command: "the elements, being changed in order among themselves, as in a psaltery the notes vary the character of the tune, yet always adhering to the sound." In the words of A. T. S. Goodrick: "Even miracles are regarded by 'Wisdom' not as a derangement of the universe, but as a rearrangement of the harmony of it."[32] The understanding of history is grounded in a consistent understanding of the workings of the cosmos.

The hand of God can, of course, be discerned in the workings of the cosmos. It is precisely from the greatness and beauty of creation that the creator is recognized (13:1). Wisdom involves the recognition of God through the works of creation, since this is required by a full understanding of the world. It is the wisdom which recognizes God which leads to righteousness and immortality: "For to know thee is perfect righteousness and to know thy might is the root of immortality." Yet this knowledge is indirect, mediated by wisdom, through the cosmos. It is not given directly by the prophetic "word of the Lord" or by ecstatic revelation.

In the review of Israel's history no individual names are used. Each of the biblical characters illustrates a type, the "righteous"—in 10:4, Noah; in 10:5, Abraham; in 10:6, Lot; in 10:10 Jacob, etc.[33] The history of Israel provides a paradigmatic example of the experience of righteous individuals or a righteous people but is only an illustration of the workings of the universe. In practice, the author appears to equate the righteous with historical Israel and unrighteous with Israel's enemies. Nevertheless, the primary distinction is not between Israel and the gentiles but between the righteous and the wicked. While Israel is presented as the paradigm of the righteous, it is not necessarily an exclusive paradigm. God "does not delight in the destruction of the living, for he created all things that they might have being" (1:13–14) and has compassion over all, "because you can do all, and you overlook the sins of men with a view to their repentance, for you love all that exists and loathe nothing which you have created, for if you had hated anything you would never have fashioned it" (11:23–24). Wisdom is characterized as *philanthrōpon*, a term with broad universalist implications. These universalist principles provide the necessary corrective to the sharp attacks on the ancient Egyptians and Canaanites, which, as Winston suggests, probably reflect the tense relations of Jews and gentiles in Alexandria at the time of composition.[34] The corruption of particular individuals and peoples does not necessarily require the rejection of the non-Jewish world as such.

The Wisdom of Solomon has often been said to be law oriented in its piety.[35] The righteous man reproaches the wicked with sins against the law (2:12), and the kings of the earth are condemned because they have not kept the law (6:4). While the "law" in question may be presumed to correspond substantially with the Mosaic law, in view of the paradigmatic role of Israel, the two cannot be simply identified. As in the other Jewish Hellenistic literature, those elements of the law which are peculiarly Jewish are ignored and emphasis is placed on elements in accordance with natural law. The list of sins in 14:22–29 covers the ethical interests of the book rather completely: "All is confusion—bloody murder, deceitful theft, corruption, treachery, tumult, perjury, agitation of decent men, ingratitude, soul defilement, interchange of sex roles, irregular marriages, adultery and debauchery. For the worship of the unspeakable idols is the beginning, cause, and end of every evil." The basic sin is idolatry, which is denounced repeatedly throughout the book.[36] This is said to lead to a variety of other sins. Of these, adultery is most frequently mentioned.[37] Surprisingly, homosexuality is not prominent (a reference to interchange of sex roles in 14:26 is the closest allusion). Infanticide is naturally enough singled out in the account of the oppression of the Hebrews in Egypt (18:5). There is also a reference to "secret mysteries or frenzied revels connected with strange laws" (14:23), which were also frowned on by classical authors on occasion.[38] Otherwise, the wrongdoing of the wicked is of the type suggested in 2:10: "Let us tyrannize the poor honest man, let us not spare the widow nor reverence the elder's hair long grey." Such actions were anathema in any culture. It is significant that when the righteous is said to reproach the wicked with sins against the law the parallel verse reads, "and charges us with falseness to our training" (2:12). Similarly in 6:4, not keeping the law is paralleled by the more general charges of not judging rightly and not walking according to the will of God. There is no reference in the book to such specific Jewish laws as circumcision, sabbath observance, or the dietary laws. There is one reference to sacrifice in the story of the Exodus (18:9), but sacrifice was not, in any case, distinctive. The law of Wisdom might in practice be equated with the natural law known to all.

The thought of Wisdom on this subject is most vividly illustrated in 13:1-9. On the subject of the basic sin of idolatry we read that all men should know God from his works, "For from the greatness and beauty of created things, is their author correspondingly perceived." The argument is similar to that of Paul in Romans 1. Despite his sympathy for the weakness of human nature, the author concludes that idolators are, after all, culpable, not because of the law of Moses but because they did not apply their resourcefulness to the knowledge of God.

In all, then, the broadly based understanding of the cosmos which we find in Wisdom is designed to present a view of true religion which could appeal to Greek sympathies on the basis of natural law. The sharp contrast of Israel and its enemies in chapters 10–19 may have detracted from the propagandistic value of the work, but it provided all the more gratifying a self-understanding for the Hellenized Jews of Alexandria.

FOURTH MACCABEES

As a final example of philosophical Judaism apart from Philo we now turn to 4 Maccabees, which is presented as a *philosophōtaton logon*. Most scholars have dated the work in the mid-first century CE, but recently Breitenstein has revived the view of Dupont-Sommer that it was written in the early second century CE.[39] The same data have been adduced in support of the different positions. Bickermann, followed by Hadas, claimed that "every unprejudiced reader of IV Maccabees cannot but be impressed by the fact that the Temple and its service are regarded as existent in the book,"[40] but the passages he mentions (4:20; 14:9) do not bear out the claim. On the other hand, Breitenstein notes that 4 Maccabees avoids reference to sacrifice and the cult in cases where they are mentioned in 2 Maccabees, and concludes that the book was written after the fall of the temple.[41] This argument is equally inconclusive. The work of Jason of Cyrene was exceptional in its interest in the temple. Lack of interest in sacrifice is not surprising in a work written in the Diaspora. On the other hand, the interest of Sib Or 5 in the temple is not diminished several decades after 70 CE. In short, the attitude of 4 Maccabees to the temple and its cult is not a reliable guide to its date.

Linguistic considerations are a little more helpful. Bickermann argued that the term *nomikos* (4 Mac 5:4) in place of *grammateus* (2 Mac 6:18) pointed to the Christian era, as also the term *thrēskeia* for religion.[42] Breitenstein has underlined the degree to which the vocabulary of 4 Maccabees is paralleled in later Christian writings, but this consideration does not help to establish a precise date.[43]

The decisive consideration for Bickermann (and Hadas) lies in the title given to Apollonius in 4 Mac 4:9, where he is *stratēgos* of Syria, Phoenicia, and Cilicia. In 2 Mac 3:5 he is called *stratēgos* of Coele-Syria and Phoenicia. Cilicia was associated with Syria for administrative purposes only for a short period between 20 and 54 CE (approximately). Bickermann concludes that 4 Maccabees was written in this period.[44] Breitenstein argues that the reference in 4 Mac 4:9 must refer to a time *after* the separation of Cilicia from Syria.[45] The logic of his argument is not apparent, since the passage clearly assumes that Syria, Phoenicia, and Cilicia are under the same *stratēgos*. It would appear then that Bickermann's dating rests on firmer evidence than the later date favored by Breitenstein.

There is general agreement that the book was composed in the Diaspora, but it gives no clear indication of the particular place. Freudenthal had already raised objections against Alexandria,[46] and, indeed, the perspective of 4 Maccabees is very different from any of the Egyptian Jewish works we have considered. Hadas has argued at some length for Antioch as the place of origin, mainly because of the immediate presence of Antiochus at the tortures.[47] This, however, may be only a dramatic technique, without regard for geographical probability. It is true that church tradition localized the graves of the martyrs at Antioch.[48] This consideration certainly does not prove that all variants of the legend were developed in Antioch, but it provides some reason for suggesting Antioch as the place of origin of 4 Maccabees, while there is no evidence to favor any other specific site.

The book falls into two parts: the "philosophical" introduction in 1:1–3:18 and the discourse on the martyrs in 3:19–18:24. The latter part has the form of an *Epitaphios Logos* or commemorative speech, as has recently been shown by Lebram.[49] There has been widespread debate as to whether this speech was actually delivered on the occasion of a commemoration or was a fictive discourse, like the speeches of Isocrates, which was meant to be read.[50] Decisive criteria are hard to find. Hadas has noted a number of features suggestive of oral delivery (e.g., "at this season" in 1:10 and 3:19),[51] but these could easily have been imitated by an author. The question must be left open.

There has also been considerable discussion on the philosophical affiliation of 4 Maccabees. Heinemann thought it was Stoic,[52] a position recently modified by Renehan, who finds in it "Koine" philosophy with Stoic features.[53] Hadas emphasized its debt to Plato.[54] Breitenstein has quite correctly insisted that 4 Maccabees cannot be assigned to any philosophical school.[55] The author was a rhetorician, not a philosopher, who used philosophical ideas eclectically to embellish his case. The philosophical pronouncements are not consistently thought through. The story of the martyrs is not well integrated with its philosophical framework. "Reason" is virtually equated with keeping the law. Yet, Breitenstein's judgment that the author's "philosophy" shows him not only to lack originality but to be a *recht verständnislosen Kopf*[56] seems too severe. While 4 Maccabees is scarcely convincing as a philosophical argument that reason is master of the emotions, it provides an unusual and interesting specimen of Jewish apologetic rhetoric.

As Breitenstein and others have observed, "reason" in 4 Maccabees is virtually equated with obedience to the law. Specifically: "Reason, then, is the intellect choosing with correct judgment the life of wisdom, and wisdom is knowledge of things human and divine and of their cause. Such wisdom is education in the Law" (1:15–17). The reasonableness of the law is simply asserted. Furthermore, the law in question is not the broadly acceptable natural law of Pseudo-Phocylides or Wisdom, but the Jewish law in all its particularity: "How is it that when we are drawn to forbidden foods we turn away from the pleasures they afford? . . . When we crave sea food or fowl or quadrupeds or any sort of food which is forbidden to us according to the law, it is due to the mastery of reason that we abstain" (1:33–34). There is no attempt here to allegorize the dietary laws, as in Pseudo-Aristeas, to make them appear more reasonable. It is sufficient that they are commanded. Further, in the story of the persecution and martyrdoms, the issue is precisely fidelity to the law, specifically in the matters of circumcision and food laws (4:25–26). What the stories show is that it is possible to be faithful to the full law, even in the face of the most extreme tortures.

The reasonableness of such conduct is suggested by 4 Maccabees in two ways. First, there is the doctrine of retribution.[57] The martyrs can look forward to "the life of eternal blessedness" (17:18; cf. 15:3), "ranged in the choir of their fathers; having received souls pure and deathless from God" (18:23). By contrast, Antiochus "will endure at the hand of divine justice the condign punishment of eternal torment by fire" (9:9). There is no reference in 4 Maccabees to bodily resurrection (in contrast to its prototype in 2 Maccabees). While the exact nature of the afterlife is not discussed, it is certainly compatible with the immortality of the soul. 4 Maccabees does not exploit the support of Greek philosophy (especially Plato) on this point. Naturally, in Greek philosophy retribution after death was not related to the Jewish law, but the philosophical pedigree of the idea lent credibility to the argument of 4 Maccabees.

The hope for the afterlife does not dominate 4 Maccabees. In this it contrasts sharply with 2 Maccabees 7 where the martyrs are repeatedly sustained by the hope of resurrection. In 4 Maccabees the main motivating factor is the inherent nobility of virtue. So the second brother taunts the king: "Do you not perceive, tyrant most cruel of all, that you are being tormented more than I, when you see that your arrogant reasoning of tyranny is vanquished by our endurance in the cause of religion? In my case I lighten my pain by the joys which virtue brings" (9:30). The virtue in question is primarily mastery of the passions and emotions. It is attained by "religious reason" (*eusebēs logismos*) and by religious fidelity: "Those who take thought for religion with their whole heart, they alone are able to dominate the passions of the flesh" (7:18). The author assumes throughout that such self-control is a good in itself. This idea had ample precedent in Greek philosophy, from Plato's famous image of the charioteer and his two horses in the *Phaedrus* to the more severe attitudes of the Stoics.[58] In 4 Maccabees this virtue is an example for others (7:9; 5:33–36; 6:18–21; 16:16). It enables the brothers to overcome the tyrant by their endurance and effect the purification of the fatherland (1:11). Yet, the appreciation of virtue is not dependent on these secondary effects but is a good in itself.

The second way, then, in which 4 Maccabees contrives to make the conduct of the martyrs appear reasonable and praiseworthy is by using it as an example of the control of the passions which was widely recognized as a virtue. Strict fidelity to the law can be presented as a virtue by Greek standards. The line of argument depends on the tacit assumption that conformity with the Jewish law is indeed in accordance with reason. 4 Maccabees does not attempt to establish this point. The weight of the argument is devoted to showing how conformity with the law involves mastery over the passions. Both reason and the law require mastery over the emotions. This does not warrant a logical identification of reason and obedience to the law, but it is sufficient basis for a rhetorical identification which builds an association in the mind of the listener or reader. This kind of identification might not persuade many gentiles but it assured the Hellenized Jews that strict Torah piety was compatible with advanced Hellenization. The attempt to assure the Jewish audience that such fidelity is the very best way to impress the gentiles is reflected in the blatant fiction whereby Antiochus is said to have set up the martyrs as models for his troops (17:17–24).

In addition to the claim to philosophical virtue, 4 Maccabees could also effect a rapprochement with Hellenistic culture through the use of the *agon* motif. The device of presenting the pursuit of virtue as a struggle or contest was well known in Greek popular philosophy.[59] It was widely exploited by Philo[60] and plays a prominent part in the

Testament of Job. It was also utilized to great effect by Paul. The *agon* of 4 Maccabees is clearly stated in 17:11–14: "Divine indeed was the contest of which they were the issue. Of that contest virtue was the umpire: and its score was for constancy. Victory was incorruptibility in a life of long duration. . . . The tyrant was the adversary and humanity were the spectators" (17:11–14).[61] The use of this popular device of the philosophers enabled 4 Maccabees to be thoroughly Hellenistic even while defending the law in an uncompromising manner.

The apologetic peculiarity of 4 Maccabees lies in its combination of a rigid, uncompromising obedience to the law, in all its details, with a thoroughly Hellenized consciousness. In this respect, it is partly reminiscent of the epic of Theodotus, although it lacks the militant tone of that work. However confused its philosophy, it reflects an esteem for philosophy, and a Jewish identity which valued the claim to philosophical status. The attempt to articulate a distinctly Hellenistic Judaism without any modification of the "strange" Jewish laws makes 4 Maccabees an exceptional instance of Jewish apologetic.

Notes

1. There are five fragments of Aristobulus's work. F 1 is found in Eusebius (HE 7.32.16–18), where Eusebius is citing Anatolius, *On the Passover*. Ff 2–5 are found in Eusebius (PE 8.10 and 13.12). Part of F 5 is also found in PE 7.14. Parallels to parts of fragments 2–5 are also found in Clement's *Stromateis* 1, 5, and 6.

2. *Stromateis* 1.150.1. Anatolius dates Aristobulus to the time of Philadelphus but this is a manifest error since Aristobulus refers to Philadelphus as the forefather of the Ptolemy for whom he wrote. See N. Walter, *Der Thoraausleger Aristobulus* (TU 86; Berlin: Akademie, 1964) 13–26. A shorter treatment by Walter can be found in JSHRZ III/2, 261–79.

3. Bickermann, *Studies*, 2:137.

4. Walter, *Der Thoraausleger*, 58–86.

5. Walter, *Der Thoraausleger*, 100. The fact that the passages in question are concentrated in Aristobulus but scattered in Pseudo-Aristeas is taken as evidence of the priority of Aristobulus.

6. Walter, *Der Thoraausleger*, 146–47 argues that Pseudo-Aristeas reflects a more advanced stage of allegorical exegesis than Aristobulus since he does not confine his allegorical interpretations to biblical anthropomorphisms. Such an argument seems hazardous as the surviving fragments of Aristobulus are quite restricted in scope and may not reflect his full practice.

7. P. M. Fraser (*Ptolemaic Alexandria* [Oxford: Clarendon, 1972] 2:964) holds to the priority of Pseudo-Aristeas but dates both to the age of Philometor. M. Hengel (*Judaism and Hellenism* [Philadelphia: Fortress, 1974] 2:106–7) dates Aristobulus more specifically between 176 and 170 BCE, since this was the only period in which Philometor was

sole ruler. This however may place too much weight on the form in which the dedication has been preserved.

8. Hengel, *Judaism and Hellenism*, 1:164.

9. Walter, *Der Thoraausleger*, 43–51.

10. Ibid., 135.

11. Ibid., 150–66. The verse in question reads "And on the seventh morning we left the stream of Acheron." Since Aristobulus has to interpret this verse allegorically to make it fit his purpose, it is unlikely that he invented it.

12. Thirteen verses of a work, *Peri physeōs kosmou*, attributed to Linus, have survived. It is conceded that the first Linus verse here is a Jewish forgery, though not necessarily by Aristobulus. See Walter, 158–65. The Linus verses are attributed to Callimachus by Clement.

13. For the verses see A. M. Denis, *Fragmenta Pseudepigraphorum quae supersunt Graeca* (PVTG 3; Leiden: Brill, 1970) 161–74; discussion Walter, *Der Thoraausleger*, 172–84.

14. E. Schürer, *Geschichte des jüdischen Volkes im Zeitalter Jesu Christi* (4th ed.; Leipzig: Hinrichs, 1909) 3:454–55.

15. H. W. Attridge, *First-Century Cynicism in the Epistles of Heraclitus* (HTS 29; Missoula: Scholars, 1976) 3–39.

16. M. Hadas, *Aristeas to Philocrates* (New York: Harper, 1951) 62.

17. See the passages listed by Attridge, *First-Century Cynicism*.

18. M. Hengel, "Anonymität, Pseudepigraphie und 'Literarische Fälschung' in der jüdisch-hellenistischen Literatur," *Entretiens sur l'Antiquité Classique XVIII* (1972) 299; Hadas, *Aristeas*, 40–43; W. W. Tarn, *The Greeks in Bactria and India* (Cambridge: Cambridge University, 1938) 414–36. On the Hellenistic kingship treatises, see E. R. Goodenough, "The Political Philosophy of Philo Judaeus," *Yale Classical Studies* 1 (1928) 53–102, and P. Hadot, "Fürstenspiegel," *RAC* 7 (1970) 555–632. See further O. Murray, "Aristeas and Ptolemaic Kingship," *JTS* 18 (1967) 337–71; J. J. Lewis, "The Table-Talk Section in the Letter of Aristeas," *NTS* 13 (1966) 53–56; Tcherikover, "Ideology," 65.

19. For a contrary view, see D. Georgi, *Weisheit Salomos* (JSHRZ 3/4; Gütersloh: Mohn, 1980) 396.

20. For a summary, see J. Reider, *The Book of Wisdom* (Dropsie College Series; New York; Harper, 1957) 12–14. An early date (late second century BCE) has recently been defended by Georgi, *Weisheit*, 396.

21. D. Winston, *The Book of Wisdom* (AB 43; Garden City: Doubleday, 1979) 20–25.

22. Ibid., 18; J. M. Reese, *Hellenistic Influence on the Book of Wisdom and its Consequences* (AnBib 41; Rome: Biblical Institute, 1970) 117–21. For a contrary view, see Georgi (*Weisheit*, 394), who emphasizes Wisdom's affinities with Gnostic writings.

23. Winston, *The Book of Wisdom*, 33–40; C. Larcher, *Etudes sur le Livre de la Sagesse* (Paris: Gabalda, 1969) 181–236.

24. See the parallels adduced by Winston, *The Book of Wisdom*, 159–218, and the literature there cited.

25. J. J. Collins, "Cosmos and Salvation: Jewish Wisdom and Apocalyptic in the Hellenistic Age," *HR* 17 (1977) 123–27.

26. For parallels on the notion "friends of God," see Winston, 188–89. On the understanding of prophets in Egyptian Judaism, see Wolfson, *Philo* 2:3–72.

27. The *sorites* is imperfect, since it should conclude by joining the beginning and end: "the beginning of wisdom makes one near to God." See A. T. S. Goodrick, *The Book of Wisdom* (Oxford Church Bible Commentary; London: Rivingtons, 1913) 175.

28. See P. Grelot, "L'Eschatologie de la Sagesse et les Apocalypses Juives," *A la Rencontre de Dieu: Mémorial Albert Gelin* (Le Puy: Xavier Mappus, 1961) 165–78; L. Ruppert, *Der leidende Gerechte* (Forschung zur Bibel 5; Würzburg: Echter, 1972) 70–105; G. W. Nickelsburg, *Resurrection, Immortality and Eternal Life in Intertestamental Judaism* (HTS 26; Cambridge: Harvard, 1972) 58–62; M. Delcor, "L'Immortalité de l'âme dans le Livre de la Sagesse et dans les documents de Qumrân," *NRT* 77 (1955) 614–30.

29. J. J. Collins, "The Root of Immortality: Death in the Context of Jewish Wisdom," *HTR* 71 (1979) 188; Winston, *The Book of Wisdom*, 25–32.

30. For the division of Wis into "the book of eschatology" in chaps. 1–5, the book of Wisdom proper in chaps. 6–9, and the "book of history" in 10–19, see Collins "Cosmos and Salvation," 123–24, and the literature there cited. For different divisions, see A. G. Wright, "The Structure of the Book of Wisdom," *Bib* 48 (1967) 165–84, and Winston, *The Book of Wisdom*, 9–12.

31. P. Beauchamp, "Le salut corporel des justes et la conclusion du livre de la Sagesse," *Bib* 45 (1964) 491–526; G. Ziener, *Die theologische Begriffsprache im Buche der Weisheit* (BBB 11; Bonn: Hanstein, 1956) 135–36.

32. J. P. M. Sweet, "The Theory of Miracles in the Wisdom of Solomon," *Miracles* (ed. C. F. D. Moule; London: Mowbray, 1965) 115–26.

33. B. L. Mack, "Imitatio Mosis: Patterns of Cosmology and Soteriology in the Hellenistic Synagogue," *Studia Philonica* 1 (1972) 30–31.

34. Winston, *The Book of Wisdom*, 45.

35. So U. Breitenstein, *Beobachtungen zu Sprache, Stil und Gedankengut des vierten Makkabäerbuchs* (Basel/Stuttgart: Schwabe, 1978) 19.

36. Esp. chaps. 13–15. For an extended treatment, see M. Gilbert, *La Critique des Dieux dans le livre de la Sagesse* (AnBib 53; Rome: Biblical Institute, 1973).

37. Cf. the comments on the children of adulterers in 3:16 and 4:3.

38. Winston (*The Book of Wisdom*, 238) aptly cites Livy, *Hist* 39.8–19.

39. Breitenstein, *Beobachtungen*, 175; A. Dupont-Sommer, *Le quatrième livre des Machabées. Introduction, Traduction et Notes* (Paris: Champion, 1939).

40. E. Bickermann, "The Date of Fourth Maccabees," *Studies in Jewish and Christian History* (AGJU 9; Leiden: Brill, 1976) 1:277 (first published in 1945); M. Hadas, *The Third and Fourth Books of Maccabees* (Dropsie College Series; New York: Harper, 1953) 95.

41. Breitenstein, *Beobachtungen*, 171–74. That 4 Maccabees is dependent on 2 Maccabees seems clear enough (ibid., 19), despite the hesitation of Fischer, *Eschatologie*, 87.

42. Bickermann, "The Date of Fourth Maccabees," 276–77.

43. Breitenstein, *Beobachtungen*, 13–29.

44. Bickermann, "The Date of Fourth Maccabees," 279–80.

45. Breitenstein, *Beobachtungen*, 174.

46. J. Freudenthal, *Die Flavius Josephus beigelegte Schrift über die Herrschaft der Vernunft (IV Makkabäerbuch) eine Predigt aus dem ersten nachchristlichen Jahrhundert* (Breslau: Skutsch, 1869) 112.

47. Hadas, *The Third and Fourth Books*, 109–13.

48. See U. Kellermann, *Auferstanden in den Himmel, 2 Makkabäer 7 und die Auferstehung der Märtyrer* (SBS 95; Stuttgart: KBW, 1979) 17, and the literature there cited, esp. Cardinal Rampolla, "Martyre et sépulture des Machabées," *RAC* 48 (1899) 290–305; 377–92; 457–65.

49. J. H. C. Lebram, "Die literarische Form des vierten Makkabäerbuches," *VC* 28 (1974) 81–96.

50. For a review of the debate, see H. Thyen, *Der Stil der jüdisch-hellenistischen Homilie* (Göttingen: Vandenhoeck & Ruprecht, 1955) 12–14.

51. Hadas, *The Third and Fourth Books*, 102.

52. I. Heinemann, *Posidonios' Metaphysische Schriften* (Breslau: Marcus, 1921) 1:154–59; "Makkabäerbücher, Buch IV," *PWRE* 14/1 (1928) 800–805.

53. R. Renehan, "The Greek Philosophic Background of Fourth Maccabees," *Rheinisches Museum für Philologie* 115 (1972) 223–38.

54. Hadas, *The Third and Fourth Books*, 116.

55. Breitenstein, *Beobachtungen*, 132–33.

56. Ibid., 179.

57. U. Fischer (*Eschatologie und Jenseitserwartung im hellenistischen Diasporajudentum* [BZNW 44; Berlin: de Gruyter, 1978] 85–105) rightly notes that the references to afterlife are in the service of retribution.

58. See A. H. Armstrong, *An Introduction to Ancient Philosophy* (3 ed.; London: Methuen, 1957) 42–43, 54–55 (on Plato), 126 (on the Stoics). For the Stoics, see also the texts assembled in C. J. de Vogel, *Greek Philosophy III. The Hellenistic-Roman Period* (Leiden: Brill, 1959) 168–76.

59. See V. C. Pfitzner, *Paul and the Agon Motif* (Leiden: Brill, 1967) 23–37, for the motif in Greek philosophy.

60. Ibid., 38–48.

61. The metaphor of the athletic contest is also used in 6:10 and 17:12–16. Pfitzner, *Paul*, 57–64.

Chapter 6

THE MYSTERIES OF GOD

We have seen how some strands of Hellenistic Judaism attempted to relate the Jewish law to the surrounding culture by playing down its most distinctive elements, and others by seeking a common ground in Greek philosophy. A third strand went beyond these in appealing to a higher revelation of a transcendent world. This third category is not sharply distinct from the other two. Rather, it seeks a deeper foundation for the common ethic and the philosophy, and it overlaps with both.

MYSTIC JUDAISM

Mention of a higher revelation inevitably recalls the theory of a mystic Judaism propounded by E. R. Goodenough.[1] Goodenough's thesis was based on Philo and also on Jewish art from a slightly later period. The examination of his thesis as it relates to his primary evidence is beyond the scope of the present discussion.[2] Suffice it to say that he was correct in highlighting a mystical tendency in Philo.[3] However, Goodenough also claimed that the same mystic Judaism was widespread before Philo and is attested in several of the literary products of Egyptian Judaism. This claim requires an evaluation.

The discussion of mystic Judaism has been complicated by the notorious evasiveness of the term *mystic*.[4] Etymologically, the word is derived from the Greek mysteries and referred to one who had been initiated. As the word is used in relation to Hellenistic Judaism several different factors are involved.

A mystic ritual?

The mysteries usually involve rituals, which in some way symbolize the process of salvation.[5] Whether mystic rituals were practiced in the Jewish Diaspora is doubtful. Goodenough argued that "the evidence seems on the whole to suggest that they may have had their mystic initiation, baptism, like the Christians later, and a "sacred table" from which the uninitiated were rigorously kept away." Even he, however, had to admit that "the evidence for this is unsatisfactory, because scanty and not in agreement."[6] This evidence is primarily drawn from Philo's scattered allusions to food and drink, rites, and mysteries.[7] The difficulty lies in determining whether these allusions are metaphorical or refer to actual cultic practices. There is also a Roman decree in Josephus (*Ant* 14.10.8 [213–16]) which refers to the practice of common meals among the Jews of Delos, but there is nothing to indicate that these had a mystical meaning.

The meal of the Therapeutae, described by Philo in *De Vita Contemplativa* is indeed a ritual. The food is said to recall the showbread of the temple, but the ritual does not in itself symbolize the process of salvation. Afterwards, however, two choirs perform, one of men and one of women. Then "when each choir has separately done its own part in the feast, having drunk as in the Bacchic rites of the strong wine of God's love they mix and both together become a single choir, a copy of the choir set up of old beside the Red Sea" (85). Philo's comparison with the Bacchic rites and the repeated metaphor of drunkenness suggests that this ritual had a mystic character, but it is difficult to say how far he is accurately reporting the Therapeutae and how far he is intruding his own thought. The meal is preceded by an exposition of scripture, which, according to Philo "treats the inner meaning conveyed in allegory. For to these people the whole law book seems to resemble a living creature with the literal ordinances for its body and for its soul the invisible mind laid up in its wording" (78). In view of this allegorical exegesis, we might expect that the recollection of the Red Sea would be taken as an allegory of spiritual deliverance, but even Philo does not suggest this. Since we have no independent evidence about the Therapeutae we cannot say that they provide reliable evidence for a mystic ritual, since the mystic character of their celebration may only be apparent through the filter of Philo's account.

Goodenough drew further support for his thesis from a series of prayers in the Apostolic Constitutions which Bousset had claimed were Jewish with only slight Christian interpolations.[8] There is no doubt that these prayers are Christian in their present form. Accordingly, when we find instructions for preparation for baptism (F 8,

Const. 7.39.2–4) or for catechumens (F 9, Const. 8.6.5–8) we must be somewhat skeptical of Goodenough's claim that they are taken "from the rules for instructing a Jewish catechumen in preparation for initiation into the Jewish Mystery,"[9] despite the Jewish character of the actual instructions. We may agree with Goodenough that these prayers draw on Jewish material of a kind closely related to Philo (e.g., "the gnosis of the unbegotten God" and the glorification of the patriarchs). In most cases, however, we lack reliable indications as to how much of the material is Jewish and how that material was originally used. A possible exception is found in F 2 (Const. 7.36.1–6) which Bousset has called a *Sabbatgebet*. God has "created the world by Christ, and hast appointed the Sabbath in memory thereof . . . Thou hast also appointed festivals for the rejoicing of our souls that we might come into remembrance of that Sophia which was created by thee." Despite the patent identification of Christ and Sophia in the following verses, the entire emphasis on the sabbath is Jewish as can be seen from the rather awkward transition in vs. 6 ("All which the Lord's day excels"), which seeks to subordinate the sabbath to the Lord's day. It is probable, then, that Christ is substituted for Logos or Sophia in the creation of the world in vs. 1. What is suggested by this prayer is not a special set of mystic rituals but an understanding of the customary Jewish festivals, including the sabbath, which linked them with *sophia*.

In fact, Goodenough's strongest argument for a mystic liturgy lies not in the metaphorical allusions to bread and wine but in the application of Philo's allegorical mentality to the Jewish festivals: "It seems, a priori, incredible that Philo, who had to see 'something far more deeply interfused' in every word of Scripture, would then have celebrated Circumcision, the Seder, the Sabbath, New Year, the Day of Atonement, First Fruits, and the rest on a purely literal level."[10] The argument is not confined to Philo. Long before him Aristobulus linked the seventh day with wisdom and the origin of light (F 5. PE 13.12.9) and added that "all the cosmos of living beings and growing things revolves in a series of sevens" (PE 13.12.13). For Aristobulus, the sabbath was evidently laden with cosmic allusions. The prayer in Const. F 2 shows how a symbolic understanding of the sabbath persisted and passed over into Christianity.

The fact that mystically inclined Jews such as Philo would have understood the sabbath in a mystical sense does not in itself establish the existence of a mystic liturgy which was specially designed from such an understanding and from which noninitiates were excluded. Georgi has argued at length that the sabbath service was the great forum for propaganda and proselytizing in the Hellenistic Diaspora.[11] Yet, he also entertains the possibility that part of the ceremony was set aside as a mystery from which the uninitiated were excluded.[12] He bases this suggestion on the Pseudo-Orphic fragments and the four-teenth satire of Juvenal (vss. 102–4),[13] which speaks of a secret book of Moses which was designed only for the circumcised, as well as Philo's use of mystery language. The suggestion that part of the ritual was esoteric is not in itself implausible, but neither is it more than a possi-bility. None of the evidence adduced speaks explicitly of an esoteric ritual on the sabbath. Georgi notes that no special meals were associ-ated with the sabbath.[14] We will return to the question of a mystic meal in connection with Joseph and Aseneth, but there again we will find no firm evidence for a special mystic ritual.

Mystic philosophy

Goodenough readily admitted that the evidence for a mystic ritual was unsatisfactory, but added that "however much or little the Jewish Mystery may have developed its own cult practices, it seems as a mystic philosophy, to have been the heart and core of Greek Juda-ism."[15] The use of mystery language in connection with philosophy, or rather the understanding of philosophy as a mystery, is clearly exemplified already in Plato.[16] The conception is clearly formulated in the words attributed to Socrates in the *Phaedo* 80 d:

> And those who founded the mysteries seem not to be bad fellows at all, but in reality to have long ago hinted that an uninitiated man who comes into Hades would lie in the mud, but that the purified and initiated man would on his arrival there dwell with the gods. So then there are, as those who have to do with the mysteries say, "Many who bear the wand, but few Bacchi." These latter are, in my opinion, none other than those who have rightly pursued phi-losophy.

Similarly, in the *Symposium* philosophy is presented as the true mys-tery.

There is no dispute that Philo freely used the language of the mys-teries.[17] Moses is said to have initiated the Israelites into the mysteries by the covenant. Within the mysteries of Moses, greater and lesser mysteries are distinguished. Moses, the high priest, and others are at various times described as hierophants. The mysteries in question are not primarily rituals. When Moses initiates people into the mysteries he exhorts them "to practise sincerity and reject vanity, to embrace truth and simplicity as vital necessaries and to rise in rebellion against the mythical fables impressed on their souls from their earliest years" (De Virtutibus 33, 178). The lesser mysteries involve "the passage from the life of the passions to the practice of virtue" (De Sacrificiis 17, 63) and the acquisition of the knowledge of God. The higher mysteries involve a more direct knowledge of God. Throughout, the true mysteries are contained in the Jewish law. Accordingly, Wolfson rather minimalistically concludes that the use of mystery language is only a veneer on a religion which is thoroughly dominated by the Mosaic law. Goodenough, however, has rightly insisted that "the question whether Philo's use of mystic terms made his religion a true 'Mystery' depends on what Philo thought was a true mystery, not upon our definitions. . . . As Plato scorned those who only carried the thyrsus, while he looked for salvation through philosophic contemplation which would lead to the vision of the forms, Philo felt that the true mystery, the one which actually purified and elevated the soul was revealed in the Torah as allegorically interpreted."[18] In short, that which is conceived to be the supreme mystery is ipso facto a real (Goodenough says "literal") mystery, whether it involves a mystery ritual or not.

Goodenough claimed that "by Philo's time and long before, the Greek-speaking world, especially in Egypt, had been transformed into a Mystery"[19] in the sense that it was imbued with a mystical philosophy. Goodenough outlined that philosophy as follows: "The objective of this Judaism was salvation in a mystical sense. God was no longer only the God presented in the Old Testament: He was the Absolute, connected with phenomena by His Light-Stream, the Logos or Sophia. The hope and aim of man was to leave created things with their sordid complications, and to rise to incorruption, immortality, life, by climbing the mystic ladder, traversing the Royal Road of the Light-Stream."[20] To Goodenough's mind the mysticism of the Light-Stream was a widespread feature of Hellenistic religion. Accordingly, when Goodenough looked for Jewish mysticism he looked primarily for references to the Light-Stream, Logos, and Sophia. It was through these that salvation was mediated in the Jewish mystery. Yet the *hieros logos* of the mystery remained the Jewish Torah, interpreted allegorically as a wellspring of *sophia*. The mystery envisaged by Philo, then, could be described as a philosophical mystery, but Goodenough defended the "literal" reality of such a mystery and kept open the possibility that it also involved a cultic ritual.

Outside of Philo, the best evidence for this philosophical mysticism is found in Aristobulus and more especially the Wisdom of Solomon.[21] Over and above his allegorical interpretation, Aristobulus briefly refers to the cosmic priority of wisdom "for all light has its origin in it" (PE 13.12.9). The further connection of wisdom with the number seven and the sabbath also hints that wisdom has a pivotal place in Aristobulus's view of the cosmos, but what remains of his work is too fragmentary to support any reconstruction of a Sophia-mysticism from his work. Ultimately, Aristobulus's greatest contribution to our understanding of mystic Judaism was through the preservation of the Orphic fragments, which will be discussed below.

The Wisdom of Solomon provides the most substantial evidence for Philonic Judaism outside of Philo. We have noted above the pivotal place of Sophia/Logos in that work. The relevance of its conceptions for mystic Judaism is evident from two references to *mystēria*. In Wis 2:22, the wicked are misled because they did not know "the mysteries of God," which are equated with "the reward of holiness"—in effect, the fate of souls after death. The second is in 6:22: "But what wisdom is, and how she came into being, I will declare, and will not conceal from you mysteries." In short, the nature of wisdom is itself a mystery, which is penetrated only by the gift of God, who is the guide of wisdom and director of the wise (7:15). Wisdom is an emanation of the glory of the Almighty and a reflection of eternal light and even superior to light (7:25–29). It forms the bridge between human and divine by entering into holy souls. She is initiated (*mystis*) into the knowledge of God. Solomon "takes her to live with him and through her he will have immortality" (8:13). In all of this wisdom appears as an active agent which has been initiated into the mysteries of God and can be a mystagogue for others, just as, conversely, God is the mystagogue for the mysteries of wisdom. The way in which wisdom serves as guide to salvation is illustrated in the résumé of the exodus in chaps. 10–19. In all of this wisdom is the focus of a mystical philosophy. Despite the famous allusion to the cosmic significance of the high priest's garments, there is nothing to suggest a mystery cult focused on wisdom—only that the cult of the Jewish temple, whether known from pilgrimages or only from scripture, was interpreted with mystic symbolism by those who shared this philosophy.[22] The soteriology of the book fits well enough with Goodenough's outline of the mystery, although the attitude to "created things with their sordid complications" is ambiguous. On the one hand, nature provides the stepping stones to the knowledge of God. On the other, the perishable body weighs down the soul, and the ultimate salvation is immortality with God.[23]

Goodenough claimed another witness to this philosophical mysticism in the *Oratio ad Graecos* attributed to Justin Martyr.[24] This document is an apologia for abandoning traditional Greek religion in favor of the Logos. The first four chapters are devoted to denunciations of the immoralities of Greek gods and heroes. This kind of polemic was traditional in popular Hellenistic philosophy and "might have been written by a Greek sceptic or rhetorician at any time after the Third Century B. C."[25] The fifth chapter invites the Greeks to "come and partake of incomparable Sophia, and be instructed by the divine Logos and learn the incorruptible King" (*basilea aphtharton*). It goes on to speak of the soul "permeated with the power of the Logos" and claims that, while this instruction does not make philosophers or rhetoricians, "it makes mortals become immortals, human beings gods, and from the earth leads to the realms beyond Olympus." The Logos "drives from the recesses of the soul the terrible sensual affections," especially lust, and so enables the soul to return to him who made it. Goodenough rightly points out the absence of any distinctively Christian references and the abundance of parallels to Philo. His conclusion, that it is the work of a proselyte to Hellenistic Judaism, is possible, but remains very hypothetical. Whatever its origin, the *Oratio* provides a striking parallel to the philosophical mysticism of Philo.

Esotericism

A major aspect of the religion of the mysteries was their esoteric character. Esotericism may take different forms. In its simplest form it entails a secret knowledge or experience which is reserved for the initiates and may not be divulged to others. The secrecy was respected with the utmost seriousness in antiquity. Livy (31.14) tells how two youths who unwittingly intruded on the Eleusinian mysteries in 200 BCE were punished by death.[26] Within Judaism, Josephus says that the Essenes were obliged by oath to keep secret the books of the sect and the names of the angels.[27] Juvenal (*Satires*, 14:102–4) refers to the "secret volume" of Moses and secret ways for the circumcised. Occasional passages in Philo are also susceptible to the interpretation that some Jewish teaching was secret. The full knowledge of Sophia "cannot be told to all since he who reveals the Secret to the imprudent and unworthy destroys and overthrows the law of perfection of the holy Mysteries" (*Questions on Genesis*, 4.8). One of the fragments says explicitly that "It is not permitted to speak out the sacred mysteries to the uninitiated until they shall have been purified with the perfect purification"; another passage warns, "One must not share everything with everyone, that is, not teachings and practices which are especially sacred. For there are many prerequisites which must be satisfied by people who aspire to share in these things . . . in order that they may not, like intemperate youths, get drunk from surfeit and superabundance when they partake at the sacred table and so be changed for the worse: to such people it is not permitted." Even if we understand the sacred table metaphorically as instruction, these passages state clearly that not all the teachings of Judaism should be immediately available to gentiles. Of course Philo stops far short of the sworn secrecy of the mysteries, and it is difficult to know whether his opinion on these matters is representative of the practice of the Hellenistic synagogue.

Only one other passage in the Hellenistic Jewish Diaspora writings clearly suggests a secret teaching. That is the opening verse of the Orphic fragment: "I will speak to those for whom it is lawful; profane ones, close the doors." The opening injunction may be no more than a literary imitation of the mysteries, but at least it reflects a desire to present Judaism as a religion whose most important doctrines were secret.

Esotericism may also be used in a broader sense, which does not require an intention to conceal, but only de facto mysteriousness. If the true meaning of the Jewish law is known only through allegorical interpretation, then an outsider can scarcely hope to discover it without special instruction. In this sense, the entire corpus of allegorical interpretation posits an esoteric revelation, even though it is devoted to divulging the mystery. Similarly, revelation gained through dreams, visions, etc., is not publicly accessible, and so is de facto esoteric. Neither of these broader uses implies deliberate secrecy, but they do underline the *supernatural* character of the religion and claim that it involves more than can be directly known from nature without special revelation.

Heavenly revelations

This brings us to the broader use of the term *mystical* for wisdom through revelations of a heavenly world, which leads to an other-worldly salvation. In this broader use, mysticism does not necessarily involve a ritual or deliberate secrecy, and the mystical philosophy is not necessarily related to Logos or Sophia. It does, of course, involve de facto esotericism. The mystical quality lies in the (alleged) direct experience of the supernatural and the transcendent nature of salvation. Whether one wishes to use the word *mystical* for these revelations or prefers to restrict it to more narrowly defined phenomena, what is important is to recognize their affinities with the mysteries and their difference over against the other writings we have been reviewing. The locus of revelation has been moved from this world to a higher one. The medium of salvation is no longer human wisdom, philosophical or traditional, nor even the Jewish law in its literal form, but rather the revelation gained by exceptional experiences of particular individuals. It is, of course, understood that such higher revelation is not opposed to the Jewish law, or even to inductive reason, but it adds something over and above them which contributes directly to salvation and is the main focus of attention. We will find this kind of mysticism in the Hellenistic Jewish apocalypses, but also in narratives such as Joseph and Aseneth and the Testament of Job.

The appeal to higher revelation does not abandon the consistent attempt of Diaspora Judaism to find a common basis with Hellenistic culture. Such appeal to higher revelation was characteristic of the Hellenistic world, as evidenced by, e.g., the popularity of the mysteries.[28] The "mystical" Jewish writings continue to preach the common ethic of Hellenistic Judaism. No firm line can be drawn between the philosophical and the mystical in Philo or the Wisdom of Solomon, where the grace of revelation is ultimately seen as the fulfillment, not the negation of human nature. Mystical experiences were not peculiar to the Jews. It is significant that one of the earliest mystical Jewish works is ascribed pseudonymously to Orpheus.

THE PSEUDO-ORPHIC FRAGMENTS

The question of a Jewish mystery in the earliest stage of Hellenistic Judaism is raised most directly by the Pseudo-Orphic fragments. In Eusebius (PE 13.12), Aristobulus claims that Orpheus, like Pythagoras, Socrates, and Plato, imitates Moses, in verses on the *hieros logos*, for "He expresses thus concerning the maintaining of all things by divine power, their being generated and God's being over all things" and proceeds to cite a poem of forty-one hexameters (Recension E). A shorter form of this poem, consisting of twenty-one hexameters, is found in two works falsely attributed to Justin Martyr, *De Monarchia* chap. 2 and *Cohortatio ad Gentiles*, chap. 15 (Recension J). Further, there are several short quotations in Clement's *Protrepticus* and *Stromateis*. Most of these coincide with J, but some in *Stromateis*, 5.123–24 are found in E and not in J. Finally, the late Tubingen Theosophy (T) offers a compilation of J and E and runs to forty-six lines.[29]

The textual history of the Orphic poem is extremely complicated. The consensus of scholarship is that the short recension, J, is the oldest. The later recensions are directly developed from this in a number of stages. The most significant steps in the process were an "Abrahamic recension" found in Clement but not in J, which added lines 26–31, and refer to a certain "Chaldean" who is the only human to see God, and a "Mosaic recension" found only in E and T, distinguished by lines 25 and 41–42, which treats Moses as the primary figure.[30]

The view that J represents the earliest form of the poem rests on a number of arguments. Clement demonstrably knew and used Aristobulus, in the immediate context of the latter's Orphic quotation. Yet, he cites the verses that seem to refer to Abraham, but never those that clearly refer to Moses. Since the "Mosaic recension" is found only in E and T, Walter, following Elter, concludes that these verses at least were inserted after the time of Clement and before Eusebius, since Clement presumably would not have passed over an "Orphic" testimony to Moses.[31] Further, R. Keller argued that the E form of the hymn does not correspond to the introductory comments of Aristobulus, which are concerned with the role of God in creation. By contrast, Aristobulus fails to underline the explicit reference to Moses. Keller infers that the poem cited by Aristobulus corresponded to J.[32] Walter admits this as a possibility but argues that it is more likely that Aristobulus cited a completely different passage, perhaps F 168 or F 169,1–5 or F 298 of the Orphic fragments edited by Kern,[33] any of which would fit the context better, or perhaps a passage that is simply lost. This radical conclusion is not required by the texts. All the recensions provide some statement which corresponds to the introductory comments on God's role in creation (e.g., l. 10). The fact that this is not the sole theme of the poem cannot disallow the quotation. There is no reason to deny that Aristobulus quoted some variant of the Orphic hymn we have.

It is possible that the hymn quoted by Aristobulus included not only J but all the verses known to Clement. While lines 41 and 42, the Mosaic recension,[34] are not found in Clement and would not have been passed over, the case for the so-called Abrahamic recension is different. The claim that Abraham saw God might have been suppressed in the Justinian version for reasons of orthodoxy. From a stylistic viewpoint, however, J reads more smoothly without the Abrahamic verses, which cause an awkward transition from line 32 to 33. We may accept the consensus that J is prior.

There is a significant difference between the view of Judaism in the J recension and in the Abrahamic one. The theme of J is monotheism and the invisibility of God. It is closely paralleled in Sib Or 3:1–45, a passage of uncertain provenance prefixed to the Third Sibyl. The Orphic dress here has the usual apologetic effect of placing a testimony to Jewish beliefs on the lips of a figure revered by the Greeks. Yet, the choice of pseudonym is always significant. The emphasis on monotheism and invisibility was most likely to appeal to people of a philosophical bent, and reflects a similar disposition in the Jewish authors. Whether or not the J version reflects the original poem cited by Aristobulus, there is no doubt, in view of the sibylline parallel, that it represents a strand of Hellenistic Judaism. It makes no mention of the law but bases its religion on a philosophical conception of spiritual purity. Understanding of the singleness of God is the heart of this religion, and it might be attained by various means. It should be said that this kind of religion is especially close to what we find in Aristobulus and Philo.

The Abrahamic recension differs pointedly from this by asserting that there is an exception to the human inability to see God—a single man from the Chaldean race. This individual was identified as "Abraham or his son" by Clement.[35] The identification with Abraham is supported by Sib Or 3:218, which refers to the origins of the Jewish race in Ur of the Chaldees. We should note however that Philo refers to Moses as a Chaldean, and the same reference is possible here too.[36] In any case, the Chaldean is said to be knowledgeable in the astral world.[37] He surpasses Orpheus, who can only point out the traces of God on earth.[38] We are reminded of Philo's explanation of Israel as "one who sees God."[39] It does not, of course, follow that all Jews see God directly, but they can at least contemplate the description of the divine throne, which is guaranteed by Abraham's experience. This passage, then, lends a new dimension to the understanding of the J recension. In view of the parallel in the *Exagōgē* of Ezekiel we may confidently claim that the Abrahamic hymn also represents a strand of Judaism which dates back to the second century BCE or possibly even the late third.

Finally, the Mosaic recension rather resembles Sir 24:23 ("all this is the book of the law of the Lord") in attempting to bring diverse material under the aegis of the Torah (cf. also the reference to divine laws in line 2, which is found only in E and T).[40] The effect of the addition is ambiguous, as is also the case in Sirach: does the law now take precedence over the heavenly experience of the Chaldean, or is that experience precisely what is significant about the law? While Judaism is more clearly related to the Torah, the hymn could be taken as an invitation to interpret the Torah in the light of Abraham's experience. The dominant image of the poem is still that of God seated on his throne. The Torah is no more than the mediator of that vision. Whether we should further think of two levels of Torah interpretation, as Georgi suggests,[41] is not certain. It is not required by the expression *kata diplaka nomon*, which may simply refer to the two tablets. However, such an interpretation is encouraged by the prominence of allegorical interpretation in Aristobulus and the later Alexandrian tradition, and is quite compatible with the view that what is important in the Torah is the vision of God. If the final recension is understood in this way, then the "Mosaic recension" may have only been making explicit the dependence of Orpheus on Moses which was already presumed by Aristobulus.

The "mystical" character of these Orphic fragments lies in their explicit esotericism and, in the Abrahamic recension, the higher revelation of Abraham's vision. The pseudonym of Orpheus lent itself readily to esotericism. While the older elaborate reconstructions of

Orphism are now viewed with skepticism,[42] *Orphika* are linked with *Bacchika,* or Bacchic rituals, as early as Herodotus, and Orpheus is linked with Bacchic behavior (*baccheuein*) in Euripides.[43] While the name of Orpheus need not in all circumstances evoke the Bacchic mysteries, it was widely associated with them. The Bacchic mysteries are associated with the hope for an afterlife already in the classical period.[44] Such a concern is also implied in the view that the body is a tomb, which Plato attributes to "Orpheus and his followers" in the *Cratylus* (400c). Surprisingly, the Jewish Orphic fragments do not touch at all on the subject of afterlife, although the divine throne is often associated with the rewards and punishments of the afterlife in the Jewish apocalyptic literature. The Jewish Orphic fragments exploit the connection with Orpheus only in presenting the monotheistic teaching as a mystery from which the profane are excluded. Judaism is set above Orphism by the claim that Abraham enjoyed the vision of God.

EZEKIEL THE TRAGEDIAN

Another early specimen of "mystical" Judaism is found in the drama on the Exodus by Ezekiel, which, at 269 lines, is the most extensive remnant of the Greco-Jewish poets apart from the sibylline oracles.[45] Ezekiel is described as a writer of tragedies in Eusebius and Clement, but no fragments of any other work have survived. He is usually assumed to have written in Alexandria.[46] The only clue to his date is a description of the phoenix (PE 9.29.254–69), which goes beyond the biblical text and may have been prompted by the appearance of the bird in Egypt in the reign of Ptolemy III Euergetes I.[47] This, of course, is very tentative, but there is nothing in the fragments against a date towards the end of the third century BCE. The terminus a quo is provided by the LXX, on which Ezekiel clearly relies.[48]

While Ezekiel was not a great poet, he constructed a competent drama in accordance with the classical conventions,[49] and his vocabulary "attests a full knowledge of tragic and particularly Euripidean usage."[50] The use of such a typically Greek form does not necessarily require that the work was written with a gentile audience in mind.[51] It may equally have served to reassure Hellenized Jews that their tradition was capable of expression in a Greek form.[52]

Ezekiel follows the biblical story rather closely, but his occasional departures are significant. So, in his treatment of the Passover, he neglects to mention the requirement of circumcision.[53] Judaism for Ezekiel is not constituted by its distinctive markings. It can compete with other traditions on a common stage. The treatment of Moses' marriage to Zipporah has also been taken to reflect a universalist attitude. Only two lines refer to this episode, but they note that Zipporah was given "to a stranger." Such a statement must be taken to imply a positive attitude towards mixed marriages.

The two major departures from the biblical text concern the dream of Moses and the description of the phoenix. The dream has attracted more scholarly attention than any other aspect of the play and has been taken by Cerfaux and Goodenough as evidence for a Jewish mystery cult.[54] The dream begins with a vision of a great throne above Mt. Sinai. Then the figure on the throne beckons to Moses, gives him a scepter and crown, and enthrones him. He himself vacates his throne. Moses enjoys a view of the entire earth round about and also the regions above the heaven and below the earth. A multitude of stars fall at his feet. Then Raguel interprets the dream, saying that Moses will cause a certain great man (*megan tina*) to rise from a throne and will himself be judge and leader, and will see "what is, what was before and is to come."

The use of a dream is a familiar element of Greek tragedy and the dreams of Joseph provide a biblical precedent. Recently, Holladay has suggested that the installation of Moses on the throne establishes him as a Greek *mantis* by analogy with Apollo, who is installed on a throne by Zeus.[55] However, Zeus does not vacate his throne for Apollo, and the "mantic throne" is not described in royal terms as is the case in Ezekiel. The most striking aspect of the dream is that the figure who initially occupies the throne (presumably God) vacates it. This element goes far beyond what we find in such visions as T Lev 8, which may be fairly close to it in time. The nearest parallel is perhaps the Similitudes of Enoch, where "that son of man" is installed on a throne and given the function of judge.[56] The parallel with Enoch is all the more striking because in the present form of the Similitudes "that son of man" is identified as Enoch, the seer who is given knowledge of what is above the heaven, what is and is to come in the course of his visions. The tradition of a vision on Mt. Sinai in which Moses was made king is found several times in later writings, most notably in Philo but also in the midrashim.[57] There is little doubt that the tradition was inspired by midrashic reflection on such scriptural passages as Exod 7:1 ("I have made you a god to Pharaoh").[58] This exegetical basis is not evident in Ezekiel, so he quite probably drew on a tradition which was already current.[59] In Jethro's interpretation, the figure who rises from the throne is presumably pharaoh.

More important than the source of the imagery in the dream is its function and significance. Meeks has suggested that "the most common function of ascension stories in literature of the period and milieu we are considering is as a guarantee of esoteric tradition,"[60] but he admits that Moses' kingship is scarcely related to this function. Yet, the kingship of Moses is evidently of central importance in Ezekiel. The particular combination of motifs which we find here must be understood within the context of the drama itself.

In view of the fragmentary state of the text it is of course difficult to propose a view of the whole. Trencsényi-Waldapfel has offered a plausible reconstruction, according to which the drama consisted of five acts and was confined to the first fifteen chapters of Exodus. Act One introduces Moses in Midian, where he meets the maiden at the well. Act Two is set at the house of Jethro, where Moses recounts his dream to Jethro and is given Zipporah in marriage. Act Three describes the encounter with God on Mt. Sinai, and gives a description of the plagues in advance. Act Four involves the actual departure from Egypt and the report of the incident at the sea. Act Five corresponds to Exod 15:23–25 and concludes with the arrival at Elim.[61] Whether or not the details of this reconstruction are accepted, it is clear that Moses' dream is recounted early in the drama and has a decisive role in the development of the action since it wins the support of Jethro. The function of the dream is indeed to guarantee knowledge that could not otherwise be available. The knowledge so revealed is the kingship of Moses but also, in Jethro's interpretation, the fact that Moses is endowed with all-encompassing vision.

The dream is fulfilled in the story of the Exodus where Moses leads his people out of Egypt and pharaoh is overthrown. The tragic climax comes with the destruction of the Egyptians at the sea. Then the drama concludes with a peaceful scene at Elim. Significantly the story is not extended to Mt. Sinai, although the giving of the law would have provided a satisfactory dramatic finale.[62] Instead, the concluding scene is marked by the second deviation from the biblical text, the description of the phoenix.[63]

The introduction of the phoenix into the story of the Exodus is most immediately prompted by the reference to the palm trees at Elim. Since the Greek word *phoenix*, which means both "phoenix" and "palm tree," is used in the LXX, it provides the obvious point of contact. However, the phoenix (*bennu*) had ancient symbolic significance in Egypt, where it was associated with the creator god and the renewal of life but also with Osiris and with the renewal of life through death.[64] In Ezekiel's drama it is coupled with the biblical imagery of the twelve springs of Elim, which suggest abundance and life. This scene is presented as the report of a scout. It is not yet present, but it suggests a promised land of renewed life and possibly of immortality.

The symbolism of the phoenix opens the possibility that the Exodus may be understood allegorically as a journey, not to Canaan but to eternal life, which is completed under the guidance of Moses. Such an allegorical understanding would of course be in keeping with the thought of Philo, some centuries later. There is no explicit allegory in Ezekiel. The symbols are not interpreted. It is possible that the phoenix only symbolizes the vitality of the promised land of Israel. However, in view of Moses' dream-vision, which grounds Moses' authority in his supernatural knowledge, we should not exclude the possibility that a transcendant salvation is envisaged.

We may now return to the theories of Cerfaux and Goodenough that Ezekiel's drama is representative of a Jewish mystery. There is no warrant for any assumption that the drama was performed in a ritual context.[65] Further, we cannot say that Moses' ascent had a paradigmatic significance for his followers, in the sense that Philo's Moses was paradigmatic.[66] However, we have seen that there is some reason to believe that the entire story had symbolic significance and dramatizes in a veiled way the process of salvation. Also the authority of Moses is not, at least in the fragments we have, related to the law but to his heavenly journey. One might, then, speak of a Jewish mystery in the extended sense that Judaism here is based on knowledge which is not publicly accessible and on a spiritual or deeper understanding of events. Moses is the leader of such a religion because of the special knowledge given to him by God.

The Judaism of Ezekiel is different from the other fragments preserved by Alexander Polyhistor. It is not primarily a national romance—it does little to show that Israel outshines its neighbors in the manner of Eupolemus or Artapanus. Again, it is not explicitly centered on the law. It is based on an acceptance of Moses as the authoritative leader because of his knowledge, but the association of Moses with the law is not noted. The only specific Jewish custom noted is the celebration of the Passover, and there the requirement of circumcision is omitted. Moses' dream is interpreted by a foreigner in direct reversal of the biblical custom (contrast Joseph and Daniel). The fact that Raguel gives his daughter to a stranger (Moses!) has obvious implications for marriage customs in the Diaspora. The Exodus evokes a confession from the Egyptian messenger. While Ezekiel holds to the superiority of Judaism, it is not understood as an exclusive religion. It is accessible to anyone guided by the heavenly knowledge of Moses. For want of a better label we may call this religion the Jewish mystery, with the understanding that no ritual practice is necessarily implied.

JOSEPH AND ASENETH

Among the most intriguing documents relevant to the question of mystic Judaism is the story of Joseph and Aseneth. The first editor, Batiffol,[67] regarded the work as Christian and he was followed in this judgment by Brooks, who did the English translation, among others.[68] The Jewish origin of the work was defended already in the review of Batiffol by L. Duchesne,[69] and at length by P. Riessler in 1922.[70] Since the articles of Kilpatrick, Jeremias, and Kuhn in the 1950s, the Jewish provenance has been generally accepted.[71] The alleged references to eucharist and confirmation are significantly different from the Christian sacraments and lack any distinctively Christian note.[72]

Joseph and Aseneth consists of two distinct though related stories, the conversion of Aseneth (chaps. 1–21) and the jealously of pharaoh's son.[73] The second story has been discussed above in Chapter 2. Each story has a point of departure in scripture. The first responds to the problem of Joseph's marriage to an Egyptian woman. The second, less clearly, explains how Joseph came to be ruler over all the land of Egypt (Gen 45:26), although it goes beyond the biblical account in actually making Joseph sovereign for a time after the pharaoh's death. This exegetical aspect of the genesis of the story is, naturally, important but it is by no means the only key to the meaning of the work. While the language of Joseph and Aseneth is heavily dependent on the LXX,[74] the structure and many motifs are drawn from the Hellenistic romances.[75] This widely acknowledged fact has two important consequences for our understanding of Joseph and Aseneth. First, despite the ubiquity of biblical phrases we cannot agree that Aseneth has a purely Jewish profile.[76] At the very least, she is also a character in a Hellenistic romance. Second, while we must be skeptical of claims that the romance genre is inherently related to the mystery religions,[77] the fact remains that Aseneth's conversion to Judaism is simultaneously her romantic attraction to Joseph and climactic marriage to him. The homology of these two strands of the story cannot be denied. Just as the quest for philosophical truth is depicted by the analogy of love in Plato's *Symposium*, so the quest for religious truth is depicted here.

The question of Jewish identity arises with unusual directness in the story of Aseneth's conversion. As Philonenko has outlined well, there is a fundamental antithesis between Jews and Egyptians, despite the mediating presence of sympathizers and proselytes.[78] The antithesis is most clearly marked by Joseph's refusal to eat with the Egyptians and to kiss Aseneth because she worshipped idols. The prohibition of intermarriage is evidently implied in Joseph's initial rejection of Aseneth. In both the matter of table fellowship and of kissing the decisive point is the worship of idols, "for it is not fitting that a pious man who worships with his mouth the living God and eats the blessed bread of life and drinks the blessed cup of immortality and is anointed with the blessed ointment of incorruption, should kiss an alien woman, who blesses with her mouth dead, dumb idols and eats from their table bread of strangling, drinks from their libations a cup of treachery and anoints herself with the ointment of perdition" (8:5). Again in Aseneth's prayer the major fault acknowledged, before her personal sin of pride, is that of idolatry, and her mouth is defiled from eating the sacrifices of the idols. It would seem then that Judaism is primarily a strict monotheism, which rejects idol worship.

The sharp antithesis between Jews and Egyptians is mediated by the presence of sympathizers and proselytes. Pentephres, father of Aseneth, and pharaoh, are both sympathizers in the sense that they are well disposed to Joseph and his religion.[79] They are not necessarily God-fearers, although they respect the God of Joseph, as there is nothing to indicate that they follow any Jewish laws. Their sympathy for Judaism does not exempt them from Joseph's separation in table fellowship, as they still worship the gods of the Egyptians. Aseneth, by contrast, definitively breaks with her ancestral religion and becomes a proselyte. Thereafter, she, like Joseph, can claim Jacob as father

(22:3). Once she has rejected the idols of the Egyptians, the impediments to her union with Joseph are overcome.

The conversion of Aseneth involves none of the rituals later associated with proselytism—circumcision, baptism, or the offering of a sacrifice in the temple.[80] Circumcision was not relevant in the case of Aseneth, but we have noted its near absence in the literature of the Hellenistic Diaspora. Sacrifice in the Jerusalem temple was, again, scarcely relevant in a Diaspora setting especially in view of the fictional setting of the story before the time of Solomon. Proselyte baptism is never attested in Hellenistic Judaism.[81] The question then arises whether conversion to Judaism was simply conceived as the rejection of idolatry or whether it still involved some ritual elements.

Ritual elements in Joseph and Aseneth?

The question of ritual is raised by two passages in Joseph and Aseneth. The first is the formulaic reference to eating the bread of life, drinking the cup of immortality, and anointing with the oil of incorruption, which occurs twice, in 8:5–6 and 15:4. The second is the mysterious honeycomb in chapters 16–17. The formulaic character of the references to the bread, wine, and oil has been taken by some as sufficient evidence that they refer to a ritual.[82] Yet, attempts to elucidate the references by analogies with the Christian eucharist, the Qumran meal, or the meal of the Therapeutae have been unsuccessful.[83] The inclusion of the anointing is problematic since it seems to come *after* the blessing of the bread and the wine.[84] Consequently, Philonenko is forced to posit a ritual which has no exact parallel in ancient Judaism, but which he then relates to initiation into Judaism as a mystery.[85] Burchard, by contrast, abandons the idea of a ritual meal and suggests that the formula refers to the entire Jewish way of life.[86]

The context in which the formula is first introduced in chapter 8 is significant at this point. Joseph explains his rejection of Aseneth by reference to their respective food, drink, and ointment. Since the eating, etc., is predicated of Joseph as a pious man it is evidently not, or at least not only, an initiation ritual. Rather, it is the habitual practice of the pious.

The possibility remains that the formula refers to a recurring ritual practice. There is an inescapable analogy with 1 Corinthians; "are not those who eat the sacrifices partakers in the altar. . . . you cannot drink the cup of the Lord and the cup of demons; you cannot partake of the table of the Lord and the table of demons" (1 Cor 10:18, 20–21). The table of the Lord for Paul is of course the eucharist. Joseph and Aseneth does not refer to the table of the Lord, but the contrast with the table of idols suggests that a cultic meal is involved. However, there is no known example of a ritual meal in which anointing comes after the bread and the cup. It is possible that Joseph and Aseneth is the unique witness to such a ritual, but it is also possible that the formula doesn't reflect a ritual, but is rather, like the OT formula "the grain, the wine and the oil,"[87] a summary of the staples of life. Even in this case, special significance is attached to eating, drinking, and anointing as the representative actions. Joseph's separatism in table fellowship lends support to the idea that meals have a special significance. The formula in Joseph and Aseneth gives a sacramental significance to eating, drinking, and anointing in any Jewish meal where a blessing is pronounced.[88] The use of oil for cleaning the hands at the end of a meal is attested, though not widely, in rabbinic Judaism, so the anointing has at least possible significance in this context.[89] In all, then, Joseph and Aseneth does not provide adequate reason for positing a mystic ritual which is otherwise unknown, since the formulaic language can be referred to the everyday rituals of Jewish life.

Group membership

The bread, the wine, and the oil are presented in Joseph and Aseneth as symbols of immortality and incorruption. Participation in the rituals of Jewish life, however understood, is the key to salvation, which is immortality. Table fellowship and group membership are of the utmost importance here. A pious man may embrace his mother, his sister from the same tribe, and his wife, who bless with their mouth the living God. E. P. Sanders concludes that "outside of Judaism there is no salvation."[90] Yet it is important to note how the group membership is defined. The basic requirement is acknowledgment of the living God, not ethnic descent. In the idiom of the story, one may marry into the family of Jacob, provided that one rejects the idols of the Egyptians. The second story in Joseph and Aseneth 22–29 shows that ethnic membership does not guarantee right conduct. Further, it is not clear that observance of the full Jewish law is required. In practice, the law is reduced to monotheism, rejecting of idolatry, chastity before marriage, and avoidance of social or sexual intimacy with "aliens"—i.e., people who worship other gods. It is noteworthy that even before her conversion Aseneth is devoted to chastity and shuns aliens. It would seem that the author regards "ethnic purity" as a virtue in its own right even when practiced by an Egyptian, except that Joseph and his family transcend the usual distinctions of race and are defined rather by worship of the true God. In short, true religion is equated with worship of the living God and avoidance of idols. This confers the right to table fellowship and group membership with Joseph and his family, and also the ultimate salvation of immortality. In 13:10 Aseneth confesses that she had not known that Joseph was God's son, for she had been told that he was the son of a shepherd from Canaan. Jacob's significance is not his ethnic origin. Aseneth feels kinship with Joseph's kin because Joseph is a son of God. The traditional criteria for Jewish identity, descent or circumcision (which is here conveniently avoided because of Aseneth's sex), are no longer decisive. The label Judaism is not in use. While the religion of Joseph and Aseneth preserves sharp boundaries over against polytheism, it is, nevertheless, a universal religion freed from the restrictions of race. It is a distinct religion, but one which can appeal to the reasonable gentile.

The episode of the honeycomb

We have argued that the bread, cup, and anointing refer to the ongoing life of the "pious" rather than to an initiation ritual. In fact, Aseneth's conversion is not marked by a ritual meal. Instead, it involves an encounter with "a man from heaven"[91] and a honeycomb. The man tells her that the mysteries of God (ta aporrēta tou theou, 16:7) have been revealed to her. Those who turn to the Lord in metanoia will eat from this honeycomb, for it is made by the bees in paradise, the angels of God eat from it and whoever eats from it will never die. Then the man eats some of the honey and gives some to Aseneth. The symbolism of the honey is not entirely clear. Philonenko relates it to the manna, which tasted like honey (Exod 16:31).[92] It may also be associated with the goddess Neith, whose symbols included the bee.[93] Its significance in its present context is quite explicit: it is the food of the angels, which gives immortality. Philonenko and Burchard quite rightly interpret this as the revelation of the true significance of the bread, wine, and oil which Aseneth will share after her conversion.[94] The episode with the honey shows that the food of the pious is really the food of angels. Therein lies the mystery. This food confers immortality like the bread from heaven in John 6. Such food imagery is often used to symbolize wisdom.[95] In Joseph and Aseneth the revealed understanding lies not only in the knowledge that those who convert in *metanoia* will never die but also in the true significance of "the bread of blessing and cup of immortality."

The salvation attained by Aseneth is immortality. The full realization of this salvation is presumably still future, but it has a strong present component. Joseph is already a "son of God" and Aseneth now becomes a "daughter of God" (21:3). The similarity in appearance between Joseph and the angel (14:8), and the knowledge that the pious share the food of angels, indicates that those who worship the living God are already living an angelic life. This conception is strikingly similar to what we find in the Qumran Hodayot.[96] The assertion that those who eat of the honeycomb will never die is reminiscent of the Wisdom of Solomon (3:2) where the righteous only seem to die. The mysteries of God in Joseph and Aseneth are the way to immortality, as also in Wisdom. Just as Joseph is a "son of God" and resembles the angel in appearance, so also the righteous man in Wisdom is a son of God (2:13, 16, 18) and is numbered among the holy ones (5:5). The symbolism of the honeycomb in Joseph and Aseneth recalls the symbolism of wisdom, which is sweeter than the honeycomb (Sir 24:20), and suggests that the transformation to the quasi-angelic state is due to the nourishment of wisdom. The main difference between Joseph and Aseneth and Wisdom is that the latter uses a philosophical idiom while Joseph and Aseneth relies on narrative symbolism.

The representative roles of Joseph and Aseneth

Joseph and Aseneth has an evident allegorical quality which has repeatedly been noted by scholars. The attempts to construe the work as a specifically Christian allegory, taking Joseph as Christ, have been rightly rejected.[97] Yet, Joseph has an obvious representative quality as the embodiment of the true (Jewish) religion, who is uncompromising on the matter of idolatry but is in all respects virtuous, admired by the leading men of Egypt and desired by the women. The representative quality of Aseneth is more explicitly stated in 15:6 where she is told that in future she will be called city of refuge, that many nations will take refuge in her, and that those who attach themselves to the Lord through repentance will be protected by her "wall." This passage applies to Aseneth a constellation of biblical prophecies—those to Abraham in Genesis, to Zion in Zech 2:15 (LXX) and Isa 62:4. Burchard concludes that Aseneth is "das Zion der Proselyten," although he insists that she is not an allegory for the proselytes.[98] Burchard is quite right that Aseneth does not lose her own individuality in the story to become a mere cipher, but she is, nonetheless, the representative proselyte. By illustrating a model proselyte experience she becomes a paradigm for proselytes who can take hope and reassurance from her story.[99]

A corpus permixtum

The conversion of Aseneth is described throughout in strongly biblical terms, which invoke the language of creation, emergence from darkness to light, and from death to life (10:18–20; 12:2–3). D. Sänger has argued that it is an actualization of the Exodus, but his argument rests on the presumed technical sense of the verb *exagein*.[100] A Jewish reader might well correlate the exodus of Aseneth from idolatry with that of Israel from Egypt, but the correlation is not highlighted in the text. Rather, the main biblical analogies are with the process of creation—evidently a more immediately acceptable conception in an Egyptian context. Further, the presence of biblical imagery cannot exclude the allusions to the Egyptian goddess Neith, noted by Philonenko, which are, at least, clearly present in the episode of the bees. The significance of the Egyptian symbolism is that Aseneth has at once both a Jewish and an Egyptian profile. She does not lose her Egyptian identity when she converts. It is because of her enduring Egyptian characteristics that she can remain an effective paradigm for proselytes.

The presentation of Aseneth as a refuge for proselytes lends Joseph and Aseneth a more obvious missionary character than is the case in many of the documents of Hellenistic Judaism. While only a Jewish reader could appreciate the full flavor of the biblical references, the story could be readily appreciated by an Egyptian. Indeed, a Jewish reader unfamiliar with Egyptian tradition would miss some of the flavor too. The story is surely meant to encourage proselytes, both those who have not yet converted and those who have. This is not to deny that its main readership may in fact have been Jewish. The presentation of Judaism as a nonethnic religion of monotheism is a statement of Jewish identity addressed to all interested parties, both Jewish and gentile. In the phrase of Dieter Sänger, Judaism is recognized as a *corpus permixtum*.[101]

Lack of sectarian character

A final question concerns the precise milieu within Judaism in which Joseph and Aseneth was composed. The mystical character of the work has led many scholars to posit a sectarian origin. The hypotheses of Essene or Therapeutae authorship have been widely rejected because of the lack of correspondence on points of central importance.[102] Philonenko's hypothesis of an unknown mystic sect rests on the assumption that a peculiar ritual is attested in Joseph and Aseneth, which we have seen reason to doubt.[103] In fact, Joseph and Aseneth gives no more impression of sectarian provenance than does Philo. The strong interest in the conversion of gentiles, but not of Jews, and the lack of distinctive laws apart from table fellowship weigh against a sectarian origin. To be sure, not all Jews would have shared the mystical view of Judaism embodied in this work, but it does not posit any significant division within the Jewish community.

THE PRAYER OF JOSEPH

Joseph and Aseneth is restrained in its allusions to the heavenly or spritiaul world. The "man from heaven" in chapters 14–17 is exceptional in the story and is also deliberately mysterious. Other documents of Hellenistic Judaism are more explicitly mythological. One of the most intriguing of such documents is the fragmentary Prayer of Joseph.[104]

The central point in the main surviving fragment of the Prayer of Joseph is that Israel is an angel of God: "I, Jacob, who am speaking to you, am also Israel, an angel of God and a ruling spirit. Abraham and Isaac were created before any work. But I, Jacob, whom men call Jacob but whose name is Israel, am he whom God called Israel, i.e., a man seeing God, because I am the firstborn of every living thing to whom God gives light" (F 1). Jacob goes on to interpret the struggle with the angel of Genesis 32 as a conflict with Uriel, who told him "that I had descended to earth and I had tabernacled among men and that I had been called by the name Jacob." Uriel envied Israel and disputed his rank, but "I told him his name, and what rank he held among the sons of God: 'Are you not Uriel, the eighth after me, and I, Israel, the archangel of the power of the Lord and the chief captain among the sons of God?" The paraphrase in Philocalia 23.19 says that Israel recognizes his true identity while doing service in the body, being reminded of it by the archangel Uriel.

We do not know the full extent of the Prayer of Joseph. The second fragment would seem to indicate that the book had an apocalyptic component: "For I have read in the tablets of heaven all that shall befall you and your sons." Further, it is questionable whether Origen's paraphrase in the Philocalia accurately reflects his source when he suggests that Israel was unaware of his heavenly origin until he was reminded of it by Uriel. In view of the brevity of the surviving fragments any interpretation must be tentative. J. Z. Smith has proposed on the basis of religio-historical parallels that "the myth may be ritually appropriated by its believers, that the 'objective' narrative has a 'subjective' correlative. That which is accomplished by the paradigmatic figure of the Patriarch Jacob-Israel may, presumably, also be achieved by the 'sons of Jacob' " by a mystical ascent to the vision of God.[105] He finds confirmation of this in the "Prayer of Jacob" which prays: "Fill my heart with good things, Master, because I am an angel on earth, because I have become immortal, because I have received the gift from thee,"[106] and in 2 Enoch, where Enoch returns to earth *after* he has ascended to heaven and become an angel. The case of Israel is especially important because of the natural paradigmatic extension of the role of Israel to the people of Israel.

What then does the Prayer of Joseph say about Jewish identity? While any conclusion is tentative, it would appear that the true Israelite is an embodiment or representative of the angelic Israel, whose true rank and destiny are in heavenly glory. This is not to say that every Israelite is a preexistent angel, but that he participates in Jacob in the way that the righteous man participates in wisdom when she "tabernacles among men" (Sir 24:8–12). The "sons of Israel" in this mystical sense are not necessarily identical with the sons of Israel according to the flesh, but the Prayer is too fragmentary to permit us to elaborate on their identity. The conceptions of the Prayer of Joseph are remarkable but have enough in common with the Philo and other documents from the turn of the era to support Smith's thesis that it is indeed a product of Hellenistic Judaism.

THE TESTAMENT OF JOB

The supernatural world is also given explicit mythological expression in the Testament of Job.[107] There is now general agreement that T Job was composed in Greek, as is evident from the use of the LXX.[108] The Egyptian provenance can scarcely be doubted since Job is said to be king of all Egypt (28:8).[109] The Jewish origin of the work is now generally granted in view of the lack of specifically Christian elements,[110] but there is little agreement about the date. A terminus a quo of about 100 BCE is suggested by dependence on LXX Job, but a terminus ad quem is difficult to find. General similarity to such works as Joseph and Aseneth and the Testament of Abraham support the common view that the work was composed in the broad period between 100 BCE and 150 CE, but a precise dating is not possible.[111]

T Job is a retelling of the story of Job but involves considerable development over and above the biblical text.[112] The story is presented as the deathbed discourse of Job to his children.[113] Most significant is the new understanding of Job's sufferings. Satan is no longer a neutral figure as in the biblical Job but a prince of evil whom Job has infuriated. Moreover, Job is aware from the outset of the reason for his suffering.

The struggle with Satan

Like Joseph and Aseneth, T Job involves a conversion to the worship of the one true God. Job, called Jobab, used to live near a venerated idol, and had come to question whether this was the God who made heaven and earth.[114] One night "a voice in a great light" informed him that the idol was not God but the "power of the devil by which human nature is deceived." Job immediately asks for authority to raze the shrine, but he is warned:

> If you attempt to destroy and you destroy the place of Satan
> he will angrily rise up against you for battle
> except that he will not be able to bring death upon you. . . .
> But if you endure, I shall make your name renowned
> in all earthly generations until the consummation of the age.
> And you will be raised up in the resurrection
> and you will be like an athlete who spars and endures hard
> labors and wins the crown [4:4–9].[115]

Job proceeds to raze the temple anyhow, and so the drama of Job's suffering is set in motion.

The introductory story of Job's conversion in chapters 2–5 provides the framework for the rest of the book, and points clearly to one aspect of the book's message. Job is an exemplary athlete of virtue who wins a crown by endurance. This motif is a common one in Hellenistic Judaism.[116] We have seen in Chapter 4 above that the Testaments of the Twelve Patriarchs typically inculcate specific virtues. The virtue of endurance is highlighted in the first part of the book (chaps. 2–27) where Job is directly involved in conflict with Satan. In 1:3 Job introduces himself as one who exhibits complete endurance. Again in chapter 27 Satan repeats the athletic image in acknowledging his defeat by Job. Job draws the moral in 27:10 by exhorting his children to patience.

However, endurance is not an end in itself. Job describes himself in 18:6–7 as a merchant at sea who is prepared to lose all he has if only he can reach a certain city and share in its riches. So, says Job, "I also now considered my possessions as nothing compared to approaching the city about which the angel had spoken to me." In fact, the angel had not told Job of a city but had promised retribution, fame, and a share in the resurrection, all of which were given to Job in the LXX. The author of T Job feels free to substitute the heavenly Jerusalem for these more traditional rewards.

It is clear from T Job 18 that Job's endurance is based on the knowledge imparted to him by the angel of the future hope/heavenly reality of the "city." The athletic metaphor for the conflict between Job and Satan refers on a deeper level, to the conflict between revealed knowledge and Satanic deception, which was already implied in the initial situation. So Satan repeatedly takes on disguises in an effort to deceive Job, first as a beggar (chap. 7), then as king of the Persians (chap. 17), then as a great storm (20:5), and finally as a seller of bread (chap. 23). Job is able to penetrate the disguises. His knowledge gives rise to endurance and so he triumphs.

The confrontation with the friends

The second part of T Job (28–44) describes Job's confrontation with his friends (which makes up nearly all the biblical book). The (non-biblical) lament of the kings for Job (chap. 32) introduces the major motif of the second half of the book by its refrain: "where now is the glory of your throne?" Job replies that his throne and his glory are in heaven and that earthly kings and their glory will pass away. We have, then, a twofold contrast. First, there is a contrast between Job's misery and his former prosperity; second, between the fragility of the earthly kingdom and the heavenly throne.

The real issue between Job and his friends is awareness of heavenly reality. Job has insight into heavenly things while the friends have not. This point is well illustrated by the extraordinary exchange between Baldad and Job in 35–38. Job's assertion that he has a throne in heaven raises a very natural problem for Baldad. Has Job, as a result of his prolonged suffering, gone mad? The response to his first question must have increased his doubt—Job says that his heart (mind) is not on earth but in heaven. This prompts Baldad to ask him about heavenly realities. Why does this God in whom Job trusts allow a faithful servant to suffer? And how does the sun which sets in the west proceed to rise in the east again?

The correlation between the two questions is not immediately evident. Baldad might be thought to have answered his own first question. However, in both questions Baldad is challenging Job's claim to know heavenly realities. His remarks on the impossibility of judging the ways of God indicate his own belief that heavenly knowledge is impossible. Job's reply seems to agree with Baldad, but is ironic. He by no means retracts his claim to heavenly knowledge, but that knowledge is not natural to man. It requires special revelation and is certainly not accessible to one so earthly minded as Baldad. Job proceeds to reaffirm his knowledge of heavenly realities with another vision in chapter 40.

Elihu, in chapter 41, goes beyond the others in seeking to expose Job's "non-existent portion." He is said to be "filled with Satan." The struggle is still between Job and Satan and the issue is faith in the heavenly reward of Job.

Job's confrontation with his friends is resolved by the theophany, which is dealt with very briefly here. The three friends are reconciled to God through the mediation of Job. This is in accordance with the biblical story, but it now carries the implication that those who lack heavenly revelation depend on the intercession of those who enjoy it.

Elihu, however, as the representative of Satan, is condemned to permanent destruction. His fate is spelled out in a hymn on the lips of

Eliphaz in chapter 43. Elihu now becomes the counterpart of Job.
Even as Job is restored, Elihu's "kingdom has passed away, his throne
has decayed, and the honor of his pretense is in Hades" (43:5).

The role of the women

Job's insight into heavenly realities is shown also through a series of
contrasts with women. In chapter 7, Job's servant fails to recognize
Satan and thereby highlights Job's ability to recognize him. In chapters 24–26, Job's wife, who has given the hair of her head to buy food
for Job, fails to see the devil standing behind her until Job calls him
forth. In chapter 39, Job's wife again shows her lack of insight by
asking the kings to recover the bones of her children. Job opposes her,
saying that the children have been taken up to heaven. Both his wife
and the kings then see the children in heaven. The women are not
evil. Like the three kings, but not Elihu, they are victims rather than
agents of deception. Neither Job's wife nor his servant definitively
transcends the state of deception (although Job's wife sees her children in heaven and then dies in peace). After the theophany, however,
we find a remarkable account of the inheritance of Job's daughters
(46–50). The daughters are given the bands which God gave to Job
when he bade him gird up his loins like a man. When they gird
themselves, their hearts are changed so that they no longer think
earthly thoughts but speak the language of the angels. Further, their
inheritance causes them to "live in heaven" (47:3). Womankind, in T
Job, symbolizes, like the three kings, the human state of ignorance,[117]
which is transformed at the end through the mediation of Job into
heavenly knowledge and heavenly life. Job's own soul is carried up to
heaven on a chariot at the end.

The religion of the Testament of Job

Salvation for T Job is immortality in heaven and it is attained
through endurance, which is made possible by heavenly knowledge
such as is given to Job. Since this knowledge is not generally accessible, it is in effect a mystery.[118] T Job does contain some advice that is
not mysterious. The account of Job's good deeds in chapters 9–15 is
evidently exemplary. The main emphasis falls on generosity to the
poor. The endurance and patience of Job is also exemplary. Finally, in
chapter 45, Job exhorts his children before his death:

Above all, do not forget the Lord.
Do good to the poor, do not overlook the helpless.
Do not take wives for yourselves from foreigners.

Apart from devotion to God and the general attitude of generosity to the poor, the only specific conduct prescribed in T Job is the avoidance of intermarriage.

The lack of more specific instructions is all the more noteworthy since Job is presented as a gentile king who is converted to the worship of the true God. There is no ritual of conversion and no reference to circumcision. Job is never called an Israelite or a Jew and such a designation would be implausible for a ruler of Egypt. What then is the group identity protected by the prohibition of intermarriage? It would appear to be the fellowship of those who worship the true God. Ethnic considerations play an even lesser role than in Joseph and Aseneth. It is not clear that T Job distinguishes between Jews and God-fearers, provided that the latter unambiguously reject idolatry. The basis of the religion is not the Mosaic law[119] but the heavenly revelations and the rejection of idolatry. So, while T Job represents a religion which is not universally accessible and that has definite boundaries, it is nonetheless universalist in that it is not restricted by ethnic or political factors.

Philonenko has suggested that T Job originated in a community of Therapeutae.[120] The prominence of hymns might be thought to accord with the singing of the Therapeutae and the ecstatic speech of Job's daughters with the inclusion of women in the choirs (*Vit Con* 80). Neither of these points of contact is unambiguous, however, and there is no parallel in T Job for the meal of the Therapeutae or indeed for their contemplative life.[121] Given the paucity of our information on the Therapeutae, there is not sufficient evidence to attribute T Job to that group. Despite the emphasis on mysteries and revealed knowledge, there is no evidence that T Job originated in a sectarian context.

THE BOOKS OF ADAM AND EVE

Closely related to the Testament of Job are the Apocalypse of Moses and the Life of Adam and Eve, two recensions of the story of Adam and Eve which overlap in about half their material.[122] The shorter of these, the Apocalypse of Moses, is primarily an account of the death of

Adam. Adam, like Job, summons his children and tells of the crucial events of his life, in this case the story of the Fall.[123] In Apoc Mos 15–29 this story is recounted a second time, in far greater detail, by Eve. As in T Job, Satan appears as a deceiver. Also as in T Job, the woman is especially vulnerable to his deception, and in Apoc Mos the woman bears the primary responsibility for the Fall.[124] Unlike Job, however, Adam succumbed to the temptation, so that the example provided by Adam and Eve is a negative one.[125] At the end, a chariot comes to Adam. The account of Adam's translation is much more elaborate than that of Job. God promises to transform him to his former glory and set him on the throne of his deceiver.[126] Adam, and also Abel and finally Eve, are buried in Paradise, in the third heaven (Apoc Mos 37:5), to await the resurrection. The books of Adam and Eve are unusual insofar as they do not envisage the immediate enjoyment of immortality after death. Yet, they do have many points of contact with the apocalypses, especially 2 Enoch.[127] The affinities with the apocalypses are more conspicuous in the Life of Adam and Eve, which contains an account of the fall of Satan (chaps. 12–17) and an ascent of Adam into Paradise, where he is informed of his coming death. He also eats of the tree of knowledge and so knows and perceives what will come to pass in this age (chaps. 25–29).[128]

In the books of Adam and Eve the transgression of the commandments has a central role. Both books devote considerable attention to the repentance of Adam and Eve.[129] The drama of disobedience is given a supernatural backdrop through the role of the Satanic deceiver. The ultimate resolution of the story lies in the promise of resurrection and this involves a supernatural revelation of the fate of Adam. The oil of mercy is denied to Adam for the present but is promised at the resurrection.[130] The apocalyptic hope provides the premises for obedience and for repentance. Yet, within their supernatural framework the books of Adam and Eve conform to a pattern of covenantal nomism and place less emphasis on the heavenly revelations than T Job or the apocalypses.

The provenance of either Apoc Mos or the Life of Adam and Eve is far from clear. Their affinities with such works as T Job and 2 Enoch support an origin in the Hellenistic Diaspora,[131] but there are indications of a Semitic original, or at least of Semitic sources underlying the Greek.[132] The supernatural and apocalyptic elements in these books were widespread both in Palestine and in the Diaspora.

THE TESTAMENT OF ABRAHAM

Another story of the death of a patriarch is found in the Testament of Abraham. This work is not a testament and is, in fact, characterized by Abraham's failure to make a testament.[133] Instead, we have an extended narrative of Abraham's death, including a full-blown apocalypse in the account of his ride on the chariot, which puts the narrative in the perspective of the heavenly revelation.[134]

The Testament of Abraham survives in two recensions. There is no consensus as to which is earlier. Nickelsburg has argued persuasively that "numerous elements *which are simply present* in Rec B *with no clearly delineated function, are of the essence* of the structure and plot of Rec A," and that therefore the longer recension A better preserves the outline of the story.[135] There is wide agreement that T Abr is a Jewish work,[136] written in Greek.[137] Egyptian provenance is suggested by several parallels to Egyptian mythology and to other Egyptian Jewish literature.[138] The date is usually put in the first century BE on the basis of parallels to other Hellenistic Jewish writings.[139]

Nickelsburg has shown that Rec A is "neatly divided into two parallel and symmetrical parts," 1–15 and 16–20.[140] In the first part, Michael comes to take Abraham, in the second part, *Death*. In both cases, Abraham refuses to go and asks for a revelation, as a stalling tactic. In the first part, the revelation is a ride on a chariot "over all the inhabited world" (10:1). In the second part it is the revelation of the rottenness of Death and the variety of his forms. In both cases, Abraham persists in his refusal, even after the revelation, and in the end he is taken by deceit.

The Testament of Abraham has rightly been called "a veritable parody on the biblical and traditional Abraham."[141] The parody lies not only in Abraham's refusal to die, but in the ironic treatment of his character. At the outset, Abraham is characterized by "quietness, gentleness and righteousness" and "the righteous man was extremely hospitable" (chap. 1). Yet, his refusal to go with Michael is construed in chapter 8 as setting himself up against God. Abraham denies this but asks to see the whole inhabited world. The ensuing ride on the chariot brings about the ultimate revelation of Abraham's character. Whenever Abraham sees people sinning, he asks God to destroy them by having the earth swallow them or fire devour them. God himself is moved to protest:

O Archistrategos Michael, command the chariot to stop and turn
Abraham aside lest he see the whole inhabited world, for if he
sees all those who act in sin, he would destroy the whole creation.
For behold, Abraham has not sinned and he has no mercy on
sinners. I, in contrast, made the world and I do not wish to destroy
any one of them, but I await the death of the sinner, until he turns
and lives [chap. 10].[142]

Abraham is then taken up to see the judgment where he learns the
need for mercy. When a soul is saved by Abraham's prayer, he is
moved also to pray for the sinners who were destroyed at his request,
for "now I know that I sinned before the Lord our God" (chap. 14).
God forgives Abraham and recalls to life those who were destroyed,
because "I do not requite in death those whom I destroy living upon
the earth."

The revelation of the judgment plays a crucial role in the Testament
of Abraham. It convinces Abraham that excessive zeal for the destruction of sinners is itself a sin. It also underlies the revelation in the
second part of the book, of the varieties of Death. Abraham's sin was
the destruction of life. Death boasts that he is the destroyer of the
world. The boast of Death puts Abraham's sin in perspective and
shows its alignment with the forces of destruction.[143] However, the
judgment scene also undercuts the power of Death, since we have
already been told that God does not wish destruction and does not
further punish those who have been struck down on earth.

The perspective on death

The purpose of the Testament of Abraham is to provide perspective
on the perennial menace of death and judgment. The reader is invited
to identify all the more easily with him because he is shown to have
his flaws and need forgiveness and because his reluctance to die persists to the end. Yet, while even Abraham remains reluctant to die, the
heavenly revelation is consoling. The terror of death is mitigated by
the realization that, while only one of seventy-two deaths is just, God
does not again destroy those who are struck down on earth. The terror
of the judgment is mitigated by the revelation that God does not share
the severity of "righteous" humans, such as Abraham, and accepts
intercession. The second revelatory passage, on the nature of Death,
is reassuring rather than terrifying because it is seen in the perspec-

tive provided by the judgment scene. The judgment scene also determines the book's ethical message: mercy rather than severity is pleasing to God.

The view of Judaism

The message of T Abr is shaped to a great degree by the heavenly revelation of the judgment scene. Therein lies the apocalyptic dimension of the work. Yet, this revelation is not in the service of an esoteric view of Judaism. Rather, as E. P. Sanders has remarked, it represents "a kind of lowest common denominator Judaism."[144] The principal characteristic of this view of Judaism is the lack of any distinction between Jew and gentile. The judgment is on the children of Adam, and there is nothing to indicate that Abraham's intercession is restricted to his own children. The sins which are mentioned are universal ones, such as murder, fornication, and theft. There is no mention of circumcision, dietary laws, or sabbath observance. The virtue of hospitality was scarcely distinctive to Jews. Sanders has noted that T Abr is extreme in its lack of distinctive requirements. There is no emphasis on group membership, such as we find in Joseph and Aseneth, or even on the rejection of idolatry which is basic to T Job. Of the writings we have considered thus far, only Pseudo-Phocylides shows less distinctive coloring than T Abr, insofar as that work is ascribed to a gentile author, while T Abr at least presupposes a tradition which venerates the patriarchs.

In view of this rather extreme universalism, it is unlikely that T Abr is the product of a sectarian group.[145] It represents a particularly tolerant formulation of what we have called the common ethic of Hellenistic Judaism. The apocalyptic component, which plays a crucial role in the book, provides a framework for the broadly universalist ethic. The framework is itself significant: salvation is located in the life after death and the understanding provided by Abraham's revelation is necessary if we are to see this life in proper perspective. Yet, Judaism here is a universal religion where little significance could be attached to the distinction between Jews and God-fearers. Abraham is depicted in such a way as to emphasize that he is part of sinful humanity. What he learns on his journey is precisely his solidarity with the rest of humanity, a solidarity already indicated in the opening lines of the book.

2 ENOCH

A similar universalistic ethic within an apocalyptic framework is found in 2 (Slavonic) Enoch. Despite the arguments of J. T. Milik, who regards it as a Christian work of the ninth or tenth century,[146] the majority opinion clearly favors Jewish authorship and an early date.[147] There is no clearly Christian element in the shorter recension B, which has been recognized as the older recension since the edition of Vaillant.[148] Further, the peculiar requirement that the four legs of a sacrificial animal be tied together (2 Enoch 15 and 21, Vaillant, pp. 59, 67) would be difficult to explain in a Christian work. In view of its affinities with Philo and other Hellenistic Jewish writings, and the allusions to Egyptian mythology in its cosmology, 2 Enoch is widely believed to have originated in Egyptian Judaism in the first century CE.[149]

2 Enoch is primarily an account of a heavenly journey. At the beginning of the book, Enoch is weeping and grieving. When he is asleep, two angelic "men" come to escort him on a heavenly tour. Before he departs, Enoch gives a brief exhortation to his sons, to practice sacrifice and avoid idolatry. In chapters 3–9 Enoch is guided through the seven heavens in turn. In the first he sees the angels who govern the stars and the elements. In the second, the place of punishment of the angels who rebelled against the Lord. In the third, the paradise which is at once the original garden of Genesis and the place prepared for the just. On the north of this heaven he sees the place of torture and punishment prepared for sinners. In the fourth heaven he sees the movements of the light of the sun and the moon and the regulation of time. In the fifth he encounters the Egrigori or Watchers who are mourning the fall of their fellow angels. Enoch tells them that he has seen their condemned brethren and exhorts them to resume their service of God. In the sixth heaven he sees seven angels who supervise the order of the world. Finally, in the seventh heaven he comes into the heavenly court. There he is anointed and given garments of glory and he becomes like one of the glorious angels.

There follow two episodes in which Enoch is given direct instruction. First, the angel Vreveil dictates to him "all the works of heaven and earth" and Enoch writes them down in 360 books. Second, God tells Enoch how he created the world. The account is remote from that of Genesis and involves quasi-mythological creatures, Adoil (from whom the great aeon is born) and Arouchaz (who becomes the foundation of creation).

At this point, God commands Enoch to return to earth for thirty days to instruct his children and pass on his writings to them. There follows the instruction of Enoch to his sons. This falls into three parts: (1) a lengthy exhortation by Enoch, without introduction (chaps. 13–14), (2) a similar address to Methusalem and his brothers which appears directly as Enoch's parting testament, and (3), finally, a similar address to a multitude of two thousand men who were assembled to see him. Then Enoch is taken up to heaven (apparently to the seventh) and Methusalem proceeds to offer sacrifice. This concludes the story of Enoch. The legend of Melchizedek is formally a distinct unit, independent of the apocalypse, whether or not it was originally juxtaposed with it in a single composition.[150]

The hortatory message

The message of 2 Enoch is most clearly formulated in the frequent exhortations. The apocalyptic heavenly journey provides a supporting framework.[151] In that journey, two kinds of material are emphasized, evidence of the order of creation and evidence of an eschatological judgment. The first of these is found in the first, fourth, and sixth heaven. Enoch is shown that the sun and moon follow a regular orderly course. The elements are not at the mercy of chance but each has an angel directing it, and these in turn are supervised from the sixth heaven. The ultimate basis for this entire order is the creation, which God describes to Enoch in chapter 11. The implications of this order for human conduct are quite clear. When God is dispatching Enoch to the earth he tells him: "explique à tes fils tout ce que je t'ai dit et tout ce que tu as vu depuis le ciel inférieur jusqu'au mon trône: toutes les milices, c'est moi qui les ai faites, il n'y a pas qui s'oppose à moi ou ne se soumette pas, et tous se soumettent à ma monarchie et servent ma seule puissance" (Vaillant, p. 33). Humanity, evidently, should do likewise. God specifies for Enoch the purpose of his mission: that they may know the creator of all things and know that there is no other apart from him.

In the course of his exhortations Enoch frequently refers back to the created order of the universe. The basis for human respect is that the Lord made man in his own likeness (p. 47). Enoch begins his testament to Methusalem and his brothers by reminding them of the relations between man and beast established at creation (p. 57). His final exhortation to the assembled multitude begins by recounting how God created everything, including humanity (p. 61). An understanding of the order of the world is the first underpinning of Enoch's message.

The exhortations of Enoch are not based solely on the order of creation. They also appeal to an eschatological judgment. Eschatology figures prominently in the heavenly journey. The third heaven is occupied by Paradise and the place of punishment. The second heaven is the place of punishment for the fallen angels, who are paradigmatic for humanity. The sojourn in the fifth heaven with the Egrigori recalls the fate of the fallen angels as a warning for others. Finally, the transformation of Enoch into the likeness of the angels in the seventh heaven has clear eschatological implications. These eschatological revelations figure prominently in the exhortations of Enoch. The contrasting places of reward and punishment in the third heaven provide the main context in which virtues and vices are articulated. Enoch repeatedly refers to a final judgment. The actual content of the exhortations is remarkably simple. It is mainly concerned with natural justice—clothing the naked and feeding the hungry. The basic principle is that whoever offends "the face of man" offends "the face of God" (Vaillant, p. 47). There are warnings to serve and fear the Lord and avoid idolatry, but there are no allusions to circumcision or distinctively Jewish customs. Only one element in the exhortations involves a highly specific practice. This is the repeated insistence on sacrifice, with the peculiar requirement that the four legs be tied. Pines has noted that the practice is declared contrary to usage by the Mishna Tamid and he suggests that "it may have been an accepted rite of a sect, which repudiated the sacrificial customs prevailing in Jerusalem."[152] Yet, there is no attempt in 2 Enoch to polemicize against other groups and, while monotheism is required, no distinction is made between Jews and gentiles.

2 Enoch is far more speculatively inclined than T Abr and spends far more time on the description of the heavenly world. The transformation of Enoch into an angel has evident paradigmatic significance, and the understanding provided by Enoch's revelation is the necessary aid towards that transformation. The persuasiveness of the message depends on the acceptance of, or belief in, the reality of the "other world" revealed by Enoch. Faith, in the sense of insight into the heavenly world, is the basis for the future hope and present action.

Yet, here too the heavenly revelations are not an end in themselves but provide the basis for an ethical message. That message does not promote Judaism as a group apart. It promotes monotheism, rejects idolatry, and fosters an attitude of human respect which is based on the order of creation, not on the history of Israel. Once again, the higher revelation is in the service of universalism.

3 BARUCH

A third Hellenistic Jewish apocalypse, closely related to T Abr and 2 Enoch is found in 3 Baruch.[153] The Jewish origin of 3 Baruch is not in doubt, despite Christian insertions in chapters 4 and 11–15.[154] There is also a consensus that it originated in the Hellenistic Diaspora because of its allusions to Egyptian and Greek mythology and its affinities with other products of Egyptian Judaism.[155] Since the apocalypse begins with Baruch lamenting the destruction of Jerusalem, a date after 70 CE, but not too long after, seems plausible. Origen (*De Principiis*, 2.3.6) refers to a book of Baruch which treats of seven heavens. 3 Baruch mentions only five. Most scholars assume that two were lost in transmission, but we cannot be certain that Origen is referring to the same document.[156]

3 Baruch, in its present form, is a shorter and more simple composition than 2 Enoch, and consists of the heavenly journey, with a brief introduction and conclusion. The introduction gives the circumstances leading up to the revelation: Baruch was grieving over the destruction of Jerusalem. Then an angel appears to show him "the mysteries of God." In the first heaven he sees men who have "the faces of oxen, and the horns of stags, and the feet of goats and the haunches of lambs" (2:3), and are identified as those "who built the tower of strife against God" (2:7). In the second heaven are men whose appearance was like dogs and their feet like those of stags, and are identified as "they who gave counsel to build the tower" (3:5). The contents of the third heaven are most complex (chaps. 4–9). They include Hades and a dragon which devours the bodies of the wicked.[157] They also include the sun and moon and a phoenix that shields the earth from the sun. In the course of his tour of this heaven, Baruch inquires about "the tree which led Adam astray" and thereby occasions a digression on the vine and the dangers of wine. In the fourth heaven he sees multitudes of birds which sing the praises of God and is told that this is where the souls of the righteous come. The

birds are generally assumed to represent the souls of the righteous.[158]
Finally, the fifth heaven is marked by a locked gate which is opened
by the archangel Michael. In this heaven the angels bring the merits
of humanity in baskets to Michael, who takes them up to God (presumably in a higher heaven). Humanity is rewarded for its merits and
punished for the lack of them. The apocalypse ends when Baruch is
returned to his place, gives glory to God, and exhorts his listeners to
do likewise.

Unlike Enoch, Baruch does not spell out his message in an explicit
exhortation at the end. The work still has a hortatory effect, through
the list of vices associated with the fruit of the vine in 4:17 and another
list of sins that defile the rays of the sun in 8:5. Much of the revelation
focuses on rewards and punishments in the afterlife. So the fate of the
animallike builders of the tower and their advisers in the first two
heavens stands in contrast to that of the birdlike righteous in the
fourth, and the climax of the revelation is the judgment of the merits of
humanity by God. All of this is evidently designed to discourage vice
and promote virtue.

The attitude towards Jerusalem

3 Baruch addresses the problem of Jewish identity more directly
than T Abr or 2 Enoch. The lists of sins are concerned with such
universal matters as murder, fornication, and theft, although idolatry
is also included in 8:5. More significant is the attitude towards Jerusalem. At the beginning of the book Baruch asks God: "Lord, why did
you burn your vineyard and lay it waste? Why did you do this? And
why, Lord, did you not requite us with another punishment but hand
us over to such nations as these, so that they reproach us and say:
'where is their God?' " The angel's reply is surprising: "Understand,
O man beloved and do not trouble yourself so much over the salvation
of Jerusalem. . . . Come and I will show you the mysteries of God."
The revelations which follow contain no vision of Jerusalem restored,
such as we find in the contemporary Judean apocalypse 4 Ezra (10:27,
44) or even in the contemporary Egyptian Jewish Sib Or 5:420–32.
How then does God respond to Baruch's initial question?

George Nickelsburg has pointed out that 3 Bar 16:2 is "a paraphrase, verging on a quotation of the LXX of Deuteronomy 32:21."
Reference to punishment at the hands of a "non-nation" and a "foolish
nation" responds to the seer's question in 1:2: "Why did you deliver

us to *nations* such as these?" The use of the language of Deuteronomy 32 indicates that the scattering of the people and the destruction of Jerusalem is viewed as a punishment for the people's sins.[159] 3 Bar 16 does not specify that the "sons of men" who are to be punished are simply the Jews, and may have a broader reference in mind. If we do apply this passage to the fate of Jerusalem, however, it is still surprisingly harsh. Baruch has been told not to trouble himself about the salvation of Jerusalem (1:3), not because that salvation is assured but because the destruction of Jerusalem is deserved.

J. C. Picard has suggested that the rejection of Jerusalem here goes even further. In 1:2 Jerusalem is the *vineyard* of the Lord. In chapter 4, the vine is the tree that led Adam astray, but was saved from the flood and now causes all mankind to sin. Picard argues that the vine in chapter 4 symbolizes Jerusalem, like the vineyard in chapter 1. So the apparent digression on the vine is a symbolic condemnation of Jerusalem and responds directly to the author's problem.[160] This passage is interrupted by a promise that the fruit of the vine will become the blood of God and that salvation will come through Christ, but this Christian passage is an evident interpolation, since the chapter concludes with a strong condemnation of the fruit of the vine and a statement that nothing good is established by it (4:17). The negative connotations of the vine in this chapter must be regarded as part of an original Jewish composition.

Picard's interpretation, that the vine in chapter 4 still refers to Jerusalem, is not explicit in the text, and so must be regarded as less than certain. However, there is no doubt that the apocalypse diminishes the significance of the fall of Jerusalem. In 1:3 Baruch is told not to worry so much about the salvation of Jerusalem. His transition from grief to glorifying God involves no assurance that Jerusalem will be restored. While the apocalypse begins with an opposition of Jerusalem and the nations, it ends with a contrast between individuals who have merits and those who have not. The fate of Jerusalem is of little consequence for the judgment of individuals. It is of interest to note that even the "builders of the tower" and their advisers are not punished for destroying Jerusalem but for cruelty (in refusing to release a woman for childbirth) and for attempting to discover the nature of heaven. It is not clear whether a specific group of people is symbolized by the tower builders, but we cannot assume that they are simply the gentile enemies of Judaism.[161]

A *system of individual rewards*

3 Baruch replaces the traditional opposition of Israel and the nations with a system of individual rewards and punishments. When the archangel Michael takes up the merits of humanity and brings back their reward, no distinction is made between Jew and gentile. The significant division is between good and bad. Apart from the sin of idolatry which is mentioned in 8:5, the ethical code is of a highly general nature. As in 2 Enoch, the ethical message of the book is given a supporting framework by the revelation of the heavens and the eschatological judgment. The apocalypse provides an entire *système du monde*[162] which seeks to integrate its eschatology into the order of the universe. The cosmology of the apocalypse, like the eschatology, requires supernatural revelation and therein lies the mystical aspect of 3 Baruch. Supernatural knowledge provides the understanding of the way to salvation. The actual conduct required by the apocalypse, however, is not esoteric at all but conforms to the common ethic which would have been acceptable even to enlightened gentiles.

The revelation of 3 Baruch puts the fall of Jerusalem in perspective, as T Abr did with the problem of death. It provides an assurance, in chapter 16, that the destruction was a just punishment, but the primary response is that Jerusalem is insignificant in comparison with the "mysteries of God"—the cosmology of the heavens and the judgment of all humanity. We are reminded of the book of Job, where God's speech from the whirlwind does not respond directly to Job's complaint but puts it in perspective by reciting the mysteries of creation.

3 Baruch, then, resolves the problem of the destruction of Jerusalem by virtually breaking its connection with Jerusalem. This step was in some respects the logical culmination of the tendency which we have seen in Hellenistic Judaism to emphasize what was held in common with the gentiles. Yet, we need only contrast 3 Baruch with Sib Or 5, which was written about the same time and which still subscribed to the "common ethic," to see how radical 3 Baruch's solution appears, even within the Egyptian Diaspora. The author of 3 Baruch could have little sympathy with the Diaspora revolt. We may suspect that he came from the upper classes, but there is little in the book to indicate social status. Yet 3 Baruch is more explicitly Jewish than Pseudo-Phocylides. At least the pseudonym and the angelology presuppose the Jewish tradition. In abandoning Jerusalem the author was not

abandoning Judaism. He testifies to the range of conceptions of Jewish identity which were still possible in the Diaspora in the period between the revolts.

CONCLUSION

The works we have considered in this chapter are diverse in character, ranging from hymns and drama to narratives and apocalypses. What they all have in common is the appeal to higher revelation. The saving acts of God in the history of Israel no longer provide an adequate basis for religion. True understanding depends on some supernatural knowledge which is not accessible to all.

This appeal to supernatural knowledge does not of itself determine the pattern of religion. The books of Adam and Eve still represent a pattern of covenantal nomism. In the great majority of cases, however, the emphasis on true understanding shifts the focus away from the specific demands of the law. In virtually all cases the distinctive Jewish requirements such as circumcision and the dietary laws are ignored. Further, the significance of membership in the actual Jewish community becomes ambiguous. The main requirement for salvation is the right understanding of wisdom, and in nearly all cases this explicitly entails the rejection of idolatry. The Jewish authors may generally have assumed that true wisdom was found primarily within the Jewish community, as Philo surely did. Yet, in principle, the wise and righteous do not necessarily correspond exactly to those who are circumcised. So a document like T Abr can ignore the distinction between Jews and gentiles and 3 Baruch need not trouble himself too much over the salvation of Jerusalem. Where the basic understanding was derived from supernatural revelation rather than the traditional formulation of the covenant, the basis for communal identity had been altered and had become more elusive.

Notes

1. E. R. Goodenough, *By Light, Light: The Mystic Gospel of Hellenistic Judaism* (New Haven: Yale, 1935), and *Jewish Symbols in the Greco-Roman Period* (12 vols.; New York: Random House, 1953–68).

2. See the incisive review article by M. Smith, "Goodenough's Jewish Symbols in Retrospect," *JBL* 86 (1967) 53–68.

3. On the mysticism of Philo, see D. Winston, "Was Philo a Mystic?" *SBLASP* (1978) 1:161–80.

4. See F. C. Happold, *Mysticism. A Study and an Anthology* (Baltimore: Penguin, 1963) esp. 35–39; S. Spencer (*Mysticism in World Religion* [Baltimore: Penguin, 1963]) reviews the major historical manifestations of mysticism and concludes with "A Survey of Tendencies" but no definition.

5. M. Nilsson, *Geschichte der Griechischen Religion* (München: Beck, 1950) 2:85–96; 329–53; 651–72; G. Bornkamm, *"Mystērion," TDNT* 4 (1967) 803–8.

6. Goodenough, *By Light, Light,* 8.

7. Ibid., 260–61. The (inconclusive) evidence of the symbols can be found in *Jewish Symbols,* passim.

8. W. Bousset, "Eine jüdische Gebetssammlung im siebenten Buch der apostolischen Konstitutionen," in *Nachrichten von der K. Gesellschaft der Wissenschaften zu Göttingen,* Phil-Hist Kl. (1915/1916) 435–85; Goodenough, *By Light, Light,* 306–58.

9. Goodenough, *By Light, Light,* 326.

10. *Jewish Symbols,* 12:21.

11. D. Georgi, *Die Gegner des Paulus im 2. Korintherbrief* (WMANT 11; Neukirchen-Vluyn: Neukirchener Verlag, 1964) 83–137.

12. Ibid., 134–37.

13. Whatsoever Moses hath delivered in the secret volume,
    Not to show the ways, unless to one observing the same rites,
    To lead the circumcised only to a sought for fountain.

14. *Die Gegner,* 83–137.

15. Goodenough, *By Light, Light,* 8.

16. Goodenough, "Literal Mystery in Hellenistic Judaism," *Quantulacumque. Studies Presented to Kirsopp Lake,* 259–64; Bornkamm, "Mystērion," 808–10; A. E. Harvey, "The Use of Mystery Language in the Bible," *JTS* 31 (1980) 320–36.

17. See H. A. Wolfson, *Philo* (Cambridge: Harvard, 1947) 1:43–55.

18. Goodenough, *Jewish Symbols,* 20.

19. Goodenough, *By Light, Light,* 7.

20. Ibid.

21. Ibid., 268–82.

22. Cf. the description of the Jerusalem cult in Ep Arist 99, where again the point at issue is how the ceremonies are perceived.

23. See Collins, "The Root of Immortality: Death in the Context of Jewish Wisdom," *HTR* 71 (1979) 177–92.

24. Goodenough, *By Light, Light,* 298–305.

25. Ibid., 299.

26. Nilsson, *Geschichte,* 2:86.

27. JW 2.8.7 (142).

28. See M. Hengel, *Judaism and Hellenism* (Philadelphia: Fortress, 1974) 1:210–18; H. W. Attridge, "Greek and Latin Apocalypses," *Semeia* 14 (1979) 159–86.

29. For the texts, see A. M. Denis, *Fragmenta Pseudepigraphorum qua supersunt graeca* (PVTG 3; Leiden: Brill, 1970) 163–67. Line references are to this edition.

30. N. Walter, *Der Thoraausleger Aristobulus* (TU 86; Berlin: Akademie, 1964) 103–15; 202–61.

31. Ibid., 104–8.

32. R. Keller, *De Aristobulo Judaeo* (Phil. Diss.; Bonn, 1948), summarized by Walter, *Der Thoraausleger Aristobulus,* 109.

33. O. Kern, *Orphicorum Fragmenta* (Berlin: Weidmann, 1922).

34. These verses refer to a "water-born" one (*hydogenēs,* an emendation for *hylogenēs*) who received a twofold law from God.

35. *Stromateis* 5.14.123.

36. Philo, *De Vita Mosis* 1.5. He also refers to Abraham as a Chaldean, *De Virtutibus* 39, 212.

37. Cf. the tradition of Abraham's ascent, which is often repeated in the pseudepigrapha, most obviously in the Apocalypse of Abraham and the Testament of Abraham, but also in 4 Ezra 3:13–14; 2 Bar 4:5; Pseudo-Philo, 18:5.

38. Ll. 19–20 (ET). See Georgi, *Die Gegner*, 73. Georgi emends l. 25 to read: *lepton emoi, pasin de dekaptychon anthrōpoisin.* Orpheus says that a cloud blocks the vision of God. It is a light one for him, but a tenfold one for all humanity.

39. Goodenough, *By Light, Light*, 177. *Praem* 43–46.

40. The word *dekaptychon* in l. 25 has often been taken as a reference to the decalogue but may simply mean manifold, as a counterpart to *lepton*, following Georgi's reading of the line.

41. Georgi, *Die Gegner*, 75.

42. For a succinct statement of the status quaestionis, see W. Burkert, *Orphism and Bacchic Mysteries: New Evidence and Old Problems of Interpretation* (Berkeley: Center for Hermeneutical Studies, 1977). For older reconstructions, see E. Rohde, *Psyche. Seelencult und Unsterblichkeitsglaube der Griechen* (Leipzig: Mohr, 1894, 1898); A. Dieterich, *Nekyia, Beiträge zur Erklärung der neuentdeckten Petrusapokalypse* (Leipzig: Teubner, 1893). See further W. K. C. Guthrie, *Orpheus and Greek Religion. A Study of the Orphic Movement* (2 ed.; London: Methuen, 1952) and, on the Hellenistic period, Nilsson, *Geschichte*, 2:232–37.

43. Herodotus 2.81; Euripides, *Hippolytus*, 952–54; Burkert, *Orphism*, 4.

44. See now the gold plate from Hipponion in southern Italy (ca. 400 BCE), which relates the way of the dead to that of the *mystai* and *bacchoi*. See further Burkert, *Orphism*, 2–4, for evidence from inscriptions and art.

45. PE 9.28; 29.4–16. A passage in Epiphanius, *Haer* 64.29.6, on the serpent, was attributed to Ezekiel by J. Scaliger in 1658 (see A. M. Denis, *Introduction aux Pseudépigraphes Grecs d'Ancien Testament* [SVTP1; Leiden: Brill, 1970] 275). The text is printed by Denis with the undisputed fragments but there is no solid basis for the attribution.

46. P. M. Fraser, *Ptolemaic Alexandria* (Oxford: Clarendon, 1972) 1:707; J. Wieneke, *Ezechielis Iudaei poetae Alexandrini fabulae quae inscribitur Exagōgē fragmenta* (Münster: Monasterii Westfalorum, 1931) 124–26.

47. K. Kuiper, "Le poete juif Ezechiel," *REJ* 46 (1903) 171; Fraser, *Ptolemaic Alexandria*, 1:708; Wieneke, *Ezechielis Iudaei*, 121. On the appearance of the phoenix in the time of Euergetes I, see Tacitus, *Annals*, 6.28.

48. Wieneke, *Ezechielis Iudaei*, 2–25; Dalbert, *Die Theologie*, 53.

49. A. Kappelmacher, "Zur Tragödie der hellenistischen Zeit," *Wiener Studien* 44 (1924–25) 69–86; I. Trencsényi-Waldapfel, "Une Tragédie Grecque à Sujet Biblique," *Acta Orientalia* 2 (1952) 143–63; B. Snell, "Ezechiels Moses-Drama," *Antike und Abendland* 13 (1967) 150–64; J. Strugnell, "Notes on the Text and Metre of Ezekiel the Tragedian's 'Exagoge,' " *HTR* 50 (1967) 449–57. The fragments of Ezekiel are the longest remnants of Hellenistic tragedy.

50. Fraser, *Ptolemaic Alexandria*, 1:708.

51. Contra C. R. Holladay, "The Portrait of Moses in Ezekiel the Tragedian," *SBLASP* 10 (1976) 447–52.

52. Trencsényi-Waldapfel ("Une Tragédie," 160–61) saw a polemic against Ezekiel in Ep Arist 136, where a tragic poet named Theodektes was afflicted with a cataract when he was about to use a biblical theme. However, Pseudo-Aristeas is primarily concerned to show why the Jewish Torah is not better known to the Greeks, and does not necessarily disapprove of Jewish use of tragedy as a means of expression.

53. J. B. Segal, *The Hebrew Passover from the Earliest Times* (London: Oxford, 1963) 24; Wieneke, *Ezechielis Iudaei*, 124.

54. Cerfaux, "L'Influence des Mystères," 85–88; Goodenough, *By Light, Light*, 288–91.

55. Holladay, "The Portrait," 451–52. Cf. esp. Aeschylus's *Eumenides*, 17–19; also 609–21, where Apollo functions in a judicial role.

56. J. Theisohn, *Der auserwählte Richter* (SUNT 12; Göttingen: Vandenhoeck & Ruprecht, 1975) 38–99.

57. W. Meeks, "Moses as God and King," *Religions in Antiquity* (Essays in memory of E. R. Goodenough; ed. J. Neusner; Leiden: Brill, 1968) 354–59.

58. Ibid., 355.

59. For traditions of enthronement, see F. T. Fallon, *The Enthronement of Sabaoth* (Leiden: Brill, 1978). For apocalyptic throne visions, I. Gruenwald, *Apocalyptic and Merkavah Mysticism* (Leiden: Brill, 1979) 32–72.

60. Meeks, "Moses," 367.

61. Trencsényi-Waldapfel, "Une Tragédie Grecque," 154–55; Kuiper ("Le poete juif," 166–67), followed by Kappelmacher ("Zur Tragödie," 82), would extend the drama to allow for the reunion of Moses and Zipporah.

62. In view of this, Trencsényi-Waldapfel's view, that the kingship of Moses is realized in the law, must be rejected ("Une Tragédie," 156).

63. The identification of the bird in Ezekiel as the phoenix is based on the repetition of the entire passage in Pseudo-Eustathius (Migne, *PG*, vol. 18, col. 729), where it is stated to be a description of the phoenix. The identification is guaranteed by the similarity to the description in Herodotus 2.73 and the obvious play on the word for palm trees.

64. M. Walla, *Der Vogel Phoenix in der antiken Literatur und in der Dichtung des Laktanz* (Wien: Notring, 1969) 1–50, esp. 16 and 30. The legend of the phoenix rising from its own ashes is attested only in later Roman writings (Walla, 62–81).

65. Wieneke (*Ezechielis Iudaei*, 119) argues that the tragedy was probably never performed because there were too many changes of scene.

66. *De Vita Mosis* 1.158; Meeks, "Moses," 355.

67. P. Batiffol, "Le Livre de la Prière d'Aseneth," *Studia Patristica* (Paris: Leroux, 1889–90) 1–115.

68. E. W. Brooks, *Joseph and Asenath. The Confession and Prayer of Asenath Daughter of Pentephres the Priest* (Translations of Early Documents II. Hellenistic-Jewish Texts 7; London: SPCK, 1918). For a list of scholars espousing Jewish or Christian authorship, see C. Burchard, *Untersuchungen zu Joseph und Aseneth* (Tübingen: Mohr, 1965) 99.

69. *Bulletin critique* 10 (1889) 461–66.

70. P. Riessler, "Joseph und Aseneth. Eine altjüdische Erzählung," *Theologische Quartalschrift* 103 (1922) 1–22, 145–83.

71. G. D. Kilpatrick, "The Last Supper," *ET* 64 (1952/53), 4–8; K. G. Kuhn, "The Lord's Supper and the Communal Meal at Qumran," *The Scrolls and the New Testament* (ed. K. Stendahl; New York: Harper, 1957) 65–93; J. Jeremias, "The Last Supper," *ET* 64 (1952/53) 91–92.

72. For a detailed refutation of the theory of Christian authorship, see C. Burchard, *Untersuchungen zu Joseph und Aseneth* (Tübingen: Mohr, 1965) 99–107; M. Philonenko, *Joseph et Aséneth. Introduction, Texte Critique et Notes* (Leiden: Brill, 1968), 99–109. The more recent attempt of T. Holtz ("Christliche Interpolationen in 'Joseph und Aseneth,'" *NTS* 14 [1967/68] 482–97) to establish the presence of Christian interpolations has been sharply rejected. See the refutations by Burchard, *Der dreizehnte Zeuge* (FRLANT 103; Göttingen: Vandenhoeck & Ruprecht, 1970) 59; "Joseph et Aséneth: Questions Actuelles," *La Littérature Juive entre Tenach et Mischna* (ed. W. C. van Unnik; Leiden: Brill, 1974) 96–97; E. P. Sanders, "The Covenant as a Soteriological Category and the Nature of Salvation in Palestinian and Hellenistic Judaism," *Jews, Greeks and Christians. Essays in honor of W. D. Davies* (ed. R. Hamerton-Kelly and R. Scroggs; Leiden: Brill, 1976) 24–25.

73. Study of Joseph and Aseneth is hindered by the lack of a complete critical edition. The old editions of Batiffol and Istrin have been outdated by further manuscript discoveries. Burchard (*Untersuchungen*, 18–23) distinguished four textual families, *a*, *b*, *c*, *d*. Philonenko regards the shortest of these, *d*, as the oldest, *b* as a first long recension, *c* a second, and *a* a third. Accordingly, his edition is based on the short text *d*. Batiffol's edition had been based on a manuscript of the family *a*. For Burchard, the best and oldest text is preserved in the family *b*. *a*, *c*, and *d* are later, but independent of *b*, so that it is possible to reconstruct an eclectic text which is better and older than *b*. For the present, we follow Philonenko's text and numbering of chapters while taking note of the longer text in Batiffol and Burchard's preliminary edition in *Dielheimer Blätter* 14

(1979) 1–53. See further Burchard, "Zum Text von Joseph und Aseneth," *JSJ* 1 (1970) 3–34, and "Joseph et Aséneth: Questions Actuelles," 77–84.

74. Philonenko, *Joseph et Aséneth*, 28; G. Delling "Einwirkungen der Sprache der Septuaginta in 'Joseph und Aseneth,' " *JSJ* 9 (1978) 29–56.

75. Philonenko, *Joseph et Aséneth*, 43–48; Burchard, "Joseph et Aséneth," 84–96; *Der dreizehnte Zeuge*, 59–86; S. West, "Joseph and Asenath: A Neglected Greek Romance," *CQ* 24 (1974) 70–81.

76. Contra D. Sänger, "Bekehrung und Exodus. Zum jüdischen Traditionshintergrund von 'Joseph und Aseneth,' " *JSJ* 10 (1979) 11–36, esp. 31. Sänger's study is too narrowly focused on the prayer in chap. 12.

77. This claim is made esp. by R. Merkelbach, *Roman und Mysterium in der Antike* (München: Beck, 1962); also K. Kerenyi, *Die griechisch-orientalische Romanliteratur* (Tübingen: Mohr, 1927). It has been sharply rejected by R. Turcan, "Le roman 'initiatique': A propos d'un livre récent," *RHR* 163 (1963) 149–99; B. E. Perry, *The Ancient Romances: A Literary-Historical Account of their Origins* (Berkeley: University of California, 1967) 336 n. 17; also A. D. Nock, review of Kerenyi in *Gnomon* 4 (1928) 485–92. For a thorough critique of the alleged affinities of Joseph and Aseneth with mystery initiation rituals, see D. Sänger, *Antikes Judentum und die Mysterien* (WUNT 2/5; Tübingen: Mohr, 1980.

78. Philonenko, *Joseph et Aséneth*, 48.

79. Philonenko (*Joseph et Aséneth*, 51) regards Pentephres and pharaoh as sympathizers. Sanders ("The Covenant," 23) takes issue with this position but allows no distinction between sympathizers and God-fearers.

80. G. F. Moore, *Judaism* (New York: Schocken, 1971) 1:331.

81. Sib Or 4: 165 is often regarded as a reference, but incorrectly so.

82. Philonenko, *Joseph et Aséneth*, 91.

83. Ibid., 91–92. See further Kilpatrick, "The Last Supper";Jeremias, "The Lord's Supper"; Kuhn, "The Lord's Supper and the Eschatological Meal at Qumran." Kuhn defends a relation with Qumran.

84. T Lev 8:4–5 mentions bread, wine, and anointing, among other elements, in the investiture of Levi, but the anointing comes before the bread and wine.

85. Philonenko, *Joseph et Aséneth*, 93.

86. Burchard, *Untersuchungen*, 126–33.

87. Hosea 2:8, 22. See further Burchard, *Untersuchungen*, 128–29.

88. See already Jeremias, "The Last Supper," 91–92.

89. So, b Ber 53b; 42a; 43b; Burchard, *Untersuchungen*, 128; Philonenko, *Joseph et Aséneth*, 93.

90. Sanders, "The Covenant," 23.

91. Philonenko (*Joseph et Aséneth*, 97) relates this figure to the *daimon paredros* of the magical papyri. The more obvious parallels are with the ubiquitous angelophanies of the Jewish literature of this period, but the fact that the angel shares heavenly food with Aseneth is exceptional in the Jewish literature.

92. Ibid., 96. So also Burchard, *Untersuchungen*, 130. See also Philonenko, "Initiation et Mystère dans Joseph et Aséneth," *Initiation* (ed. C. J. Bleeker; Supp Numen 10; Leiden: Brill, 1965) 147–53.

93. Ibid., 65–66.

94. Ibid., 96; Burchard, *Untersuchungen*, 129.

95. E.g., Sir 24:19–22 (wisdom's inheritance is sweeter than the honeycomb); Prov 9:2–5 ("eat of my bread, drink of the wine I have mixed"). Note that in Burchard's reconstruction of the text of Aseneth's prayer she thanks God for giving her the bread of life and the cup of wisdom. Burchard, *Untersuchungen*, 86, 90.

96. See H. W. Kuhn, *Enderwartung und Gegenwärtiges Heil* (SUNT 4; Göttingen: Vandenhoeck & Ruprecht, 1966); G. W. Nickelsburg, *Resurrection, Immortality and Eternal Life* (HTS 26; Cambridge: Harvard, 1972) 146–56.

97. The designation "son of God" is applied to the righteous man in Wis 2:13, 16, 18. Burchard, *Untersuchungen*, 112–17.

98. Burchard, *Untersuchungen*, 119.

99. U. Fischer (*Eschatologie und Jenseitserwartung, im Hellenistischen Diasporajudentum* [BZNW 44; Berlin: de Gruyter, 1978] 115–23) argues that Aseneth is identified with the heavenly Jerusalem. The argument is based on parallels with 4 Ezra 9:38–10:56 and esp. Rev 21, and the imagery of walls and foundations (some of which is poorly attested textually, see Fischer, 118). It is true that the salvation which Aseneth attains is heavenly, but it is significant that there is no explicit reference to Jerusalem. The Zion/Jerusalem imagery, both earthly and heavenly, is transferred to Aseneth. She represents a form of salvation which replaces that traditionally associated with Jerusalem. So the traditional imagery lacks the specific concrete reference to Jerusalem which Fischer posits.

100. Sänger, "Bekehrung," 26. Sänger argues that 12:1–2, the beginning of Aseneth's psalm, is a *Lobpsalm* and that the *Lobpsalm* is often used with reference to the Exodus. It does not, however, follow that the imagery necessarily implies a reference to the Exodus here.

101. Sänger, "Bekehrung," 35.

102. Joseph and Aseneth has been attributed to the Therapeutae by M. Delcor, "Un roman d'amour d'origine thérapeute: Le Livre de Joseph et Aséneth," *Bulletin de Littérature Ecclésiastique* 63 (1962) 3–27. See Burchard, *Untersuchungen*, 107–12; Philonenko, *Joseph et Aséneth*, 102–8; H. C. Kee, "The Socio-Religious Setting and Aims of 'Joseph and Aseneth,' " *SBLASP* (1976) 183–92.

103. Philonenko, *Joseph et Aséneth*, 105.

104. J. Z. Smith, "The Prayer of Joseph," *Religions in Antiquity*, 253–94. There are two fragments preserved by Origen, *Comm. in Ioann.* 2.31 (F 1) and Philocalia 23.15 (F 2). There is also a quotation from the second fragment and a paraphrase of the first in Philocalia 23.19.

105. Ibid., 288.

106. Ibid., 290. The Prayer of Jacob is found in Berlin P. gr. 13895. (Preisendanz, *PGM* 2:148–49). See also Goodenough, *Symbols*, 2:203.

107. For text and translation, R. A. Kraft, *The Testament of Job* (T&T 5; Pseudepigrapha Series 5; Missoula: Scholars, 1974).

108. B. Schaller, *Das Testament Hiobs* (JSHRZ III/3; Gütersloh: Mohn, 1979) 307.

109. The hesitation of Schaller (ibid, 311) seems unwarranted.

110. Ibid., with references to the earlier debate. M. R. James regarded T Job as the work of a Jewish Christian (*Apocrypha Anecdota 2* [Texts and Studies 5/1; Cambridge: University Press, 1897]).

111. M. Delcor ("Le Testament de Job, la prière de Nabonide et les traditions targoumiques," *Bibel et Qumran* [Berlin: Evangelische Hauptbibelschaftgesellschaft, 1968] 72–73) argued for a date about 40 BCE, taking the "king of the Persians" in 17:1 as a reference to Pacorus, but the negative connotations of this title were traditional in Egypt. See J. J. Collins "Structure and Meaning in the Testament of Job," *SBLASP* (1974) 1:50. Schaller prefers a date in the early second century CE.

112. Hence the common but loose designation "midrash" (e.g., K. Kohler, "The Testament of Job, An Essene Midrash on the book of Job," *Semitic Studies in memory of A. Kohut* [Berlin: Calvary, 1897] 264–338; D. Rahnenführer, "Das Testament Hiobs und das NT," *ZNW* 62 [1971] 68–69).

113. On the testament form in T Job, see Collins, "Structure," 37–39.

114. Cf. the conversion of Abraham in Jub 12:12 and in Apoc Abr.

115. The resurrection of Job is found already in LXX Job 42:17a.

116. Pfitzner, *Paul and the Agon Motif*, 38–72. See also I. Jacobs, "Literary Motifs in the Testament of Job," *JJS* 21 (1970) 1–3.

117. The portrayal of women in T Job as lacking heavenly insight is in accordance with Philo's use of female imagery for the irrational soul. See R. A. Baer, *Philo's Use of the Categories Male and Female* (Leiden: Brill, 1970) 40–53.

118. The affinites of T Job with merkavah mysticism are emphasized by Kee, "The Socio-Religious Setting," 1:53–76.

119. In this respect the affinities with the apocalypses are noteworthy, esp. since the knowledge given to Job is in large part eschatological.

120. M. Philonenko, "Le Testament de Job et les Therapeutes," *Semitica* 8 (1958) 41–53; "Le Testament de Job," *Semitica* 18 (1968) 9–24. So also R. Spittler, *The Testament of Job* (Diss. Harvard, 1971) 53–83. Spittler suggests a possible Montanist redaction in view of the ecstatic behavior of Job's daughters, but this is unnecessary.

121. See the sharp critique of the Therapeutae hypothesis by Schaller, *Das Testament*, 309–11.

122. L. S. A. Wells, "The Books of Adam and Eve," *APOT* 2:123–54; G. W. Nickelsburg, "Some Related Traditions in the Apocalypse of Adam, the Books of Adam and Eve and 1 Enoch," *The Rediscovery of Gnosticism. Vol. 2. Sethian Gnosticism* (Studies in the History of Religions 41; ed. B. Layton; Leiden: Brill, 1980) 515–39; *Jewish Literature Between the Bible and the Mishnah* (Philadelphia: Fortress, 1981) 253–57. For the Greek text of Apoc Mos, see K. von Tischendorf, *Apocalypses Apocryphae* (Hildesheim: Olms, 1966, reprint of 1866 edition) 1–22. For the Latin text of the Life of Adam and Eve, see J. H. Mozley, "Documents: The 'Vita Adae," *JTS* 30 (1929) 121–49.

123. Apoc Mos 5–8; Life, 30–34. The testamentary elements are stressed by Nickelsburg in his treatments.

124. In Apoc Mos 21:6. Adam exclaims after eating the fruit: "O wicked woman what have I done to thee that thou hast deprived me of the glory of God?" In the Life (9–11), Eve is deceived by Satan and abandons her penitence until Adam rebukes her.

125. Apoc Mos 30:1: "Now then, my children, I have shown you the way in which we were deceived, and do ye guard yourselves from transgressing against the good."

126. Apoc Mos 39:2; Life, 48:3.

127. Wells ("The Books of Adam and Eve," 126) notes the parallels in the conception of the tree of life, the sacred oil, the sin of Eve, the lake of purification, the seven heavens, etc.

128. This passage includes a Christian interpolation.

129. Life, 1–11; Apoc Mos 32.

130. Apoc Mos 13; Life, 40–42.

131. So Wells, "The Books," 129–30.

132. Ibid., esp. the note by Charles on p. 130.

133. A. B. Kolenkow, "The Genre Testament and the Testament of Abraham," *Studies on the Testament of Abraham* (ed. G. W. Nickelsburg; SCS 6; Missoula: Scholars, 1976) 139–52.

134. On T Abr as an apocalypse, see J. J. Collins "The Genre Apocalypse in Hellenistic Judaism," *Apocalypticism* (ed. D. Hellholm; Tübingen: Mohr, forthcoming).

135. G. W. Nickelsburg, "Structure and Message in the Testament of Abraham," *Studies*, 92. The references here are to recension A. For the text and translation, see M. E. Stone, *The Testament of Abraham* (T&T 2; Missoula: Scholars, 1972).

136. Christian authorship was defended by a number of older scholars, such as M. R. James and Schürer, but has found no recent followers. See E. Janssen, *Testament Abrahams* (JSHRZ V/1; Gütersloh: Mohn, 1974) 199.

137. M. Delcor, *Le Testament d'Abraham* (SVTP 2; Leiden: Brill, 1973) 34; Janssen, *Testament*, 198–99. R. A. Martin ("Syntax Criticism of the Testament of Abraham," *Studies on the Testament of Abraham*, 95–101) suggests that "the producer of Recension A (and probably also the producer of Recension B) is editing a Greek text which was earlier translated from a Semitic language" but allows that some "additions" may not go back to a Semitic original.

138. Delcor, *Le Testament*, 67–68.

139. Delcor (*Le Testament*, 47–51) emphasizes affinities with T Job. E. P. Sanders ("The Testaments of the Three Patriarchs," *The Pseudepigrapha* [ed. J. H. Charlesworth; Garden City: Doubleday, forthcoming]) relates T Abr to 2 Enoch and 3 Bar. So also Collins, "The Genre Apocalypse."

140. Nickelsburg, "Structure and Message," 85.

141. Ibid., 87.

142. Cf. Wis 1:4; 11:21–26, on the mercy of God the creator. David Winston has drawn my attention to a similar story about R. Simeon b. Yohai in b Shabbat 33b.

143. Kolenkow, "The Genre Testament," 146.

144. Sanders, "The Testaments."

145. Ibid., provides a good critique of the repeated attempts to link T Abr with the Essenes or Therapeutae (e.g., Delcor, Le Testament, 69–73).

146. J. T. Milik, The Books of Enoch (Oxford: Oxford University, 1976) 107–16.

147. J. C. Greenfield, "Prolegomenon," in H. Odeberg, 3 Enoch or the Hebrew Book of Enoch (New York: Ktav, 1973) XVIII–XX; Fischer, Eschatologie, 38–41. The terminus ante quem is supplied by Origen (De Principiis, 1.3.2), which refers to a book of Enoch à propos of the creation of the world.

148. A. Vaillant, Le Livre des Secrets d'Hénoch, texte slave et traduction francaise (Paris: Institut d'Etudes Slaves, 1952). The older translations, including that of Charles (APOT 2:425–69), presupposed the priority of the longer recension. Recently, J. H. Charlesworth reports that F. Andersen now questions Vaillant's views on the two recensions ("The SNTS Pseudepigrapha Seminars at Tübingen and Paris on the Books of Enoch," NTS 25 (1979) 315–323.

149. Charles, APOT 2:426; M. Philonenko, "La cosmologie du 'Livre des Secrets d'Hénoch,'" Religions en Egypte Hellénistique et Romaine (Paris: Presses Universitaires de France, 1969) 109–16; Fischer, Eschatologie, 40. There is a consensus that the book was written in Greek. See A. Rubinstein, "Observations on the Slavonic Book of Enoch," JJS 13 (1962) 1–21.

150. The Melchizedek legend is omitted in some manuscripts. See R. H. Charles and W. R. Morfill, The Book of the Secrets of Enoch (Oxford: Clarendon, 1896) xiii; Fischer, Eschatologie, 40.

151. Collins, "The Genre Apocalypse."

152. S. Pines, "Eschatology and the Concept of Time in the Slavonic Book of Enoch," Types of Redemption (Numen Supp XVIII; R. J. Z. Werblowski and J. C. Bleeker; Leiden: Brill, 1970) 75.

153. Collins, "The Genre Apocalypse." A further Diaspora apocalypse, the Apocalypse of Zephaniah, will be left aside here because of its fragmentary and problematic character. For a summary and statement of the problems, see J. H. Charlesworth, The Pseudepigrapha and Modern Research (SCS 7; Missoula: Scholars, 1976) 220–23. Two other apocalyptic works which may incorporate Egyptian Jewish elements are the Apocalypse of Elijah and the Narration of Zosimus, but both are Christian in their present form.

154. J. C. Picard, Apocalypsis Baruchi Graece (PVTG 2; Leiden: Brill, 1967) 75–78; W. Hage, Die griechische Baruch-Apokalypse (JSHRZ V/1; Gütersloh: Mohn, 1974) 17–20; H. M. Hughes, "3 Baruch or the Greek Apocalypse of Baruch," APOT 2:527–41.

155. Picard, Apocalypsis, 77–78; Fischer, Eschatologie, 75.

156. Picard (Apocalypsis, 77) denies that 3 Bar ever referred to more than five heavens.

157. The relation between Hades and the dragon is confused. See Fischer, Eschatologie, 80–82.

158. Hughes (APOT 2:539) cites Sanhedrin 92b, "And the soul may say: the body has sinned; for since I separated from it, I fly in the air like a bird."

159. Nickelsburg, Jewish Literature, 302.

160. J. C. Picard, "Observations sur l'Apocalypse grecque de Baruch I: Cadre historique et efficacité symbolique," Semitica 20 (1970) 77–103.

161. Nickelsburg (Jewish Literature, 302–3) implies that the builders are the Romans. Picard ("Observations," 79) sees an allusion to Greek sophists.

162. Picard, "Observations," 95–96.

CONCLUSION

It should be apparent from the foregoing chapters that there was no simple normative definition which determined Jewish identity in the Hellenistic Diaspora. There are however some persistent tendencies. All these attempts to articulate Jewish identity move between two poles. On the one hand, there are the constraints of the Jewish tradition. On the other are the values of the Hellenistic world. All the material we have surveyed can be viewed in one aspect as a spectrum of attempts to strike a balance between these competing factors and overcome the dissonance between them.

The Jewish tradition could be construed in various ways. The pattern of "covenantal nomism" which E. P. Sanders had posited as the dominant construction of Judaism was certainly represented in the Diaspora, in such diverse works as the chronicle of Demetrius, Fourth Maccabees, and the books of Adam and Eve. Yet it was not the only, or even the dominant, factor in the religion of Hellenistic Judaism. The Jewish tradition could also be construed as the story of a glorious past which fostered ethnic pride with little regard for religious laws or for anything that could be called nomism, as we found most conspicuously in Artapanus. It could also be construed as a moral system which prized universal human values and attached little importance to distinctive laws such as circumcision. The Jewish people might still be regarded as the paradigm for righteous humanity, but a righteous gentile was preferable to an unrighteous Jew. A work like Pseudo-Phocylides makes no explicit reference to Judaism. What matters is the code of conduct, not allegiance to a given people. In the Testament of Abraham and 3 Baruch there is ultimately no distinction between Jew and gentile at the judgment. These are admittedly extreme examples. Loyalty to the Jewish community is evidently an important factor in the great majority of cases (3 Maccabees is a striking example). Yet, there was a soft boundary line between Jew and gentile. The God-fearers and sympathizers may not have been a well-defined class, but they are important because they illustrate the gray area where the boundary between Jew and gentile becomes unclear and loses much becomes unclear and loses much of its importance.

The political identity of the Diaspora Jews is also achieved through balancing traditional loyalty with their new allegiance. Jerusalem enjoys symbolic importance, as it provides the Jews with a venerable center which is peculiarly their own. Yet even a work like Sib Or 3, which glorifies the Jerusalem temple, does so without diminishing its loyalty to the gentile rulers of Egypt. For Philo and his like the status of Jews in Alexandria was a more urgent concern than the prospect of eschatological restoration in Judea. Only in the traumatic period after 70 CE do we find a movement to abandon the Diaspora and return to Jerusalem. Even then this aspiration may not have been shared by the upper-class Jews, and it is only in this period that we find significant social division within the Diaspora. At the same period, we find a diametrically opposite view in 3 Baruch, who is prepared to abandon his concern for the welfare of Jerusalem.

Even the most conservative strands of Diaspora Judaism still attempt to strike a balance with Hellenistic culture. So Demetrius attempts to satisfy the standards of critical historiography and 4 Maccabees makes full use of Greek rhetoric. Sib Or 5, which exhibits the most far-reaching rejection of the gentile world still uses a traditional Greek form of expression and the pseudonym of the sibyl. Evidently this pervasive use of Hellenistic forms of expression cannot be adequately understood as a device to attract the gentiles. For most of its history, Diaspora Judaism did attempt, with varying degrees of success, to win adherents and sympathizers. The use of Hellenistic forms, however, and even the very desire to win gentile adherents, sprang from the self-identity of the Jews as respectable civilized members of Hellenistic society.

The common thread of Jewish identity, however, comes from the reliance, in whatever form, on the Jewish tradition. The author of 3 Baruch still uses the pseudonym of a Hebrew prophet. Artapanus may pay scant attention to Deuteronomic law, but he is determined to glorify the ancestors of the Jews. Philo's philosophy may be basically derived from the Greek tradition but he expresses it through exegesis of the Jewish Torah. Even Pseudo-Phocylides, who makes no explicit references to Judaism, betrays his identity by his use of the Septuagint. This common reliance on the tradition, rather than any specific interpretation of it, is what enables us to distinguish Jew from gentile in the Hellenistic Diaspora.

The attempt of Jews to find common ground with their gentile neighbors suffered a severe setback in the tragic revolt in the time of Trajan. The tradition was not entirely terminated: the Jewish sibylline oracles continue for centuries after the revolt. Yet, the attempt at cultural synthesis was undermined and could never again be pursued with such vigor. The legacy of the Hellenistic Diaspora was inherited not by Judaism but by the emerging Christian church. The Hellenistic Jews failed to win the respect and acceptance they desired from the Hellenistic world. Yet, their endeavor should not be judged a failure because of its historical outcome. The debacle of the great revolt was not a result of the Hellenization of Judaism but of social and political tensions within the Roman empire over which Jews had little control. The endeavor to find common ground between Athens and Jerusalem remains a noble effort, which attests a faith in the human community which transcends national, ethnic, and religious boundaries. The attempt to articulate a common ethic, acceptable to diverse traditions, and to relate individual traditions to universal values remains a worthy goal which must still be pursued in our own day. It is in the search for a universal common bond that the future of humanity lies.

INDEX OF SUBJECTS

INDEX OF MODERN AUTHORS